ADVANCE PRAISE FOR

A Guide to LGBTQ+ Inclusion on Campus, Post-PULSE

"LGBTQ+ inclusion starts on college campuses. *A Guide to LGBTQ+ Inclusion on Campus, Post-PULSE* is timely, comprehensive, and action-oriented. I look forward to using it in my principal training courses as well as in my scholarship."
—Hilary Lustick, Professor, Educational and Community Leadership,
Texas State University

"As a long-term advocate, ally, educator, and consultant on creating welcoming, affirming, and inclusive educational spaces, *A Guide to LGBTQ+ Inclusion on Campus, Post-PULSE* is both, a much-needed resource, and a breath of fresh air. The information and personal stories contained in this volume offer constructive, positive, and pedagogically sound information to foster LGBTQ+ inclusion in higher education. The particular dedication to the PULSE nightclub victims sends a message of hope to the world, especially at times when it feels as if we are moving backward. In addition, as a Latina, the homage to the PULSE victims—mostly Latinxs—reminds us of the diversity within our community. The multiple and diverse voices, guidance, and insights in this volume offer both theoretical underpinnings and practical guidance to implement immediate and long-term changes to make our campuses more LGBTQ+ inclusive for all. We will embrace each other. No matter our differences, we will support each other. We will not be stopped. We will continue to get stronger, get better, get more united, get more inclusive."
—Graciela Slesaransky-Poe, Professor and Founding Dean,
School of Education, Arcadia University

"We cannot change what we cannot name. We cannot disrupt bigotry and bias without deconstructing, rejecting, and then transforming what we have traditionally taught—binary privilege. In Virginia Stead's new collection, *A Guide to LGBTQ+ Inclusion on Campus, Post-PULSE*, Brandon L. Beck, Katherine Lewis, and Susan M. Croteau suggest that we can strengthen inclusion on campuses by doing what we do best—teaching courses that reject ratification or endorsement by a binary power structure. We are not obligated to reinforce a gender hierarchy where the binary is the privileged position of the central figures in our texts and syllabi. Kerry James Marshall inspired this transformation in art history curriculum in Britain by making black people the central figures in his work. Now Beck, Lewis, and Croteau call upon all of us to do the same. Bravo! There is no better word for what they have written in our behalf as college student educators."
—Cindi Love, Executive Director, American College Personnel Association,
College Student Educators International

Lane Community College
Women's Program
4000 E. 30th Avenue
Eugene, OR 97405

"As someone who has been a part of campus life for the last fifty years, both as a student/faculty member and as a member of the LGBTQ academic community, I have witnessed the emergence of our community and the many challenges it has faced. That a book like this can be written is a remarkable testament to the struggles and achievements of our community. We have successfully established ourselves as an active and creative presence in academic life. Equally significant, the authors represented in this collection give us a sense of the many challenges and struggles that still exist, and importantly, they give us ideas that we need to confront and dismantle them. *A Guide to LGBTQ+ Inclusion on Campus, Post-PULSE* can be read as a roadmap for the future."
—Fred Fejes, Professor, School of Communication and Multimedia Studies;
Center for Women, Gender and Sexuality Studies;
and Fellow of the Peace, Justice and Human Rights Initiative,
Florida Atlantic University

"Relevant and enlightening, *A Guide to LGBTQ+ Inclusion on Campus Post-PULSE* will be a welcome tool for all campuses whose goals are to enhance and elevate the quality of services for LGBTQ students. The book encompasses bold topics not previously presented together in a single volume, and the authors show a leap of courage in their forthright and clear presentations of real and current issues. This guide is a must-read for all faculty, staff, and student affairs educators whose missions include the commitment to the development of the whole student."
—Doris Ching, Emeritus Vice President for Student Affairs, University of Hawai'i System,
Former Interim Chancellor at University of Hawai'i—West O'ahu

A Guide to LGBTQ+ Inclusion on Campus, Post-PULSE

EQUITY IN HIGHER EDUCATION
THEORY, POLICY, & PRAXIS

Virginia Stead, H.B.A., B.Ed., M.Ed., Ed.D.
GENERAL EDITOR

vol. 7

The Equity in Higher Education Theory, Policy, & Praxis series
is part of the Peter Lang Education list.
Every volume is peer reviewed and meets
the highest quality standards for content and production.

PETER LANG
New York • Bern • Frankfurt • Berlin
Brussels • Vienna • Oxford • Warsaw

A Guide to LGBTQ+ Inclusion on Campus, Post-PULSE

Edited by Virginia Stead

PETER LANG
New York • Bern • Frankfurt • Berlin
Brussels • Vienna • Oxford • Warsaw

Library of Congress Cataloging-in-Publication Data
Names: Stead, Virginia, editor.
Title: A guide to LGBTQ+ inclusion on campus, post-Pulse /
edited by Virginia Stead.
Description: New York: Peter Lang, 2017.
Series: Equity in higher education theory, policy, and praxis; vol. 7
ISSN 2330-4502 (print) | ISSN 2330-4510 (online)
Includes bibliographical references.
Identifiers: LCCN 2017025675 | ISBN 978-1-4331-4628-2 (hardback: alk. paper)
ISBN 978-1-4331-4625-1 (paperback: alk. paper) | ISBN 978-1-4331-4648-0 (ebook pdf)
ISBN 978-1-4331-4649-7 (epub) | ISBN 978-1-4331-4650-3 (mobi)
Subjects: Sexual minority college students—United States.
Homosexuality and education—United States.
Education, Higher—Social aspects—United States.
Gay college students—United States.
Lesbian college students—United States.
Bisexual college students—United States.
Transgender college students—United States.
Classification: LCC LC2574.6 .G85 2017 | DDC 378.0086/640973—dc23
LC record available at https://lccn.loc.gov/2017025675
DOI 10.3726/b11502

Bibliographic information published by **Die Deutsche Nationalbibliothek**.
Die Deutsche Nationalbibliothek lists this publication in the "Deutsche
Nationalbibliografie"; detailed bibliographic data are available
on the Internet at http://dnb.d-nb.de/.

The paper in this book meets the guidelines for permanence and durability
of the Committee on Production Guidelines for Book Longevity
of the Council of Library Resources.

© 2017 Peter Lang Publishing, Inc., New York
29 Broadway, 18th floor, New York, NY 10006
www.peterlang.com

All rights reserved.
Reprint or reproduction, even partially, in all forms such as microfilm,
xerography, microfiche, microcard, and offset strictly prohibited.

Printed in the United States of America

In Memorium

Victims of the PULSE Nightclub Massacre
June 12, 2016, Orlando, FL

This book is dedicated to those who perished because of the June 12, 2016 massacre at the PULSE nightclub, Orlando, Florida. They died through no fault of their own. Their murder inspires us all. Their legacy includes a massive new wave of pro-LGBTQ+ activism. We extend our thoughts and prayers to all who loved the following victims:

Angel L. Candelario-Padro (28), Juan Chevez-Martinez (25), Luis Daniel Conde (39), Cory James, Connell (21), Tevin Eugene Crosby (25), Deonka Deidra Drayton (32), Simon Adrian Carrillo Fernandez (31), Leroy Valentin Fernandez (25), Mercedez Marisol Flores (26), Peter O. Gonzalez-Cruz (22), Juan Ramon Guerrero (22), Paul Terrell Henry (41), Frank Hernandez (27), Miguel Angel Honorato (30), Javier Jorge-Reyes (40), Jason Benjamin Josaphat, (19), Eddie Jamoldroy Justice (30), Anthony Luis Laureanodisla (25), Christopher Andrew Leinonen (32), Alejandro Barrios Martinez (21), Brenda Lee Marquez McCool (49), Gilberto Ramon Silva Menendez (25), Kimberly Morris (37), Akyra Monet Murray (18), Luis Omar Ocasio-Capo (20), Geraldo A. Ortiz-Jimenez (25), Eric Ivan Ortiz-Rivera (36), Joel Rayon Paniagua (32), Jean Carlos Mendez Perez (35), Enrique L. Rios, Jr. (25), Jean C. Nives Rodriguez (27), Xavier Emmanuel Serrano Rosado (35), Christopher Joseph Sanfeli (24), Yilmary Rodriguez Solivan (24), Edward Sotomayor Jr. (34), Shane Evan Tomlinson (33), Martin Benitez Torres (33), Jonathan Antonio Camuy Vega (24), Juan P. Rivera Velazquez (37), Luis S. Vielma (22), Franky Jimmy Dejesus Velazquez (50), Luis Daniel Wilson-Leon (37), and Jerald Arthur Wright (31). (Retrieved from: http://globalnews.ca/news/2756440/mass-Casualties-after-florida-nightclub-shooting-police-say-gunman-is-dead/)

Table of Contents

List of Tables and Figures xi
Foreword: Reflections on a History of Queer Life in Higher Education........... xiii
    Warren J. Blumenfeld
Acknowledgments xxiii

Introduction: Powerful Lessons for Making All Campuses LGBTQ+ Inclusive........1
    Virginia Stead

Part One: Beyond the Campus Gates: How State Sanctioned Practice Impacts LGBTQ+ Communities............................... 3
Chapter One: If Gender Isn't Binary: A Legal Review of Titles VII and IX 5
    Barbara Qualls
Chapter Two: Just Another Gay Day in the Campus Three Year Old Room....... 17
    Robin K. Fox and Erica Schepp
Chapter Three: Checking the Pulse Early: LGBTQ-Inclusive Curriculum
    in Elementary Schools.. 27
    Dominic Grasso and Traci P. Baxley

Chapter Four: When Secondary Schools Fail: LGBT Issues in the
   Juvenile Justice System. 41
   Shiv R. Desai

**Part Two: Systemic Campus Failures to Include the
LGBTQ+ Community** 53

Chapter Five: LGBTQ Marginalization or Inclusion? Troubling Institutional
   Assertions of Commitment to Social Justice 55
   valerie a. guerrero and Kari J. Dockendorff

Chapter Six: Big U Knows Best: Patronizing Queer Campus Culture 67
   S. Gavin Weiser and Travis L. Wagner

Chapter Seven: "It's Not Natural!" 79
   Wahinkpe Topa (Four Arrows) aka Don Trent Jacobs

Chapter Eight: Writing from Queer Silos: Implications of Tokenizing
   Queer Identities in Counsellor Education 85
   Christopher A. Cumby

**Part Three: LGBTQ+ Faculty and Student Narratives of
Profound Campus Exclusion** 97

Chapter Nine: Our Morning after PULSE: A Parent/Teacher Educator's
   Experience of Protection, Invisibility, and Action 99
   Sarah Pickett

Chapter Ten: Embodying Queer Pedagogy on Campus:
   Autoethnographic Explorations after Orlando, FL 111
   Kerri Mesner

Chapter Eleven: Liminal Living Liberates 121
   Alan Smith

Chapter Twelve: Fear and the Unknown: Harrowing Experiences of
   LGBTQ Students in Higher Education 129
   Eric J. Weber and Karin Ann Lewis

**Part Four: Contrasting Examples of Leadership Training for
LGBTQ+ Inclusiveness** 139

Chapter Thirteen: Preparing Social Justice Leaders to Deconstruct
   Heterosexual Privilege 141
   Karen (Karie) K. Huchting, Jill Bickett, and Emily S. Fisher

Chapter Fourteen: Increasing Gender and Identity Competency Among
    Student Affairs Professionals... 159
    Angela Clark-Taylor, Kaitlin Legg, Carissa Cardenas, and Rachael Rehage

Part Five: Moving Forward: Inclusive LGBTQ+ Policy Implementation.... 173
Chapter Fifteen: George Washington University: One Campus Takes
    Comprehensive Action Against Hate Crimes............................. 175
    Carol A. Kochhar-Bryant
Chapter Sixteen: Beyond Safe Zones: Disruptive Strategies Towards
    LGBTQ Inclusion on Campus 191
    Pietro A. Sasso and Laurel Puchner
Chapter Seventeen: Supporting Queer Survivors of Sexual
    Assault on Campus.. 209
    Nicole Bedera and Kristjane Nordmeyer
Chapter Eighteen: Stories of LGBTQ+ Hate, Fear, Hope, and Love in the
    University of Hawai'i System: Twenty Years of the Marriage Equality
    Movement 219
    Rae Watanabe, Tara O'Neill, and Camaron Miyamoto

**Part Six: Reaching Out: Transformative LGBTQ+ Curriculum and
    Pedagogy 239**
Chapter Nineteen: Creating an Inclusive Learning Environment for
    LGBT Students on College Campuses.................................... 241
    Clayton R. Alford
Chapter Twenty: Transgender/Gender Non-Binary Inclusion in
    Higher Education Courses... 255
    Brandon L. Beck, Katherine Lewis, and Susan M. Croteau
Chapter Twenty-One: "How Do You Ally?" Redefining the Language
    We Use in Ally Education 267
    Laura D. Gentner and Kristen Altenau Keen
Chapter Twenty-Two: Utilizing Indigenous Pedagogies to Uproot
    Racism and LGBTQ+ Intolerance: A Student Affairs Perspective............. 277
    Camaron Miyamoto, Dean Hamer, Joe Wilson, and
    Hinaleimoana Wong-Kalu
Chapter Twenty-Three: Dialogues on Diversity: A Curricular Option to
    Promote LGBTQIA Inclusion on Campus 287
    Paul S. Hengesteg

Chapter Twenty-Four: Remember PULSE: LGBT Understanding and
    Learning Serves Everyone 301
    Pamela Ross McClain

Conclusion … and a Call to Action: LGBTQ+ Inclusion: Getting It Right on
    Our Own Campuses... 313
    Virginia Stead

Afterword: Ending the Erasure of Trans* and Non-Binary Students
    Through Higher Education Policy... 315
    Kari J. Dockendorff

About the Contributors... 323

Tables and Figures

Tables

Table 3.1. Suggestions for LGBTQ-Positive K to 5 Curriculum.....................34
Table 3.2. Suggestions for LGBTQ-Positive 3 to 5 Curriculum 35
Table 18.1. Campus Pride Index 2014 Survey Results............................230

Figures

Figure 11.1. A Self-Reflective Portrait 122
Figure 11.2. EGO! 124
Figure 18.1. UH Commission on the Status of LGBTI Equality Survey 232
Figure 23.1. Student Survey..294

Foreword

Reflections on a History of Queer Life in Higher Education

WARREN J. BLUMENFELD

I travel around the United States and to other countries giving presentations and training workshops on college, university, and high school campuses and at professional conventions on topics around social justice issues.

Recently, after I spoke about heterosexism and cissexism at an east coast university, a student asked me what my undergraduate LGBT student group was like. "Was there much resistance from the administration and from other students?" she inquired. More questions followed: "Did the women and men work well together?" "Were bisexuals and trans people welcomed?" "Was the group's focus political or mainly social?" "Was there a separate 'coming out' group for new members?" "What kinds of campus activities did your group sponsor?"

As she asked me these questions, my head began to whirl with visions of my undergraduate years. I stopped long enough to inform her that I graduated with my B.A. degree on June 13, 1969—15 days before the momentous Stonewall rebellion, an event generally credited with sparking the modern movement for LGBT liberation and equality.

Though I later learned that some universities like Cornell, Stanford, and Columbia had officially recognized LGBT student groups before 1969, as a graduating senior, the concept of an "out" person, let alone an organized, above-ground student organization was not even in my range of possibilities.

HETEROSEXISM IN THE COLD WAR

I was born during the height of the Cold War era directly following World War II, a time when any sort of human difference was held suspect. On the floor of the U.S. Senate, a young and brash senator from Wisconsin, Joseph McCarthy, loudly proclaimed that "Communists corrupt the minds, and homosexuals corrupt the bodies" of good, upstanding Americans, and he proceeded to purge suspected Communists and homosexuals from government service.

When I was only 2 years old, my parents suspected that I might be gay, or to use the terminology of the day, "homosexual." Shy, withdrawn, I preferred to spend most of my time alone. Later, on the playground at school, children called me names like "sissy", "fairy", "pansy", "little girl", and "fag" with an incredible vehemence and malice that I did not understand.

My parents sent me to a child psychologist from 1951, when I was only 4 years old, until I reached my 13th birthday, with the expressed purpose of making sure that I did not grow up "homosexual." Each session at the psychologist's office, I took off my coat and placed it on the hook behind the door, and for the next 50 minutes, the psychologist and I built model airplanes, cars, and trains—so-called age-appropriate "boy-type toys." It was obvious that the psychologist confused issues of gender with sexuality believing that one could prevent homosexuality by imposing "masculine" behaviors.

During high school in the early 1960s, I had very few friends and never dated. It was not that I did not wish to date, but I wanted to date some of the other boys. I could not even talk about this at the time, for the concept of high school Gay/Straight Alliance was still many years in the future. In high school, the topic of homosexuality rarely surfaced officially in the classroom, and then only in a negative context. I graduated high school in 1965 with the hope that college life would somehow be better for me. I hoped that people would be more open-minded, less conforming, and more accepting of difference.

SOMETHING WAS MISSING

To a great extent, things were better. In college, I demonstrated my opposition to the war in Vietnam with others. I worked to reduce racism on campus, and I helped plan environmental ecology teach-ins. Nevertheless, there was still something missing for me. I knew I was gay, but I had no outlet of support through which I could express my feelings. As far as I knew, there were no openly LGBT people, no support groups, no organizations, and no classes or library materials that did anything more than tell me that homosexuality was "abnormal" and that I needed to change.

In 1967, I finally decided to see a therapist in the campus counseling center, and I began what for me was a very difficult coming out process. And then during my first year of graduate school in 1970, I experienced a turning point in my life.

In my campus newspaper, *The Spartan Daily*, at San José State University, I saw the headline in big bold letters: "GAY LIBERATION FRONT DENIED CAMPUS RECOGNITION." The article stated that the chancellor of the California State University system, Glenn Dumke, under then Governor Ronald Reagan's direction, had denied recognition to the campus chapter of Gay Liberation Front.

In the ruling, Dumke stated that:

> The effect of recognition ... of the Gay Liberation Front could conceivably be to endorse or to promote homosexual behavior, to attract homosexuals to the campus, and to expose minors to homosexual advocacy and practices ... belief that the proposed Front created too great a risk for students—a risk which might lead students to engage in illegal homosexual behavior.

CURIOSITY AND FEAR

This was the first I had heard of such a group, and the first time I had heard about other LGBT people on my campus. I called the coordinator of the group, and she invited me to the next meeting. Since the chancellor did not permit group members to hold meetings on our campus, they met at a little diner on a small side street a few blocks off campus. Unfortunately, this only confirmed my fears of the underground nature of LGBT life. As I approached the door to enter the meeting, I felt as if I were a member of the French resistance during the Nazi occupation.

Upon entering, I saw around 15 people. I recognized one man from my chemistry class, but the others were strangers. I saw a near even mix of men and women, which made me feel a bit easier. In my mind, I had envisioned 50 men waiting to pounce on me as I entered, but I soon discovered that they were all good people who were concerned about me. They invited me to their homes, and before too long, I relaxed in their presence.

I left San José in 1971 to work for a progressive educational journal, *EdCentric*, at the National Student Association in Washington, DC. Within a few months after arriving, I founded and became the first director of the National Gay Student Center, a national clearinghouse working to connect and exchange information between the newly emerging network of LGBT campus organizations within the United States.

One year after leaving San José, I read that students at Sacramento State University, represented by the student government, had sued the chancellor in Sacramento County Superior Court and won the case forcing the university officially to recognize their group. The court upheld the students' First Amendment rights to free speech and freedom of association by affirming their contention that, "... to justify suppression of free speech, there must be reasonable grounds to fear that serious evil will result if free speech is practiced; there must be reasonable ground to believe that the danger apprehended is imminent."

I had the opportunity to talk with Marty Rogers, one of the founding members of the LGBT group at Sacramento State University, who described how the denial of recognition and eventual court battle were instrumental in the group's organizing success:

> Being denied recognition, being decreed invisible, reactivated in most group members other similar and painful incidents in their lives. The difference this time was that there was mutual support—from the campus newspaper and from the student government. Two faculty members openly acknowledged their homosexuality through letters to the Acting College President and the campus newspaper—they insisted on being seen. For once, homosexuals were not running and hiding. Publicly announcing one's homosexuality, an issue which had not really been confronted previously, became an actuality as a result of the denial of recognition.

Fortified by this precedent-setting case, other campus groups throughout the country have waged and won similar battles.

ONE YEAR "SICK" AND THEN NOT

While living in Washington, DC, I became an active member of the Gay Liberation Front. One demonstration in particular sticks out in my mind. We had been jointly planning our tactics over the past month. I and my compatriots of the Gay Liberation Front and Gay May Day collective, friends from the Mattachine Society, and members of the newly formed Gay Activists Alliance were to gather on this bright morning during the first week of May in 1971, and carpool up Connecticut Avenue in northwest Washington, DC to the Shoreham Hotel. Also uniting with us were people from out-of-town who joined us as part of Gay May Day as we attempted to shut down the federal government for what we considered to be an illegal and immoral invasion into Vietnam.

We parked about a block away since we didn't want hotel security and attendees at the American Psychiatric Association (APA) annual conference to notice a rather large group of activists sporting T-shirts and placards announcing "Gay Is Good", "Psychiatry Is the Enemy", and "Gay Revolution." Half the men decked themselves in stunning drag wearing elegant wigs and shimmering lamé dresses, glittering fairy dust wafting their painted faces.

A year before, at the APA conference held in San Francisco, activists demonstrated outside and a few got inside. As a result, conference organizers conceded to permit a panel to lead a discussion workshop at the 1971 annual conference in DC under the title, "Lifestyles of Nonpatient Homosexuals." The panelists (below, from left to right), included Dr. Franklin Kameny, Director of Mattachine DC; Barbara Gittings, Director of the Philadelphia office of Daughters of Bilitis; and Jack Baker, University of Minnesota, who was the first "out" U.S. student body president.

In their capacity as official conference panelists, these three were granted inside access to all proceedings, including admission to the annual Convocation of Fellows, in which all attendees were to hear U.S. Attorney General Ramsey Clark deliver the keynote address in the hotel's over-the-top Regency Ballroom. Earlier in the week, some of us checked out the hotel's layout. The day before, a comrade placed a wedge in a doorway coming from the Rock Creek Park woods into the hotel, where we gained access.

All along, the panelists were to serve as our Trojan Horses. After the Convocation was called to order, and half-way through Clark's address, our insiders opened the doors and in we poured, chanting, waving, and shouting. On stage, we witnessed a stunned Attorney General surrounded by similarly stunned and also upset APA officials, and seated in the front rows we noticed elderly men who wore gold medals around their necks. When they saw us, they stood and began beating us with their medals while shouting "Get out of here. We don't want any more people like you here!" Others yelled: "You're sick, you're sick you faggots, you drag queens!" Other psychiatrists stood up from their seats and attempted to push us physically from the hall. I was able to escape their grasp, and I sat locking arms with a contingent on the floor just beneath the stage.

I then saw Franklin Kameny rush the stage and grab the microphone, his booming voice cracking through the pandemonium even after the technician cut the power. "Psychiatry is the enemy incarnate", he yelled, the anger seemingly oozing from his pores. "You may take this as a declaration of war against you!"

And this was, indeed, our intent: To declare war on the psychiatric profession for the atrocities, the colonization, the "professional" malpractice it had perpetrated over the preceding century in the name of "science", and the biological and psychological pathologizing of sexual and gender transgressive people. From the so-called "Eugenics Movement" of the mid-19th century though the 20th century CE and beyond, medical and psychological professions have often proposed and addressed, in starkly medical terms, the alleged "deficiencies" and "mental diseases" of lesbian, gay, bisexual, and transgender (LGBT) people.

The Eugenics Movement in science was coined by Francis Galton in England in 1883 from the Greek word meaning "well born" or "of good origins or breeding", and it codified the socially constructed hierarchical concept of "race." Using this concept, some members of the scientific community viewed people attracted to their own sex as constituting a distinct biological or racial type—those who could be distinguished from "normal" people through anatomical markers.

For example, Dr. G. Frank Lydston, an American urologist, surgeon, and Professor from Chicago, in 1889 delivered a lecture at the College of Physicians and Surgeons in Chicago in which he referred to homosexuals as "sexual perverts" who are "physically abnormal." He continued:

> ... the unfortunate class of individuals who are characterized by perverted sexuality have been viewed in the light of their moral responsibility rather than as the victims of a physical and incidentally of a mental defect. ... Even to the moralist there should be much satisfaction in the thought that a large class of sexual perverts are physically abnormal rather than morally leprous.

Also, the American medical doctor, Allan McLane Hamilton, wrote in 1896 that "the [female homosexual] is usually of a masculine type, or if she presented none of the 'characteristics' of the male, was a subject of pelvic disorder, with scanty menstruation, and was more or less hysterical and insane."

In another example, Physician, Perry M. Lichtenstein, published in 1921 that: "A physical examination of [female homosexuals] will in practically every instance disclose an abnormally prominent clitoris" (p. 372).

Furthermore, in France in 1857, Ambroise Tardieu wrote that: "This degeneracy is evidenced in men who engage in same-sex eroticism by their underdeveloped, tapered penis resembling that of a dog, and a naturally smooth anus lacking in radial folds."

In addition, and rather than considering homosexuality, bisexuality, and gender non-conformity merely as emotional, gender, and sexual differences along a broad spectrum of human potential, some sectors of the medical and psychological communities forced pathologizing language onto people with same-sex and both-sex attractions, as well as on those who cross traditional constructions of gender identities and expression. Dr. Sigmund Freud (1986), for example, saw homosexuality as a developmental disorder, a fixation at one of the intermediate "pregenital" stages. He believed this was caused, at least in part, by an incomplete resolution in males of the Oedipal complex.

Another respected expert, the Swiss physician, August Forel, wrote in 1905:

> The [sexual] excesses of female inverts exceed those of the male ... and this is their one thought night and day, almost without interruption. [Male inverts] feel the need for passive submission ... and occupy themselves with feminine pursuits. Nearly all [female and male] inverts are in a more or less marked degree psychopaths or neurotics.

Educational opportunities for primarily middle-class women improved somewhat during mid-19th century in the United States. Although they were locked out of most institutions of higher learning, a number of women's colleges were founded, such as Mt. Holyoke College, Vassar, Smith College, Wellesley College, and Bryn Mawr. There were, however, many conservative critics who attacked this new trend, warning that educated women would be unfit to fill their traditional roles in society. Some, like Dr. Edward Clarke, in 1873 warned that study would interfere with women's fertility, causing them chronic uterine disease. And Dr. Havelock Ellis (1939) concluded that:

> Women's colleges are the great breeding ground of lesbianism. When young women are thrown together, they manifest an increasing affection by the usual tokens. They kiss each other fondly on every occasion. They learn the pleasure of direct contact … and after this, the normal sex act fails to satisfy them. (quoted in Faderman, 1991, p. 49)

Ellis (1939) also posited that female homosexuality was increasing because of the rise of feminism, which taught women to be independent of men.

All of this has resulted in members of the medical professions committing lesbians, gay males, bisexuals, and those who transgress so-called "normative" gender identities and expressions (often against their will) to hospitals, mental institutions, jails, and penitentiaries, where they have been forced to undergo pre-frontal lobotomies, electroshock, castration, and sterilization. As well, we have been made to endure "aversion therapy", "reparative therapy", "Christian counseling", and genetic counseling.

The first *Diagnostic & Statistical Manual of Mental Disorders* (DSM-I) (the APA-sponsored and endorsed handbook of mental disorders) published in 1952, listed homosexuality, for example, as "Sociopathic Personality Disorder." The "updated" 1968 DSM-II described homosexuality as "Sexual Orientation Disorder (SOD)."

The physician Irving Bieber co-authored a study in 1962, "Homosexuality: A Psychoanalytic Study of Male Homosexuals" sponsored by the New York Society of Psychoanalysts, in which he concluded that homosexuality constituted a psychopathology that could be cured or prevented with psychoanalysis. Bieber later was quoted in 1973 saying: "A homosexual is a person whose heterosexual function is crippled, like the legs of a polio victim" (Bieber's 1973 quote from *New York Times*).

In addition, the psychiatrist Charles Socarides (1968), founder of the National Association for Research & Therapy of Homosexuality (NARTH), argued that homosexuality is an illness, a neurosis, possibly caused by an over-attachment to the mother, which he too argued could be treated. Bieber and Socrarides became the "authoritative" and often-referenced researchers in the areas of "causation" and "treatment" of homosexuality.

The year following our storming the Shoreham Hotel's Regency Ballroom, APA held its annual conference in Dallas, Texas. No activist propped open a side entrance, and no multi-group contingent burst into the assemblage, for something seemed to have changed within the organization over the intervening year. Barbara Gittings and Franklin Kameny again presented their views and facilitated a workshop discussion, this time joined by "Dr. H. Anonymous" (a.k.a. psychiatrist Dr. John E. Fryer, wearing a costume mask to hide his identity) who discussed his experiences as a gay psychiatrist and member of the APA.

By 1973, the American Psychiatric Association had finally changed its designation of homosexuality for those comfortable with their sexual orientation, asserting that it did not constitute a disorder: "[H]omosexuality *per se* implies no impairment in judgment, stability, reliability, or general social or vocational capabilities." Two years later, in 1975, the American Psychological Association followed suit and urged mental health professionals "to take the lead in removing the stigma of mental illness that has long been associated with homosexual orientations."

In 2013, the American Psychiatric Association made what they considered a big change in the labelling of transgender people. That year they published the DSM-V which replaced the 1980 DSM-III diagnosis of "gender identity disorder" with "gender dysphoria", a concept they described as a more neutral designation, one that was descriptive rather than diagnostic and pathologizing.

In the case of LGBT people, the scientific community has consistently deployed the "medical model" to investigate and pathologize the "other." In this way, heteronormativity and cissupremacy (oppression and colonization against trans people) become perceived as the unremarkable or "normal" standards, unquestioned hegemonic norms against which all others are judged. Heterosexual and cisgender norms justify and explain away the otherwise unacceptable persecution and oppression of non-conforming sexual and gender identity groups, while evading issues of domination, privilege, subordination, and marginalization.

Thus the "medicalization" of homosexuality, bisexuality, and gender non-conformity only serves to strengthen oppression and heterosexual and cisgender privilege through its relative invisibility. Given this invisibility, issues of oppression and privilege are neither analysed nor scrutinized, neither interrogated nor confronted by members of the dominant group.

I am very proud of the actions we took during those difficult and also exciting times. We contributed our small piece to the large jigsaw puzzle of queer history, a piece that, when interlocked with all of the other pieces as we comrades interlocked arms to prevent the outraged psychiatrists from evicting us from the Regency Ballroom, has exposed the biases and, most importantly, the foundational power dynamics in the social constructions of "abnormality", "disease", "mental illness", "hysteria", "disability", and "immaturity", for us and for so many other marginalized groups, including women, people who are differently abled, young people, and elders.

Following our successful and historic zap on the APA psychiatrists that day in May, 1971, we exalted comrades returned to the GLF commune at 1620 S Street in northwest DC, and we sang in unified and joyous harmony "When the Gays Go Marchin' In." And in fact, we did!

HOPE FOR THE FUTURE

A few years ago, I boarded a subway train on the Green Line in Boston bound for Boston University where I was scheduled to present a workshop on LGBT history at an annual Northeast LGBT student conference. Also entering the car were four young male students *en route* to the conference, one whom I remembered from a workshop I had given the previous day.

Once on board, they sat two by two in rows directly in front of me. After a few moments of animated talk and without apparent concern or self-consciousness, one of them reached out his hand and gently stroked the hair of the young man seated next to him. The other man welcomed and accepted the gesture.

Witnessing this scene, I thought about how far LGBT people had come from the time I attended college as an undergraduate. Tears came to my eyes as I thought back to the pain of coming out of a closet of denial and fear. I saw before me memories of the hard and often frightening work so many of us have been doing to ensure a safer environment so that young people are able to display seemingly simple acts of affection for someone of their own sex, acts which different-sex couples routinely take for granted.

Through my travels to college and university campuses, and despite some progress, I come away with the sense that conditions remain somewhat difficult for some LGBT and questioning young people. Support systems in many places have been set firmly in place on campuses, and students today appear more self-assured and exhibit a certain joyous and feisty rebellion not seen only a decade or so ago.

Therefore, I realize that though school is still not a particularly "queer" place to be, it is a great deal better than ever before. In solidarity, then, we need to keep up the struggle.

REFERENCES

Bieber, I. (1973, December 23). In "The A.P.A. ruling on homosexuality." An interview with two psychiatrists, Dr. Robert L. Spitzer and Dr. Irving Bieber, *The New York Times*.

Ellis, H. (1939). *Psychology of sex*. London: William Heinemann.

Faderman, L. (1991). *Odd girls and twilight lovers: A history of lesbian life in twentieth-century America*. New York, NY: Penguin Books.

Forel, A. (1905). La Question sexuelle (traduit dans de nombreuses langues), réédité en 2012: La question sexuelle exposée aux adultes cultivés, préface de Christophe Granger, Éditeur: AUTREMENT.

Freud, S. (1986). *The essentials of psycho-analysis: Selected by Anna Freud*. New York, NY: Penguin Books.

Hamilton, A. M. (1896). The civil responsibility of sexual perverts. *American Journal of Insanity, 52*, 503–509.

Lichtenstein, P. (1921). The "fairy" and the lady lover. *Medical Review of Reviews, 27*, 369–374.
Lydston, G. F. (1889, September 7). Clinical lecture: Sexual perversion, satyriasas, and nymphomania. *Medical and Surgical Reporter, LXI* (10), 553–557.
Socarides, C. (1968). *The overt homosexual.* Lanham, MD: Jason Aronson.
Tardieu, A. (1857). *Étude medico-légale sur les attentats aux moeurs.* Paris: J.-B. Baillière.

Acknowledgments

The Editor wishes to thank everyone who has helped bring this manuscript to fruition. Of the several volumes in the series, *Equity in Higher Education Theory, Policy, and Praxis*, this one has been the most heart-breaking to assemble and edit. Special appreciation therefore goes out to those who circulated the call for chapter proposals, to the hopeful authors who submitted proposals, and to the dedicated 45 whose courageous research appears in the pages that follow.

At Peter Lang Publishing, I am particularly grateful to the professional support team whose patience and gentle guidance have contributed to our safe navigation of the company's new and improved policies following the ownership change in 2015. In New York, Dr. Farideh Koohi-Kamali, Senior Vice President of Peter Lang Publishing/USA, has helped with the really tough decisions, while Sarah E. Bode, Acquisitions Editor for the Education list, and Editorial Assistant Tim Swenarton have shouldered the week to week exigencies of developing a world class text. Elsewhere, gratitude extends to Dr. Anna DiStefano for her insightful, challenging, and expedient peer review of the book prospectus. To my academic friends and colleagues, thank you for giving so much of your time and insightful criticism as the project developed.

Now for the best of all. This book would have been impossible to imagine, much less construct and refine without the steady love and encouragement of my family. To my sisters-in-law, Kathleen Stead and Jo-Anne Stead, thank you for being there when the going got tough. To my daughter, Julia Stead, your belief in my work and brilliant suggestions have been an invaluable part of this project.

Thank you for easing the journey and lighting the path. Finally, to my spouse extraordinaire, Robert Edward Stead, oceans of thanks for being so supportive and patient, for generously discussing picayune differences in meaning, for keeping me fed and watered, for making such thoughtful use of your headphones, and for loving me so well.

Introduction

Powerful Lessons for Making All Campuses LGBTQ+ Inclusive

VIRGINIA STEAD

This is the seventh volume in the *Equity in Higher Education* series. Courageous researchers, including queer folk and allies of the LGBTQ+ community, have created a text that explicitly describes how to transform LGBTQ+ campus exclusion into inclusion. Whether you are a long-time researcher of LGBTQ+ experience, a familiar explorer, or a novice in the field, what follows will give you many of the tools to extend current research and strengthen pro-LGBTQ+ activism at multiple levels across any campus.

The dedication is uniquely poignant given the June 16, 2016 targeted murder of 49 innocent victims at the PULSE nightclub, a LGBTQ+ refuge in Orlando, FL. Motivated by unexpectedly intense senses of loss and rage, several colleagues jumped at the idea of developing a book that would support LGBTQ+ inclusion on campus. Amherst Professor turned blogger, Warren J. Blumenthal, agreed to provide the Forward, *Reflections on a History of Queer Life in Higher Education*. His evocative writing style and extensive experience offer an insightful and informative background to LGBTQ+ academic life.

The chapters are grouped into six distinct sections: (1) Beyond the Campus Gates: How State Sanctioned Practice Impacts LGBTQ+ Communities, (2) Systemic Campus Failures to Include the LGBTQ+ Community, (3) LGBTQ+ Faculty and Student Narratives of Profound Campus Exclusion, (4) Contrasting Examples of Leadership Training for LGBTQ+ Inclusiveness, (5) Moving Forward: Inclusive LGBTQ+ Policy Implementation, and (6) Reaching Out: Transformative LGBTQ+ Curriculum and Pedagogy.

In Section One, Qualls does a masterful review of Titles VII and IX, Fox and Schepp describe how to talk to three-year-olds about same-sex parenting, Grasso and Baxley give examples of LGBTQ+ elementary curriculum, and Desai depicts painful reminiscences of high school years spent within the juvenile justice system.

In Section Two, guerrero and Dockendorff unpack lip-service commitments to social justice, Weiser and Wagner unveil queer culture patronization, Wahinkpe Topa reminds us all of the eternal normalcy of LGBTQ+ existence, and Cumby challenges the tokenization of LGBTQ+ support in counsellor education.

In Section Three, Pickett illuminates the inseparable experiences of LGBTQ+ parents and teacher education instructors in the wake of the PULSE attack on the queer community. Mesner likewise explores the nature of queer pedagogy on campus, and Smith proffers an intimate narrative of personal exclusion. In addition, Weber and Lewis elucidate episodes of fear and the unknown among LGBTQ+ students in higher education.

In Section Four, Huchting, Bickett, and Fisher share positive ways for social justice leaders to address heterosexual privilege, and Clark-Taylor, Legg, Cardenas, and Rehage describe LGBTQ+ competency training among student affairs professionals.

In Section Five, Kochhar-Bryant elucidates how campus hate crimes can be prevented, Sasso and Puchner disrupt LGBTQ+ exclusionary practice, Bedera and Nordmeyer describe much-needed strategies for supporting queer survivors of campus sexual assault, and Watanabe, O'Neill, and Miyamoto offer insights into LGBTQ+ marriage equality on campus.

In Section Six, Alford describes inclusive learning environments, Beck, Lewis, and Croteau broaden course transformation to include transgender/gender non-binary identities, Gentner and Keen illuminate ally language and skills, Miyamoto, Hamer, Wilson, and Wong-Kalu inform student affairs training with Indigenous pedagogies, Hengeseng offers LGBTQIA inclusive curriculum strategies, and McClain invokes an all-gender perspective on the universal benefits of LGBT inclusion.

In my Conclusion, and with a nod to our peer reviewer, Dr. Anna DiStefano, I discuss connections among the 24 chapters and suggest ways in which activists might proceed to make their campuses LGBTQ+ inclusive. As well, and in the most timely of ways, Dockendorff's Afterword offers insights, strategies, and encouragement to those work toward ending the erasure of trans* and non-binary students in higher education policy. As a final step, I post the link to a recommended gender dictionary for novice and seasoned researchers who encounter academic terms whose meaning they wish to clarify: https://www.theguardian.com/world/2015/dec/29/gender-dictionary-2015. May the power of well-chosen words continue to deepen our understanding, clarify our communication, and strengthen our pro-LGBTQ+ activism.

PART ONE

Beyond THE Campus Gates

How State Sanctioned Practice Impacts LGBTQ+ Communities

CHAPTER ONE

If Gender Isn't Binary

A Legal Review of Titles VII and IX

BARBARA QUALLS

INTRODUCTION

Not so long ago, the verbal minefield of political correctness as it relates to gender was simple: Did a woman want to be called Mrs., Miss, or Ms.? Those terms seem almost antique when today we juggle an alphabet soup of acronyms, a jumble of psychological terms, a mixture of legal terminology, as well as newly coined words that have meaning only to those who have coined them. Although there are many different and equally valid aspects of the social, educational, and legal evolution of the sex/gender discussion, the most fundamental parameter of change is how the law deals with sex and gender. The focus of this chapter requires another narrowing of the discussion through the examination of one particular group of individuals who are impacted by the sex/gender debate, those who identify as transgender. The construct of transgender applies to spectrum behavior, which may include overt manifestation or not, may include transient identification or not, and may include attempts at biological alteration, or not. There is little surprise that case and statutory law grapples with such a fluid concept.

For schools and the people who operate them, the implications of transgender law are complex. The obligation to educate everybody in a relatively nonrestrictive atmosphere becomes undefinable when one group of students behaves in the manner their self-identity demands and that, in turn, causes another group of students to experience fear or debilitating discomfort. Adding to the complexity is a transgender definition that itself is vague, as well as the complications arising from discrimination based on that vague construct. As pharmacological and medical advances make sex more easily aligned with gender, and as social tolerance for those advances continues to vacillate, advisory direction for educators and their legal advisors is more nuanced than ever before and has a shorter shelf life.

WHAT IS TRANSGENDER?

Given that sexuality is best examined as a spectrum concept, transgender individuals are not just men who have some effeminate characteristics or women who display some masculine traits. Even during the turbulent social changes of the late 20th century, medical science defined transgender as a disorder, and "Gender Identity Disorder" was a classification in the Diagnostic and Statistical Manual of Mental Disorders (American Psychological Association, 1980).

Over three decades later, a comprehensive study of the effect of sex hormones on brain activity was conducted at the Medical University of Vienna and the results were definitive: gender identity is a complex neurological event, one that is not always linked to physical sex, is not "immediately discernible and primarily established in the psyche of a human being" (How our gender influences us, 2016). As a neurological event, gender identity is also partially claimed, studied, and parsed by psychological academics. Rands (2009) recognizes five gender-based terms that, while related, differ a great deal in research use, and presumably could have legal implications. These are *gender identity* (how one self-identifies), *gender expression* (how one dresses, acts, presents to the world), *gender attribution* (how one is gender-identified by the world), *gender roles* (social expectations assigned to a specific binary gender), and *gender assignment* (official social designation by gender). It is the last term in particular that has clear legal implications because conflict over gender identity primarily occurs when a societal institution and its policy enforcers require or prohibit a behavior that an aggrieved individual believes is contradictory to their gender identity.

Today, *transgender* may still not have a clinically pristine a definition, but recognizing its spectrum nature and understanding that it is both a psychological and a biological construct is a distinct improvement over early connotations of the term. For example, *transgender* is different from *straight, lesbian, gay, bi-sexual, asexual, queer,* and other terms associated with sexual identity and behavior. Stryker and Whittle (2006) pointed out that early use of the term identified primarily those individuals who wore clothing and assumed behaviors of the sex other than their birth assignment, usually without any implication of attempts at body changing. Today, *transgender* is still an ambiguous term but it does include identification and presentation, and often implies some changes of the physical self. The most common form of physical transformation is hormone therapy whereas the most invasive form is surgical alteration of both external and internal sex and reproductive organs.

There is legal reason to consider the physical process utilized by transgender individuals. Hormone therapy dramatically alters physical attributes such as strength, weight, and stamina. As a result, competitive situations that are dependent on those physical attributes are ripe for charges of discrimination or competitive advantage. Likewise, the requirements for some types of employment include physical components. For those reasons, the areas of law most often impacted by transgender identity and discrimination are employment law and competitive athletics. The gifted female South African Olympian track star, Semenya Caster, whose physicality and power might have allowed her to compete successfully in men's or women's events, are often cited as an example of the need for more sophisticated markers for gender than those currently used by the International Olympic Committee (IOC Consensus Meeting on Sex Reassignment and Hyperandrogenism, 2015).

THE CIVIL RIGHTS ACT: TITLE VII AND TITLE IX

The two pillars of law that impact the litigation of transgender discrimination are the similarly named, but different in focus, Title VII and Title IX. The wide umbrella of the Civil Rights Act of 1964 included several references to sex discrimination, but Title VII specifically targets discrimination in employment practices. Later amendments to the 1964 legislation allow for recovery of compensatory and punitive damages and include similar discrimination associated with the Americans with Disabilities Act and section 501 of the Rehabilitation Act (Civil Rights Act [CRA], 1964). While there is a Title IX included in the CRA of 1964, the Title IX that impacts discrimination litigation is the Title IX portion associated with the Education Amendments of 1972. Title IX specifically prohibits exclusion from participation, denial of benefits, or discrimination *on the basis of sex* in any education program or activity that accepts federal financial aid (Education Amendments, 1972).

These two major components of the discrimination law, when taken together, create a formidable legal weapon for application in transgender disputes. Neither Title VII nor Title IX was written specifically with transgender people in mind, and certainly not with guidance for the legal disputes about toilet and locker room access that have arisen during the second decade of the 21st century. Specifically, Title VII's fundamental purpose is to prohibit employment discrimination based on membership in one of several protected classes. Sex is one of these groups, but given its drafting in 1964, this section likely meant binary sex, not transgender. In fact, for several decades, transgender and all non-gender-conforming cases were not protected under Title VII. Slowly, the judiciary has embraced a more inclusive definition of sex.

Similarly, Senator Birch Bayh (the "Father of Title IX") probably did not anticipate transgender bathroom usage when he advocated strongly for equality of athletic programs for women in higher education. Indeed, the original intent of Title IX's discrimination prohibition now includes unwanted sexual behavior, up to and including assault and rape, and can be litigated, at least in part, as sex discrimination cases under Title IX.

EMPLOYMENT LAW DISCRIMINATION

Before the Civil Rights Act of 1964 and its component Title VII, employees had some recourse when experiencing discrimination, but such protection was usually articulated through broad stroke Constitutional coverage, such as the Fifth and Fourteenth Amendments. Issues related to pay, working conditions, and union membership were addressed in the Fair Labor Standards Act and other statutory law. In addition, individual states also had protections for employees. Title VII, however, specifically brought sex discrimination into pointed consideration, although the several manifestations of sex and gender identification (transgender) was not singularly addressed.

Transgender Discrimination and Employment Law

The legal and social paths to understanding how the law applies to transgender individuals are neither short nor straight. In order to arrive at a reasonable examination of some of the legal questions surrounding cases of transgender public school students, cases that involve their access to bathrooms and locker rooms, it helps to understand how the applicable law has evolved. In the 1960s, terms such as *integration, segregation, discrimination, prejudice, equality,* and *tolerance* became so widely used that popular culture absorbed them and, as a result, lost some level of clear definition. Over time, as the left and right ends of the 1960s' initial socio-political schism came closer together, legislation eventually codified what a majority of the nation could live with. It achieved this in terms of new ways of considering how racial differences, religious differences, ethnic differences, and sexual differences would be dealt with in the legal domain.

That overarching codification was the Civil Rights Act of 1964. Proving that some leaders do, indeed, grow into their office, the ultimate insider and Southern Democrat, President Lyndon Baines Johnson shepherded the sweeping civil rights reform that ultimately put Titles VII and IX into the everyday vocabulary of lawyers, civil rights advocates, educators, and millions of Americans who were, in some way, "different" from the societal norm.

Titles VII and IX in Employment Law

Title IX at its inception referred to binary male-female designations to define sex, and until recently, transgender (sometimes still called *transsexual*) which was not included in the list of classes under civil rights protection (*Ulane v. Eastern Airlines*, 1984). The Supreme Court has broadened some aspects of that original exclusion, though, most notably in inclusion of consideration of incidents of employment law discrimination (*Price Waterhouse v. Hopkins*, 1989).

In 2000, two Circuit courts (Nine and One) broke new legal ground by recognizing transgender plaintiffs as members of protected classes for purposes of Title VII non-discrimination. Actually, the recognition included a larger genre of gender non-conforming individuals, not just transgender (*Schwenk v. Hartford*, 2000 and *Rosa v. Park West Bank & Trust*, 2000). Of equal value in the evolution of transgender civil rights protection, district courts at the federal level during that same time period accepted more Title VII claims from transgender plaintiffs (*Doe v. United Consumer Financial Services*, 2001).

Significant Employment Law Cases

Doe v. United Consumer Financial Services: Transgender woman was terminated because employers could not tell her gender "just from looking".
Price Waterhouse v. Hopkins: Employer may not discriminate against a transgender woman who appears (clothing and behavior) too masculine.
Rosa v. Park West Bank & Trust Co.: Transgender woman was denied loan application because she was not dressed as a man.
Schwenk v. Hartford: Transgender woman was assaulted by a guard while she was incarcerated. Argument went to whether the assault was a sexual assault or animus toward transgender.
Ulane v. Eastern Airlines, Inc.: Title VII does not prohibit discrimination against those with sexual identity *disorder*.

Because a significant amount of societal evolution occurs in the work place, Title VII and the Equal Employment Opportunity Commission (EEOC) that enforces it, need a clear and unambiguous meaning for the key terms included in the statute. For a time, a Band-Aid approach was taken by merely adding "sex" in the list of protected classes. Often, social trends outpace law and such was the case with the Title VII definition of key terminology. For that reason, the strong feminist movement of the 1980s had laid the foundational groundwork so that by the time *Price Waterhouse* was heard by the Supreme Court, the decision to find for the transgender woman plaintiff was not seriously in doubt. Clearly, in 1989, no employer could discriminate against an employee for simply appearing insufficiently masculine or feminine. After *Price Waterhouse*, the tortured language associated with the term "sex" in legal terminology had made great strides in evolution (Feldblum, 2013).

EDUCATION LAW DISCRIMINATION

Public education functions as an extension of the state, thus all applicable employment prohibitions on discrimination in governmental settings is in place in public schools, both P-12 and higher education. In addition, Title IX further encompasses all private or for-profit institutions that accept federal funds. While several agencies and statutes address protection against discrimination for some vulnerable populations, litigation that impacts sex discrimination in educational practice is, like employment discrimination, most impacted by the application of Title VII and Title IX. Equally like employment law, application of Title VII and Title IX in educational discrimination litigation still grapples with specifics of discrimination involving non-conforming gender cases.

Title VII and Title IX in Education Law

Consideration of transgender discrimination in education allowed the evolution of Title IX, by introducing the protected civil rights class status of transgender to be considered in determining equal protection claims. A ground-breaking case that established transgender as a protected class was one tried in New York federal district court that allowed a transgender woman to sue New York University in a sexual harassment case, citing her rights under Title IX, specifically as it prohibits sex discrimination in a public educational institution that accepts federal funding. The university's claim that the plaintiff was a biological male in transition to female, thus could not claim sexual harassment in the person of a male professor. That claim was discounted by the court.

> The simple facts are ... that Professor Eisen was engaged in indefensible sexual conduct directed at plaintiff which caused her to suffer distress and ultimately forced her out of the doctoral program in her chosen field. There are no conceivable reasons why such conduct should be rewarded with legal pardon just because, unbeknownst to Professor Eisen and everyone else at the university, plaintiff was not a biological female. (*Miles v. New York University*, 1997)

With "Sex" Defined, What About Bathrooms?

As can be seen from the evolution of Titles VII and IX litigation, the original intent was to inform employment law (Title VII) and education equity (Title IX).

Access to bathrooms and locker rooms has become a symbol of the newest battle in the increasingly more ambiguous, complex—and confusing—sexual revolution (*Johnston v. University of Pittsburgh*, 2015). Not so long ago, discussion about sex discrimination in education could use the terms "gender" and "sex" interchangeably. Disputes almost exclusively had to do with whether girls' programs were treated in a manner on par with boys' programs. While all arguments freely used the term *equality* in defence of various positions, most combatants really meant "more stuff for my side." And everybody meant that "girls" were biologic females with XX chromosomes and "boys" were biologic males with XY chromosomes (*Kastl v. Maricopa County Community College*, 2009). While there remains argument about exactly what "equality" means in some fact-specific situations, in general, the legal, psychological, financial, and curricular definition of equality has been determined.

Title IX of the Education Amendments Act of 1972 put a hefty price tag on sex discrimination for institutions that accepted federal funding. It took seven more years for the (then) Department of Health, Education and Welfare to establish a three-prong test for compliance:

- athletic participation opportunities that are substantially proportionate to student enrolment;
- continual expansion of athletic opportunities for the underrepresented sex; and
- accommodation of the interest and ability of underrepresented sex.

The courts have varied wildly in describing transgender as a medical, biological, and psychological condition—but have generally settled on Gender Identity Disorder (*Glenn v. Brumby*, 2011). It was not until 2014 that the new and improved Department of Education refined Title IX compliance, where institutions were instructed to treat students "consistent with their gender identity", superficially appeared to be dealing with the issue, but in reality, created more questions.

In employment settings without mandatory attendance, regimentation according to sex may be quite different from the educational world. Schools are often divided around gender and certainly are tasked with promulgating social skills that are usually shaped by societal expectations of gender-specific behaviour. Title IX 1972 however, intends that "no person in the United States shall, on the basis of sex, be excluded from participation in, be denied the benefits of, or be subjected to discrimination under any education program or activity [that] is receiving Federal financial assistance." A straightforward reading of that statement would appear to cover transgender, thus to claim discrimination under Title IX, an individual would be required to demonstrate that their grievance occurred as a result of their gender—because he or she was being a "male" or "female" (Shults, 2005). However, that observation still reflects the use of gender as a binary construct.

Without too much argument, one could assume that when public bathrooms are segregated by sex, transgender people should be able to use the bathroom that matches their gender identity. However, in the early test cases of transgender bathroom and locker room access in public school settings, the objections of community members and parents of "straight" students play a large role, both in the decisions and policies of the schools and in the litigation strategy when those cases move to court. In May 2016, the Education Department (through its Office of Civil Rights) and the Justice Department's Civil Rights Division sent a joint Dear Colleague letter to all public schools in the United States, clarifying the intent of Title IX to allow transgender students to use the bathrooms and locker rooms that aligned with their gender identity. Almost immediately, parental and political voices decried the federal executive overreach of such an edict (Suk, 2016). The parental objection tended to focus on safety, privacy, comfort for gender-conforming students. Political objection was, in large part, opportunistic. The chance to criticize Washington and stand loud and proud for "family and traditional" values was almost like an election year gift.

While the criticism of federal overreach was not unexpected, it was also not unreasonable. The effect of such a departmental rule, with the implicit threat of enforcement by withholding funds, is equivalent to creating law without any input from voters or by elected representatives. In litigation, it has been established that the Dear Colleague letter does not rise to the level of application of the *Chevron* deference, a legal principle by which a court is not required to agree with an administrative regulation, but must respect such regulation as having been created by experts in the field, who presumably have depth of knowledge and responsibility to establish a reasonable regulation. The absence of both *Chevron* deference and public input contributes to the pushback that the Dear Colleague letter has generated.

Protecting and Litigating Rights to Bathroom and Locker Room Access

To some observers of the transgender legal movement, bathroom and locker room access is at the forefront, both as a real issue of concern as well as serving as a symbol of the entire protest against sexual/gender discrimination. Transgender student cases are currently active in several parts of the country, some pre-dating the Education Department's Dear Colleague letter, but several more because of that missive. In what may be considered a landmark decision in the debate about the definition of gender and sex for the purposes of use of public bathrooms, *G.G. v. Gloucester County*, 2015 (the *Gloucester* case), a high school student in Virginia has brought a face to the discussion. G.G. is a transgender boy who entered high school as a female, but after beginning treatment for gender dysphoria, requested that his masculine name be reflected on his school records, that he be addressed with masculine pronouns, and that accommodations for bathroom usage be established. The high school met all his requests, specifically by allowing G.G. to use the bathroom in the nurse's office. He later asked to be allowed to use bathrooms designated for boys because the use of the nurse's bathroom singled him out.

Shortly after this arrangement was established, the school's governing board held a public hearing on a proposed resolution requiring bathroom usage according to biological sex. Many citizens spoke to their support of the resolution, as well as G.G. himself in opposition. The resolution passed and G.G. filed suit in district court asking for an injunction that would allow him to continue to use the boys' bathroom until conclusion of the litigation. He further claimed violation of Title IX protection against sex discrimination. The Department of Education issued an Amicus Curiae brief in support of G.G.'s position that Title IX protects the right of bathroom usage choice for transgender students. The court dismissed G.G.'s Title IX claim, which in turn made moot the injunction request.

On appeal (*G.G. v. Gloucester County*, 2016), the circuit court reversed the 2015 decision of the district court concerning Title IX protection, stating that transgender students are protected from sex discrimination under the provisions of the Department of Education's Section 106.33 regulations language that indicates only binary sex designation. That decision also allowed G.G.'s injunction request to stand.

Today's interpretation of application for Title IX regulations concerning sex discrimination is quite different from what Congress must have thought they were approving, although it is not hard to imagine that with exposure to the intervening three decades of social evolution they might have been pleased. How to deal with transgender discrimination and harassment issues, and whether transgender is a protected class under Title IX, fuel just the latest chapter in that evolution. The crux of the new discussion is couched in the language that originally called for equal facilities for men and women in institutions that accepted federal funding: "A recipient may provide separate toilet, locker room, and shower facilities on the basis of sex, but such facilities provided for students of one sex shall be comparable to such facilities provided for students of the other sex" (34 C.F.R. § 106.33, 2000).

The Dear Colleague letter issued by the Education Department and the Justice Department has a counterpart issued by the EEOC and Office of Civil Rights (OCR). A "Fact Sheet: Bathroom Access Rights for Transgender Employees Under Title VII of the Civil Rights Act of 1964" gives employers guidance on transgender employees, generally defining "sex" as "gender identity." It goes further, though, in specifically citing prohibited behavior as including discrimination based on hostility, desire to protect persons of a particular gender, stereotyping, or *the desire to accommodate other people's prejudices or discomfort* (emphasis added). The last section is very important because one of the focus factors of the *Gloucester* case is the strong community complaint against allowing G.G. to continue using the bathrooms that align with his gender identity. However, the "Fact Sheet" is designed for guidance of workplace behavior and impacts employment law, not yet applied to Title IX and transgender issues in schools.

THE NATIONAL FUTURE OF BATHROOM AND LOCKER ROOM WARS

In years to come, when transgender bathroom and locker room issues are definitively decided through judicial action, the *Gloucester* case is likely to be the cited landmark simply because it is the one most likely to be presented to the Supreme Court first. It is important to note that similar cases are lodged in California, Wisconsin, and Maryland. Likewise, coalitions of states have challenged the Education Department Dear Colleague letter, claiming executive overreach. It is not completely clear how the several individual cases and the collective challenges will resolve. In late 2016, several mitigating factors are influencing resolution, but whether they *should* or not is another issue. These include the schismatic politics of an unprecedented presidential campaign, the waning but still vocal influence of hard line right wing social politics, and the effort of the courts to parse language to limit appellate repudiation. For example, since *Gloucester* has progressed further in the judicial process, some other cases have cited the *Gloucester* findings and decisions, but have not succeeded in doing so because *Gloucester* facts are restricted to bathroom access, not to locker room usage rights.

Just as the legal and procedural issues surrounding segregation were legally resolved, but still have far to go in resolution of attendant social issues, it is likely that a judicial or legislative resolution for transgender bathroom and locker room access will appear. It is equally likely that, decades after that resolution, human issues of prejudice and misunderstanding will still abound.

REFERENCES

American Psychological Association. (1980). *Diagnostic and statistical manual of mental disorders* (3rd ed.). Washington, DC: Author.
Civil Rights Act of 1964 § 7, 42 U.S.C. § 2000e et seq (1964).
Doe v. United Consumer Financial Services, Case No. 1:01CV1112 (N.D. Ohio 2001).
Education Amendments of 1972 § 9, 20 U.S.C. § 1681 et seq (1972).
Feldblum, C. (2013). Vulnerable population: Law, policies in practice and social norms: Coverage of transgender discrimination under sex discrimination law. *Journal of Law in Society, 14*(1), 1–20.
G.G. v. Gloucester County. G.G. ex rel. Grimm v. Gloucester County School Board, 132 F. Supp. 3d 736 (E.D. Va. 2015).

G.G. v. Gloucester County. G.G. ex rel. Grimm v. Gloucester County School Board, 822 3d 709 (4th Cir. 2016).
Glenn v. Brumby, 724 F. Supp. 2d 1284 (N.D. Ga. 2010), aff'd, 663 F. 3d 1312 (11th Cir. 2011).
How our gender influences us. (2016, August 22). *Medizin & Wissenschaft.* Retrieved from https://www.meduniwien.ac.at/web/en/press-meduni-vienna/press-release-german-only
International Olympic Committee: IOC Consensus Meeting on Sex Reassignment and Hyperandrogenism (2015). Retrieved from https://www.olympic.org/
Johnston v. University of Pittsburgh, 97 F. Supp. 3d 657 (W.D. Pa. 2015).
Kastl v. Maricopa County Community College District, 325 Fed. Appx. 492 (9th Cir. 2009).
Miles v. New York University, 979 F. Supp. 248 (S.D.N.Y. 1997).
Price Waterhouse v. Hopkins, 490 U.S. 228 (1989).
Rands, K. (2009). Considering transgender people in education. *Journal of Teacher Education, 60*(4), 419–431. doi:10.1177/0022487109341475
Rosa v. Park West Bank & Trust Co., 214 F. 3d 213 (1st Cir. 2000).
Schwenk v. Hartford, 204 F. 3d 1187 (9th Cir. 2000).
Shults, E. (2005). Sharply drawn lines: An examination of Title IX, intersex, and transgender. *Cardozo Journal of Law and Gender, 12*, 337–351.
Stryker, S., & Whittle, S. (Eds.). (2006). *The transgender studies reader.* New York, NY: Routledge.
Suk, J. (2016, May 24). The transgender bathroom debate and the looming Title IX crisis. *The New Yorker.* Retrieved from http://www.newyorker.com/news/news-desk/public-bathroom-regulations-could-create-a-title-ix-crisis#
Ulane v. Eastern Airlines, 742 F. 2d 1081 (7th Cir. 1984).

CHAPTER TWO

Just Another Gay Day IN THE Campus Three Year Old Room

ROBIN K. FOX AND ERICA SCHEPP

THE SETTING

It is a "typical" day in the three year old classroom at the University's Children's Center. "Typical" meaning there are twelve children involved in activities, families are dropping off children, teacher assistants and student teachers are working with children as the lead teacher talks to a faculty member about a research project at a child size table. At one of the tables the teacher assistant is playing with three children as they sort objects by color, size, texture, etc. The children are talking about their families. One of the children states that she has two dads and one of the other children says "You can't have two dads. Who is your mom?" to which the first child responds "I don't have a mom. I have two dads." This back and forth goes on for a while and then the children turn to the teacher assistant who hasn't spoken. They appear to be looking for her to offer information. She responds by asking them if they can think of other ways to sort the objects in front of them.

As the teacher assistant is clocking out for the day, the lead teacher follows her out of the classroom and asks her how she felt things went with the children. With a quivering voice, the teacher assistant said she got nervous when the children talked about having two dads and didn't know what to say. The lead teacher said she had overheard the exchange and rather than jumping in and taking over the teacher decided to wait and talk to the teacher assistant at the end of her shift. They talked about why the teacher assistant was nervous, how by saying nothing she may have made the children feel like this was something they shouldn't talk about and that it would be most poignant if the teacher assistant did some thinking, reviewed some resources and then either brought in a book to read to the children to enter back into this conversation or thought of how to engage all of the children in a discussion about families and preparing herself for the questions the children may have.

The teacher assistant accepted the challenge of reviewing resources and did research on her own so she was prepared to talk to the children. And a couple of days later she asked the same children if she could talk to them. The teacher assistant asked the lead teacher to listen to the discussion and give her feedback. The feedback shared was that the teacher assistant handled questions well, she gave information and it was a calm conversation. But what happened beyond the three year old classroom was that this teacher assistant, who was majoring in Social Work, then took what she learned at the Center and used it when a discussion in one of her courses about same sex marriage emerged. She was able to discuss statistics, laws, and information about the LGBTQ community. Through this experience she became a knowledgeable, thoughtful, ally who continued her work advocating for the children whose parents are members of the LGBTQ community all because some three year olds asked questions and a staff member gave her the gift of learning.

CAMPUS CHILDREN'S CENTERS AS LGBTQ SPACES

With over 1,400 campus children's centers in the United States (www.education-department.org/daycare.php) we would be remiss if we didn't include them in any discussion about campus climate as related to LGBTQ issues. Children's centers serve a variety of purposes from childcare for faculty, students and staff; to research sites for teacher education faculty; to practicum sites for teachers in training along with being an employment opportunity for students. Many of the campus children's centers are nationally accredited and are considered model programs which follow the National Association for the Education of Young Children's *Developmentally Appropriate Practices* (Copple & Bredekamp, 2009) and *Anti-Bias Education* (Derman-Sparks & Olsen Edwards, 2010).

DEVELOPMENTALLY APPROPRIATE PRACTICES AS A STARTING POINT

There are three core considerations of *Developmentally Appropriate Practices* that teachers of young children are to consider when developing learning activities and environments. Those three principles are:

- What is known about child development and learning-referring to knowledge of age-related characteristics that permits general predictions

about what experiences are likely to best promote children's learning and development?
- What is known about each child as an individual-referring to what practitioners learn about each children that has implications for how to best to adapt and be responsive to that individual variation?
- What is known about the social and cultural contexts in which children live-referring to the values, expectations, and behavioural and linguistic conventions that shape children's lives at home and in their communities that practitioners must strive to understand in order to ensure that learning experiences in the program or school are meaningful, relevant, and respectful for each child? (Copple & Bredekamp, 2009, pp. 9–10)

These core considerations could just as well have been written for university instructors, residence hall personnel, campus activities programmers, health and counselling staff working at universities, etc. This idea that when we plan for activities (a lecture, a program developed by a hall director, Freshmen Convocation, etc.) we consider the appropriateness of what we are planning based on general understanding of the developmental level for whom the activity is planned along with specific needs of individuals while always considering the culture and lived experiences of the individuals. It is important to note that Copple and Bredekamp do not write about the responsibility of the children or even the families to make sure the activities take into consideration these three tenets and yet when working with university students we do expect the students to often speak up. For example, campus childcare center staff who adhere to these three tenets and specifically the third one related to culture and lived experiences would not wait for a child who has two moms or two dads or a parent who is transgender before including age appropriate children's literature about members of the LGBTQ community. The staff would view this as their responsibility so when LGBTQ members enter their space they see representations of their lived experiences. On the other hand, we have often heard university personnel say things like "I would include gay literature in my course if someone asked me to but no one ever has." There can be an expectation that the solving of the issue is somehow the responsibility of the student or staff member who is LGBTQ.

USING ANTI-BIAS EDUCATION WITH CHILDREN AND AT UNIVERSITIES

The *Anti-Bias Education* was developed by Derman-Sparks and Olsen Edwards (2010) and for many in the early childhood profession it is seen as the partner to *Developmentally Appropriate Practices*. There are four goals of the Anti-Bias Education:

- Each child will demonstrate self-awareness, confidence, family pride, and positive social identities;
- Each child will express comfort and joy with human diversity; accurate language for human differences and deep, caring human connections;
- Each child will increasingly recognize unfairness, have language to describe unfairness, and understand that unfairness hurts;
- Each child will demonstrate empowerment and the skills to act, with others or alone, against prejudice and/or discriminatory actions. (pp. 3–5)

Just as with the goals of *Developmentally Appropriate Practices*, the goals of the *Anti-Bias Education* could just as easily be written for the work we do with university students. Of course it would be the hope that by the time students enter the university these goals have been partially achieved related to LGBTQ issues. But for many students whose experience with "out" members of the LGBTQ community is limited, the university may be the first time they get to know a fellow student who is openly gay or they meet someone who is out as transgender or they may have a faculty member who writes about and lectures about being lesbian in a small town, or the student may come to understand or accept or come out as a member of the community. The goals of the *Anti-Bias Education* pertain to young children and university students and everyone in between and beyond.

THE POTENTIAL IMPACT IN CHILDCARE CENTERS AND ON CAMPUS

High quality early childhood education has long been cited as having positive impacts on the lives of the children and at times their families (Duncan & Magnuson, 2013) and because of the potential influence campus children's centers are where discussions about social justice, equity, heteronormativity, noticing and celebrating differences should take place as the impact reaches beyond the children who receive care at the centers. Campus children's centers are in a unique situation that allows the youngest on campus to lead the way to more inclusive, welcoming and celebratory spaces for members of the LGBTQ community both on and off campus. The tenets of high quality early childhood teaching and social justice practices in early childhood education can be generalized to the broader university community.

If campus children's centers adhere to the goals of *Developmentally Appropriate Practices* and *Anti-Bias Education* how and what is taught there has potential to open up spaces for dialogue across campus. For example, if a child says to another child "that is so gay" and a teacher intervenes having a calm discussion about the hurtfulness of such a statement it is not only the children who hear this dialogue.

There are student teachers, volunteers, researchers, teaching assistants who also overhear the discussion and might take that experience and use a similar tactic the next time they overhear a peer, student or instructor use a hurtful word or phrase. Additionally the families of the children may be privy to such interactions or told about it after the fact by their child or the teacher. It might be that the parent is a member of the LGBTQ community and now knows how situations like this are handled and in turn feels supported by the center staff. The parent might even be empowered to raise their hand in class and ask about when gay centered curriculum will be incorporated, or go to the Registrar's office and request that a university form be changed to be more LGBTQ friendly or may use pronouns in a writing assignment they haven't used before.

INCREASING NUMBERS: CHILDREN, PARENTS, STUDENTS, FACULTY, STAFF

Families with two moms, two dads, polyamorous family combinations, parents who are transgender and combinations other than a biological mom and dad are becoming more visible in our children's centers (Beren, 2013). Children are "coming out" as it relates to gender identity and expression (gender fluid) at younger ages (Payne & Smith, 2014) and although young children may not "come out" in preschool as lesbian, gay or queer, many people share that at a very early age they felt "different" which as adults attribute to knowing they were gay. Statistically, based solely on the increased number of people (children, university students, staff, parents) associated with campus children's centers who are LGBTQ, it makes sense that center staff recognize and address the needs of members of the LGBTQ community.

> Our daughter was in a four year old kindergarten room at a childcare center. The center staff knew we were a two mom family and we thought they were comfortable with our family. In our daughter's classroom they used themes so when the "Family Week" theme came up we asked the teacher to please have books in the classroom about families that looked like our family (specifically, two mom or two dad families).
> At drop off and pick up time the first day of the week we noticed that *And Tango Makes Three* was displayed on the bookshelf. Our family loves that book and although it was about a two dad penguin family we recognized that for some teachers it might be more palatable than a book about a two person family. What we weren't prepared for is when we talked to our daughter after Family Week was over and she said that no one read the book all week although she was certain that most of the other books about families (with a mom and dad) were read. We felt like it was almost worse to have the book on display and NOT read it than to have it there and no one touch it all week. Clearly our daughter was watching.
> When we did a walk through at a university childcare center we saw not only were there books already in the classrooms about two mom families but there was someone

reading one of the books to a small group of children. The children asked questions and the teacher answered the questions. It was amazing to see and we felt like we didn't have to do all of the educating of the staff.

BEYOND DISPLAYING THE BOOKS AND HETERONORMATIVE DISCOURSES

This parent attempted to disrupt the heteronormative narratives that are played out in early childhood settings by requesting children's literature which included LGBTQ characters. Heteronormative discourses are found in many aspects of early childhood settings (Blaise & Taylor, 2012) from the songs that are sung (*The Farmer in the Dell*) to the books read (*Berenstain Bear* series) to the posters on the walls. And the same can be written regarding university campuses.

Heteronormative narratives are so embedded in the culture of campuses that often they go unnoticed or unchallenged. For the university children's center the parents toured, it may be easier to dismantle some of those heteronormative discourses as a childcare center is smaller than the university as a whole. It can be easier to work with a staff of 50 teachers and teacher assistants within the confines of four early childhood classrooms than to change an entire university campus and rid it of all examples of heteronormativity. Some examples are Homecoming King and Queen, pictures of couples which appear to be male/female in marketing materials, the continuation of locker rooms for males and females or bathrooms for females or males which a smattering of "all gender" single stall bathrooms, wings in residence halls for females or males but not both, etc.

Even more powerful are the more explicit examples our students tell us about, such as questions about sexual activity and type of birth control used from the health center assuming that all students who are sexually active require birth control, or comments from a professor to a student about their "boyfriend" (the student appears to be female) or the activity in a biology course about heredity that includes tracking a student's mom and dad to see what traits are dominant (this type of activity also implies that there is a mom and dad, that the parents are the biological parents of the student, that the biological parents are "known," etc.).

But universities don't have to do this work alone. There are numerous resources for working toward more LGBTQ friendly spaces, curriculum, policies and procedures. One such resource that may be helpful for university administrators is Campus Pride and specifically looking at what a university student who identifies as a member of the LGBTQ community would be looking for when determining if a campus is "friendly" (Windmeyer, 2012). By using a simple questionnaire a campus could quickly see where there are areas to be improved upon and where they embrace areas of strength.

Just like in early childhood centers, it is not enough to have the books with LGBTQ themes and characters that go untouched or unread in a child's classroom the same is true for university libraries that have books with LGBTQ themes or by authors who are LGBTQ but no required readings from these texts. It is not enough to have a poster or two around campus in which the people in the photo could be read as members of the LGBTQ community while hundreds of other visual artifacts depict what appears to be a man and a woman as a couple.

It is not enough for some members of the campus community to have *Safe Zone* placards on their office doors while numerous faculty and staff doors do not have this sign of safety. And it is not enough that topics related to LGBTQ issues are on course syllabi to be covered at the end of the semester (as faculty we are well aware that what is listed at the end of the semester is often times not covered because other topics have taken longer than expected).

Just as early childhood is a time when children are "forming cultural identities, friendships, developing opinions and appreciating others" (Flores, 2014, p. 117) so too are the university years a time of potential growth in developing cultural competency which includes the LGBTQ culture. Consider the following experience of one campus childcare leader:

> I was a new director of a campus childcare center. One of the first things I did was to change the registration form. The form I inherited had a line for "mother" and a line for "father." At the time I would have, if asked, defined myself as an ally so I knew the form should be changed to better meet the needs of families with two moms or two dads. So I changed the form and took off "mother" and "father" instead adding the words "parent/guardian" under each of the lines.
>
> One day I gave a tour to a parent who was interested in the program for her child. The parent talked about her partner who was a woman and about the father of the child. I can remember thinking I was proud of the posters around the classrooms in which phrases like "Teach peace and celebrate diversity" were displayed. At the end of the tour I gave the parent the forms to complete and asked her to contact me with any questions. I was surprised when she called the next day and told me that although the tour was helpful in understanding the philosophy of the center she felt like maybe it wasn't the right fit for her family. She shared that although the enrolment form didn't have a place for a mother and father it made her feel like her family didn't belong.
>
> This mother needed more; two lines on the application form and my attempt at inclusion seemed to have been quite a fail. In hindsight I get it—I was still thinking of a family as the typical two parent grouping. I knew then that I had a lot of work to do in helping people feel welcomed and included. And of course I changed the form again—no more lines—just large spaces for people to define "family" in the way that worked best for them. I used this example during staff trainings for many years after the experience to share with those at the center that there is always more to learn about helping people to feel welcomed and included. I share often how embarrassed I was that this parent had to teach me what I should have already known.

We use this example to illustrate that even someone working at an accredited university children's center with the best intentions and professional training in *Developmentally Appropriate Practices* and *Anti-Bias Education* can make mistakes when attempting to do the work of welcoming and supporting members of the LGBTQ community. Likewise, making changes to the culture of large universities or even small community colleges to be more inclusive and welcoming to the LGBTQ community is undoubtedly a vast undertaking in which there may be some mistakes but just as the childcare director did in the story above university personnel need to take on these challenges, being open to critique and change.

BACK TO THE THREE YEAR OLD CLASSROOM

We return to the story at the beginning of this chapter. There is so much to learn from what happened in this situation and much to be generalized to the broader campus community. The children were in a safe place where they could talk about their lived experiences and they were not silenced. Although the teacher assistant didn't know how to enter the conversation there was a lead teacher to guide her afterward. The lead teacher viewed "teaching children to view cultural diversity as an asset" (Bauml & Mongan, 2014, p. 4) and encouraged the teacher assistant to gain the tools to initiate further discussion with the children. The teaching assistant took the time to learn and then she returned to the children to engage with them using what she had learned. What happened in this classroom could happen throughout every college campus—making a safe space to talk about lived experiences, having thoughtful mentors for our students, faculty and staff to offer tools and support for learning and finally not expecting everyone to have all of the answers but for everyone to care enough for and about each other to enter into difficult conversations.

And what about the child who was silent during the initial exchange? He was not the child who had two dads or the child who said that type of family configuration didn't exist. Instead he was silent. What would he have learned if the teacher assistant didn't revisit the discussion? If he grew up and defined himself as part of the "straight" world he may have learned that silence is ok, that he had no role to play in these types of discussion, or that it wasn't ok to have difficult conversations. Any of the children in this scenario, without an adult intervening, could interpret an adult's silence in any number of ways which over time could manifest in continued silence, apparent distain for the LGBTQ community or worse. Or if he grew up and identified with the LGBTQ community, he may have felt like Brian Silveira did. He stated that his teachers should have taken the time:

> … to discuss fairness, equality, and the contributions made by gay people so that I could be proud of myself. I should have grown up with their support and love because it was their

ethical responsibility to me, a 5-year-old gay boy in their care. (Burt, Gelnaw, & Lesser, 2010, p. 111)

University children's centers are the spaces on our campuses where our youngest family members spend their days. The families who use the centers find the services invaluable but these centers can have an impact on the larger campus community. We implore members of campus communities who may be struggling with how to have difficult conversations about LGBTQ issues to look to the tenets of *Developmentally Appropriate Practices* and *Anti-Bias Education* which although written for educators of young children could be a launching pad to think about meeting the needs of the LGBTQ community on their campuses.

A PERSONAL NOTE FROM ROBIN

It is not long after the horrific events at Pulse that my wife and I are laying down with our eight year old daughter at the end of a busy day, when she starts to cry. Her tears are gut wrenching and not simply the tears of an over tired child. When she is able to speak she says, "I don't want to get killed. I don't want you to get killed. People are killing brown people and people who are gay."

In that moment my heart broke again for the 49 members of our community we lost. I imagined them all as children being loved by their families and I thought about the depth of sadness, loss and anger this tragedy has left. And my heart broke for our child. We must do better. We must do better for our children so that bedtime discussions are not about a fear of being killed but can be stories of celebration and acceptance. And we must do better for all members of the LGBTQ community and we must never forget that forty-nine people lost their lives and to them we are responsible for continuing to make change in this world.

REFERENCES

Bauml, M., & Mongan, K. (2014). Getting to know you: Sharing time as culturally relevant teaching. *Dimensions of Early Childhood, 42*(2), 4–11.

Beren, M. (2013). Gay and lesbian families in the early childhood classroom: Evaluation of an online professional development course. *Learning Landscapes, 7*(1), 61–79.

Blaise, M., & Taylor, A. (2012). Research in review: A queer eye for early childhood. *Young Children, 61*(1): 88–98.

Burt, T., Gelnaw, A., & Lesser, L. K. (2010). Creating welcoming and inclusive environments for lesbian, gay, bisexual, and transgender (LGBT) families in early childhood settings. *Young Children, 65*(1): 97–102.

Copple, C., & Bredekamp, S. (2009). *Developmentally appropriate practice* (3rd ed.). Washington, DC: National Association for the Education of Young Children.

Derman-Sparks, L., & Olsen Edwards, J. (2010). *Anti-bias education for young children and ourselves*. Washington, DC: National Association for the Education of Young Children.

Duncan, G. J., & Magnuson, K. (2013). Investing in preschool programs. *Journal of Economic Perspectives, 27*(2), 109–132. doi:10.1257/jep.27.2.109

Flores, G. (2014). Teachers working cooperatively with parents and caregivers when implementing LGBT themes in the elementary classroom. *American Journal of Sexuality Education, 9*, 114–120. doi:10.1080/15546128.2014.883268

Payne, E., & Smith, M. (2014). The big freak out: Educator fear in response to the presence of transgender elementary school students. *Journal of Homosexuality, 61*, 399–418. doi:10.1080/00918369.2013.842430

Windmeyer, S. L. (2012). *Campus Pride's factors to consider in choosing a university*. Retrieved August 24, 2016 from https://www.campuspride.org/resources/factors-to-consider

CHAPTER THREE

Checking THE Pulse Early

LGBTQ-Inclusive Curriculum in Elementary Schools

DOMINIC GRASSO AND TRACI P. BAXLEY

It was approximately 7:45 a.m. and I was preparing my classroom materials for the day ahead. Students were starting to file down the hallway after eating breakfast in the cafeteria. I was writing on my whiteboard, when all of a sudden, I heard the door to my classroom open, and saw a familiar 5th grade student poke his head in. He looked at me, and I looked at him, knowing that he wasn't supposed to be in my room at this time. Before I could open my mouth to direct him to go to his homeroom class, he looked at me, shouted "faggot," began laughing, closed the door, and proceeded to march merrily down the hallway to his class. (Grasso, 2016)

OUR MOTIVATION FOR WRITING

I (Dominic) cannot pinpoint what exactly it was about that specific incident that it left such a lasting impression on me. At first, it was the fact that I had been degradingly insulted by a 5th grade student, but then I realized that I might have been more upset that I was totally unsure of how to respond. It has been well documented that teachers in schools across the nation are hearing similar anti-gay slurs used regularly (Kosciw, Greytak, Palmer, & Boesen, 2014). Perhaps just as troubling, is the fact that many teachers may not know what to do, or how to respond to a student in elementary school when they overhear students using antigay slurs, or witness a student being bullied because of their gender expression.

Fast forward to the tragic events that took place inside Pulse Nightclub, Orlando's premiere Lesbian, Gay, Bisexual, Transgender, and Queer/Questioning

(LGBTQ) nightclub during the early morning hours of June 12th, now characterized as the deadliest shooting in modern American history. At approximately 2:00 a.m., shooter Omar Mateen opened fire inside the nightclub, leaving 49 innocent people dead and wounding 53 others. While the details of the tragic event, as well as the motivation behind Mateen's actions continue to be explored, it is believed that severe homophobia may have been the underlying cause of Mateen's actions.

We began to focus on these two incidents, their commonalities, and on what we saw as systemic failures in education that contributed to such extreme absence of empathy and hostility toward differences in human identity. We began asking ourselves hard questions:

> What is the role of public education in addressing homophobic views?
> How could we build heteronormativity into mainstream curriculum?
> How prepared are teachers to talk about LGBTQ issues in their classrooms?
> How can teachers move beyond their personal biases to support and advocate for the LGBTQ student and community?

Writing this chapter gives us the opportunity to propose curricular and instructional practices that address prevailing heteronormative thoughts and the beliefs that are often woven, implicitly and explicitly, into classroom norms.

THE DANGER OF WAITING UNTIL CHILDREN ARE OLDER TO TEACH ABOUT SEXUALITY AND GENDER

In our diversity and multicultural education courses we introduce conversations about LGBTQ issues in order to help facilitate anti-bias classrooms that build consciousness, compassion, and a commitment to advocating for children and their families. One of the foundations for creating an anti-bias, caring classroom community is for teachers to:

> ... intentionally introduce issues of fairness and unfairness, and coach children to think critically and to take action. Teachers learn about children's families and cultural identities and integrate those identities into the daily life of the classroom, at the same time as they acknowledge the ways in which their own cultural identities shape their teaching. (Pelo, 2008, pp. ix–x)

To make the greatest impact, we encourage our pre-service teachers and graduate students to begin developing these equitable classrooms as early as preschool and elementary grades. Wollman-Bonilla (1998) observed a tendency in teacher candidates to avoid talking about serious issues with young children; for fear that the content will upset or damage them. It is this proclivity, to shelter or prevent students from engaging in potentially controversial topics that can lead to stereotyping, misunderstanding, and ignorance about others. While educators may question the idea of engaging elementary level students in conversations about diverse families and gender non-conformity, we believe that it is essential in order to interrupt pervasive biased or prejudiced views towards the LGBTQ community (Sleeter & Grant, 2009). In other words, Vasquez (2007) argues that,

> ... we cannot afford for [young] children not to engage in some tough conversations if they are to learn to become critical analysts of the world who are able to make informed decisions as they engage with the world around them. (p. 6)

Guiding children to be reflective and actively engaged in their communities enables them not just to acquire the skills needed to be successful academically, but it supports their skills in self-efficacy and being agents for social change. We maintain that educating students about diversity and inclusion early, can play a significant role in combatting and preventing homophobic beliefs that unchecked, can lead to catastrophic incidents like that of the Pulse Nightclub.

We aim to present solutions that may support the transformation of school curriculum into a more just and equitable experience for all students. This chapter will mainly discuss the role of elementary schools in regards to educating youth about the LGBTQ community through the lens of queer theory and equity pedagogy, and will discuss potential barriers and benefits that elementary level teachers believe to be associated with the inclusion of LGBTQ-themed curriculum. Finally, this chapter will conclude by suggesting practical strategies and recommendations that elementary level educators can implement in their own classrooms as part of a critical multicultural curriculum that will allow students to begin to combat heteronormative ideologies, as well as deconstruct hegemonic gender binaries.

THEORETICAL FRAMEWORK

Our LGBTQ-themed curriculum is grounded in critical radical theory, equity pedagogy, and queer theory. Critical radical theory (Freire, 2006; Sweet, 1998) promotes the humanization of all people and seeks to transform the world by transforming the way people think about the world and their role in it. Equity pedagogy is a process that places the student at the center of instruction. Teachers who engage in equity pedagogy employ a habit of critical self-reflection, culturally responsive teaching strategies, and a classroom environment that centers on social equity. When effectively implemented, equity pedagogy "enriches the lives of both teachers and students and enables them to envision and create a more humane and caring society" (Banks & Banks, 1995, p. 157).

Deriving from principles found within critical theory, queer theory developed in response to the gay liberation movement during the 1980s and was heavily influenced by the seminal works of Michel Foucault (1990), Judith Butler (1990) and James Sears (1992). The central goal of queer theory is to deconstruct and eliminate binary identities in regards to gender and sexuality (Butler, 1990; Foucault, 1990; Greene, 1996; Shlasko, 2006). Queer theorists contend that by labeling groups of people by sexual and gender expression identities (heterosexual vs. homosexual, masculine vs. feminine), we are perpetuating the discourse that heterosexual is normal and homosexual is abnormal (Greene, 1996; Pinar, 1998; Shlasko, 2006). By eliminating and deconstructing labels in reference to gender and sexuality such as heterosexual/homosexual, masculine/feminine, etc., individuals who may identify as queer can express themselves freely and fluidly across the gender and sexuality spectrum, instead of restricting themselves to one binary category. Queer theorists posit that when individuals are labeled within a binary category in regards to gender and sexuality, it perpetuates oppression by shifting power to the majority binary category *heterosexual* and away from the minority binary category *homosexual*.

This framework supports our assertion that teachers should provide opportunities that (a) critically reflect on their own biases and notions of equity with LGBTQ issues and community; (b) develop the background knowledge needed to take on the challenge of engaging students in the practice of challenging heteronormative binary categories in the classroom; and (c) engage students in inclusive curricula and instruction that includes LGBTQ-themed materials for students in elementary grades. Teachers that choose to adopt our equity pedagogy will provide opportunity for their students to investigate, question, and construct new knowledge trough inquiry and dialogue.

THE ROLE OF ELEMENTARY SCHOOLS IN RE/CREATING SOCIAL JUSTICE

Framed upon the concepts and thinking of critical theory, equity pedagogy, and queer theory, we will now discuss the role elementary schools play in facilitating the social justice education that is needed to transform the heteronormative discourses that have marginalized the LGBTQ community. It is important to note that there is a divide in thinking between queer theorists in regards to the idea of including LGBTQ language and themed literature and curricula in schools. Some queer theorists (Britzman, 1995; Luhman, 1998; Morris, 2005) believe that by including and introducing labels such as lesbian, gay and bisexual to students, whether through literature or through open discussions, teachers are actually only adding to the already overwhelming heteronormativity found in educational settings. According to Luhman (1998), to include representations of gay and lesbian people in the curriculum assumes that the problem of homophobia stems from ignorance, and by including LGBTQ representations, teachers are not addressing the real issue of heteronormativity. The thinking behind this relates to the work of Foucault (1990) and his concept of discourse. By engaging in a classroom discourse that identifies and distinguishes binary categories such as heterosexual and homosexual, teachers might actually be giving light to, and enforcing these binary constructs of identity, which could possibly perpetuate the already rigid heteronormative framework of educational institutions.

Other queer theorists (Blackburn & Pascoe, 2015; Rasmussen, 2004) posit that by introducing LGBTQ-themed literature in elementary classrooms, educators are in fact "queering" the curriculum, which they regard as highly beneficial for students. Rasmussen (2004) explains that because the themes that students will be exposed to in LGBTQ books are so different than themes that might usually be covered in elementary curriculums, educators are indeed pushing their limits, and questioning their reading practices, ultimately linking the tenets of queer theory into their practice. Teachers willing to engage in more inclusive practices, even beyond discussing anti-LGBTQ remarks with students, could begin with the introduction of LGBTQ-themed literature and curriculum in the elementary level classroom in hopes that educating students about diverse topics early can prevent bullying (cyber, verbal, and physical).

Topics inclusive of LGBTQ themes and families as well as gender nonconformity are typically excluded from elementary school curriculum. Kosciw, Greytak, Palmer, and Boesen (2014) found that only 18% of students are exposed to positive representations of gay and lesbian people in school curriculum. When asked to consider the inclusion of LGBTQ themes in their classroom, many educators, especially those teaching at the elementary level, immediately question why that is relevant to students, or jump to the conclusion that they are being asked to teach about gay and lesbian sex.

Throughout our years of teaching, we have heard *many* students use anti-gay terms in a variety of settings, situations and contexts. Many teachers, like me, have heard anti-LGBTQ slurs used regularly in the elementary school setting. Kosciw et al. (2014) reported that nationally, 71.4% of students heard "gay" used in a negative way frequently or often at school, and 64.5% of students heard other homophobic remarks such as "dyke" or "faggot" frequently or often. Usually, at this age, students are referring to something they do not like, and are using the anti-gay slurs as synonyms for something they consider to be "stupid," or "dumb." However, the specific incident in the opening of the chapter was the impetus that refuelled my passion and desire to promote the importance of including LGBTQ-themed literature and curriculum in elementary school classrooms. Incidents like this one can lead to a significant rationale promoting the inclusion of LGBTQ themes and issues in a well-balanced multicultural curriculum: students are not as innocent or naive as we once believed them to be.

In the 1990s, James Sears, one of the leading scholars in the field of queer theory, proposed the radical idea of "queering" the elementary curriculum. At the time, his reasoning behind it was simple: kids are not as innocent when it comes to issues of gender and sexuality, as most adults frequently believe them to be. "Childhood innocence is a veneer that we as adults impress onto children, enabling us to deny desire comfortably and silence sexuality" (Letts & Sears, 1999 p. 9).

Assumptions today about children not being aware of gender or sexuality are outdated. We are living in an age in which LGBTQ issues (Pulse Nightclub shooting, Supreme Court ruling on Gay Marriage, North Carolina Bathroom Bill) and people (Michael Sam, Caitlyn Jenner, Anderson Cooper) are constantly seen on TV, written about in magazines, and discussed on the radio. Furthermore, the vast expansion of social media has seemingly expedited how and when students are exposed to people and topics revolving around gender and sexuality (Grasso, 2016).

Additionally, research projects such as the documentary, *It's Elementary* (Chasnoff & Cohen, 1996), and *The No Outsiders Project* (Atkinson & DePalma, 2010) have proven that students at young ages know a great deal more about gender and sexuality than most adults might predict. In elementary school, a student typically is exposed to anti-LGBTQ remarks, and although they might not know exactly what they are saying, they do know that their words have a negative connotation to them. As early as elementary school, peer enforcement or acceptance of binary gender roles through homophobic harassment and name-calling has become common (Bickmore, 1999; Sears, 1998). *Welcoming Schools*, (2009) a project of the Human Rights Campaign, explains why discussing family diversity, teasing, name calling, and gender in elementary school is so important. "To help all children feel safe and welcome, schools must pro-actively address all name-calling and hurtful teasing. Anti-gay and gender-based teasing begins in elementary school and can become pervasive at this age" (p. 2).

Many teachers say nothing when they hear students using anti-LGBTQ slurs. *Welcoming Schools* (2009) suggests that when teachers overhear students use words such as "gay," "faggot," or "dyke" it is essential that teachers take the time to create a teachable moment, and educate students in regards to the words they are using.

Learning in the context of the classroom what a word such as "gay" means clarifies students' understanding. Instead of only hearing these words on the playground as put downs, children can ask questions and get information to help dispel stereotypes that can lead to insults and physical harassment (p. 2). Essentially, by fostering courageous classroom conversations and including literature about LGBTQ topics, teachers can educate students in a way that dispels stereotypes and helps prevent verbal and physical harassment (Welcoming Schools, 2009).

Past research has indicated that elementary teachers identify parental backlash, and insufficient training as significant barriers preventing them from including LGBTQ-themed literature and curriculum in their classrooms (Bouley, 2011; Flores, 2009). Due to teachers having insufficient training on how to include LGBTQ-themed literature appropriate for elementary students, many teachers are under the guise that LGBTQ books contain sexually explicit materials (Bickmore, 1999). This could not be further from the truth, as the majority of elementary level LGBTQ-themed books focus on topics such as: alternative family types, gender nonconformity, bullying, and social exclusion (Bickmore, 1999; *Welcoming Schools*, 2009).

Interestingly enough, Bickmore (1999) writes that the vast majority of stories included in an elementary school classroom *already* quietly include sexuality in the form of normalized nuclear families, characters, and heterosexual relationships. Bickmore (1999) points out that often times books considered multicultural due to the characters' exclusion from the dominant culture in other ways (race, religion, etc.) tend to particularly emphasize the protagonists' heterosexuality. Societal heteronormative practices are normalized in our daily interactions. It is this type of regulated thinking and behaving that "others" groups in society.

STRATEGIES FOR PROMOTING LGBTQ-INCLUSIVE ELEMENTARY CLASSROOMS

The next section of this chapter will include several practical recommendations for how elementary level teachers might make their classroom and curriculum more LGBTQ-inclusive. *It's Elementary* (1995) and *Welcoming School* (2009) were two research projects that began to develop strategies and lesson plans for implementing LGBTQ-themed literature in elementary level classrooms. Tables 3.1 and 3.2 include materials and ideas adapted from Grasso (2016) and the *Welcoming Schools Guide* (2009). As well, the Appendix is an annotated bibliography of LGBTQ-themed picture books that embody inclusive elementary curriculum.

SUMMARY

A curriculum that includes LGBTQ-themed literature is grounded in equity pedagogy as well as queer theory, and is intentionally designed to address the need for exposure, awareness, and empathy for a marginalized group in society. Literature addressing LGBTQ issues that confront biases and stereotypes allow for the building of critical practices and personal reflections for teachers. These dialogues in the classrooms create safe spaces for students and teachers to learn, reflect, experience, develop empathy, and provide opportunities for transformative education to take place.

Table 3.1. Suggestions for LGBTQ-Positive K to 5 Curriculum.

Grades	Materials	Subjects/Themes	Student Activities
K-2	Red- A Crayon's Story by Michael Hall The New Girl and Me by Jacqui Robinson	Language Arts/Social Studies: Themes: *Welcoming Classroom Environment *Respect *Diversity	1. Read the two trade books. 2. Lead a discussion of the themes of each book. 3. Have students draft a new set of class rules that set the tone for a more inclusive classroom environment for all students and encourages students to be themselves. 4. Have students create a Venn diagram discussing times they have felt "unwelcomed" at school and times they have felt "welcomed" at school and how they can act towards others to make their classmates feel welcomed.
K-5	I am Jazz by Jessica Herthel and Jazz Jennings Jacob's New Dress by Sarah and Ian Hoffman The Sissy Duckling by Harvey Fierstein	Language Arts/Social Studies: Themes: *Gender *Bullying *Expressing Yourself *Families	1. Read one or more of the trade books. 2. Using critical conversations, lead a class discussion regarding gender roles and bullying. 3. Primary students can compare and contrast how the characters in the book responded to the problem of not conforming to their genders. 4. Intermediate students can conduct a character analyses of the protagonists and explain how the theme of bullying is developed and explained through the plot.

Table 3.2. Suggestions for LGBTQ-Positive 3 to 5 Curriculum.

Grades	Materials	Subjects/Themes	Student Activities
3–5	And Tango Makes Three by Justin Richardson and Peter Parnell	Language Arts/ Science: Themes: *Animal Adaptations *Animals in Captivity *Different Animal Families *Diverse Human Families	1. Read the picture books. 2. Discuss the big ideas in the story with students. 3. As a science activity, discuss animal adaptations, such as adaptations that penguins have that help them survive in the arctic environments and connect how the unique family structure presented in the book have help the penguins to survive. 4. Students can conduct research reports on animals that have unique adaptations or unique family structures. 5. Using critical conversations, students can debate the pros and cons to keeping animals in captivity versus allowing animals to remain in their natural habitats.
3–5	Various children's biographies on famous LGBTQ people including: • Elton John • Barney Frank • Ellen Degeneres • Frida Khalo • Melissa Etheridge • Sir Ian McKellen • John Ameachi • Michael Sam • George Takei • Walt Whitman • Oscar Wilde	Language Arts/Music/ Physical Education/Drama Themes: *Role Models *Important People *Diversity	1. Have student to conduct research on famous LGBTQ individuals who have had influential lives as artists, actors, musicians, or athletes. 2. After conducting their research, students can create a poster board, brochure or visual presentation highlighting their chosen individual's accomplishments and how they have impacted the lives of many others.

We join with other scholars who also call for the inclusion of LGBTQ curriculum in in the classroom so teachers and students will dialogue about being othered and heteronormative practices. Finally, we believe that elementary teachers that adopt equity pedagogy and LGBTQ-themed curriculum will vigorously involves learners in a practice of knowledge construction and those students will become actively engaged in social justice … even in elementary grades.

APPENDIX

Annotated Bibliography of Elementary School Books with LGBTQ Themes

Byran, J. (2006). *The different dragon*. Two Lives Publishing. Ridley Park, PA: Alyson Publications.
This book is a story about a boy, Noah, who lives with his two mothers and their cat Diva. While his Go-Ma is telling him a bedtime story, Noah and Diva encounter a fierce fire-breathing dragon. Unfortunately, the dragon does not fit in with the other dragons because he does not want to be mean, fierce, and breathe fire anymore. Noah teaches the dragon that there is not just one way to fit in as a dragon, and that there are all types of different dragons out there who should be treated as equals.

deHaan, L., & Nijland, S. (2000). *King and king*. New York, NY: Tricycle Press.
A classic fairy tale with a new twist. The queen in the story declares that her son has been single for long enough and needs to get married. She sends out for all of the eligible princesses in the surrounding lands to come visit her son as eligible suitors, even though he tries explaining to his mother, the queen, that he has never been interested in princesses. Eventually, he turns down all of the eligible princesses, and falls in love with the brother of one of the eligible suitors. A wedding is held and they become King and King.

dePaola, T. (1979). *Oliver button is a sissy*. Orlando, FL: Harcourt.
The story of a boy named Oliver who does not conform to the typical gender activities associated with boys. Instead, Oliver would rather play dress up, jump rope, or learn to tap dance. Oliver is constantly teased at school by the other boys until he performs at the school talent show and is finally recognized for being the star he is.

Elwin, R., & Paulse, M. (1990). *Asha's mums*. Toronto, ON: Women's Press.
A short story about a girl named Asha and her class who are about to go on a field trip to a science center. When Asha brings back her permission slip back signed by her two moms, her teacher, Mrs. Samuels tells her that her form is not filled out correctly and she won't be able to go on the trip if her form is not filled out correctly. Asha becomes very upset and the next day at show and tell discussing families, a discussion about different types of families occurs.

Fierstein, H. (2002). *The sissy duckling*. New York, NY: Simon & Schuster.
Meet Marmee and Meema: two of the most loving, caring mothers a young reader will encounter, and their family of three adopted children. This book is a look at the "surprisingly normal" life of children who are raised in a same sex parent household. The book revolves around the children's interactions with the other children who live on the same block, and showcases how supportive the rest of the block is of Marmee and Meema's family. Of course, there is one neighbor on the block who simply does not approve of Marmee and Meema.

Newman, L. (1989). *Heather has two mommies*. Los Angeles, CA: Alyson Publications.
This is the story of a girl named Heather who grows up in a family with two mothers and no fathers. She joins a playgroup and the teacher, Molly, reads the group a story about a boy whose father is a veterinarian. After the story, as the other students in the play group are talking about their fathers, Heather realizes for the first time that she does not have a father, and feels excluded. A discussion about the many different types of diverse families then occurs.

Newman, L. (2004). *The boy who cried fabulous*. New York, NY: Tricycle Press.
A rhyming poetry story about a boy who gets into trouble because he cannot stop observing how "fabulous" every little detail in the world around him is. Readers will enjoy joining Roger on his every day journey and how optimistic he is about everything "fabulous" that he encounters along the way.

Polacco, P. (2009). *In our mother's house*. New York, NY: Penguin Young Readers.
Readers will meet Elmer- a boy duck who does not enjoy participating in any "typical" boy activities. Instead of playing sports, Elmer enjoys cooking and playing with dolls. Soon enough, Elmer becomes the victim of Drake Duckling (the forest bully) and when Elmer does not stand up for himself, even his own father calls Elmer a "sissy." Disheartened by his father's words, Elmer runs away from home and starts to live life on his own. However, when a group of hunters injure Elmer's father, it's up to Elmer to save his Father and show the flock of ducks that he is strong enough to be the first duck to survive a winter in the forest.

Richardson, J., & Parnell, P. (2005). *And tango makes three*. New York, NY: Simon & Schuster.
The book takes place in the Central Park Zoo and describes several of the different animal families that you might see in the zoo. The book talks about the penguin families in the zoo, and two particular penguins in the zoo, Roy and Silo, who are both boys, who do everything together (just as if boy and girl penguins would). Eventually, the zookeeper, Mr. Gramzay notices that they must be in love. Eventually, the zookeeper plants an egg in Roy and Silo's rock nest, and eventually the egg hatches into a baby penguin that they name Tango.

Valentine, J. (1991). *The duke who outlawed jelly beans and other stories.* Los Angeles, CA: Alyson Publications.

A collection of classic fairy tales that are each given slight twists to reflect LGBT themes, especially different types of families (two mothers, two fathers). For example, in the story *The Duke Who Outlawed Jelly Beans*, the Duke takes over a kingdom and begins to make ridiculous rules, including outlawing eating of jelly beans and banishing children who don't come from one mother one father "correct" homes. The children from all types of diverse families, including divorced parents, stepparents, grandparents, and same sex parents ban together to outsmart the duke.

REFERENCES

Atkinson, E., & DePalma, R. (2010). Undoing homophobia in primary schools by the *no outsiders project*. Oakhill: Trentham Books Unlimited.

Banks, C. A. M., & Banks, J. A. (1995). Equity pedagogy: An essential component of multicultural education. *Theory into Practice, 34*(3), 152–158.

Bickmore, K. (1999). Teaching conflict and conflict resolution in school: (Extra-) curricular considerations. In A. Raviv, L. Oppenheimer, & D. Bar-Tal (Eds.), *How children understand war and peace* (pp. 45–69). San Francisco, CA: Jossey-Bass.

Blackburn, M. V., & Pascoe, C. (2015). K–12 students in schools. In G. L. Wimberly (Ed.), *LGBTQ issues in education: Advancing a research agenda* (pp. 89–105). Washington, DC: AERA.

Bouley, T. (2011). Speaking up: Opening dialogue with pre-service and in-service teachers about reading children's books inclusive of lesbian and gay families. *Journal of Praxis in Multicultural Education, 6*(1), 1–19.

Britzman, D. (1995). Is there a queer pedagogy? *Educational Theory, 45*(2), 151–165.

Butler, J. (1990). *Gender trouble: Feminism and the subversion of identity.* New York, NY: Routledge.

Byran, J. (2006). *The different dragon.* Two Lives Publishing. Ridley Park, PA: Alyson Publications.

Chasnoff, D., & Cohen, H. S. (1996). *It's elementary: Talking about gay issues in school* [video]. San Francisco, CA: Women's Educational Media.

deHaan, L., & Nijland, S. (2000). *King and king.* New York, NY: Tricycle Press.

dePaola, T. (1979). *Oliver button is a sissy.* Orlando, FL: Harcourt.

Elwin, R., & Paulse, M. (1990). *Asha's mums.* Toronto, ON: Women's Press.

Fierstein, H. (2002). *The sissy duckling.* New York, NY: Simon & Schuster.

Flores, G. (2009). Teachers' attitudes in implementing gay-themed literature as part of a balanced multicultural education curriculum. (Doctoral dissertation). Retrieved from ProQuest Dissertations and Theses database (UMNI No. 3370947).

Foucault, M. (1990). *A history of sexuality, an introduction* (Vol. 1). New York, NY: Vintage Books.

Freire, P. (2006). *Pedagogy of the oppressed.* (Revised). New York, NY: Continuum International Publishing Group.

Grasso, D. (2016). It's never too early: The (in)visibility of LGBTQ curriculum in the elementary classroom. In K. A. Waldon & T. P. Baxley (Eds.), *Equity pedagogy: teaching diverse student populations.* Dubuque, IA: KendallHunt.

Greene, F. (1996). Introducing queer theory into the undergraduate classroom: Abstractions and practical applications. *English Education, 28*(4), 323–339.

Kosciw, J. G., Greytak, E. A., Palmer, N. A., & Boesen, M. J. (2014). The 2013 national school climate survey: The experiences of lesbian, gay, bisexual and transgender youth in our nation's schools. New York, NY: GLSEN.

Letts, W. T. IV, & Sears, J. T. (Eds.). (1999). *Queering Elementary Education: Advancing the Dialogue about Sexualities and Schooling*. New York, NY: Rowman & Littlefield.

Luhman, S. (1998). Queering/querying pedagogy? Or, pedagogy is a pretty queer thing. In W. Pinar (Ed.), *Queer theory in education* (pp. 141–156). Mahwah, NJ: Earlbaum.

Morris, M. (2005). Queer life and school culture: Troubling genders. *Multicultural Education, 12*(3), 8–13.

Newman, L. (1989). *Heather has two mommies*. Los Angeles, CA: Alyson Publications.

Pelo, A. (2008). Introduction: Embracing social justice in early childhood education. In A. Pelo (Ed.), *Rethinking early childhood education* (pp. ix–xiii). Milwaukee, WI: Rethinking Schools Publication.

Pinar, W. (1998). *Queer theory in education*. Mahwah, NJ: Lawrence Erlbaum.

Polacco, P. (2009). *In our mother's house*. New York, NY: Penguin Young Readers.

Rasmussen, M. L. (2004). "That's so gay!" A study of the deployment of signifiers of sexual and gender identity in secondary school settings in Australia and the United States. *Social Semiotics, 14*(3), 289–309.

Richardson, J., & Parnell, P. (2005). *And Tango makes three*. New York, NY: Simon & Schuster.

Sears, J. T. (1992). Educators, homosexuality, and homosexual students: Are personal feelings related to professional beliefs? In K. M. Harbeck (Ed.), *Coming out of the classroom closet: Gay and lesbian students, teachers, and curricula* (pp. 29–79). Binghamton, NY: Haworth Press.

Shlasko, G. (2006). Queer (v.) Pedagogy. *Equity and Excellence in Education, 38*(2), 123–134.

Sleeter, C. E., & Grant, C. A. (2009). Making choices for multicultural education: Five approaches to race, class, and gender. Hoboken, NJ: John Wiley & Sons.

Sweet, S. (1998). Practicing radical pedagogy: Balancing ideals with institutional constraints. *Teaching Sociology, 26*, 100–111.

Valentine, J. (1991). *The duke who outlawed jelly beans and other stories*. Los Angeles, CA: Alyson Publications.

Vasquez, V. (2007). Using the everyday to engage in critical literacy with young children. *New England Reading Association Journal, 43*(2), 6–11.

Welcoming Schools. (2009). The Welcoming Schools Guide: An inclusive approach to addressing family diversity, gender stereotyping and name-calling in K-5 learning environments. Washington, DC: The Human Rights Campaign.

Wollman-Bonilla, J. (1998). Outrageous viewpoints: Teachers' criteria for rejecting works of children's literature. *Language Arts, 75*(4), 287–295.

CHAPTER FOUR

When Secondary Schools Fail

LGBT Issues in the Juvenile Justice System

SHIV R. DESAI

INTRODUCTION

While the overrepresentation of black and Latinx youth in our Juvenile Justice System (JJS) has been well-documented (Alexander, 2011; Stevenson, 2014), it is important to note that Lesbian, Gay, Bisexual, & Transgender (LGBT) youth are also significantly overrepresented. In fact, nearly 300,000 LGBT youth are arrested and/or detained each year. The intersectionality of race and sexuality become even more apparent when 60% of these arrests are of black and/or Latinx youth. Simply put, in a nation where LGBT youth constitute a mere 7% of the overall youth population, they comprise 15% of those currently incarcerated (Hunt & Moodie-Mills, 2012; Irvine, 2010; Majd, Marksamer, & Reyes, 2009; Weiss, 2015).

Furthermore, LGBT youth face harsher sentences, are frequently labeled as sex offenders due to their sexual orientation, and are more often adjudicated on minor nonviolent offenses (Maccio & Ferguson, 2016; Wilson, 2014). More importantly, once they are in detention and/or correctional facilities, LGBT youth do not have access to a safe environment as a result of verbal and physical harassment. Additionally, many LGBT youth experience segregation because of their sexual orientation. Therefore, the purpose of this chapter is to discuss the issues LGBT youth face within the JJS through a case study of one youth of color who identifies as being gay and is part of the youth juvenile justice council that I facilitate and advise.

First, I discuss how the school-to-prison pipeline impacts LGBT youth. Next, I discuss Positive Youth Development (PYD)/Community Youth Development

(CYD) (Watts & Flanagan, 2007) as my theoretical framework because it complements my research methodology, which utilizes Youth Participatory Action Research (YPAR). YPAR teaches young people how to critically examine complex power relations, histories of struggle, and oppression (Cammarota & Fine, 2010). More importantly, YPAR and PYD/CYD challenges "traditional" research practices by building on the idea that youth should take part in critical inquiry and action because they are key knowledge holders who can formulate relevant questions, engage in ongoing reflection, analyze data, obtain results, and suggest solutions that are transformative (Bautista, Bertrand, & Morrell, 2013; McIntyre, 2000; Torre, 2009; Watts & Flanagan, 2007). In my findings, I examine the experiences of one gay youth whose experiences in the JJS mirror that of many LGBT who find themselves ensnared by the JJS due to family abandonment. I conclude by sharing strategies that can greatly assist LGBT incarcerated youth.

SCHOOL BULLYING, FAMILY ABANDONMENT, AND THE JUVENILE JUSTICE SYSTEM

While there are several factors that contribute to making LGBT youth vulnerable to the school-to-prison pipeline, I will focus on two key causes: school bullying (Blackburn, 2004; Kosciw, Greytak, Palmer, & Boesen, 2014), and family abandonment, rejection and/or abuse (Maccio & Ferguson, 2016).

School Bullying

For LGBT youth, schools are not always safe, welcoming spaces. According to the Lesbian and Straight Education Network's (GLSEN) National School Climate Survey (2013), nearly 60% of LGBT students felt unsafe at school and 65% frequently heard homophobic remarks (Kosciw et al., 2014). Furthermore, 74% and 36% of LGBT youth reported being verbally or physically harassed, respectively, due to their sexual orientation. With the prevalence of social media (e.g., Facebook), almost half of LGBT youth stated they experienced electronic harassment. Moreover, 57% of LGBT students who were harassed or assaulted in school, did not report the incident to school staff because they did not believe there would be an effective intervention. Many believed that school officials would only exacerbate the situation by making it worse. More disturbing, 62% of LGBT students who did report an incident indicated that the school staff did not do anything to address the issue.

In a ground breaking study, Himmelstein and Brückner (2011) utilized data from the National Longitudinal Study of Adolescent Health to highlight the disproportionate rates non-heterosexual adolescents suffer punishments from school and criminal-justice authorities. They found LGBT youth had up to three times greater odds than their heterosexual peers of experiencing harsher school discipline even when they engaged in similar transgressive behaviors as their heterosexual counterparts. What makes matter worse is teachers often overlooked harassment of non-heterosexual students by their peers and frequently blamed them for their victimization. Even more problematic, is when LGBT youth do try to stand up for or try to defend themselves against school bullying, it often results in them being punished or criminalized. A hostile school climate leads to higher rates of truancy, absenteeism, and dropping out for LGBT youth (Blackburn, 2004; Wilson, 2014), as well as higher levels of depression and/or anxiety (Himmelstein & Brückner, 2011; Snapp, Hoenig, Fields, & Russell, 2015). In addition to schools pushing out youth, family rejection is another leading cause for their overrepresentation in the JJS.

Family Abandonment, Abuse and Rejection

Numerous studies have indicated that between 20–40% of homeless youth self-identify as LGBT, and the primary cause for being homeless is family rejection, abandonment and/or abuse (Gattis, 2013; Snapp et al., 2015; Wagaman, 2016). Indeed, 26% of LGBT youth leave their family due to conflicts over their sexual orientation and 30% suffer family violence after "coming out" (Himmelstein & Brückner, 2011). The dire consequences for LGBT homeless youth is that they report higher rates of being physically or sexually victimized, higher rates of attempted suicide, use illicit substances and greater mental health concerns (Acevedo-Polakovich, Bell, Gamache, & Christian, 2013; Tyler, Hagewen, & Melander, 2011). Furthermore, once they are homeless, they face numerous challenges in accessing adequate shelter or permanent housing.

LGBT youth find themselves cast onto the streets leaving them emotionally and physically vulnerable. In order to face these obstacles, they may turn to survival sex or other sex work to support themselves. Unfortunately, this dangerous behavior leaves them susceptible to abuse, increases potential health concerns, and further victimization, along with putting them at risk for arrest. Research demonstrates that LGBT youth are twice as likely to be arrested and detained for nonviolent offenses (Irvine, 2010; Maccio & Ferguson, 2016; Majd et al., 2009) such as violating curfew and sleeping in public space laws. Thus, family support is critical for LGBT youth well-being (Detrie & Lease, 2007; Shilo & Savaya, 2011) so they do not end up homeless and become entrapped by the JJS.

LGBT and the Juvenile Justice System

According to some studies, on any given day, there can be up to 69,000 youth that are held in correctional placements, and 26,000 that are held in juvenile detention centers (Irvine, 2010; Majd et al., 2009). As much as 13–15% of this population identifies as being LGBT. Until recently, there had not been extensive studies that examined the experiences of LGBT youth within the JJS. Irvine's (2010) study examines the findings from 2,100 surveys that were administered in six jurisdictions across the nation. Irvine found that approximately 11% of the boys and 23% of the girls identified as being LGBT. The main findings were that LGBT youth were twice as likely to have been removed from their homes because someone was hurting them, as well as twice as likely to have been in foster care. In addition, LGBT youth were twice as likely to have been detained in juvenile facilities for running away, and four times more likely to be detained for prostitution.

The Equity Project (Majd et al., 2009) study gave a survey to more than 400 legal professions and interviewed 65 of them. In addition, 55 youth were interviewed. Two-thirds of youth respondents believed strongly that they experienced bias from court personnel, and 70% of them indicated they experienced police mistreatment due to their sexuality. Furthermore, Majd et al. (2009) documented how LGBT youth are overcharged with sex offenses and are often categorized as sex offenders, which further perpetuates heterosexist notions that being queer is a form of deviancy.

The Equity Project found that 32% of boys and 40% of girls were homeless due to lack of support, and 20% of boys and 33% of girls were removed from their homes because someone was hurting them. Family rejection or abandonment often underlies many of the offenses with which LGBT are charged with such as running away, survival crimes (i.e., shoplifting and prostitution), substance use, and domestic disputes. Domestic violence charges LGBT youth encounter is another key point because in many cases they are simply defending themselves against family members who attacked them because of their sexuality.

In 2006, an unprecedented lawsuit challenged the egregious treatment of LGBT youth confined in the Hawai'i Youth Correctional Facility (HYCF) (Majd et al., 2009). The court found that the HYCF failed to protect the plaintiffs from physical and psychological abuse, used isolation as a means to protect LGBT youth from abuse, and did not provide the necessary training to protect LGBT youth. The Equity Project found that LGBT youth safety was still a serious problem for both youth and staff: 80% of youth said it was a serious problem and 50% of detention staff reported that they were aware of situations where LGBT youth were being mistreated because of their sexual orientation. Moreover, they found that bullying and harassment was a pervasive issue for LGBT youth in detention and correctional institutions.

In sum, there are many challenges that LGBT youth encounter in detention and correctional facilities. From being forced to take showers separately to being segregated for their own protection (Irvine, 2010), there is much work that needs to be done within the JJS in order to make LGBT youth feel safe and protected.

POSITIVE AND/OR COMMUNITY YOUTH DEVELOPMENT

I employ a Positive Youth Development (PYD)/Community Youth Development (CYD) framework for this study because LGBT youth have been silenced for far too long. Such a framework, complements a YPAR methodology, which teaches youth to be agents of change and fight for social justice (Cammarota & Fine, 2010).

Watts and Flanagan (2007) explain how liberation psychology can be useful to this framework since it helps youth examine social injustices while imagining just societies, promotes self-determination and solidarity with others, and focuses on ending oppression as well as unearthing healing in the process. PYD/CYD offer a dynamic model to engage youth in civic participation because it considers multiple ways to incorporate youth knowledge. Furthermore, it promotes a more holistic framework that nurtures emotional, mental, and spiritual development. PYD/CYD offers "authentic collaboration" by enabling youth to take lead, while adults are in the background assisting, mentoring and facilitating. Through this process, youth act as community organizers who focus on the roots of the social problem, which empowers them in identifying the key solutions to the social issue. To that end, Watts and Flanagan (2007) offer four key components on PYD/CYD that emphasizes liberation: (1) Worldview and social analysis, of which critical consciousness is a central part, (2) Sense of Agency, which is empowerment, (3) Opportunity structure, which permits action based on one's analysis, and (4) Societal Involvement Behavior (SIB), which is sociopolitical activism.

As you can see PYD/CYD enriches YPAR by building on the idea that youth should take part in critical inquiry and action because they are key knowledge holders who can formulate relevant questions, engage in ongoing reflection, and analyze data (McIntyre, 2000; Quijada Cerecer, Cahill, & Bradley, 2013; Rodríguez & Brown, 2009; Torre, 2009). YPAR also promotes a collective process between the researcher and youth, allowing both parties to contribute meaningfully in all areas of research. Most importantly, YPAR fosters critical consciousness.

METHODOLOGY

A case study is a type of empirical inquiry with the purpose of investigating a bounded case, which can be a situation, instance, or person, narrowed in scope and focus that will examine real life context for contemporary phenomenon (Savin-Baden & Major, 2013). Zach, a bi-racial (white and Latino) gay male is a member of Leaders Organizing 2 Unite & Decriminalize (LOUD). LOUD was created as a partnership between a grassroots community organization and a county Juvenile Justice System in the Southwest. Through a juvenile justice youth council, LOUD has direct impact on juvenile justice policies and is able to conduct a YPAR study that examines the experiences of incarcerated youth. While the larger YPAR study examines youth activism and empowerment through YPAR, for the purposes of this chapter, I focus specifically on data that I collected on Zach since his story speaks to the intersectionality of the JJS and the LGBT community.

Data was collected during the 2015–2016 academic year, and included field notes, individual interviews and transcripts from the usually two-hour weekly meetings. The purpose of the weekly meetings was to review and plan YPAR projects. Additionally, I conducted three semi-structured individual interviews with Zach, which lasted 45–90 minutes and discussed our work with the YPAR project, the JJS, his sexuality, and his schooling experiences.

All data sources were examined through horizontalization, the "process of laying out all the data for examination and treating the data as having equal weight; that is, all pieces of data have equal value at the initial data analysis stage. The data is then organized into clusters or themes" (Merriam, 2009, p. 25–26). Themes were organized into 14 main categories such as the following: gender, culture, education, family, sexuality, JJS, and activism. The data was organized using these categories and aided in the creation of thematic memos that were used for analysis. It is important to note that Zach reviewed this chapter to ensure accuracy and to make sure confidentially was not violated.

FINDINGS AND DISCUSSION

In this section, I focus on data that reveals Zach's schooling experience, dealing with family abandonment, surviving homelessness, and his experiences in the JJS.

Schooling Was Painful

Bullying at school started for Zach in elementary school; however, he does not necessarily think it was for being gay because he did not know he was gay in elementary school. Rather, it was because he "hung out" with girls only. Seventh grade was a pivotal year because this was when he first truly identified as being gay. Zach said that kids would say he was gay based on how he talked and his voice. In other words, he explained how his mannerisms would be identified as "being gay." Schooling was extremely painful as this point. He remarks, "It took me a long time to accept it. So, I was like, 'I didn't want to be gay.' Like I had times in my life I was like, 'I don't want to be this thing.' Like I cried. I cut myself. I did not want to be gay because it makes life so much harder." To make matters worse, his guidance counselor told him to "try not to be too open about it." Zach expressed anger and stated that he was telling me basically not be myself. This example supports the

GLSEN's National School Climate Survey (2013) findings that LGBT youth do not feel supported at school and are often frustrated by school official's response to their being bullied (Kosciw et al., 2014). Plainly, school was not a welcoming place for him.

Zach has tried repeatedly going back to school. However, each time, he ends up leaving because of harassment. He is in the process of trying to find a GED program because he still values his education and has aspirations of going to college. When I mentioned that his high school had a Gay/Straight Alliance club, he said that he was not aware of it. However, he also said that this club was not enough because you only had a few spaces where you would feel accepted. This key point suggests that schools need to create more inclusive institutional policies where LGBT students feel strongly supported.

Domestic Violence

Research demonstrates that LGBT youth are significantly more likely to experience family rejection, abandonment, and/or abuse, which often leads to homelessness (Maccio & Ferguson, 2016). The main reason why Zach became system involved was due to a domestic violence incident. At 14 years old, he was attacked by his step-dad due to his sexuality. Zach explained,

> [Cops] told me that it was all my fault, [and] that I shouldn't have done like what I did and they believed my parents ... my [step-]dad held me down, like he was hurting me, like I had bruises and I got arrested that night ... I was confused with the whole situation and I was terrified.

After his arrest, he has not been welcomed back home; effectively, making him homeless for the last two years. It is important to note that Zach also believes that the reason he is not welcomed back is because he had stolen money from his mom before. Zach's incident, similar to other youth in the study, points out a major flaw in our domestic violence laws, in which youth are silenced, both literally and figuratively. Zach was not allowed to tell his side of the story even when there was a clear indication of abuse (e.g., bruises). Perhaps, even more disturbing is that his mother is still his legal guardian—even though she has abandoned him. She still has tremendous influence on how his probation gets administered. The many hardships that Zach has had to endure due to being homeless will be examined.

Castaway on the Streets

For many LGBT youth who are homeless, they may engage in "survival sex" to get by (Gattis, 2013). Zach describes his time being homeless with tremendous sorrow, "I did everything I could to stay alive and it was a horrible thing that I was doing [survival sex]." What made matters worse was that he was absconding from probation at this time, which has prolonged his probation. Interestingly, he was in contact with his probation officer who knew his family was not supporting him and as a result he was in constant search for shelter. This begs the question as to why the Children, Youth, and Family Department (CYFD) did not intervene and hold his mom accountable for abandonment. Moreover, why this issue is not raised by him court to impede further punishment.

Below is a powerful exert from our interview about surviving on the streets and how it impacts him to this day:

> Like there's parts of me that I still don't like and I'm facing it and I'm like, well, towards like the whole soliciting myself, I cannot face that. I thought I got over it, [but] I didn't. Like I played it off and it just comes back and back and back and it hits harder every time. Like I had people, my own best friend told me that I was a complete garbage, like they told me I was trash ... They started dating someone who like outed what I was doing on Facebook and [was] just talking shit. They broke my skateboard and burned it, like fucked up shit, all because of like what I was doing, I guess. Like other people are telling me I'm worthless, that my life isn't worth living, that I should kill myself ... I'm not trying to kill myself over doing that. ...

Family and peer support is essential for LGBT youth well-being (Detrie & Lease, 2007; Shilo & Savaya, 2011). Regrettably, during this time in his life Zach was not getting enough support. This was a primary reason for why he joined LOUD. Through LOUD, he was able to find critical support, housing, and assistance with his probation agreement. Zach emphatically states that if it was not for LOUD he does not know where he would be. As a result, he is in a much more stable place now.

Another flaw in the JJS that Zach's story illustrates is that juvenile probation officers often are not aware of how to support LGBT youth. In Zach's case, his probation officer did not assist in finding shelters or transitional living programs. Furthermore, he was more interested in making sure Zach complied with the conditions of probation rather than assisting Zach confront the grave obstacles of homelessness and family abandonment. Again, when such instances occur it is no longer a JJS issue, but rather, a CYFD issue. In our case, my co-facilitator and I reported this concern to CYFD. Sadly, they did not act. During the course of our interview, Zach and I stated we believed that CYFD did not act because he was system involved and believed the JJS should be responsible.

Being Gay in the Detention Center

Being in the detention center (D-Home) was a frightening experience for Zach who has been in there multiple times. He remarked, "Being gay, being in the detention center sucks. Like people [correctional officers], other youth, they me treat me like shit." While he was glad to have food and a bed, Zach also recognized the D-Home was a hostile environment. Zach described, "[T]hey [youth] think that you're just a fucking … fag. … Like I'm not going to hit on you.… I had people like threatening to rape me." He also stated that one of the staff was helpful by suggesting he could move to another unit. However, Zach felt he would encounter the same issues again. Additionally, he mentioned that one of the senior staff addressed his grievance when that individual heard negative and homophobic comments from other staff members who discussed how they would react if their son or daughter was queer.

Zach did explain that staff in the D-Home ask youth to self-identify if they are gay. However, if you do *come out* you make yourself a target and could be isolated for your own protection. Consequently, Zach tried to hide his sexual identity. Nevertheless, he felt at times that staff were aware that he was gay. When this occurred, he felt they would "talk kind of like low key, kind of talk shit" and "just like joke about it." Thus, his experience reinforces previous findings about LGBT youth in detention (Irvine, 2010; Majd et al., 2009), particularly about the insensitivity of staff, segregation of LGBT youth, and harassment based on sexual identity.

CONCLUSION

While previous studies have mentioned the need for training, awareness, and developing equitable treatment of LGBT, Zach's case study really offers the need to develop protocols and interventions for family rejection, abandonment and/or abuse since his main problems stem from his family rejecting his sexual identity. As stated previously, Zach needed CYFD to intervene rather than the JJS, and should have been allowed to voice his side of the domestic dispute. His probation has been extended primarily due to being homeless, which has caused him to abscond to find permanent shelter. In addition, programs such as LOUD have provided a safe space for him to be himself and find his voice.

Through LOUD, he has been able to provide feedback on the new probation agreement that is being developed by the state, among other important initiatives. One key recommendation was being able to provide an alternative safe place for youth to reside in if they could no longer live at home. Finally, he said that just because detention staff show the Prison Rape Elimination Act (PREA) video, it does not mean that they are creating a safe environment and addressing the needs of LGBT youth. What he would like to see is training staff on recognizing homophobia and/or heterosexist attitudes as well as including efforts to educate both the adults and youth to be more inclusive.

REFERENCES

Acevedo-Polakovich, I. D., Bell, B., Gamache, P., & Christian, A. S. (2013). Service accessibility for lesbian, gay, bisexual, transgender, and questioning youth. *Youth & Society*, *45*(1), 75–97. doi:10.1177/0044118X11409067

Alexander, M. (2011). *The new Jim Crow: Mass incarceration in the age of colorblindness*. New York, NY: New Press.

Bautista, M., Bertrand, M., & Morrell, E. (2013). Participatory action research and city youth: Methodological insights from the council of youth research. *Teachers College Record*, *115*(October), 1–23. Retrieved from http://www.tcrecord.org/DefaultFiles/SendFileToPublic.asp?ft=pdf&FilePath=c:\WebSites\www_tcrecord_org_documents\38_17142.pdf&fid=38_17142&aid=2&RID=17142&pf=Content.asp?ContentID=17142

Blackburn, M. V. (2004). Understanding agency beyond school sanctioned activities. *Theory Into Practice*, *43*(2), 102–110. doi:10.1207/s15430421tip4302_2

Cammarota, J., & Fine, M. (Eds.). (2010). *Revolutionizing education: Youth participatory action research in motion*. New York, NY: Routledge, Taylor and Francis Group.

Detrie, P. M., & Lease, S. H. (2007). The relation of social support, connectedness, and collective self-esteem to the psychological well-being of lesbian, gay, and bisexual youth. *Journal of Homosexuality*, *53*(4), 173–199. doi:10.1080/00918360802103449

Gattis, M. N. (2013). An ecological systems comparison between homeless sexual minority youths and homeless heterosexual youths. *Journal of Social Service Research*, *39*(January 2015), 38–49. doi:10.1080/01488376.2011.633814

Himmelstein, K. E. W., & Brückner, H. (2011). Criminal-justice and school sanctions against nonheterosexual youth: A national longitudinal study. *Pediatrics*, *127*(1), 49–57. doi:10.1542/peds.2009-2306

Hunt, J., & Moodie-Mills, A. C. (2012). *The unfair criminalization of gay and transgender youth*. Retrieved from http://www.americanprogress.org/wp-content/uploads/issues/2012/06/pdf/juvenile_justice.pdf

Irvine, A. (2010). "We've had three of them": Addressing the invisibility of Lesbian, Gay, Bi-Sexual and Gender Non-conforming youths in the Juvenile Justice System. *Columbia Journal of Law and Gender*, *19*(3), 675–699.

Kosciw, J. G., Greytak, E. A., Palmer, N. A., & Boesen, M. J. (2014). The 2013 National School Climate Survey: The experiences of lesbian, gay, bisexual and transgender youth in Our Nation's Schools. New York, NY: Gay, Lesbian & Straight Education Network (GLSEN).

Maccio, E. M., & Ferguson, K. M. (2016). Services to LGBTQ runaway and homeless youth: Gaps and recommendations. *Children and Youth Services Review*, *63*, 47–57. doi:10.1016/j.childyouth.2016.02.008

Majd, K., Marksamer, J., & Reyes, C. (2009). *Hidden injustice: Lesbian, gay, bisexual, and transgender youth in Juvenile Courts*. San Francisco, CA: Equity Project Partners.

McIntyre, A. (2000). Constructing meaning about violence, school, and community: participatory action research with urban youth. *The Urban Review*, *32*(2), 123–154. doi:10.1023/A:1005181731698

Merriam, S. A. (2009). *Qualitative Research: A Guide to Design and Implementation*. San Francisco: John Wiley & Sons.

Quijada Cerecer, D. A., Cahill, C., & Bradley, M. (2013). Toward a critical youth policy praxis: Critical youth studies and participatory action research. *Theory Into Practice*, *52*(3), 216–223. doi:10.1080/00405841.2013.804316

Rodríguez, L. F., & Brown, T. M. (2009). From voice to agency: Guiding principles for participatory action research with youth. *New Directions for Youth Development, 2009*(123), 19–34. doi:10.1002/yd.312

Savin-Baden, M. & Major, C. H. (2013). Qualitative research: The essential guide to theory and practice. Florence, KY: Routledge.

Shilo, G., & Savaya, R. (2011). Effects of family and friend support on LGB youths' mental health and sexual orientation milestones. *Family Relations, 60*(3), 318–330. doi:10.1111/j.1741-3729.2011.00648.x

Snapp, S. D., Hoenig, J. M., Fields, A., & Russell, S. T. (2015). Messy, butch, and queer: LGBTQ youth and the school-to-prison pipeline. *Journal of Adolescent Research, 30*(301), 57–82. doi:10.1177/0743558414557625

Stevenson, B. (2014). *Just mercy: A story of justice and redemption.* New York, NY: Spiegel and Grau.

Torre, M. E. (2009). Participatory action research and critical race theory: Fueling spaces for nos-otras to research. *The Urban Review, 41*(1), 106–120. doi:10.1007/s11256-008-0097-7

Tyler, K. A., Hagewen, K. J., & Melander, L. A. (2011). Risk factors for running away among a general population sample of males and females. *Youth & Society, 43*(2), 583–608. doi:10.1177/0044118X11400023

Wagaman, M. A. (2016). Promoting empowerment among LGBTQ youth: A social justice youth development approach. *Child and Adolescent Social Work Journal*, 1–11. doi:10.1007/s10560-016-0435-7

Watts, R. J., & Flanagan, C. (2007). Pushing the envelope on youth civic engagement: A developmental and liberation psychology perspective. *Journal of Community Psychology.* doi:10.1002/jcop.20178

Weiss, J. (2015). Equal justice for all: Care of LGBT youth in the juvenile justice system. *European Psychiatry, 30*, 155. doi:10.1016/S0924-9338(15)30129-2

Wilson, H. (2014). Turning off the school-to-prison pipeline. *Reclaiming Children and Youth, 23*(1), 49–53. doi:10.1515/commun-2014-0010

PART TWO

Systemic Campus Failures TO Include THE LGBTQ+ Community

CHAPTER FIVE

LGBTQ Marginalization or Inclusion?

Troubling Institutional Assertions of Commitment to Social Justice

VALERIE A. GUERRERO AND KARI J. DOCKENDORFF

CAMPUS CONTEXT

When controversy occurs on campus, the faculty, staff, and student body often look to campus leadership to both understand the institution's assessment of the event and to guide individual responses. The aim of this chapter is to explore an institution's response to protests of an honorary degree leading up to commencement; we employ queer theory and critical race theory (CRT) to unpack the chain of events, the campus responses, and explore alternate institutional responses and future options to engage campus constituents in meaningful dialogue that allows for the "varying and variable subjectivities, identities, and the specific meanings attached to 'differences'" (Brah & Phoenix, 2016, p. 258). For our purposes, we define "campus response" as statements released by spokespersons of the institution as well as any public campus actions.

We will examine the impact of these responses on the perception and enactment of the university's strategic action plans and the overall campus climate. Throughout this chapter, special attention will be paid to the ways in which pointing to past efforts on racial inequality fails to address emerging and evolving complexities of race, gender, and sexuality on campus. Our critique of the campus' responses through the lens of queer theory and CRT, seeks to embrace Harper's (2012) call for recognition of one's own complicity in racism and erasure of the "minoritized." We use the term "minoritized," instead of "minority," to emphasize Harper's assertion that

> ... persons are not born into a minority status nor are they minoritized in every social context (e.g., families, racially homogeneous friendship groups, or places of worship). Instead, they are rendered minorities in particular situations and institutional environments that sustain an overrepresentation of Whiteness. (p. 9)

Simultaneously, we emphasize and acknowledge that racialized campus environments require institutional actions *in addition to*, rather than only through a focus on individual intentions or actions.

SETTING AND SITUATION

The University of Utah (the U) is a large, research institution set in the intermountain region of the country. The university is largely a commuter campus, with a small percentage of students living on campus, and students of color making up roughly a quarter of the student population. The backdrop for the institution is a large urban area that is home to the dominant religion in the region. Policy, legislation, and social expectations are particularly influenced by the dominant faith in the region.

In the months leading up to the spring 2016 commencement activities, the U announced that it would award an honorary doctoral degree to an individual who served on the board of directors of two organizations that The Southern Poverty Law Center (SPLC, 2015, October 21) classified as hate groups who had committed hate crimes. A hate crime is a criminal offense motivated in whole or in part by the offender's bias against a race, religion, disability, ethnic origin, or sexual orientation. Immediately, there was backlash from lesbian, gay, bisexual, trans, queer, and other (LGBTQ+) community supporters who pointed to the nominee's contributions to these organizations. Despite protests and concerns from individuals within and outside of the university, campus leadership decided to proceed with plans to confer the honorary degree because of the nominee's "humanitarian efforts." However, the decision was made to delete any mention of the nominee's affiliation with these hate groups from their biography on the university website.

During the commencement ceremony, graduating students protested by standing and turning their backs to the stage as the nominee was awarded the degree, while numerous faculty present wore rainbows on their regalia in support of LGBTQ+ students. After two months of silence, campus leaders responded to the community in the days after the convocation ceremony. In an open letter, they offered a general apology, stated that the LGBTQ+ community was a valued part of the campus community, and, as proof of the institution's "commitment to diversity," pointed to a campus-wide dialogue on racial climate that had taken place during the fall semester. This correspondence ended senior administrations discussion of the situation.

THE INFLUENCE OF CAMPUS CLIMATE

Through the study of organizations, we understand that an institution's mission shapes its purpose, conveys the priorities of that institution, and frequently offers a version of a commitment to diversity and/or inclusion (Smith, 2015). Consistently, research findings have indicated that the perception of an institution's commitment to diversity is related to student success and impacts both retention and student satisfaction (Astin, 1993; Berger, 2002; Rankin, 2005). In addition to the values made explicit, an institution's commitment can be conveyed through "decisions that are made, visual cues about what is important, responses to incidents, language developed for a wide variety of purposes, and everyday behavior" (Smith, 2015, p. 230). Symbolic components of the campus environment, such as traditions, logos, stories, ceremonies, and celebrations, also express institutional norms and expectations (Berger, 2002).

Individuals experiencing marginalization are especially cognizant of gaps between rhetoric and practice, of how institutional commitment to inclusion is or is not threaded throughout its culture, and of how these elements within campus culture impact student success (Smith, 2015). In the above case, the institutional symbolism of an honorary degree to an individual who repudiates the validity and humanity of LGBTQ+ individuals signalled an acceptance and allegiance with those values by campus leadership.

The qualifications for the nomination of an honorary degree at the U include "unusual distinction in service to the University and/or society in such areas as research, scholarship, education, the arts, humanities, the professions, business, government service, civic affairs, human rights, humanitarian outreach, social activism, innovation and invention" (Procedure, 2010). In bestowing a university honor upon an individual who served on the leadership boards of multiple organizations classified as hate groups by the Southern Poverty Law Center, the institution condoned this participation as distinguished service to society (SPLC, 2015, October 21). To award a leader within an organization that views families led by same-gender couples as the catalyst for "catastrophic population decline, economic contraction, and human tragedy" (Carlson & Mero, 2005, p. 30), communicates that the institution is in alliance with these beliefs.

Considering the symbolism of the award and its public nature, members of the campus community were confused by the mixed messages being communicated. Over the last few decades, the institution had taken various levels of action in an effort to support the success of students from minoritized groups including women, students of color, and LGBTQ+ students. These steps ranged from efforts to positively impact the day to day experiences of minoritized students to initiatives that furthered academic disciplines validating the marginalized. Some of these indications of inclusion are: the annual celebration of Pride week; an LGBT Resource Center staffed with a director and administrative support; a queer positive women's resource center; an Associate Vice President for Diversity who reports to the chief academic officer; an institutional division that supports inclusion and diversity; an office to further inclusive excellence through campus training for faculty and staff ; a Gender Studies department; a School for Cultural and Social Transformation; and multiple resource centers devoted to supporting historically minoritized ethnic and racial groups.

Collectively, these components of the institution suggest a welcoming, safe campus that is intentional in its efforts to cultivate both a positive campus climate and the academic success of students minoritized as a result of their gender, sexual orientation, race, and/or ethnicity. However, by embracing and defending this egregious misalignment of institutional practice and rhetoric, the institution both diminished and undermined its previous efforts (Berger, 2002; Smith, 2015).

THROUGH THE LENS OF CRITICAL RACE THEORY

On college campuses, discussions about race are often limited to reactions or responses to crises and they frequently focus on individual actions and incidents rather than how racism is deeply embedded in U.S. educational systems (Harper, 2012; Harper & Hurtado, 2017; Harper & Patton, 2007; Ladson-Billings, 1998). Such incidents are typically restricted to actions that could be characterized as hate crimes, ethnoviolence, or microaggressions. Ethnoviolence is the result of systemic and socially constructed norms that allow dominant cultures to engage in actions that are exploitive, violent, and intimidating toward marginalized groups. Microaggressions are the less obvious but more pervasive, everyday acts of racism that are largely ignored and unreported (Pierce, 1969; Yosso, Smith, Ceja, & Solorzano, 2009).

Although offenders often claim that they acted out of ignorance rather than malice, "many people, including college students, administrators, and faculty, make racist statements; engage in racially oppressive actions; and maintain exclusive memberships in racially segregated networks" (Harper & Patton, 2007, p. 1). The concept of White supremacy is not limited to extreme manifestations of aggression or explicit racism; instead, it is a taken for granted normalization of Whiteness (Gillborn, 2016). In the current situation, we assert that racism and White supremacy played a role in the campus response and turn to CRT to emphasize the erasure of numerous minoritized communities.

Originating from critiques of critical legal studies (Bell, 1992; Delgado & Stefancic, 1993), CRT provides tools to examine the issue at hand while centering racism and White supremacy as well as their impact upon marginalized groups within higher education (Parker & Lynn, 2016). The development of CRT allowed legal scholars, activists, and lawyers to critique the role of the U.S. legal system in reifying White supremacy and continuing to limit the Civil Rights of Black Americans (Delgado, 1984; Delgado, Stefancic, & Liendo, 2012). When applied to education, a CRT lens "challenges the myth of racelessness and explicitly names racism/White supremacy in areas such as college access, curriculum, and policy" (Patton, 2015, p. 316). In applying this lens to the aforementioned nomination and subsequent campus responses, we are able to "disrupt the ordinary, predictable, and taken for granted ways in which the academy functions as a bastion of racism/White supremacy" (Patton, 2015, p. 317). We aim to highlight passive and active responses from the University which served to divide and diminish the power of minoritized communities, while reifying the standards and expectations of White supremacists.

Before applying CRT, it is crucial to highlight the tenets we will foreground in this examination. First, racism is endemic to society resulting in race and racism being deeply embedded within U.S. educational systems (Bell, 1992; Delgado & Stefancic, 1993). Its entrenched nature makes racism appear to be a normal occurrence that is difficult to recognize, much less remedy. The second tenet driving our exploration is Bell's (1980) concept of interest convergence that claims racial equity only gets advanced when it benefits White people. Essentially, White and complicit leaders will entertain advances for campus constituents of color as long as the changes do not cause large disruptions to the status quo. The third tenet we employ, intersectionality, is both central to CRT and a theory in its own right, that provides a process to analyze one's multiple lived identities and experiences within historical, political, and social contexts (Crenshaw, 1989, 1995). Collectively, these tenets guide our use of CRT while allowing an exploration of identity that differs from queer theory.

THROUGH THE QUEER THEORY LENS

Queer theory provides us with one set of tools for exploring the institutional response in this situation. On the surface, queer theory allows us to question what is normal (Dilley, 1999; Talburt, 2011), but it also allows us to "analyze a situation or a text to determine the relationship between sexuality, power, gender, and conceptions of normal and deviant" (Dilley, 1999). Queer theory can be used to highlight the fluidity of identity and the ways in which "our multiple differences—not just sexual orientation and gender identity, but race, class, religion, sex, immigration status, etc.—are critical to how 'we are'" (Lugg & Murphy, 2014, p. 1185). Through this lens, it is clear that the university must find ways to acknowledge the *many* salient identities of students, faculty, and staff, rather than ignoring one set of identities, for example, the set, by pointing to existing reactive efforts related to the negative racial climate on campus.

By using its institutional power to award an honorary degree, the university is placing value on all work of the nominee, from their humanitarian involvement abroad to their leadership within anti-LGBT organizations. In taking up this lens, we can "highlight how society accepts and promotes heterosexuality, and disapproves of and denigrates homosexuality, through inverting what is considered normal and proper" (Dilley, 1999, p. 466). Thus, we are able to point out how the university champions heteronormativity by erasing the nominee's anti-LGBT work and instead pointing to their strong humanitarian efforts, as if the two are separate.

EXAMINING CAMPUS RESPONSES THROUGH CRT AND QUEER THEORY

Rather than pro-actively enacting systemic interventions or explicitly acknowledging the reification of racism and White supremacy in education, campus leaders continue to foster a campus climate where these undertones thrive (Davis & Harris, 2015; Patton, 2015). In utilizing language that invokes the notion of racelessness in education, we engage in ahistoricism which both "celebrate[s] oppressors and den[ies] the voices of those who experienced oppression" (Patton, 2015, p. 319). In this instance, rather than engaging hurt and enraged community protesters the first campus response literally erased the history of the nominee and their participation in the social war against LGBTQ+ individuals and communities in order to proceed with celebrations as usual. In sanitizing the nominee's biography, the institution strengthened feelings of invisibility and exclusion of LGBTQ+ individuals by asserting that the individual's "humanitarian" accomplishments outweighed their continued crusade against LGBTQ+ individuals and families.

Delving more deeply into the implications of ahistoricity, it is important to note two relevant tenets of CRT. A university spokesperson announced that the nominee's biography was scrubbed because the committee did not include this information in their decision and instead focused on the nominee's work "promoting health, education, and economic development" in Africa (Logue, 2016; Wood, 2016). This narrowed focus actually indicates the value placed on colonialism and White supremacy by this dominating faith and its supporters (Davis & Harris, 2015; Patton, 2015). Not only does this reflect the tenet that racism is normalized to society at large, but it is also aligned with CRT's call to challenge dominant ideology (for example, claims of colorblindness, neutrality, objectivity) asserting and supporting a majoritarian agenda (Gillborn, 2016). In celebrating the nominee's contributions to promoting western notions of health, education, and economic prosperity, the focus became the nominee's success in reifying cultural superiority and global colonization through Eurocentric ideals (Feagin, 2013; Gillborn, 2016). By glorifying these "humanitarian" efforts, the campus aligned itself with the goals of colonialism and its efforts to wipe out indigenous ways of being and knowing (Patton, 2015).

To reiterate, this case occurs in a context where religious faith has a unique control over economic prosperity and social capital. Considering that (a) the nominee and their family have extensive ties to the region's dominant faith; (b) the nominee's spouse is an official authority within their faith; and (c) their faith recently welcomed the world-wide annual conference of one of the hate-groups linked to the nominee, it is naive to assume that campus administration did not factor this environmental influence into their decisions (Keiter, 2015; Logue, 2016).

More specifically, to rescind the nomination would have invited conflict with the groups and individuals holding the most power and influence in the region. Electing to ignore community protests and avoid any public requests to rescind the nomination, not only symbolically aligned the institution with ideals represented by these individuals and groups, but also signified a key tenet of CRT: interest convergence. In this case, rather than making gains toward justice as a result of benefits to the institution, campus leadership deemed economic and social gain through continued support of the nominee more valuable than the gains possible from supporting LGBTQ+ communities.

The preference to invoke race and not gender or sexuality is evident in the campus' official (second) response to community protests. As stated, in an open letter to the community, campus leadership directed attention to "thirteen immediate responses" that effectively places communities categorized as "diverse" in competition with one another for campus resources. Specifically, LGBTQ+ individuals and (presumably) constituents of color or individuals expressing racial marginalization are directed to the same set of suggestions to validate and support their lived experiences on campus. Furthermore, while we understand through queer theory that identity is fluid (Lugg & Murphy, 2014), there are still unique experiences and needs that must be directly addressed. This strategy communicates two primary messages to the reader: (1) an assumption that these categories of identity (LGBTQ+, racially, and ethnically minoritized) are mutually exclusive, and (2) the suggestion that strategies to improve racial climate would be akin to those that might improve campus inclusion for LGBTQ+ individuals.

Applying the tenet of intersectionality illuminates the challenge of validating the complex lived experiences of minoritized individuals (Crenshaw, 1989, 2003). Often, individuals with multiple minoritized identities are forced by individuals and systems of power to acknowledge only one identity at a time (Crenshaw, 1995, 2003). In this case, concerns about racial climate were addressed with miniscule mention of minoritized genders, sexualities, socio-economic classes, or other social identities that frequently experience a hostile campus climate. To direct LGBTQ+ community members to find hope in a list of immediate responses that do not acknowledge their full identities only contributes to their erasure. LGBTQ+ identities are not only absent from the list, they are reminded that these 13 responses to the racial dialogue were "immediate," while those protesting the nominee were not acknowledged until two months after the announcement and once the honorary degree had already been awarded.

Lastly, it is important to revisit the influence of interest convergence. As indicated in "13 immediate responses," the term "diverse" seems to describe and refer only to people who hold non-dominant identities with emphasis on the racially and ethnically minoritized. Such use of "diverse" is indicative of the institution's view of diversity as representing bodies numerically. Improving public perceptions of campus diversity often leads to an increased number of individuals categorized as diverse on campus, resulting in financial benefits for the institution. The goal of increasing and supporting diversity thus becomes an instance of interest convergence, with little effort toward transforming the campus environment for the minoritized. In the open letter "Regarding honorary degrees," the authors highlighted the *diverse bodies* that will arrive in the upcoming academic year. Rather than using the situation as an opportunity to facilitate sustained engagement with inclusive beliefs and strategies, their commitment to their own financial interests are boasted. Despite a trend of actions that convey a materialistic support for minoritized identities, there are numerous ways the institution could genuinely validate all campus constituents. Smith (2015, p. 235) asserts, "If the institution wishes to convey commitment to student success in an environment in which a community does not feel included, then it will need to be clear that the community is seen, appreciated, and valued."

RECOMMENDATIONS FOR INCLUSIVE CAMPUS RESPONSES TO CRISIS SITUATIONS

There are numerous ways a campus can effectively respond to crises and actively address and improve campus climate. Specifically, apology-letters should "include an action-oriented nature that firmly states how the campus and specific ... groups are working to address the subsequent issues, past, present, and future, from the incident" (Davis & Harris, 2015, p. 74). In examining the passive and active responses in this case (Davis & Harris, 2015; Harper, 2012; Patton, 2015), we are able to identify: (a) an avoidance in acknowledging how the degree conferral actively hurts LGBTQ+ communities, (b) an absence of specific action-oriented language to address and correct the harm done, and (c) inadequate reference to future structural change to interrupt everyday actions that maintain White supremacy and heterosexism. The following are suggestions promoting a proactive response that validates the breadth of experiences for students.

To begin, despite acknowledging the negative feedback about the nominee selection and thanking the community for their "heartfelt perspectives," the apology component ended by asserting that these "voices have been clearly heard and we are truly sorry." Rather than conveying genuine remorse, this apology actually reminds protesters that while their voices were "heard," the institution did not take any action indicating such. Similarly, nothing is said to own the ahistoric actions of the institution when erasing and ignoring portions of the nominee's legacy. Without details acknowledging that the institution actively chose to proceed with conferring the degree after objections, an apology recognizing the hurt caused by their unwavering decision falls short.

Next, the most effective follow-up to an apology outlines specific actions that address and aim to correct the harm enacted by the institution (Davis & Harris, 2015). While the letter invoked the institution's diversity statement, reminding the community that the institution "values the rights and dignity of all ... LGBTQ people," no detailed suggestions are offered related to how the institution will seek to mend or compensate for the damaged trust. Visionary language reminding readers that positive change can come from pain is used throughout the response, but offers no new actions as a direct result of the situation. Providing vague references to future transformation means little when a concrete plan is not articulated.

Finally, the most detailed portion of the response is the thoughtful reaction to the open dialogue on racial climate which occurred more than six months earlier. These "13 immediate responses" were the result of ongoing cross-campus collaboration. Numerous departments and units contributed suggestions and commitments to begin a positive shift in the racial climate. While some efforts provided were not new and actually represented years of labor from dedicated campus constituents, the collection of responses begin to offer the hope of future change. However, these suggestions merely begin to scratch the surface of changing everyday actions that perpetuate the status quo, namely the impact of White supremacy and heterosexism on campus. Without direct countermeasures to interrupt systemic oppression, the institution remains complicit in their maintenance (Harper, 2012; Patton, 2015). Such measures might include a council of representatives from all constituencies that respond to campus incidents through a well communicated protocol. Though creating an advisory council could be helpful, without a meaningful charge and an informed, intentional action-plan, systemic change is not possible.

CONCLUSION

Despite rhetoric that education is the great equalizer, higher education "from its genesis, has been a primary force in persistent inequities" (Patton, 2015, p. 318). By taking up queer theory and CRT, we can identify the myriad ways minoritized identities continue to be systematically marginalized in higher education. In this case, the University of Utah had an opportunity to not only acknowledge LGBTQ+ campus constituents, but to directly address concerns raised by the community via commencement protests. Instead, through use of its institutional power, the university chose to ignore anti-LGBT actions and involvement in order to proceed with conferring an honorary degree for a nominee's "humanitarian" efforts. While pointing to the open dialogue on campus racial climate as evidence of the university's commitment to *doing good work* may seem like a winning strategy, the response fails to acknowledge the LGBTQ+ community directly and pits one marginalized group against another.

REFERENCES

Astin, A. W. (1993). Diversity and multiculturalism on the campus: How are students affected? *Change, 25*, 44–49. doi:10.1080/00091383.1993.9940617

Bell, D. A. (1980). Brown v. Board of Education and the interest-convergence dilemma. *Harvard Law Review, 93*(3), 518. doi:10.2307/1340546

Bell, D. A. (1992). Racial realism. *Connecticut Law Review, 24*, 363–379.

Berger, J. B. (2002). The influence of the organizational structures of colleges and universities on college student learning. *Peabody Journal of Education, 77*(3), 103–119. doi:10.1207/s15327930pje7703_3

Brah, A., & Phoenix, A. (2016). Ain't I a woman? Revisiting intersectionality. In E. Taylor, D. Gillborn, & G. Ladson-Billings (Eds.), *Foundations of critical race theory in education* (2nd ed. pp. 251–259). New York, NY: Routledge.

Carlson, A. C., & Mero, P. T. (2005). The natural family: A manifesto. In *The family in America 19 (3)*. Rockford, IL and Salt Lake City, UT: Spence Publishing. Retrieved from: http://worldcongress.org/pdf/The%20Natural%20Family%20-%20A%20Manifesto.pdf

Crenshaw, K. (1989). Demarginalizing the intersection of race and sex: A Black feminist critique of antidiscrimination doctrine, feminist theory, and antiracist politics. *The University of Chicago Legal Forum, 1989*, 139–168.

Crenshaw, K. W. (1995). Mapping the margins: Intersectionality, identity politics, and violence against women of color. In K. Crenshaw, N. Gotanda, G. Peller, & K. Thomas (Eds.), *Critical race theory: The key writings that formed the movement* (pp. 357–383). New York, NY: The New Press.

Crenshaw, K. W. (2003). Demarginalizing the intersection of race and sex: A black feminist critique of antidiscrimination doctrine, feminist theory, and antiracist politics. In A. K. Wing (Ed.) *Critical race feminism: A reader* (2nd ed., pp. 23–33). New York, NY: New York University Press.

Davis, S., & Harris, J. C. (2015). But we didn't mean it like that: A critical race analysis of campus responses to racial incidents. *Journal of Critical Scholarship on Higher Education and Student Affairs, 2*(1), 6. Retrieved from http://ecommons.luc.edu/jcshesa/vol2/iss1/6

Delgado, R. (1984). The imperial scholar: Reflections on a review of civil rights literature. *University of Pennsylvania Law Review, 132*, 561–578.

Delgado, R., & Stefancic, J. (1993). Critical race theory: An annotated bibliography. *Virginia Law Review, 79*(2), 461–516. doi:10.2307/1073418

Delgado, R., Stefancic, J., & Liendo, E. (2012). *Critical America: Critical race theory: An introduction* (2nd ed.). New York, NY: NYU Press. Retrieved from http://www.ebrary.com.ezproxy.lib.utah.edu

Dilley, P. (1999). Queer theory: Under construction. *International Journal of Qualitative Studies in Education, 12*(5), 457–472. doi:10.1080/095183999235890

Feagin, J. T. (2013). *The White racial frame: Centuries of racial framing and counter framing.* New York, NY: Routledge.

Gillborn, D. (2016). Education policy as an act of White supremacy. In E. Taylor, D. Gillborn, & G. Ladson-Billings (Eds.), *Foundations of Critical Race Theory in Education* (2nd ed., pp. 43–59). New York, NY: Routledge.

Harper, S. (2012). Race without racism: How higher education researchers minimize racist institutional norms. *The Review of Higher Education, 36*(1), 9–29. doi:10.1353/rhe.2012.0047

Harper, S. R., & Hurtado, S. (2007). Nine themes in campus racial climates and implications for institutional transformation. *New Directions for Student Services, 120*, 7–24. doi:10.1002/ss.254

Harper, S. R., & Patton, L. D. (2007), Editors' notes. *New Directions for Student Services, 2007*, 1–5. doi:10.1002/ss.253

Keiter. (2015, October 27). SLC hosts World Congress of Families; conference has anti-gay agenda, gay rights activists say. *Fox13 Now.* Retrieved from: http://fox13now.com/2015/10/27/slc-hosts-world-congress-of-families-conference-has-anti-gay-agenda-gay-rights-activists-say/

Ladson-Billings, G. (1998). Just what is critical race theory and what's it doing in a nice field like education? *International Journal of Qualitative Studies in Education, 11*(1), 17–24.

Logue, J. (2016, May 2). Honorary degree questioned. *Insider Higher Ed.* Retrieved from: https://www.insidehighered.com/news/2016/05/02/u-utah-scrubs-references-antigay-groups-biography-honorary-degree-recipient

Lugg, C. A., & Murphy, J. P. (2014). Thinking whimsically: Queering the study of educational policy-making and politics. *International Journal of Qualitative Studies in Education, 27*(9), 1183–1204. doi:10.1080/09518398.2014.916009

Parker, L., & Lynn, M. (2016). What's race got to do with it? Critical race theory's conflicts with and connections qualitative research methodology and epistemology. In E. Taylor, D. Gillborn, & G. Ladson-Billings (Eds.), *Foundations of critical race theory in education* (2nd ed., pp.143–153). New York, NY: Routledge.

Patton, L. D. (2015). Disrupting postsecondary prose: Toward a critical race theory of higher education. *Urban Education, 51*(3), 315–342. doi:10.1177/0042085915602542

Pierce, C. (1969). Is bigotry the basis of the medical problem of the ghetto? In J. Norman (Ed.), *Medicine in the Ghetto* (pp. 301–314). New York, NY: Meredith Corporation.

Procedure 9–002: Honorary Degrees. (2010, November 9). Retrieved from: http://regulations.utah.edu/community/procedure/P9-002.php

Rankin, S. R. (2005). Campus climates for sexual minorities. *New Directions for Student Services, 2005*, 17–23. doi:10.1002/ss.170

Smith, D. G. (2015). *Diversity's promise for higher education: Making it work*. Baltimore, MD: JHU Press.

Southern Poverty Law Center. (2015, October 21). Everything you need to know about the anti-LGBTQ World Congress of Families (WCF). Retrieved from https://www.splcenter.org/news/2015/10/21/everything-you-need-know-about-anti-lgbtq-world-congress-families-wcf

Talburt, S. (2011). Queer theory. In B. J. Bank (Ed.), *Gender and higher education*. Westport, CT: Greenwood Publishing Group.

Wood, B. (2016, April 28). University of Utah removes references to anti-LGBT groups from bio of honorary degree recipient. *The Salt Lake Tribune*. Retrieved from http://www.sltrib.com/news/3827168-155/university-of-utah-removes-references-to

Yosso, T., Smith, W. A., Ceja, M., & Solorzano, D. G. (2009). Critical race theory, racial microaggressions, and campus racial climate for Latina/o undergraduates. *Harvard Educational Review, 79*(4), 659–690.

CHAPTER SIX

Big U Knows Best

Patronizing Queer Campus Culture

S. GAVIN WEISER AND TRAVIS L. WAGNER

"If GSA can help one or two people a semester come out, feel comfortable and grow personally, then we are doing more than any other organization on campus."
—ROBBY THOMPSON, BIG U'S GAY STUDENT ASSOCIATION VICE-PRESIDENT, 1983 (BEDENBAUGH, 1983)

ORIENTATION: HISTORIES OF EXPLOITATION AND EXCLUSION OF QUEER CAMPUS FOLX

A southern institution surviving upon the labor and capital of its marginalized groups is how one institution has survived the thirty years of queer justice. Reflecting on this move toward a more inclusive campus environment, reveals that each increment has been accomplished not by institutional leaders, but by those most affected by the intolerance. At each juncture, a critical moment for change was championed by those seemingly without agency, but who found that inner strength to make their community more inclusive despite the regressive tenor of regional and state politics.

At each one of these critical moments of time, how has a large state institution of post-secondary learning reacted? Often the labor has been thrust upon the marginalized. This assumption upon the shoulders of the marginalized signifies a deep violence upon the assumed. Institutions of higher education represent the dominant, as they have agency and thus the power to act. The two ways in which institutions reify their domination are through gifts and debts (Bourdieu, 1977).

These gifts and debts are symbolic forms of violence that reinstantiate the role of a benevolent father figure, old, wise, and wizened, whose force upon the student is to maintain the status quo. It is these "gentle, hidden exploitation[s that are] the form taken by man's exploitation of man whenever overt, brutal exploitation is impossible" (Bourdieu, 1977, p. 192).

In a shift from the campus of yesterday, administrators can no longer remove queer students from campus, institutions must deploy strategy (in the de Certeau construction) to maintain their habitus of normality (Bourdieu, 1977; de Certeau, 1984). This habitus becomes embodied by queer students, not only as they need the work to be done, but as they see their work as the only way it will be done.

Take as an example the quote from Robby Thompson above. Thompson, then vice-president of Big U's Gay Student Association (GSA), spoke to the labor required by a then "controversial" group of students and faculty to educate both members of the university and the larger community on what it means to exist as queer within the hostility of the 1980s American South. Occurring alongside a hostile relationship between the university and its persons of color, this advocacy showed that work was done not by university initiatives, but by the wills of oppressed communities. Theoretically, the university was fine with communities existing, but affirming existence and deeming rights to such persons were hardly practiced. Indeed, only months earlier the University denied validity to GSA by arguing that it "advocated conduct that [was] illegal in South Carolina" (Staff and Wire Reports, 1983). It was only due to the actions of an ACLU lawsuit that GSA was allowed to function and then, as Thompson states, it became the singular duty of GSA to advocate for inclusion.

The university has since fostered iterations of organizations like the GSA and included representation within the larger queer spectrum, however, these changes rarely came quickly, often involving direct confrontation with the implicit heteronormative logics of institutional practices. Whether it be unenforced guidelines for respecting pronouns of queer students or the false coupling of sexual orientation with gender identity in health services information, such acts serve to remind queer folks that their presence is at odds with campus-defined "normalcy." The result is repeated attempts to dismantle queer mobility on campus both implicitly and explicitly. Facing adversity in regards to such demobilizing practices, the queer community stood their ground, creating outlets and alternative means with which to build their own safe spaces. Frustratingly, such work, when successful, was often insidiously co-opted for the benefit of the university's image. The unsupported labor of queer folks became the product of campus pride. The irony resting here in the pride of the university, being at odds with pride as it pertains to the community it proclaims to protect.

This chapter looks critically at one large, southern state institution's movement at the intersection of hate and fear that impacts the lives of students, faculty, staff, and community members. This site provides glimpses into the temporal specifics of a grouping of people, but not the totality of the queer experience. The chapter analyses the university's enactment of sub-institutional documents and practices with regards to their inclusivity. This approach borrows from Sarah Ahmed who asks inclusivity practitioners to decentralize inclusivity as "management strategy" from the nature of diversity itself (2012, p. 53). For Ahmed, it is the difference between acknowledging practices of inclusivity and talking directly about those "being included." This chapter examines inclusive discourses at the aforementioned institution, asking how inclusivity fails when the university merely gives lip service to inclusivity within a neoliberal agenda. Each practice will be examined for approaches to queer inclusion. Focus will be given to moments where express identities are mentioned and where mention fails to either account for the totality of queer inclusivity or rejects the basic rights and needs of queer persons. These critiques are made with a constant acknowledgment that such failures result due to underlying desire for heteronormative comfort within traditional, Westernized modalities of university system structures. While specifically a critique of queer inclusivity, such oppressive and exclusionary practices could hold true for other marginalized groups as well, though instantiations change in unique ways. Finally, the chapter concludes with alternative approaches towards university inclusivity while also acknowledging the uncomfortable conversations about universities' problematic history.

RESEARCH 101: A REVIEW OF LITERATURE ON CAMPUS INCLUSION AND HETERONORMATIVE REGIMES

Often queer inclusivity is a function of neo-liberal agendas. Liberal multiculturalism too is part of the "disciplinary apparatus of the state" forcing its subjects into boxes (Puar, 2007, p. 212). Furthermore, in looking at LGBTQIA+ justice, we cannot cleave apart queer issues from other aspects of identity politics. By forcing subjects into boxes, this precisely becomes the outcome and thus we must be cognizant of this move, so as not to create division amongst oppressed populations, as well as internalized oppression.

The early movement for queer justice was explicitly a justice for the gay white man, a demand to reinstate his white privilege; contemporary movements seek to implicitly reinscribe white privilege (Puar, 2007). This assumption of homonormativity further marginalized queer and trans voices of color (Duggan, 2012). At play within discourses of justice is the division between the role of recognition within oppressed communities and the function of acknowledgment of difference. Is it, as Ahmed states, a "management strategy" or is it actually serving to discuss the operative roles of difference (2012)? Moreover, early queer justice cannot be severed from the necropolitics of the AIDS epidemic (Mbembe, 2003). Contemporary reactions to violence within the queer community hold resonance against these early acts of state violence against the queer community. This is most recently seen clearly in the blood donation ban that enacted a psychological toll upon gay men wanting to help their community after the PULSE tragedy in Orlando, FL.

In the university archives of the student newspaper, as well as the city newspaper, little prior to the early 1980s was written about queer students. Little surprise exists that some of the earliest evidence of the queer community comes in the form of speaking to the impact of AIDS upon the community. In a 1985 article, the director of student health services says that the university has to be realistic, that "we have gays. There is a very distinct possibility AIDS will show up in one form or the other" (Salahuddin, 1985, p. 1-C). This same piece later goes on to interview the president of the GSA wherein he remarks that their group serves to ensure that "gay students fit into the community and be at ease with themselves" (Salahuddin, 1985, p. 6-C). Moreover, historically the students at the institution who developed AIDS "would likely be asked to go home" (Salahuddin, 1985, p. C–6). This is due to the understanding of the institution that these students would "likely be too sick to keep up with school work" (Salahuddin, 1985, p. C–6).

By removing these students from the place that has been their home serves as a form of exile from their community. Giorgio Agamben speaks to the history of the exile of a class of people in his seminal work Homo Sacer, or the *Sacred Man* (1998). This exile of people creates a subset of individuals of whom have no rights and are in some regards freed to act without regard to law. This fosters a sense of freedom to act beyond legality, something not in the best interest of the institution. We argue that due to this exteriority to university policies, the university deemed it prudent to keep these students under their juridical control, and thus end the university exile for queer students.

Beyond a historical approach to the medicalization of sexuality, today we are hosting LGBT Open Houses through the health center for students. The invitation to this event reads: "Student Health Services is the patient-centered medical home for ALL *Big U* students. We invite students from the LGBTQ community and their allies to join us for a drop-in reception at the *Named* Student Health Center" (Student Health Services, 2016). Hosting a drop-in reception for students who are explicitly part of the queer community is a vestige of the medicalization of queerness. In the 19th century, queer people became people, and not just people engaged in a sex act. As Foucault stated, "sexuality was a medical and medicalizable object, one had to try and detect it" (1990, p. 44). Sarah Ahmed points out that welcoming events for historically marginalized groups reinforce ownership of space, and thus those who are welcomed in are not the original owners, or even new owners, but guests of the privileged (Ahmed, 2012).

Such consistent messaging by the university on the topic of queer members of the community and their connection to HIV/AIDS commits a symbolic violence against these communities (Bourdieu, 1977). The agency to control death, or necropolitics, dictates who lives, who dies, and whose narrative gets centered (Mbembe, 2003). For the queer students, and those impacted directly by HIV and AIDS, this constant reminder of how they are branded as diseased outsiders means university success for these students is of a secondary concern to both the individual and the institution.

SPECIAL TOPICS SEMINAR: A CASE STUDY OF QUEER EXCLUSION AT ONE SOUTHERN UNIVERSITY

College is meant to be a learning space. Students feeling a sense of connection to university life has proved to be instrumental to the success of these students (Astin, 1999). When students do not feel part of the community, they are more apt to leave the institution (Rankin, Weber, Blumenfeld, & Frazer, 2010). Several experiences of student involvement at our site prove to have the opposite impact upon queer students. One of the largest events to take place at many large state institutions, homecoming, serves as a re-inscription of heteronormativity in the role of king and queen. Moreover, this institution hosts an annual competitive blood drive in competition with an athletic rival, once again, excluding queer men. While the policy that prohibits queer men from blood donation is not specific to the university in question, it does not resist by standing up to the event.

Not all programs at the site are exclusionary. However, in tradition with putting the impetus upon the oppressed, we see the events that largely involve the queer community are led by the queer community. As discussed above, the university's queer student group was founded (as is common) by queer students on campus. Beyond the founding of this student organization, it was students that advocated for a full-time student affairs position that would serve specifically queer students. This was finally accomplished in the fall of 2013 after many other universities had accomplished such a position. With the position came the implementation of the LGBTQ Community Development Program spearheaded by members of the student senate and Ben Muller (2012). In reflecting on his work to build the program, Muller notes that he "experienced the harsh realities of inequality many times" within the university system and that his work not merely to acknowledge the queer community as a "remainder of the population." Understanding that even with the inclusion of an office and staff, the programming and presence of a queer community only truly came at the demands of queer students. This is also reflective of the founding of a minority serving office, which would one day find itself home to the queer student services administrator.

The institution and the students in contemporary times prides itself that the largest event on campus, unrelated to a sporting event, is the GSA's annual spring drag show. This event, which began by students in the late-90s serves as a spectacle for the non-queer community, coming in to observe the queer community (Ladenheim, 1998). Even today, in 2016, this event still has ties to the AIDS crisis, teaching those in attendance about condoms and other STI prevention materials. The constant barrage of misinformation about the promiscuity of queer students on campus not only perpetuates stereotypes but alienates queer students who do not fit into this stereotypes that many students have internalized of what it means to be queer.

Many university library collections include a variety of online resources for students hoping to do research, often colloquially called library guides. Amongst the guides included at our institution's library is a section for "Women/Gender Studies" (Women's and Gender Studies: Welcome, 2016). Navigating the guide a user is met with a handful of tabs on how to engage with women's and gender studies research and a final tab reading "LGBT issues." Delving into this tab reveals the ways in which the university comprehends issues almost exclusively from a research standpoint, seeing queer populations not as agents with knowledge, but as objects for study.

One instance includes a listing on the opening page of information regarding literature and videos on queer populations and links to "overview sources." The only information available of any potential benefit to queer students, rather than queer or queer-interested scholars, is a suggested link to the Office of Multicultural Student Affairs. Furthermore, the link leads to said office's homepage, but not to the express portions of the website concerning queer campus populations. Like the community events and engagements mentioned above, even the research provided within this library guide orient towards a narrative of AIDS and its cultural impact, reinstating this narrative's dominance within queer groups. Even guidance on research within databases remains ineffectual as library personnel often suggest terms that are supposed to help navigate subject headings within database searches. Essentialist and exclusive of many within the queer community, terms like queer or agender are not subject headings and thus hinder research within the library catalogue. Admittedly, the challenge of subject headings is not solely the onus of the university and is symbolic of a larger queer exclusion within information systems which has a well-explored history (Adler 2013; Berman 1993; Drabinski, 2013; Olson 2001).

However, the offering of these limited options without explanation as to the failings of an organizational structure speaks to the manner in which this institution implicitly chooses to account only for those queer groups accepted within *current* notions of equality. The fact that no mention is made of persons who may be queer, intersex, or agender identifying shows a limited concern for recognition of queer inclusivity. In line with theories of "library anxiety," such a lack of appropriate terminology can lead to a queer user feeling "helpless" when encountering such a library guide and subsequently reading the entire library as an "overpowering" place which induces "fear" (Mellon, 1986). Pair this failure with the lack of a single gender neutral bathroom within the entirety of the university's library and the space becomes latently violent.

Finally, the aforementioned library guide offers its prospective users a link to explore "coming out resources." The page, while full of useful LGBTQIA+ coming out resources, *only links to organizations outside of the university's walls*. Specifically, the link to a counselling center links to the University of Illinois (U of I) Urbana-Champaign. A person needing immediate support would fail to find any direct links to counselling services on the part of the university. Instead, they are met with a link to a physical site in which they can schedule appointments on weekdays between 9 a.m. and 5 p.m., assuming students have the means to traverse the over seven hundred miles necessary to get between this institution and the U of I Urbana-Champaign (Women's and Gender Studies: Welcome, 2016). In all likelihood, the library guide's creator intended to link out to a specific document or guide for coming out that has since been relocated within the university's web page, or removed, and fails to load. In fact, with further investigation, one can find the U of I Urbana-Champaign site which has its own *Coming Out* series that guides individuals through the challenges of coming out.

While likely unintentional, this failure is indicative of a larger misguided attempt at institutional concern for their marginalized queer students. First, the dead link shows a clear indifference to the need to make sure that resources for LGBTQ students are both timely and, more importantly, accessible. Second, the presumed resource is neither free, nor wholly representative of the queer spectrum. By providing such a venue as the "idealized" version of a coming out resource, this institutional document negates the need for institution-specific resources (Coming Out, 2015).

One can read this failure to properly link to this institution's own resources as an aggravated version of Ahmed's (2012) understanding of diversity existing merely "by virtue of being addressed." It also validates Ahmed's concern for acts of inclusion as being "shared objects" that can be repeated and reused as shallow affirmations without actualized validity (p. 56). Ultimately, by including the coming out resources of other entities, this institution can give voice to *concern* for the safety of its queer community; instead, it leaves the labor required to obtain safe, easily locatable spaces for coming out as the burden of queer students.

Returning to previous discussions of health and queer identities, another information resource at the institution shows the troubling relationships between the university's prescribed understandings of queerness and the actual lived experiences of the queer folks at the institution. Within the student health section of the university's website resides a section focused on "wellness, prevention, and advocacy services," which links into a section for "sexual health" (Sexual Health & Relationship Communication, 2016). The online resource offers many of the expected resources for an individual seeking sexual health information about STD and HIV tests, contraceptive access, and a hotline to discuss issues.

Aside from the binary structuring of sexual supplies offered, the extended explanation of the hotline's services includes the offering to talk about HIV/AIDs, partner communication, one's sexual orientation, and navigating one's gender identity and expression. While it is certainly crucial that each of these topics can be considered crucial to health and well-being, the conflation of these terms into one hotline under the umbrella term of sexual health suggests implicit singular relationships between one's sex, one's sexual orientation, and one's gender identity. Here the university, through an attempt to include more diverse components of interest to the queer community, ultimately suggests essentialist ties between distinct moments of queerness.

By placing such components of an individual's identity in the same textual space as words like sexually transmitted infections (STIs) and AIDs, the hotline implies an adversity to such identities and expressions. To return to Foucault, relating gender identities and sex to the act of sex itself, suggests not a concern with the psychological well-being of a student grappling with their gender identity, but instead, a tying of that gender identity to the potentials in which they may *do* sex differently. For as Foucault asserts, when sexual acts become "obsessions" they no longer represent individual acts, but things to describe ad nauseum, envisioning every "image" and "modulation" that could be feasible within these acts themselves. Earlier, Foucault states that this shift in identifying sex as a thing to be named, meant that those engaging in non-reproductive sex fell into a state of mandated confession, regardless of their practices (1990, p. 63). Accordingly, sex becomes a way to codify difference and individuals whose embodiment and lived experience represent the perception of difference become doubly tied to their respective sexualities. By including connotations of sexual deviancy such as STIs within the same space as one's gender, the two are conflated and the juxtaposition affirms a preoccupation with a queer person's sexual behavior.

GRADUATION: THE FUTURE OF QUEER INCLUSION IN THE ACADEMY

A neoliberal reading of the queer movement at this institution, like at most institutions, is to understand that while the work for queer justice has been put on the backs of the oppressed, queer justice is never accomplished without a convergence of interests between the oppressed and the oppressors (Bell, 1995). This is most commonly seen at this site with the addition of a full-time staff person to work to serve queer students. While this was certainly a benefit for the queer students at the institution, this move allows the institution to use this as a talking piece in respect to the credibility of its diversity and inclusion. Often, this commitment to inclusion can serve as little more than a tick-box for institutions, leaving the real work of inclusion not only unfinished but truly unstarted. Something as simple as an underfunded office serves merely as a way for an institution to maintain an illusion of commitment, leading the institution to maintain a post-oppression perspective regarding issues of hate on their campus (Ahmed, 2012).

Universities are built upon a European tradition, so it is no surprise that the "language of diversity becomes easily mobilized as a defence of reputation (perhaps even a defence of whiteness)" (Ahmed, 2012, p. 151). In a contemporary landscape, moving for queer justice, when cleaved apart from racial and/or intersectional justice becomes another tool of white supremacy, arguing for the HRC model of LGB justice. This is to be expected, as Jasbir Puar concludes that "queerness [is] indebted to modernity, and modern sexual identities are built on the histories of colonialism, nation formation and empire, and racialization, the nation is founded on the (homo) sexual other" (Puar, 2007, p. 49). But the acceptable, homonormative queer has become the liberal fantasy of college administrators.

The new homonormativity proffered by Lisa Duggan ensures that the homonormative queer is apt to accept dominant norms "while promising the possibility of a demobilized gay constituency and a privatized, depoliticized gay culture anchored in domesticity and consumption" (2003, p. 50). A clear example of Duggan's homonormativity emerges in the aforementioned institutional artifacts, and it can occur within the failure of the library to have information resources that cover non-normativised queer persons. Alternatively, it can happen through accepting and idolizing the homonormative queer allows for university administrators to tout their own attempt at inclusion, while still keeping at bay the undesirable, no less than they did in the 1980s by keeping at a distance those impacted by HIV/AIDS. Each iteration is unique, but as a whole they reflect a concern, not for those they aim to aid, but instead a systemic, microaggressions which serve to block mobility and place the university as a place of unattainable access.

While this site is specific, the realities herein are less so. University administrators must continue to push boundaries for inclusion. We need to move beyond the welcome events, to a space wherein queer students arrive on campus and feel as if their presence has been expected, as opposed to a burden that must be shouldered, in part by their peers. In order to make this a reality, institutions of higher learning may need to shrug off conservative legislatures which demand the removal of funding for these spaces, for the censorship of queer reading materials, for the requirement of heteronormative binary housing assignments, and finally institutions must acknowledge their past failures and a plan of action to be more intentional to challenge and change their community.

REFERENCES

Adler, M. (2013). Paraphilias: The perversion of meaning in the Library of Congress catalog. In *Feminist and queer information studies reader* (pp. 309–323). Sacramento, CA: Litwin Books, LLC.

Agamben, G. (1998). *Homo sacer: Sovereign power and bare life* (D. Heller-Roazen, Trans.). Stanford, CA: Stanford University Press.

Ahmed, S. (2012). *On being included: Racism and diversity in institutional life*. Durham, NC: Duke University Press.

Astin, A. (1999). Student involvement: A developmental theory for higher education. *Journal of College Student Development, 40*(5), 518–529.

Bedenbaugh, A. (1983, November 9). Gay student group forms speakers Bureau. *The Daily Gamecock*, p. 3.

Berman, S. (1993). *Prejudices and antipathies: A tract on the LC subject heads concerning people*. Jefferson, NC: McFarland.

Bell, D. A. (1995). Brown v. board of education and the interest convergence dilemma. In K. Crenshaw (Author), *Critical race theory: The key writings that formed the movement*. New York, NY: New Press.

Bourdieu, P. (1977). *Outline of a theory of practice*. Cambridge: Cambridge University Press.

Coming out. (2015, December 29). *Student affairs at Illinois counseling center*. Retrieved from https://web.archive.org/web/*/http://counselingcenter.illinois.edu/brochures/coming-out

de Certeau, M. (1984). *The practice of everyday life* (S. Rendall, Trans.). Berkeley, CA: University of California Press.

Drabinski, E. (2013). Queering the catalog: Queer theory and the politics of correction. *The Library, 83*(2), 94–111.

Duggan, L. (2012). *The twilight of equality? Neoliberalism, cultural politics, and the attack on democracy*. Boston, MA: Beacon Press.

Foucault, M. (1990). *The history of sexuality: An introduction, volume I* (Robert Hurley, Trans.). New York, NY: Vintage.

From Staff and Wire Reports (1983, February 4). USC violated gay organization's rights, judge rules. *The Daily Gamecock*, p. 1.

Ladenheim, S. (1998, October 23). Metropolis drag queens entertain. *The Daily Gamecock*, p. 1.

Mbembe, A. (2003). Necropolitics. *Public Culture, 15*(1), 11–40. doi:10.1215/08992363-15-1-11

Mellon, C. A. (1986). Library anxiety: A grounded theory and its development. *College & Research Libraries, 47*(2), 160–165.

Muller, B. (2012). *LGBTQ community development program* (Bachelor's Honors Thesis). Retrieved from Columbia Cooper Honors Theses Collection.

Olson, H. A. (2001). The power to name: Representation in library catalogs. *Signs, 26*(3), 639–668.

Puar, J. K. (2007). *Terrorist assemblages: Homonationalism in queer times*. Durham, NC: Duke University Press.

Rankin, S., Weber, G., Blumenfeld, W. J., & Frazer, S. (2010). *2010 state of higher education for lesbian, gay, bisexual & transgender people*. Charlotte, NC: Campus Pride

Salahuddin, M. (1985, November 4). Colleges say AIDS posing no problems, *The State*, pp. C–1, C–6.

Sexual health and relationship communication (2016, June 2). *In University of South Carolina Student Health Services*. Retrieved from https://web.archive.org/web/20160602105210/https://www.sa.sc.edu/shs/cw/students/sexualhealth/

Student Health Services. (2016, August 25). Join us for the LGBTQ Open House Wednesday, Aug. 31, 5–7 p.m. at the Thomson Student Health Center to answer any questions you might have about our general and LGBTQ-specific services! More information about UofSC's LGBTQ support services at ow.ly/P0F4303vJkN. [Facebook status update]. Retrieved from http://bit.ly/2bzbU3R

Women and gender studies: *Welcome*. (2016, July 12). *In University of South Carolina University Libraries*. Retrieved from http://guides.library.sc.edu/women

CHAPTER SEVEN

"It's Not Natural!"

WAHINKPE TOPA (FOUR ARROWS) AKA DON TRENT JACOBS

IN THE BEGINNING

I am guessing that many readers upon first reading the title of this paper are taken aback, at least for a moment. Perhaps it seems I am taking a position contrary to the purpose of this volume. Of course, I chose it because not only is it the most common argument against sexual or gender diversity that I hear, I intend to make the case that this argument itself is not natural. As an Indigenous author I find such a position to be as anti-Indian as much as it is anti-gay. Both represent a gross misunderstanding or even a rejection of Nature as teacher. Nor is a coincidence that Christian orthodoxy influences both negative attitudes. For example, the perspective that being gay is not natural can be found in the Scriptures of all three of the Abrahamic religions:

> The Old Testament: Leviticus 18:22: "You shall not lie with a male as one lies with a female; it is an abomination."
> The New Testament: Corinthians: 6:9: "Or do you not know that the unrighteous shall not inherit the kingdom of God? Do not be deceived; neither fornicators, nor idolaters, nor adulterers, nor effeminate, nor homosexuals."
> The Quaran (7:81): "For ye practice your lusts on men in preference to women: ye are indeed a people transgressing beyond bounds."

Those who may pick and choose from Scriptures might ignore such passages. Many support the rights of Lesbian, Gay, Bisexual, Transgender, Queer, and

Intersexual (LGBTQI) folks and abhor the prejudice and other violence committed against them. However, I wonder how many would not go as far as to say LGBTQI is "natural." Gay marriage supporters honor the importance of love, equality, tolerance, and the legal right for people to be who they are, but I reckon that they would feel uncomfortable thinking that gay marriage is as natural as heterosexual marriage. They might disagree with those who want to make same-sex marriages illegal, but they would be uncomfortable if their gay child chose to marry.

A NATURAL COURSE OF DIVERSITY

All this is to say that, of the many people who adhere primarily to our dominant worldview, whether supportive or hostile to LGBTQI behaviors, very few would find that the only thing unnatural about the topic is the inability to see these behaviors as a natural course of diversity, which in fact it is. It is furthermore exactly how we understood this aspect of diversity for 99% of human history, before we separated ourselves from Nature around eight thousand years ago (Four Arrows, 2015). The problem now is that Nature is no longer a teacher of truth in our world. Religions have made sure of this. Consider how Biblical Scripture supports anti-Indianism. In Luke 12:1–7, Jesus makes it clear that man was more valuable than sparrows. In Indigenous worldview, such a hierarchy value does not exist. Once we assign a power ranking to any aspect of creation, we set the stage for looking down on and devaluing anyone who is different.

Yet just this kind of hierarchy is made especially clear in Genesis 1:26 where we are told humans are made in God's image so "they may rule over the fish in the sea and the birds in the sky, over the livestock and all the wild animals, and over all the creatures that move along the ground." Couple this with John 14:6 where Jesus says, "I am the way, and the truth, and the life. No one comes to the Father except through me," and we see the basis for Pope Alexander VI's 1493 Doctrine of Discovery (Gilder Lehrman Institute of American History, 2017), which led the way for the terrible atrocities that followed Columbus's voyage, including the atrocities against the Indigenous. Even today, The Doctrine continues to influence legal decisions regarding Indian lands such as the treaty lands at Standing Rock by maintaining the assumption that "non-Christian peoples who were discovered, and dispossessed, had a moral flaw that justice should take into account in ways that would rationalize injustice" (Deloria, 2006, p. 106).

If Indians in general had a moral flaw because they were not Christian, those who practiced "unnatural" sexual behaviors were especially susceptible to the Doctrine of Discovery and vulnerable to Biblical rationalization for brutality beyond description here.

Charges of cannibalism and human sacrifice were made against the Native cultures, but sodomy was an offense which, if not quite so horrifying to European sensibilities, received even more attention as a sign of Indian depravity. The Spaniards—who knew only a world in which homosexuality was excoriated, feared, and all but hidden from public view—now encountered cultures where it was not only tolerated but openly avowed and, in certain areas of Central and South America, institutionalized (Crompton, 2006).

EXPERIENCES OF BEING TWO-SPIRIT

Although a relatively recent development, male and female homosexuals and transvestites are referred to by many Indigenous American societies in their own tongues as "two spirit" people. They are respected as being a balance between masculine and feminine energies and as such are regarded as being exceptionally spiritually gifted. Many serve as spiritual leaders and healers. Effeminate males often live and dress as women, and women with masculine traits often serve as hunters and warriors along with men. When I was in North Dakota with the Water Protection effort to stop an illegal oil pipeline from crossing the Missouri River at Standing Rock, I saw the leadership and loving power of the Two-Spirit encampment. They were highly involved in all of the important actions going on there and were treated the same as everyone else. In fact, in his scholarly book on gay identity and social acceptance in Indian Country, Brian Gilley (2006) describes how transcending stereotypical sexual identities was a matter of course, even foundational to most tribal cultures.

I use *Two-Spirit* here as an Indigenous author referring to an Indigenous concept. It is best if the term not be appropriated for general use by non-Natives who do not fully comprehend the complex meaning it has in the Indigenous language. It is also a relatively new phrase that grew out of the Native American Gay and Lesbian movement, which held its first international gathering in Minneapolis, MN in 1988. In Winnipeg, MB, Canada, during the summer of 1990, those who attended the third annual gathering focused on finding a new term for Native sexualities and gender diversity. After considerable discussion, the term two-spirit was chosen, which refers to a wide variety of Native American and First Nations roles and identities past and present. The term is not intended to mark a new category of gender. Instead two-spirit is an indigenously defined pan-Native North American term that bridges Native concepts of gender diversity and sexualities with those of Western cultures.

Such pan-Indian understanding that goes across tribal affiliations is important but it also requires caution. My own work in Pan-Indianism that seeks to find common ground on many worldview considerations is always at risk of missing the main point of Indigeneity, the deep understanding of a particular place via a particular relationship to it and a unique language that describes it (Lang, 1998,

p. 164). Each place has its own unique version of understanding *two-spirit* roles and identities, whether thought of in dominant culture as gay, lesbian, transvestite, transsexual, transgender, drag queens, and butches, or in tribal languages as winkte, nádleeh, and other appropriate tribal terms. Finding a pan-Indian language that comes close to the ancient understandings in general is important, however, and can hopefully solve some self-identity problems that Native Americans and First Nations two-spirit people have faced. It allows those who live in both urban and rural areas, but not necessarily on reservations, the opportunity to use only one unambiguous term—two-spirit—for their gender identity.

NATURAL BALANCES

The natural balance between solar and lunar energies, and among male and female energies in complex but symbiotic relationships, is shaped by what individual landscapes have in common. Variety depends on the particular life entity. This natural balance is reflected in the relationships between men and women in the majority of Indigenous cultures. Women traditionally played a central role. They were seen as life-givers and caretakers of life. They were honored for their wisdom and vision. "In Aboriginal teachings, passed on through the oral histories of Aboriginal people from generation to generation, men and women were equal in power and each had autonomy within their personal lives" (Aboriginal Justice Implementation Commission, 1999, n.p.).

Women were never seen as inferior until the Europeans came to our shores and colonization's influence, policy, and reservation government brought forth their beliefs in male superiority (Howell, 1996). This is an important confirmation of the "naturalness" of sexual identity diversity. In Nature, the male and the female are equal partners; close and holistic observation of the complex ways of many creatures confirms this. In such an atmosphere, how could alternative sexual identity be seen as a threat? For men to adapt to women's roles or vice versa still preserves equal status. "Homosexual culture goes hand in hand with a strong woman-based society, and such a society was at the very heart of Indian culture that has been most under attack by white philosophy and practice" (Blackwood, 1984, p. 55).

CONCLUDING THOUGHTS

In traditional Indigenous cultures, decisions about identity choices came from dreams and visions. If a young girl had a vision to dress as a male and to do male activities, this was honored by all. Because spiritual knowledge is a major characteristic of traditional ways of being in the world, this alone would have created awareness. This knowledge was often brought into human consciousness via the teachings and examples of other-than-human creatures of a place. As well, it is important to note that contemporary biological science has documented that more than 10% of all prevailing species in homosexual behaviors. Perhaps the percentage would be even higher were it not for such high levels of species extinction.

Such knowledge challenges interpretations of Darwin that claim reproduction with the opposite sex is the only factor that counts in making it possible for humans to survive and thrive (Fereydooni, 2012). Paula Gunn Allen further supports the idea that relationships, not mere procreation, are what the harmonious life, depicted by walking the red road, is all about:

> Among American Indians, spirit-related persons are more closely related than blood-related persons. Understanding this primary difference between American Indian values and modern Euro-American values is critical to understanding Indian familial structures and the context in which lesbians functioned. For American Indian people, the primary value was relationship to the spirit world. All else was determined by the essential nature of this understanding. Spirits, gods, and goddesses, metaphysical/occult forces, and the right means of relating to them, determined the tribes every institution, custom, endeavor, and pastime. This was not peculiar to inhabitants of the Western hemisphere, it was at one time the primary value of all tribal people on earth. (1981, p. 38)

REFERENCES

Aboriginal Justice Implementation Commission. (1999). Aboriginal women. In *Report of the Aboriginal Justice Inquiry of Manitoba* (ch. 13). Retrieved from http://www.ajic.mb.ca/volumel/chapter13.html

Allen, P. G. (1981). Lesbians in American Indian cultures. *Conditions, 7,* 67–87.

Blackwood, E. (1984). Sexuality and gender in certain Native American tribes: The case of cross-gender females. *Signs: Journal of Women in Culture and Society, 10*(1), 27–42.

Crompton, L. (2006). *Homosexualtity and civilization.* Cambridge, MA: Harvard University Press.

Deloria, V., Jr. (2006). Conquest masquerading as law. In Four Arrows (Don Trent Jacobs) (Ed.), *Unlearning the language of conquest: Scholars expose anti-Indianism in America* (pp. 94–107). Austin, TX: University of Texas Press.

Fereydooni, A. (2012, March 14). Do animals exhibit homosexuality? *Yale Scientific.* Retrieved from http://www.yalescientific.org/2012/03/do-animals-exhibit-homosexuality/

Four Arrows (aka Donald Trent Jacobs). (2015). *Point of departure: Returning to our more authentic worldview for education and survival.* Charlotte, NC: Information Age.

Gilder Lehrman Institute of American History. (2017). *The doctrine of discovery, 1493: A primary source by Pope Alexander VI.* Retrieved from https://www.gilderlehrman.org/history-by-era/imperial-rivalries/resources/doctrine-discovery-1493

Gilley, B. J. (2006). *Becoming two-spirit: Gay identity and social acceptance in Indian country.* Omaha, NB: University of Nebraska Press.

Howell, C. (1996). *The impact of colonialization on the role of non-traditional Native American women.* Retrieved from http://pages.cs.wisc.edu/~caitlin/papers/native.htm

Lang, S. (1998). *Men as women, women as men: Changing gender in Native American cultures.* Austin, TX: University of Texas Press.

CHAPTER EIGHT

Writing FROM Queer Silos

Implications of Tokenizing Queer Identities in Counsellor Education

CHRISTOPHER A. CUMBY

INTRODUCTION

This chapter derives from my experiences as a Master of Education student studying Counselling Psychology. The goal of this chapter is to illuminate the experiences of tokenization experienced by lesbian, gay, bisexual, trans, queer, and other gender and sexual minority people (LGBTQ+) within educational spaces. I position myself here as a visible queer man in a space dominated by heterosexual students and faculty. Using autoethnography (see Ellis, 1997; Ellis & Bochner, 2000, 2006; Ellis, Adams, & Bochner, 2011), a critical research method that uses story to tell research, I use my experiences to attempt a deeper understanding of this phenomenon.

There are several approaches to conducting autoethnography, of which I took an approach similar to Adams (2011), whose style tends to be story written alongside academic writing in order to create something evocative and meaningful. In taking this approach, I wrote several pieces from memories of my time so far in the program which elicited a strong reaction, and chose three to examine in depth here. This process can be strife with ethical issues of including experiences involving other people. For this reason, I chose stories that were from my perspective, I chose not to use names throughout, and I received permission from my supervisor to include a conversation between the two of us. In doing so, I hope to respect the identities of those who were involved in my experiences and honour their privacy.

I note here that my experiences are not necessarily the experiences of everyone in the LGBTQ+ community, nor should it be taken as such. My community is rich with complex experiences and beautiful, wonderful people, and it is not my intention to speak for everyone, but rather to use this opportunity to provide commentary on what some of us in the community experience. Primarily, this chapter grapples with the barriers that many LGBTQ+ students face in the classroom, understanding tokenism within such spaces, navigating through microaggressions (Sue et al., 2007), and finally ending off with a thoughtful conversation about how we can (continue to) support LGBTQ+ people in education.

IN THE CLASSROOM

I walked into the classroom eager to study counselling methods; I was relatively new to the program at this point, having moved from my new home in Labrador two months ago to become a student again. Sitting around me in the small seminar room were 11 other students at various stages in the program; some were full-time students like me, while others were teachers who studied part-time.

The professor, a former primary/elementary guidance counsellor, stands in front of the class and greets us all merrily, despite our exhausted expressions which is reflected by the evening sky through the window. He begins the lecture with an invitation for us to watch a video on one-on-one counselling scenarios. With the press of a button, the video projector flickers on and we are shown the counsellor, a person of colour, as he counsels a grieving white woman whom, we are told by the narrator, comes to seek help with managing the emotional burden of having a sick mother in the hospital. "… And these Mexican nurses don't know anything. They are useless, no help at all! I can't believe my poor mother has to deal with this on top of her illness," the woman exclaims angrily over the crackling loudspeakers in the room.

"I have to interrupt for a moment, Jean; as your counsellor, and as a person of colour from a Mexican background, I'm wondering if your feelings about the capabilities of the nurses might affect how you see me in our relationship?" The conversation pauses, and the narrator asks the class if this was the right decision to make, or if there was a better way of handling the situation.

The professor stops the video, and turns to the class, "Well, what do you all think?"

"I think that the counsellor shouldn't have mentioned that right then and there. She was clearly upset and may not have meant what she was saying. It should have been brought up, but I don't think it was necessary to bring it up right now," one student says, as the classmates around me nod in agreement.

The professor echoes the student, "Yes, I would agree with you there. It didn't seem necessary to bring it up at the moment."

I pipe up as the professor turns to move on in the lecture, "I don't think that's right. As a Queer person, I've often asked myself what it would look like if I had a client that had said something homophobic. What could I do, you know? There's been so many times in my life already that I have had these kinds of things happen, it's naïve to think it wouldn't happen in counselling practice. What's more, if I were to experience this, I think I *would* bring it up immediately—what if I go on through the sessions thinking this person might be homophobic? It's not a secret that I'm queer. I am vocal and visible about that. To ignore this would be to miss the point entirely that this counsellor is a person of colour dealing with a client who has said something racist. If that person thinks that you are incompetent because of who you are as a person, then not only do you suffer, but the whole relationship between counsellor and client suffers." My heart pounds against my chest as I notice everyone looking at me blankly around the room. I suspect that my speech hasn't convinced many people, if any.

People around me voice their concerns that I am wrong about what I have just said. I am not quite sure how to respond, even less sure of my position as I feel as if I have been booed off the stage. As the conversation heats up, the professor thanks us for our comments and moves the lecture along. I quickly leave the class feeling emotionally exhausted and defeated.

(Lack of) Support

Within the Academy, support is often one of the first areas of concern regarding the success of LGBTQ+ students and staff (Vaccaro, 2012). However, there are two broader levels of support which must be considered here when conceptualizing support within educational praxis: systemic, and systematic.

Systemically, there is a general lack of awareness and knowledge about queer and trans lives, about our subculture, and the celebrations, strengths, and resiliency that comes from such a vibrant community. This lack of knowledge is often typified by not identifying, or connecting with the LGBTQ+ community in some way such as having LGBTQ+ relatives, friends. While information is readily available for interested persons, such knowledge is often centered around the tokenized queer and trans students within educational spaces. This is to say, this phenomenon often looks like a form of "Queer Gatekeeping," in which *out* LGBTQ+ students are seen as the expert of knowledge and treated in such a way. This is not necessarily new information within queer discourse, however it should be noted here to further this understanding.

Using a microcosmic lens, systemic support can often look like a lack of knowledge by peers, administrators, and staff, where no knowledge often equates to no support; ultimately lending itself to a lack of representation (Baker, Gaulke, & Smith, 2015). For example, my professor, a self-professed "old white guy," unintentionally reinforced a heteronormative, white-washed worldview for the class in failing to recognize the underlying message of the material he had presented. While this is not to suggest a lack of competence, it certainly speaks to a micro-culture which is not uncommon within education.

Systematic support, on the other hand, refers to institutional levels of support through the forms of funding, policy at the local, provincial/state, and federal levels, laws, and other mediums through which a heteronormative milieu is reinforced (Baker et al., 2015). It should be understood, then, that despite typical queer discourse, knowledge alone is insufficient to cause change. Support must necessarily come from a variety of sources, which is discussed later in this chapter. These issues should be understood in relation to one another in order to effect real action and change within educational praxis.

Being "Out" in the Classroom

Stemming from support comes the challenge of coming out, a feat that is specific to the lives of queer and trans people. Choosing to come out is political, empowering, frightening, dangerous, and important. In coming out in the classroom, one must consider the consequences of social disapproval, social avoidance, higher stress levels, and other aspects that stem from the coming out process (Corrigan & Matthews, 2003; Pitts, 2015). But why do people come out at all, given these potential risks?

As a masculine-presenting person, it can be argued that it is not necessary to come out. Given the emotional burdens of having to confront others on a frequent basis, it is important to recognize here that many people who belong to the LGBTQ+ community do not have the opportunity or ability to conceal themselves, known otherwise as "passing-privilege," in which our bodies are drawn under scrutiny and judged against prevailing notions of cisgender and heterosexual identities, subsequently deemed "passable."

Aside from the safety assured from concealing queer and trans identities (Semp, 2011), those who can "pass" may choose not to. For myself, it can be broken down into two issues: empowerment, and activism. Empowerment looks different depending on the context, but it can be likened in this case to self-representation. This is the process of being seen, and seeing others who embody similar experiences and identities represented in the space around oneself. Self-representation is important in counsellor education, as we must bring our authentic selves to the table, and indeed this drives connection, which is the foundation of counselling in itself. The benefits of this kind of empowerment involve improved psychological well-being, lower stress, and the aforementioned sense of connection (Corrigan & Matthews, 2003).

Tokenization often contributes to feelings of alienation and invisibility (Speciale, Gess, & Speedlin, 2015). The idea of difference among peers can be emotionally difficult, and the risks that come with coming out is always weighed with the risks of staying in the closet. To come out for me was an experience of tokenization, one which I felt was necessary despite this, but one which was not free of burden. Throughout school experiences, students must always negotiate this. Coming out is, of course, not a singular process, but one which happens in every classroom, in every group conversation, and in every conversation with professors and staff. Negotiating these terms inevitably contribute to student stress and burnout, especially when coupled with taking on the role of token queer in the classroom.

The second piece in considering coming out in the classroom revolves around activism. Coming out is a political act because it destabilizes the heteronormative assumptions of representation within the classroom (Adams, 2011). There are also strong feelings of responsibility and allyship when confronted with situations of invisibility such as the one described here. In this scenario, there was a feeling of *had to* rather than *should*; as the only queer-identified person in the room, there was a sense of responsibility. I had to ask myself, *If not me, who? If not now, when?* Despite the risk of coming out, and the emotional exhaustion that comes from having these frequent conversations, as students in a professional program, it is necessary to consider the possible negative effects of not responding. The next section will underline this in more detail.

CULTURAL COMPETENCY AND QUEER LIVES

I call my partner in the lobby, who is back in Labrador in our home. "But these are *counsellors*," I tell him, "I am not saying they are incompetent or stupid, but they are going to be dealing with kids and teenagers especially, and they are going to encounter students who are queer and trans. What will happen to those students? They don't know a lot, if anything, about our lives and our experiences. I got the impression from the room that no one has noticeably experienced what it feels like to be dismissed immediately because of their identity. I found that particularly odd because many of the people in the room were women, so I know they have experienced it at some time or another. Perhaps some have never known, or at least had an awareness of, what being on the outside looks like at all. Even the professor didn't seem to know much about it, although he's made clear his awareness of his bias as an older, straight, white man. It still wasn't enough because his lecture just made him complacent in this marginalization."

"What about it made you feel that way?" My partner asks, curiously.

"Well." I think about it for a moment, before continuing, "I think that as a professor in a professional counselling program, and as a student counsellor, it's important that we all be active allies to marginalized communities. With campaigns such as It Gets Better, the one about all of the LGBTQ+ suicides (Savage & Miller, 2010), more than ever people in these positions need to acknowledge their own limitations and learn more about queer and trans lives to help out."

"That's true," he replies, "Even here in Labrador, the guidance counsellor only comes one week a month, and the closest counsellor around is a four-hour drive. It's similar to other rural communities—kids usually only have limited access to their guidance counsellor. There's not many LGBTQ+ role models in the community, either, so that really exasperates it further."

"Exactly!" I exclaim, "If people come to see a counsellor and they don't know much, or anything, about queer and trans experiences, where does that leave these people seeking help? I'm worried about the implications of culturally ignorant counsellors coming out of education programs like this situation seems to be."

I pause, contemplating exactly what it meant to be a token queer voice in a room full of well-educated people. Such people who otherwise have no idea what our experiences have been and how they are so different from their own. As I think for a moment, my professor and a classmate walk past. The professor says solemnly, "Have a good evening, Chris" as they exit the building.

I don't sleep well that night.

STUDENT CULTURAL AWARENESS

Within the helping fields, the term *cultural competency* is often used to describe an understanding of diverse cultural groups. This understanding is used by health professionals to provide appropriate care for clients (Boroughs, Bedoya, O'Cleirigh, & Safren, 2015). Cultural competency with LGBTQ+ people requires an understanding of how these identities create difference in experience from the general public. Counselling discourse regarding gender and sexual minorities often looks at coming out narratives as the sole purpose for LGBTQ+ people seeking counselling; however, this should be understood as one of many ways that experiences may differentiate.

Boroughs et al. (2015) discuss some of the problems with cultural competency frameworks within education. Specifically, they suggest that cultural competency courses are often not offered in graduate level degrees, and when they are, they are not required courses. This problem lies in wake of the common ideology that there are specific counsellors who specialize in cultural counselling, and so it is unnecessary for students to require this knowledge due to the breadth of information on the subject. While this argument may be made, it should be emphasized that a base level of knowledge is important for all professionals. This knowledge reflects the realities of the complex groups of people that most professionals will work with throughout their careers, instead of limiting these people to only specialists who are already overburdened by large caseloads. Using a multicultural framework in general practice can help professionals increase their empathy skills, connect more with their clients, and be more effective in their roles.

MICROAGGRESSIONS AND TOKENISM

Microaggressions are subtle insults, verbally or nonverbally, targeting minority groups. Such insults are often automatic and unconscious, and may be unintentional (Sue et al., 2007). While this term was originally used to explain racial microaggressions, it has since been expanded to include gender and sexual minorities (see Nadal et al., 2016). Microinvalidations are a sub-type of microaggressions, which are "characterized by communications that exclude, negate, or nullify the psychological thoughts, feelings, or experiential reality of a [minority person]" (Sue et al., 2007, p. 273).

As the only out queer person in the classroom, I discussed my experiences with them, my concerns about experiencing client homophobia, and my relation to the material being shown, only to be met with disagreement and disengagement. My experiences were invalidated by the group of students around me, and this was exasperated by the lack of allyship in advocating for me, or people with similar lived experiences. When this experience of microinvalidation is considered alone, it may be easily dismissed; however, this experience does not exist within a vacuum. Indeed, experiences of microaggressions (especially in tokenized scenarios) exist as a part of a constellation of similar experiences that happen daily.

When we consider this in reference to the Minority Stress Model (Meyer, 1995, 2003), we can have a better comprehension of these experiences. The Minority Stress Model was introduced by Meyers to explain the phenomenon of people from various minority groups (i.e. out-groups) experiencing higher levels of distress due to societal stressors regarding their identity, when compared to the general public (Boroughs et al., 2015). This model explains the compounding effects of microaggressions and experiences of discrimination as determinants of negative health outcomes for LGBTQ+ people, often contributing to burnout, depression, and anxiety. When there is a lack of visibility, connection, or representation of LGBTQ+ people within education, these experiences of tokenization similarly affect marginalized gender and sexual peoples. In order to avoid conflating this point, tokenism and microaggressions both interact with each other, creating stress reactions for those who experience them. Consequently, this affects mental and physical health (Sue, 2010), which leads to lower rates of success among students when compared to cisgender and heterosexual populations.

RECOMMENDATIONS FOR MOVING FORWARD

A few weeks pass since the "classroom encounter" as I have entitled it in my head. I find myself now sitting across from my supervisor in her office. Like almost every other time that we had met, we talked about my research, courses, assistant work that I had been doing for her, as well other normal conversation topics. As we were talking about local events, I was curious to know about the lack of LGBTQ+ symbols of inclusion that were oft represented by flags, posters, and other media. We were both open about our queerness in the faculty, and she was one of the few, if only, faculty members who was open and visible—which is understandable given the sparsity of tenure-track positions juxtaposed with the multitude of teaching-term professors.

"Why aren't there any rainbow or trans flags around the building? I wondered because I've heard that the faculty is pushing toward more inclusion of minority and out-groups, but I haven't seen any of the symbol-stuff around …" I trail off.

My supervisor stops to think about this before replying, "Well … I think that there's something about teachers that makes them a little nervous to have those kind of symbols in place without something more concrete to back them up with. Many people in Education faculties come from the public school system, and I think that there is a kind of mindset that follows from that. Perhaps there is a nervousness about not having enough training, or not having enough support from senior administration—although our dean and faculty have been great on that front in my experiences—but there seems to be a need for something more concrete in place."

"Huh … I've never thought about it like that before," I reply, "But, I have to wonder what can we do to help build bridges between all of these silos? How can we start to hold each other up when there are so few of us, and so many barriers? These questions are big, and maybe we can't figure them out right now."

"No," she responds, "I agree, they can't necessarily be answered here. But you're right that there is a different kind of atmosphere. Every workplace comes with its own barriers that are unique to the space itself, and we definitely can't expect anything we come up with to help everyone. We also need to remind ourselves that activism from a silo can burn us out, and that these things won't change overnight."

"Maybe you should write some things down and see what you can found out?" She suggests.

"That's a great idea!" I respond, "I'm not sure if anything will come out of it, but I'd be interested in seeing where it takes me." I finish the meeting and head to my office, pulling a pen and notepad out as I walk. Upon reaching my desk, I have already had some ideas float into my consciousness, which I quickly jot down. "*Now,*" I think, "*What do I think educators need to know about supporting people like me?*"

As I was writing, I started thinking about the things that were already contributing to a positive environment. In Canada, we have sexual identities protected under the Human Rights Act, and in Newfoundland and Labrador, our Human Rights Commission includes Gender Identity and Expression as protected under the Act (*Human Rights Act*, 2010). The faculty had my supervisor, who helped push for a more inclusive school culture, and the rest of the staff and dean were on board from what I could tell. However, not every university, school, or community has these protections in place. Before endeavoring on any type of activist work, it may be important to conduct a cultural competency assessment to determine the local climate (Baker & Moore, 2015; Baker et al., 2015). If no policies exist, it is imperative to advocate for these protections in order to have concrete support and build an environment which welcomes gender and sexual minority communities.

I thought about the research that I had read, of which many authors argued for inclusive orientation training for students (Baker & Moore, 2015), and staff training (Bidell, 2012; Boroughs et al., 2015; Butler et al., 2016), which should be on-going, rather than a one-off event. Inclusive staff training should be one which emphasizes being an ally to marginalized communities, especially when no one is present to represent such voices; however, it is essential not to silo queer and trans voices to expect them to only do queer activism.

Allyship, then, should be considered an ongoing process of raising up the voices of those who may not otherwise have opportunities to speak. Training programs should also acknowledge that mistakes are common, and expected. In my experiences as a trainer and facilitator, those without knowledge of the LGBTQ+ community are often afraid of messing up and offending—to them I suggest recognizing when a mistake is made, apologizing, and moving on from the mistake. Once this has been established, allies should learn to recognize and interrupt microaggressions when they witness them (Speciale et al., 2015). This reinforces a stronger community, and unloads the burden of education and confrontation from LGBTQ+ people.

Educators and administration should consider making cultural competency coursework mandatory in graduate programs (Boroughs et al., 2015), and infuse current curriculum with LGBTQ+ information. To further this, educators should ask students privately how to better assist their needs in the classroom (Semp, 2011), and avoid outing them to the class. This is incredibly important to consider with trans students, as they may not have the ability to legally change their name due to financial or age restrictions, and which outing them may bring issues of safety. Finally, I argue that educators should have deep, enriching conversations with students, peers, and colleagues about discrimination and oppression.

These are just a few of the possible recommendations for enriching educational and community spaces, but this list is not exhaustive. As our community and society grows upon each other, the needs of the community will also shift. As professionals, we must keep up-to-date with research and the local community, and making ourselves visible as allied voices for the community. Above all else, we must keep holding on to each other, build on the voices of marginalized peoples, and promote a culture of compassion and acceptance.

REFERENCES

Adams, T. E. (2011). *Narrating the closet: An autoethnography of same-sex attraction*. Walnut Creek, CA: Left Coast Press.

Baker, C. A., Gaulke, K., & Smith, K. (2015). Counselor education cultural climate: Underrepresented Master students' experiences. *Journal for Multicultural Education, 9*(2), 85–97. doi:10.1108/JME-07-2014-0032

Baker, C. A., & Moore, J. L. (2015). Experiences of underrepresented doctoral students in counselor education. *Journal for Multicultural Education, 9*(2), 68–84. doi:10.1108/JME-11-2014-0036

Bidell, M. P. (2012). Examining school counseling students' multicultural and sexual orientation competencies through a cross-specialization comparison. *Journal of Counseling & Development, 90*, 200–207.

Boroughs, M. S., Bedoya, C. A., O'Cleirigh, C., & Safren, S. A. (2015). Toward defining, measuring, and evaluating LGBT cultural competence for psychologists. *Clinical Psychology: Science and Practice, 22*(2), 151–171.

Butler, M., McCreedy, E., Schwer, N., Burgess, D., Call, K., Przedworski, J., ... Kane, R. L. (2016). *Improving cultural competence to reduce health disparities* (No. 16-EHC006-EF). Rockville, MD: Comparative Effectiveness Review, Number 170.

Corrigan, P., & Matthews, A. (2003). Stigma and disclosure: Implications for coming out of the closet. *Journal of Mental Health, 12*(3), 235–248. doi:10.1080/0963823031000118221

Ellis, C. (1997). Evocative autoethnography: Writing emotionally about our lives. *Communication Faculty Publications.* 304. http://scholarcommons.usf.edu/spe_facpub/304

Ellis, C. S., & Bochner, A. (2000). Autoethnography, personal narrative, reflexivity: Researcher as subject. In N. K. Denzin & Y. S. Lincoln (Eds.), *Handbook of qualitative research* (2nd ed.) (pp. 733–768).

Ellis, C. S., & Bochner, A. P. (2006). Analyzing analytic autoethnography: An autopsy. *Journal of Contemporary Ethnography, 35*(4), 429.

Ellis, C., Adams, T. E., & Bochner, A. P. (2011). Autoethnography: An overview. *Forum: Qualitative Social Research/Sozialforschung, 12*(1), 273–290.

Human Rights Act. (2010). (Press Release). Newfoundland and Labrador: Justice Department.

Meyer, I. H. (1995). Minority stress and mental health in gay men. *Journal of Health and Social Behavior, 36*(1), 38–56.

Meyer, I. H. (2003). Prejudice, social stress, and mental health in lesbian, gay, and bisexual populations: Conceptual issues and research evidence. *Psychological Bulletin, 129*(5), 674.

Nadal, K. L., Whitman, C. N., Davis, L. S., Erazo, T., & Davidoff, K. C. (2016). Microaggressions toward lesbian, gay, bisexual, transgender, queer, and genderqueer people: A review of the literature. *Journal of Sex Research, 53*(4–5), 488–508. doi:10. 1080/00224499

Pitts, T. (2015). *A glimpse of the transgender experience: Mental health issues and implications for counsellors* (Master of Counselling).

Savage, D., & Miller, T. (2010). *It gets better project.* Retrieved from http://www.itgetsbetter.org

Semp, D. (2011). Questioning heteronormativity: Using queer theory to inform research and practice within public mental health services. *Psychology & Sexuality, 2*(1), 69–86. doi:10.1080/19419889.2011.536317

Speciale, M., Gess, J., & Speedlin, S. (2015). You don't look like a lesbian: A coautoethnography of intersectional identities in counselor education. *Journal of LGBT Issues in Counseling, 9*(4), 256–272. doi:10.1080/15538605.2015.1103678

Sue, D. W. (2010). *Microaggressions in everyday life: Race, gender, and sexual orientation.* Hoboken, NJ: John Wiley & Sons.

Sue, D. W., Capodilupo, C. M., Torino, G. C., Bucker, J. M., Holder, A. M. B., Nadal, K. L., & Esquilin, M. (2007). Racial microaggressions in everyday life: Implications for clinical practice. *American Psychologist, 67*(4), 271–286. doi:10.1037/0003-066X.62.4.271

Vaccaro, A. (2012). Campus microclimates for LGBT faculty, staff, and students: An exploration of the intersections of social identity and campus roles. *Journal of Student Affairs Research and Practice, 49*(4), 429–446.

PART THREE

LGBTQ+ Faculty AND Student Narratives OF Profound Campus Exclusion

CHAPTER NINE

Our Morning AFTER PULSE

A Parent/Teacher Educator's Experience of Protection, Invisibility, and Action

SARAH PICKETT

OUR MORNING: PROTECTION, INVISIBILITY, AND ACTION

The Pulse Massacre motivates me to write about LGBTQ+ affirming practice in K–12 educational communities, pedagogy, and teacher education settings. In positioning myself I grappled with the multiple marginalized identities represented in the Pulse tragedy that my social location does not reflect. I struggled with how to represent these marginalized communities and honour the intersectionality of the Pulse Massacre victims (Carbado, Crenshaw, Mays, & Tomlinson, 2013). Intentionally, I focus only on my lived experience within the identities I hold as white, cisgender, lesbian/queer, co-parent, and educator of educators.

I position myself within the LGBTQ+ community and use autoethnography as methodology, drawing meaningful connections between personal and cultural knowledge through evocative accounts of my experience in education that matter and make a difference (Ellis, 1999, 2004; Ellis & Bochner, 2000). My experience is not intended to nor could it represent the myriad responses that LGBTQ+ educational communities experienced after Pulse. Narrative accounts of my experience after the Pulse Massacre aim to contribute knew cultural knowledge to the question: *How can allies, K–12 educational environments, and more broadly educational institutions, such as the academy enact an ethic of care following tragedies such the Pulse Massacre?*

In attempting to answer this question a relational context becomes pivotal to the process of knowledge construction, meaning making, and co-creating preferred outcomes (Freedman & Combs, 1996; Gilligan, 2014). In closely analyzing my experience, I step back from it, while still treating it as meaningful and valuable (Ellis, 2004; Ellis & Bochner, 2006). My *first hand familiarity* as a member of the LGBTQ+ community makes noticing recurring experiences, emotions, and omissions plausible (Adams, 2011; Blumber, 1969, p. 38).

Writing retrospectively and analyzing my post-Pulse experience has resulted in more questions than answers. By witnessing my experience through text, educators are invited to critically reflect on their own approaches, ambivalence, or avoidance of difficult questions arising from the Massacre. Throughout all the narratives, overt and covert messages highlight avenues toward co-creating preferred outcomes in a relational context and within an ethic of care (Gilligan, 2014; Noddings, 1992, 1995). I leave the remaining unanswered and emergent questions inherent in this inquiry for the reader to create and ponder.

PROTECTING OUR OWN CHILDREN FROM THE PULSE AFTERMATH

To our knowledge my partner and I are the only same-gender couple/parent who are *out* at our children's school. This fact situates us within our school community on the day following the Pulse Massacre.

6:00 a.m.

I awake from sleep with rapid, racing, pressing thoughts. I'm sweating as if I've just completed a marathon and yet, I lay still in bed. What will we tell our children? How do we explain this? Do they even know the word *gay*? How do you explain massacre to a five and six year old? As a psychologist and educator why I don't feel better prepared for this conversation? I want to go back to bed. Where are the covers, where are the covers? Go back to bed Sarah, go back to sleep.

6:15 a.m.

I have to figure out what to say to them. Why didn't Kathy (my partner and co-parent) and I talk to them about this yesterday? We had such a great day, hiking, breathing in the fresh crisp air that I've come to love living in the North Atlantic seaboard. We explored cannons, and towers, and the wonderful history of this place I'm blessed to call home, this land that holds a part of our children's heritage.

6:35 a.m.

While making beds, sorting through laundry, and checking the weather, Kathy and I begin to discuss how we will approach introducing the word gay to our children. It seems strange to both of us that a word, which has had such power surrounding our lives, is not a part of our children's language. We both came out in the 1990s, a time characterized by descriptions such as Gay Pride and Gay Marriage, a moment when the word gay was a commonplace descriptor for our community, one whispered in hallways, used to harm us, and wielded as a source of shunning. In this moment we are keenly aware of how our community language has changed over the years. We now go to Pride as a family, a word that reflects the sexual and gender diversity of our community and we've had many family conversations about love, romance, marriage, friendship, gender, sex, and how families may be created without any need for the word gay.

6:45 a.m.

Precious alone-time in the shower as Kathy makes tea and coffee and I breathe in the steam, feel the pounding hot water across my back while pushing my fingers tightly into my eyes and holding my hands across my face. I'm hiding. If I stay here long enough maybe the day will pass and I won't have to go downstairs, sit at our kitchen table and explain the word gay. It's not explaining the word, that I'm dreading; it's what the word represents in this conversation. At ages five and six, they are too young to learn that some people hate our family, that someone's hatred for Mommy and Mom's love, behaviors, and sexuality led to 49 people being killed and 53 wounded in a gay bar in Orlando, FL. How do I explain a massacre of this magnitude within our community, their community? How do we keep them feeling safe in this world when our ideas of safety, equity, and progress have been profoundly called into question by this event?

7:00 a.m.

> Kathy: What are we going to tell them?
> I: Enough to question what they might hear about Pulse at school. We can't prepare them for the unknown. We can only alert them and hope they'll talk to us. Does that sound good?
> Kathy: Yes, can you explain? (slight smile, eyebrow lifted; the same look that can cajole me into just about anything)
> I: (warm smile) Yes.

7:05 a.m.

We enter the children's rooms, look softly at each other and take a deep breath. Good morning my sweets, we each say.

7:15 a.m. (Kitchen Table)

While our son takes a bite of waffle and our daughter slowly eats cut strawberries one by one, in between bids for attention from both of them to hear just one more part of their dreams, I say, I have something to talk with you both about, and it's important.

Why did I have to explain the word gay today? Because they might hear the word today, more than any other day in their life thus far. The LGBTQ+ community is in the spotlight, throughout the media, on the radio today. We as a community have been in this position before during our children's lives, but today is different.

7:20 a.m.

Phew, we made it through explaining the word gay with relative ease. To which my son asks, Can I tell you my dream now?

Almost, I say. (I dig deep, pulling on my mother's courage). I begin, the other night a person went into a place where many people who are gay go to dance and hang out together and this person hurt a whole bunch of people very badly. We don't know why the person did this, but many people died and many were hurt. (I look to Kathy for reassurance and the softness of her eyes before continuing.)

> 5-year old: They died!
> I: Yes, many people died.

Before they can ask me too many questions for which I'm not prepared, I begin again. This person hurt people because they were different. Our family doesn't believe in hurting people because we may be different or disagree.

> 6-year old: Where were they?
> I: In Orlando, Florida.
> 5-year old: Florida? Where Disneyworld is?
> I: Yes.
> 6-year old: I don't want to go to Florida.
> I: (I chime in before the fear takes over.) We are not going to Florida any time soon. We live far away from Florida. This was one person's action. Mom and Mommy, families like ours, and many families different from ours are very sad today for all the people who had someone they love die or get hurt. Mom and Mommy want you to know about what happened in case you hear about it at school.
> Both Children: Can we finish telling you our dreams?
> Kathy and I (relieved): Absolutely!

7:30 a.m.

Breakfast conversation is finally over. While our children go upstairs to get ready, we clean up, pack lunches and finishing getting ready I say to Kathy, "How'd I do? Was that okay? To above their heads? To dark? Not explicit enough? I didn't want to scare them. This is awful."

Kathy looks softly at me and says, "You did great my love. Thank you."

[Editor's Note: The term "cisnormativity" was first used in the 2000s, but its first recorded academic use was in *The Journal of the International AIDS Society* in 2012. It is a combination of the prefix cis-, as in cisgender, and the suffix -normativity, as a complement to *heteronormativity*.]

Our Morning may evoke emotional responses in relation to LGBTQ+ experience and compel educator/allies to no longer distance themselves from the impact of problematic hetero/cisnormative discourses (Nadal, Whitman, Davis, Erazo, & Davidoff, 2016; Sue, 2010). In deconstructing our experience details such as the significance of terminology, the duality of language, the need to protect, many strains of minority stress are elucidated (Meyer, 2003). As a narrative-counseling practitioner, I relish these spaces embedded in *our morning* attending to unique outcomes within stories of marginalization and domination. Spaces educators can attend to, such as how terminology may be used as a weapon—and a blanket- and the contextual nature of language (White, 2007; White & Epston, 1990).

Importantly, educators may reflexively ask, why did we feel compelled, a sense of urgency to arm our children with accurate information and prescribe for them the possible situations they may encounter? Strengths emerge within *our morning* while we, as *gay* parents, attend to the protection of our children living within the dominant hetero/cisnormative discourse. These strengths are witnessed in the nuance of *our morning*.

Universal themes such as parental responsibilities in attending to young children and the daily activities of family life are presented alongside our urgency to prepare and protect. Experiences of LGBTQ+ people may be viewed both within and outside hetero/cisnormaitve discourses (Butler, 1999; Ellis & Bochner, 2000; Freedman & Combs, 1996; White & Epston, 1990). *Our morning* both lives within and resists dominant hetero/cisnormative discourse. The *telling* of *our morning* is an act of resistance to problematic narratives that situate LGBTQ+ experience as less valuable than those of our heterosexual and cisgender peers, unworthy of discussion, and as acts of deviance (Butler, 1999; Freedmond & Combs, 1996). As colleagues and allies, educators may consider what actions may be taken to support LGBTQ+ students, families, colleagues and community within the hetero/cisnormativity of schools? "Our morning" offers educators' a venue for resisting hetero/cisnormative assumptions about LGBTQ+ families and how we are taken up or dismissed in educational environments.

INVISIBILITY AND VOICE DURING *OUR MORNING* AFTER THE PULSE MASSACRE

8:15 a.m. Elementary School

I don't know if I'm up to this today. As a lesbian, parent, and teacher educator I consistently ask myself when engaging with my children's school, is this necessary? Today, my answer is yes, that is, until I encounter the support staff. After a conversation with my son's teacher, I head toward to the school office, the hub of the school's daily functioning. I arrive at the office and ask the administrative support if I may speak with the principal. I'm told that the principal is very busy this morning and that unless it's urgent I will need to arrange a time to speak with them after school.

I wonder, is this urgent? It can't wait until school is over, that will be far too late, but is it urgent enough for me to request an unscheduled meeting with the principal? 49 people in our community were killed and 53 wounded over the weekend and there has been mass media coverage on the Pulse tragedy. Is it urgent that I speak with the principal, the teacher about how Pulse will be taken up, or not taken up with our child, the only child of *out parents* in this K-6 elementary school? How is urgency determined? What if I meet with the principal and they do not understand my fears, concerns, or the profound effect that the massacre is having on our community and our family?

I decide to sit and wait to speak to the principal. After waiting for what seemed like an hour and witnessing the principal rush around the office for what appeared to be an "urgent" situation, I'm keenly aware of the fear I have of not making it to speak to the Dean of the Faculty of Education before the education students arrive. I've got about 30 minutes. I re-approach the administrative support, "Is there another member of the administrative team available, like the guidance counselor? Perhaps what I need to speak to the principal about can be addressed then," I say.

The administrative team member I've been directed to is putting down their things as I walk in. I wonder if they are aware of the Pulse Massacre. They must be. Maybe they will start the conversation, I think. They begin the conversation with, "My apologies, I'm running a bit late this morning, I was waiting on contractors at my house and couldn't leave. What brings you in this morning?" I think: *How different our mornings have been*. I ask, "Are you aware of what happened in Orlando?" They respond with "Oh yes, it's just awful." I wait and hope that they will then make a bid for connection and say, "I'm glad you're here, I was hoping that we might talk about how we as a school community can support your community, your son, your family and our student." Silence. I then realize that although I'm *out* to the school and they are aware that our son has same-gender parents, the school community is not aware of the significant impact the tragedy is having on same-gender parents and on the LGBTQ+ community worldwide.

I deeply understand in this moment that this lack of awareness, that my invisibility is systemic. I feel the knot in my stomach tighten, my chest begin to pound, my blood begin to boil and I'm slightly dizzy; my body is talking to me. In this environment, this conversation may not be safe. My thoughts race: If the LGBTQ+ community mattered today, the school district and the school board would have made statements of support the morning after the Pulse Massacre and offered guidance to school administrative teams, including best practices in LGBTQ+ affirming school communities; the professional association of teacher educators in my province would have alerted their members about how to enact an ethic of care today for LGBTQ+ folks in the context of school communities. If any of these institutional responses had occurred, our family would have had a greater chance of being visible in this conversation.

MOVING PAST MINIMUM STANDARDS OF TOLERANCE AND TOWARD LGBTQ AFFIRMING PRACTICES

In authentically enacting our experience with the school after Pulse, I'm expanding on what Adams (2011) coined the *paradox of the closet: post-coming out*. Adams states that even if a person receives a positive response to sharing their same-gender attraction, after *coming out* they may never be acknowledged again. I expand on this theory, and situate my interaction with the school within the framework, *paradox of the closet: parental post-outness*. While the school has responded positively to my being *out* as a person, I'm acknowledged less as an *out parent*. In common with the experience of LGBTQ+ students in Catholic schools who receive the message, *it's okay to be gay, as long as you don't act on it*, the message we receive is, *it's okay to be out parents, as long as you blend in* (Callaghan, 2016).

In this context, *blending in* would mean not having and/or asserting any needs outside the hetero/cisnormativity of schools. Approaching the school after Pulse is *not blending in* as it falls outside the hetero/cisnormativity that governs schools (Bower & Klecka, 2009; Duke, 2008; Kosciw, Greytak, Bartkiewicz, Boesen, & Palmer, 2012; Taylor et al., 2011). Lack of acknowledgment of our status as *post-out parents* can be witnessed through the schools disengagement, confusion, and surprise when we don't *blend in*.

A failure to acknowledge *post-out parents*, while unintentional, is still harmful. As a marginalized group, we are left to interpret the meaning of this invisibility (Nadal et al., 2016; Sue, 2010). For example, Adams (2011) describes a *post-out paradox* when a mother asks her *out gay* son if he notices an attractive woman, stating that all men notice women. Should the son in Adams' example explain to his mother again that he is *gay* and not attracted to women? Does the mother know and intentionally dismiss her son's same gender attraction? Likewise, the lack of acknowledgement after Pules creates a *parental post-out paradox*. Am I to assume that the school chose to not respond or engage with us as *out parents?* Is the school unaware of the significance of the Pulse tragedy? All of these unanswered questions give support to the resounding message, *it' okay to be out parents, as long as you blend in!*

School communities that approach the Pulse tragedy and the LGBTQ+ community in solidarity may change our experience as *post-out parents*. Acknowledgment advances visibility and disrupts the hetero/cisnormative discourses that maintain the *post-out parental paradox of the closet*. This disruption enhances opportunities for dialogue beyond LGBTQ+ community tragedies like Pulse and toward affirmative LGBTQ+ education practices which radically impact LGBTQ+ students, families, and community affiliates (Hernandez & Fraynd, 2014; Snapp, Mcguire, Sinclair, Gabrion, & Russell, 2015).

My response to the school administrator was to educate. I shared that we'd spoken with our son about the Pulse Massacre that morning. I explained our concerns as parents that while we didn't imagine his grade would be talking about Pulse a lot, some of his classmates may have heard about it on the radio, or on TV. Some students may not have been given accurate information about what happened or make comments that hurt others. I stated that I'm concerned about homophobia, transphobia, islamophobia, and racism in relation to Pulse. I shared how my wife and I as parents, and as LGBTQ+ community members, want to be honest with our children about what happened and want to direct them to focus on love instead of hate. I explained that our son might hear a grade five or six student talking about the massacre and that we'd asked him to tell us. I wondered if the administrator grasped the significance of this event. I invited the school to consider how they could open dialogue about Pulse and honour LGBTQ+ students, families, and communities. I framed the school as a place that could help students express and share feelings, dispel myths, and get accurate, non-phobic information.

INSTITUTIONAL ACTIVISM

9:00 a.m. The Academy

One of the many roles I hold is that of Assistant Professor in a Faculty of Education where I'm also chair of the Sexuality and Gender Education Committee and Faculty Advisor to the student led Gender and Sexuality Alliance. I've intentionally been *out* since joining the faculty in 2009. Being *out* has been at times exhausting and challenging while simultaneously opening spaces for discussion with open-minded heterosexual and cisgender allies in greater positions of power. I believe in relational contexts, I foster collaborative dialogue, and I strive to create spaces where difficult conversation can thrive. I knew that I could approach the Dean on the morning after the Pulse Massacre and was confident that I would be met with openness, willingness, and engagement.

Before approaching the Dean, I scanned through the weekend and that day's university communications to see if the Pulse Massacre had been addressed. It had not. I called colleagues in other faculties on campus who are part of the LGBTQ+ community to see how their disciplines were responding. The unanimous feedback was *s i l e n c e*. Armed with this information I approached the Dean. We engaged in a collaborative conversation where I shared my sadness about Pulse, my community, and my children's future. I wondered out loud how as a faculty of education we could walk in solidarity with the LGBTQ+ students in our faculty, our LGBTQ+ teachers, and our school communities. I invited the Dean to wonder with me about the message that *silence in response to Pulse* would send to our students.

Given that the event was geographically far away, they initially struggled with how *experience near* the Pulse Massacre was for the LGBTQ+ community. I highlighted other geographically far events, such as the *Sandy Hook Elementary School Massacre*, as a bridge to understanding that geography does not in these instances equate in distancing the experiences of the victims or the responses of the world at large. The Sandy Hook Massacre evoked in our faculty a very *experience near* response, culminating in holding a vigil and actively taking care of each other as teacher educators. I shared that many in our community, the LGBTQ+ community, had worked tirelessly from positions of both institutional and radical activism with the belief that the next generation would not have to endure the victimization that we did. For those of us within the LGBTQ+ community, the Pulse Massacre challenged our beliefs, our hope, and our work.

I thanked the Dean for their time and willingness to consider our faculty response. I was pleased to be asked, not much later that day, to give feedback on a message from the Dean in response to Pulse that would be communicated to students, faculty, staff, and our educational community. It was a message of solidarity and offered information about how those in need of support could find support and reassurance. I sighed with relief and then went about the rest of my day, exhausted and withdrawn. I'm saddened yet not surprised that only one colleague in the faculty texted to ask how I was doing. It appeared that for most others around me in the education faculty *June 13, 2016* was like any other day, no different, no less safe than the rest, no more grief stricken than the day before.

EDUCATORS CHALLENGING HETERO/CISNORMATIVITY: AN ETHIC OF CARE

Later in the week following Pulse, I'm asked by a colleague who was out of town during the Massacre, how I've been. I'm unable to hold back my grief and tears any longer, and while standing in the hallway as students rush by, I breakdown. We embrace as long held back tears roll down my face. I describe my experience of loneliness, isolation, and grief alongside motivation and a sense of urgency to engage in institutional activism and the protection of my children, LGBTQ+ students, and the queer community. I'm struck by her humble response. She too wells up with tears and asks reflectively,

> Why didn't I reach out to you? Why is it that I didn't consider the impact that this tragedy was having on my colleagues, students in our faculty and the education community at home? What barriers are created through problematic and systemic hetero/cisnormative discourses? As a person with a critical awareness of my privilege, how do my own social location and privilege hinder me from recognizing pain in a colleague, in a community of students?

She apologizes and acknowledges my grief. She validates my experience of: *if not me, then who would have done this work?* My colleague honours the personal costs associated with enacting my authentic self within the positions I hold as lesbian/queer, parent, and teacher educator, as well as the setting aside of grief to foster visibility, solidarity, and action.

PRACTICING AFFIRMING LGBTQ+ PEDAGOGY

As illustrated through my conversation with a colleague, the practice of affirming LGBTQ+ pedagogy means creating space for ambivalence, approaching difficult conversations, being honest about our non-preferred behaviors, and walking beside one another. It also means acknowledging what we don't know and pausing, as the Dean of my faculty did, willing to sit in the position of learner (Cochran-Smith & Demers, 2010). The position of visible learner is not always comfortable for educators and is not reserved exclusively for allies; it is equally desirable for those who position themselves within LGBTQ+ identities.

By positioning educators, teacher educators, and school communities within a relational framework, understanding is sought, critical analysis becomes valued, and lived experience is respected as meaningful. From this relational stance profound learning may occur, learning that seeks to disrupt problematic homophobic, biphobic, transphobic, and hetero/cisnormative discourses in education. From this perspective, educators, teacher educators, and school communities may begin to co-create possibilities for LGBTQ+ students, families, and communities to be acknowledged. "We cannot live a healthy life without recognition" (Garrick, 2001, p. 96).

REFERENCES

Adams, T. E. (2011). *Narrating the closet: An autoethnography of same-sex attraction*. Walnut Creek, CA: Left Coast.

Blumber, H. (1969). *Symbolic interactionism*. Englewood Cliffs, NJ: Prentice Hall.

Bower, L., & Klecka, C. (2009). (Re)considering normal: Queering social norms for parents and teachers. *Teaching Education, 20*(4), 357–373. doi:10.1080/10476210902862605

Butler, J. (1999). *Gender trouble: Feminism and the subversion identity*. New York, NY: Routledge.

Callaghan, T. (2016). Young, queer, and Catholic: Youth resistance to homophobia in Catholic schools. *Journal of LGBT Youth, 13*(3), 270–287. doi:10.1080/19361653.2016.1185758

Carbado, D. W., Crenshaw, K. W., Mays, V. M., & Tomlinson, B. (2013). Intersecionality. *Du Bois Review, 10*(2), 303–312. doi:10.1017/S1742058X13000349

Cochran-Smith, M., & Demers, K. (2010). Research and teacher learning: Taking an inquiry stance. In O. Kwo (Ed.), *Teachers as learners: Critical discourse on challenges and opportunities* (pp. 13–43). Hong Kong: Comparative Education Research Centre, University of Hong Kong & Springer.

Duke, S. (2008). Hidden, invisible, marginalized, ignored: A critical review of the professional and empirical literature (or lack thereof) on gay and lesbian teachers in the United States. *Journal of Gay and Lesbian Issues in Education, 4*(4), 9–38. doi:10.1300/J367v04n04_03

Ellis, C. S. (1999). Heartful autoethnography. *Qualitative Health Research, 9*(5), 669–683.

Ellis, C. S. (2004). *The ethnographic I: A methodological novel about autoethnography*. Walnut Creek, CA: Altamira.

Ellis, C. S., & Bochner, A. P. (2000). Autoethnography, personal narrative, reflexivity: Researcher as subject. In N. K. Denzin & Y. S. Lincoln (Eds.), *Handbook of qualitative research* (2nd ed., pp. 733–768). Thousand Oaks, CA: Sage.

Ellis, C. S., & Bochner, A. P. (2006). Analyzing analytic autoethnography: An autopsy. *Journal of Contemporary Ethnography, 35*(4), 429.

Freedman, J., & Combs, G. (1996). *Narrative therapy: The social construction of preferred realities*. New York, NY: Norton Company.

Garrick, D. A. (2001). Performances of self-disclosure: A personnel history. *The Drama Review, 45*(4), 94–105.

Gilligan, C. (2014). Moral injury and the ethic of care: Reframing the conversation about differences. *Journal of Social Philosophy, 45*(1), 89–106.

Hernandez, F., & Fraynd, D. J. (2014) Leadership's role in inclusive LGBTQ-supportive schools. *Theory into Practice, 53*(2), 115–122.

Kosciw, J. G., Greytak, E. A., Bartkiewicz, M. J., Boesen, M. J., & Palmer, N. A. (2012). *The 2011 National School Climate Survey: The experiences of lesbian, gay, bisexual and transgender youth in our nation's schools*. New York, NY: GLSEN.

Meyer, I. H. (2003). Prejudice, social stress, and mental health in lesbian, gay, and bisexual populations: Conceptual issues and research evidence. *Psychological Bulletin, 129*(5), 674.

Nadal, K. L., Whitman, C. N., Davis, L. S., Erazo, T., & Davidoff, K. C. (2016). Microaggressions toward lesbian, gay, bisexual, transgender, queer, and genderqueer people: A review of the literature. *The Journal of Sex Research, 53*(4–5), 488–508. doi:10.1080/00224499.2016.1142495

Noddings, N. (1992). *The challenge to care in schools.* New York, NY: Teachers College Press.

Noddings, N. (1995). A morally defensible mission for schools in the 21st century. *Phi Delta Kappan, 76*(5), 365.

Snapp, S. D., Mcguire, J. K., Sinclair, K. O., Gabrion, K., & Russell, S. T. (2015). LGBTQ inclusive curricula: Why supportive curricula matter. *Sex Education, 15*(6), 580–596.

Sue, D. W. (2010). Microaggressions in everyday life: Race, gender and sexual orientation. Hoboken, NJ: John Wiley and Sons.

Taylor, C., Peter, T., McMinn, T. L., Elliot, T., Beldom, S., Ferry, A.,…Schachter, K. (2011). *Every class in every school: The first national climate survey on homophobia, biphobia, and transphobia in Canadian schools.* Final report. Toronto, ON: Egale Canada Human Rights Trust.

White, M. (2007). *Maps of narrative practice.* New York, NY: W.W. Norton.

White, M., & Epston, D. (1990). *Narrative Means to Therapeutic Ends.* Adelaide: Dulwich Centre.

CHAPTER TEN

Embodying Queer Pedagogy ON Campus

Autoethnographic Explorations after Orlando, FL

KERRI MESNER

OPENING WITH QUESTIONS

[Autoethnography starts] I start my day, as I often do, slowly waking up with a cup of tea and spending some time perusing Facebook. Facebook is an enjoyable but slippery slope for me ... one thread leads to another and suddenly an hour has passed in idle browsing.

Today is different, however. My newsfeed is peppered with posts and headlines about a mass shooting at a queer nightclub in Orlando, Florida. 49 people are dead, and 53 more are injured; most of the victims are Latinas and Latinos (Latinx) as it was a Latinx night at the club.

My response is visceral. Shock. Grief. And simultaneously, not-shock. As a queer Christian theologian and educator, I've long been aware of the climate that makes the US ripe for an attack like this. A part of me, disturbingly, is not surprised. Another part of me is reeling. A queer club. While I'm not a club goer myself, I celebrate our long history of creating sanctuary in clubs, and today, this sanctuary has been violated. If they were not safe at Pulse, who's to say we are safe anywhere?

I cry. Read queer commentary voraciously. Try to make meaning.

The next day, I am walking to the local courthouse in the small Pennsylvania town where I live, to submit paperwork for a replacement passport. It's a sunny day in this bucolic town. People move with a sense of ease, running errands, enjoying the gentle warmth of summer's arrival.

And I am wary. As a Trans/genderqueer person, my body is constantly read as different, as unintelligible, as disturbing. Normally, I hold that embodied space with pride, *even defiance. Today, I feel the risk of my body's expression. Today, for the first time in years, I would rather blend in. I realize that in the wake of the Pulse attack, my genderqueer body feels profoundly unsafe in the world. My world has changed. [Autoethnography pauses]*

This auto-ethnographic chapter seeks to explore the gifts and challenges of embodying my work as a queer educator after the Pulse attack in Orlando. In this chapter, I ask: what are the particularities of being queer identified and teaching gender/sexual diversity content after the Orlando shootings? What are the implications of choosing to bring my embodied identity into my teaching as a location/site/educational context? Even more specifically, what particularities of my experience as a Trans identified educator are impacted by the Orlando attack?

POSITIONALITY

As a queer performative auto-ethnographer, I hold a pedagogical commitment to the value of reflexivity. Indeed, as an educator, I believe that awareness of my own positionality, that is, my sociocultural location and how that location informs my beliefs, is vital for effective pedagogy, and I encourage the same kind of self-reflection in my students. In the spirit of that kind of pedagogical Transparency, I offer here a few thoughts about my own current positionality.

As a White, upper middle class educator with a doctorate, I'm aware that I hold a great deal of privilege. In a country (and continent) riddled with systemic racism, my White skin allows me both access and reprieve. I'm also aware of the gift of being able to partake in many years of university education that many do not have access too. As queer, genderqueer, and lesbian, my positionality becomes more complex. My lesbian self might seem fairly "mainstream" nowadays (although I would argue against the notion of a "post-queer" society, I simply don't think we're there yet). At the same time, my gender-queerness, my Trans-ness, means that I am consistently "read" as different, as difficult to pin down.

As a queer Christian, I seem to have a foot in at least two worlds, one the hegemonic (and oftentimes oppressive) world of contemporary Christianity, and the other in the liminal space of queer Christianity, wherein I try to subvert that same hegemony. As someone who has lived in Canada, the United Kingdom, and now the United States, I'm also aware of my sense of belonging to whilst simultaneously being an observer of American culture. Intersectionality, then, infuses my lived reality and informs my pedagogy. All of this undergirds my passionate belief that teaching is both personal and political, embodied and theoretical, and that education is a space where profound activism can take place.

NATIONAL CLIMATE

In approaching this chapter, I also locate myself contextually within the current political climate for queer folks living in the United States, particularly for Trans and gender nonconforming folks. I attempted to embody this particular contextualization in a recent performative auto-ethnographic piece, *Carry the Weight* (Mesner, 2016). In this arts based, multi-researcher live installation at the Kennedy and King Monuments in Washington DC, I worked to make sense of the current anti-Trans legislations sweeping the American political scene. The following excerpts from *Carry the Weight* illustrate that national context:

> *[Stage Directions] I stand near the entrance to the King monument with the pile of stones in between me and the gathered audience. The wind is blowing fiercely and passers-by pause, some joining in on the performance.*
>
> Kerri: I tried to imagine myself into a moment at these monuments. I tried to imagine myself into a conversation with Martin Luther King Junior. What might he have to say to me, to us, now?
>
> Kerri: Somehow, there was simply no way for me to avoid looking to North Carolina as I shaped my piece for today's presentation. And I wonder not only about King, but also about Bayard Rustin, a key advisor and organizer with King, who was gay. What would Rustin have to say to me, to us now?
>
> Kerri: And as I looked to North Carolina, somehow, there was simply no way for me to divorce my body from the words that needed to be spoken. The reference to North Carolina in this piece points to the passing of The Public Facilities Privacy & Security Act, officially called An Act to Provide for Single-sex Multiple Occupancy Bathroom and Changing Facilities in Schools and Public Agencies and to Create Statewide Consistency in Regulation of Employment and Public Accommodations (commonly known as HB2), the infamous "bathroom bill" that impacted Trans, gender nonconforming, and LGBTQ communities.
>
> Kerri: I acknowledge, as a White, genderqueer woman, that I have access to privilege that many of my Trans siblings do not, Trans women of color, for instance, are at the greatest risk of anti-Trans violence, and nonetheless, I feel HB2 in my body. On my body. Attacking my body and the bodies of my Trans siblings, known and unknown.
>
> Kerri: And so, I researched. Because this is so recent, much of my research was online. And as I gathered text from the Bill, from headlines and ideas from other online sources, I felt the toxicity of this research, the way that even seeking it out, reading it, and now performing it, affects my body.
>
> Kerri: But there are words that need to be spoken. Maybe these words aren't tidy or coherent, but really, that reflects the day to day barrage that we, as Trans folks, experience from the media, from politicians, from religious leaders, sometimes even from friends and colleagues. There are words that need to be spoken.

[Stage Directions] I hand out large stones, about the size of an apple, to audience members and passers-by. There are 100 in total. Each stone has the text of anti-Trans legislation recently proposed or passed in the United States, statistics of anti-LGBTQ violence, and Biblical phrases often quoted in support of homophobia. Together, as I pass out the stones, we read some of these statements out loud.

Audience Member: "… in no event shall that accommodation result in the local boards of education allowing a student to use a multiple occupancy bathroom or changing facility designated under subsection (b) of this section for a sex other than the student's biological sex." (General Assembly of North Carolina, 2016, p. 2)

Audience Member: "He that is without sin among you, let him first cast a stone at her" (King James Version Bible: John 8:7). Love the sinner hate the sin.

Audience Member: "78% of Trans or gender nonconforming K-12 students experience harassment." (Grant et al., 2011, p. 3)

Audience Member: "Kansas State Bill 513: "Creating the student physical privacy act", introduced on March 16th, 2016: Students can sue their school for $2500 each time they encounter someone of the opposite sex in the bathroom. (Kansas State Legislature, 2016, p. 1)

Audience Member: "19 year old and 14 year old teens plead guilty to beating Transgender woman at Rosedale McDonald's. The video that was recorded by a McDonald's employee on his cellphone and posted online captured part of attack. It showed Polis being kicked and struck in the head, then dragged by her hair across the floor. She then suffered an apparent seizure as onlookers laughed." (Siegel, August 4, 2011)

Audience Member: "Seventy percent of Trans/gender nonconforming respondents reported being denied access, verbally harassed, or physically assaulted in public restrooms. These experiences impacted respondents' education, employment, health, and participation in public life." (Herman, 2013, p. 65).

Audience Member: "Human Rights Watch reports that dozens of Transgender women, including asylum seekers, are locked up in jails or prison-like immigration detention centers across the country." (Human Rights Campaign, 2016)

[Stage Directions] I invite the audience and passers-by to take a stone with them, to "share the weight" of the necessary work of change. It's brutally cold, an icy wind cutting through our clothing as we move into this third hour of presentations. I sense exhaustion from the group, and it's unclear to me if this is exhaustion borne of the weather, or of the issues under discussion. I carry many stones home to Pennsylvania with me.

MOMENTS OF IMPACT

As an explicit ethical authorial choice, all examples of students and teaching moments in this chapter are fictionalized composites drawn on multiple experiences from my work as an educator.

Months before Orlando ...

[Autoethnography resumes] It's the first week of classes ... and, as I did in my other two classes this week, I talk with my students about the multiplicity of genders, and ask them to share what they would like us to know about their own pronouns. I use myself as an example, explaining that as a woman and a genderqueer person, I am comfortable with female (she/her) pronouns, as well as gender-neutral (they/their) ones. Then, I invite them to share around the circle. As we go round, it becomes apparent that I'm the only one in the circle who (from my limited perspective at least) challenges gender normative pronouns. This is often the case, but I continue the practice in my classes, both as a pedagogical act, and also because occasionally there is a student who (explicitly or implicitly) is supported by this practice. As we reach the final student ... if I'm really honest, a tiny part of me, deep inside, sighs with the recognition of my difference ... I take a deep breath and carry on teaching. [Autoethnography pauses]

This moment, one that repeats for me in many of my classes, reminds me of both the importance of these conversations, as well as my own vulnerability each time we do this go-round. If I'm really honest, when a student does self-identify as queer in some way, I feel a little less alone, a little less exposed. I choose to use my body as a pedagogical site. As someone who incorporates substantive content about gender and sexual diversity into most of my courses, I believe that one of the most accessible ways for my students to learn is through the power of story, my own story and the stories of others. And so I choose to make my queerness visible, to make my queerness a point of discussion and learning. As Warren and Fassett (2004) put it, "I offer my body as a site for my students to question their own assumptions, their own ideas, and their own narrow-minded ideals" (p. 26).

Indeed, were I not to make this intentional curricular choice, I'm aware that my gender identity and sexuality would still nonetheless be on display, would be read and misread, by my students, colleagues, and even by strangers. Like Warren and Fassett (2004), I'm aware that:

> the classroom space ... is never safe, never free from that question about who we are, what we do, and our collective worth. Sexuality, our performance of identity, is always at play. What does it mean to be sexual in the classroom, to be a being marked by sexuality? (p. 21)

I love the discussions that emerge with my students. I'm passionate in my commitment to opening up dialogue. I'm very clear that I don't want to get pulled into a "don't ask, don't tell hegemonic undertow" (Barton, 2011, p. 440). Resisting that pull, engaging in courageous conversations with my students and colleagues, is perhaps the most important work I can do as an educator. For me, education is activism. Indeed, as a spiritually rooted minister, theologian, and practitioner, education is one form of what I think of as a "contemplative" frame of mind (Mesner, 2014a). These conversations are real ways that my activism Translates into praxis.

And yet, at the end of the day, I often find myself exhausted, a kind of soul-exhaustion that runs deeper than the typical tiredness of a professorial day. I have come to recognize this exhaustion as resulting from a kind of emotional labor. Sender (2014) states that GLBT people engage in emotional labor that "includes expressing Transformations of feeling from shame to pride through coming out narratives, managing their own emotions and relationships in their roles as queer ambassadors, and training others to be more emotionally accepting of GLBT people" (p. 221). Sender also suggests that "people in less enfranchised social positions, such as women, GLBT people, and people of color, are all unfairly burdened by the work required to handle their own feelings as well as the feelings of those around them" (p. 221). I work hard to cultivate deep roots of community and support to nourish me in this kind of labor, and most of the time, I find my work of queer pedagogy sustainable.

Summer 2016 ... after Orlando

[Autoethnography resumes] Today, I feel the risk of my body's expression. Today, for the first time in years, I would rather blend in. I realize that in the wake of the Pulse attack, my genderqueer body feels profoundly unsafe in the world. My world has changed. [Autoethnography pauses]

My worldview has radically changed. I recognize, of course, that I am still privileged with far greater safety than many in the world. I remember the deeply personal shock and outrage many Americans felt after 9/11, and, living in New York at the time, I remember being troubled by this apparent "loss of innocence." Millions of people around the world never had the luxury of that kind of innocence to begin with, oftentimes because of American interventions.

Nonetheless, amidst this intersectional complexity, my worldview has radically changed. I've never felt a naïve idealism about the state of LGBTQ activism; while there has undoubtedly been significant progress in recent years in the United States and beyond, it's always been clear to me that this kind of progress does not always trickle down to the young gay boy being harassed in a rural Midwestern town, or to the Black Trans woman in New York City. I tend to maintain a bit of cynicism about our progress in terms of queer human rights. And yet, even with this self-protective worldview, somehow, the Pulse shooting changes things for me. This shooting cuts deeply to the heart of my fiercely beloved community. It reminds me that it's dangerous to relax into an assumption of safety, that my people can be murdered anywhere, anytime. My world has changed. Warren and Fassett's (2004) description of one student's violently homophobic evaluation comment resonates here, and like the authors, "I know, I know that this moment is an attack on my body, on my soul, my spirit" (p. 27).

[Autoethnography resumes] I'm teaching another segment on gender and sexual diversity in education. This is familiar territory to me. It's material I've researched, written about, and taught, for many years. Generally, I love the material ... I love the conversations that unfold ... I love the discoveries by and with my students ... and I even love the sometimes difficult and awkward moments that inevitably emerge in my classrooms while teaching this content.

My students often have questions, statements of challenge. They want to know why we need to focus in so explicitly on gender and sexuality, amidst the range of "isms" in the world. I often need to challenge the various iterations of "we are all people" or "we are all the same," reminding my students that this is just as dangerous as approaching anti-racism work with a lens of "colorblindness." I know that encountering resistance is not uncommon in this work. Usually I have a good sense of resiliency, humor, and efficacy in meeting student resistance and engaging in these difficult conversations with compassion.

This summer, however, is different. Usually, my choice to embody my queer pedagogy is a particular strength that I bring to my work. This summer, it almost feels like a liability. How in the world do I teach this content with honesty and groundedness when, in the midst of grief and feeling my own body at risk, it's a struggle just to navigate through the day? How do I respond to resistance, and sometimes even to subtly coded homophobia and Transphobia, when I really want to respond with outrage? I try to breathe deeply. *[Autoethnography ends]*

Navigating the space between pedagogical ideal and immediate lived reality proves challenging post-Orlando. I strive to strengthen what performative auto-ethnographer Spry (2011) calls:

> ... practiced vulnerability ... strategic surrender to an in-betweenness of self and other, to a relation, to a letting go of a single story ... a space of active reflection where one inhabits the intersections of his [sic] own personal experiences with the intimate politics of others. It is the practice of being vulnerable to meaning making, to the collision and communions of our experiences with others; it is the practice of being vulnerable to the process of becoming. (pp. 168–169)

I take heart from Spry's reminder that "practiced vulnerability does not leave the performer exposed, but rather opened to the strength gained through critical reflection" (2011, p. 167). Like Warren and Fassett (2004), I strive to "teach from the heart, teach from the position of an exposed mind, body, and spirit, a mode of engagement with our students that is honest, available, and socially just" (p. 29).

NAVIGATING OPEN-HEARTEDNESS AND SOCIAL POWER

There are times, however, when my desire to teach from this open-hearted space collides with the socio-cultural realities of my classroom. Adams and Jones (2011) remind us that, "rather than being sacred spaces of pedagogical equality, our classrooms are microcosms of our culture, and we would do well as teachers to remember that fact" (p. 101). I do, indeed, try to remember that my classroom does not exist in a vacuum; it is shaped and influenced by the structural and systemic forces of homophobia and Transphobia that infuse our world. My students and I, knowingly or unknowingly, are shaped by these forces.

In light of these forces, now, more than ever, I sense the vital importance of thinking deeply about social power in the classroom. I'm concerned not simply about my own wellbeing, but the wellbeing of the lesbian undergraduate, the Trans doctoral student, the master's student with a gay son. I concur with Wilcox's (2003) suggestion:

> Rather than treating each student equally from the start, this may imply not only encouraging disempowered students to speak of their experiences but also teaching students who are heavily empowered by mainstream society to recognize that power and cede the floor … as well as to privilege in the course materials those voices that are less commonly heard in college settings. (p. 102)

And so, I find myself wrestling with multiple intersecting threads here … my commitment to embodied vulnerability as a pedagogical location bumps up against the realities of social power in my classroom … bumps up against my own grief, lack of safety, and outrage in light of the Orlando attacks. Adams and Jones (2011) remind me that, "… perhaps this is what a reflexively queer auto-ethnography adds up to, just stories, texts that tell and don't tell about 'bodies literally affecting one another: human bodies, discursive bodies, bodies of thought'" (Stewart, 2007, p. 128). I find deep wisdom and even comfort in Adams and Jones' claim that:

> The auto-ethnographic means sharing politicized, practical, and cultural stories that resonate with others and motivating these others to share theirs; bearing witness, together, to possibilities wrought in telling. The queer means making conversations about harmful situations go, working to improve the world one person, family, classroom, conference, and essay at a time. The reflexive means listening to and for the silences and stories we can't tell, not fully, not clearly, not yet; returning, again and again, to the river of story accepting what you can never fully, never unquestionably know. (pp. 111–112)

CLOSING WITH QUESTIONS

I began this chapter with questions, and I close it with deeper questions still. How does the communal trauma of an event like the Pulse shooting continue to shape and inform my experience as a Trans/genderqueer lesbian? How does it shape me as a teacher? And can I really even separate my queerness from my teaching? Would I ever want to? If not, how do I navigate my own landscape of grief, trauma, and inherent bodily risk whilst still remaining present to and with my students?

I return to the power of story. I remember, along with Adams and Jones (2011) that "stories can be insurrectionary acts if we make room for our (all of our) selves and their desires, for making trouble and acknowledging the implications of doing so, for embracing the texture of knowing without grabbing on to sure or fast answers" (p. 114). I reconnect with my commitment to make room for all of myself, all of my queerness, all of my passion for teaching, and all of my humanness. I reconnect with the frustrating beauty of the questions.

In my play, *Intervention*, (Mesner, 2014b), I tell stories of queerness and life ... trauma and grace ... humor and grief. At the end of *Intervention*, in a final moment of prayer between Kerri-the-queer-minister and God, I settle deeply into this space of ambiguity, uncertainty, and spirit. It seems a fitting closing (or perhaps opening) for this chapter.

> *[Stage Directions] The stage lights dim just slightly. Kerri looks around the empty church, pauses, then resumes the conversation with God.*
> Kerri: God, the sanctuary is silent ...
> I open my eyes
> And the sanctuary is silent.
> God, maybe silence is the only breath deep enough to give voice to what I know now ...
> And yet I don't want to rush to resurrection
> I want to practice a spirit of remaining ... (Rambo, 2010)
> Remaining in this strange place that trauma survivors know well
> A Holy Saturday kind of place ... a waiting kind of place
> With a Spirit that will not answer me, or triumph, or redeem this experience ...
> But instead a Spirit that simply remains with me
> And I breathe. I breathe and am breathed with.
> And the breath opens a space and names something without words.
> And it is enough. (pp. 166–167)

Perhaps remaining with the questions is indeed enough.

REFERENCES

Adams, T. E., & Jones, S. H. (2011). Telling stories: Reflexivity, queer theory, and auto-ethnography. *Cultural Studies/Critical Methodologies, 11*(2), 108–116.

Barton, B. (2011). My auto/ethnographic dilemma: Who owns the story? *Qualitative Sociology, 34*(3), 431–445.

General Assembly of North Carolina. Second extra session 2016 H1 House Bill 2. (2016). Retrieved from http://www.ncleg.net/Sessions/2015E2/Bills/House/PDF/H2v1.pdf

Grant, J., Mottet, L., Tanis, J., Harrison, J., Herman, J., & Keisling, M. (2011). *Injustice at every turn: A Report of the national Transgender discrimination survey*. Washington, DC: National Center for

Transgender Equality and National Gay and Lesbian Task Force. Retrieved from http://www.thetaskforce.org/static_html/downloads/reports/reports/ntds_full.pdf

Herman, J. (Spring 2013). Gendered restrooms and minority stress: The public regulation of gender and its impact on transgender people's lives. *Journal of Public Management & Social Policy, 19*(1), 65–80.

Human Rights Campaign. (March 23, 2016). *US: Transgender women abused in immigration detention: Face sexual assault, solitary confinement.* Retrieved from https://www.hrw.org/news/2016/03/23/us-Transgender-women-abused-immigration-detention

Kansas State Legislature. (2016). Creating the Student Physical Privacy Act. Retrieved from http://www.kslegislature.org/li/b2015_16/measures/documents/sb513_00_0000.pdf

Mesner, K. (2014a). Wrestling with the angels of ambiguity: Queer paths in contemplative activism. In C. Leggo, S. Walsh, & B. Bickel (Eds.), *Arts-based learning in research and pedagogy: Contemplative and artistic practices* (pp. 89–110). New York, NY: Routledge.

Mesner, K. (2014b). *Wrestling with the angels of ambiguity: Scholarship in the in-between: Queer theology/performative auto-ethnography* (Doctoral Dissertation). Retrieved from https://open.library.ubc.ca/cIRcle/collections/ubctheses/24/items/1.0135575

Mesner, K. (2016). Sharing the weight. In J. Norris, *Response abilities: Generating arts-based research with Franklyn Delano Roosevelt and Martin Luther King.* American Educational and Research Association Annual Meeting, Washington, DC.

Rambo, S. (2010). *Spirit and trauma: A theology of remaining.* Westminster, England: John Knox.

Sender, K. (2014). No hard feelings: Reflexivity and queer affect in the new media landscape. In K. Ross (Ed.), *The handbook of gender, sex, and media* (pp. 207–225). Oxford: John Wiley and Sons.

Siegel, A. (2011, August 4). *Teen pleads guilty to beating Transgender woman at Rosedale McDonald's.* The Baltimore Sun. Retrieved from http://articles.baltimoresun.com/2011-08-04/news/bs-md-co-mcdonalds-beating-plea-20110804_1_teonna-monae-brown-chrissy-lee-polis-vicky-thoms

Spry, T. (2011). *Body, paper, stage: Writing and performing auto-ethnography.* Walnut Creek, CA: Left Coast.

Stewart, K. (2007). *Ordinary affects.* Durham, NC: Duke University.

Warren, J. T., & Fassett, D. L. (2004). Spiritually drained and sexually denied. In D. Denton, & W. Ashton (Eds.), *Spirituality, action and pedagogy: Teaching from the heart* (pp. 21–30). New York, NY: Peter Lang.

Wilcox, M. M. (2003). Negotiating social power in the classroom. *Council of Societies for the Study of Religion Bulletin, 32*(4), 100–104.

CHAPTER ELEVEN

Liminal Living Liberates

ALAN SMITH

OPENING THOUGHTS

"So, do you have a girlfriend yet?" He froze as they asked him that question. The oppressed know well the domain of paralysis, helplessness, and annihilation. In what ways can we address the overwhelming air of death and destruction that shackle so many? How can we resuscitate lives? Changing the way we present information and tell stories is one important way to do so. Imprisoned by strict categorization, marginalized peoples traverse and navigate challenging territory and often create new spaces that defy easy labelling These so called gray areas are on the contrary luminous, dynamic and full of color The following autoethnography uses drawings and words to both illustrate an example of such and to challenge the alienating and isolating language of objectivity. Drawing from the work of Kumashiro, Finlay, and Ellis this autoethnography uses self-reflexive analysis and drawings as a means to paint a portrait of empowerment. My own experience with heteronormativity serves as part of the frame for the story. Weaving the work of three authors together with my own story I attempt to render a liberating picture. In the following drawing (Figure 11.1), I paint a self-reflexive picture.

My border designs connect to Ancient Greece, specifically featuring two vases depicting sexual intimacy between two males. The upper right of the page features a looming, towering figure dressed in ministerial garb. A clerical collar surrounds his neck, as he represents not just my father who is an Episcopal priest, but all of the omnipresence of Christianity in my life. Inescapable by day like a sun in

122 | ALAN SMITH

Figure 11.1. A Self-Reflective Portrait.
Source: Author.

the sky, I chose the upper right side of the page to place this figure. The border surrounding him is composed of crosses that resemble daggers, representing the stinging, piercing words, and deeds that have been directed towards me throughout my life.

It was only at night or behind a locked door that I could find the space to be my gay self, as the symbol of a key protects me and my male consort from the damning reaches of the judgmental entity in the sky. Yet even underneath the protection of the dark and the locked door, I am not free. The look on my face is a nervous one. I am on guard, with my finger to my mouth, hushing my lover. The other hand although close to his aroused member is not in a position simply to pleasure him, but rather to hide, and pleasure him at the same time. He is also completely naked and I am not, once again showing how even in the "free zone" I was still imprisoned.

My shirt emblazoned with the words "Homo Sex Is Sin" embodies my own learned self-hate, and my years of attempting to "pass publicly" as a straight man. The fold in my shirt covers the "s" in the word sin as if to show that only behind the curtain can gay sex be "in" fashion. I am speaking to myself telling myself in a moment of hindsight that simply moving that which hides can change everything, ultimately for the better. It is a "truth shall set us free" moment.

My narrative relies not on a clock to guide the reader. This particular journey through my life is event driven. There are two naked figures drawn one at the top and one at the bottom that depict a struggle. Reminiscent of Keith Haring's (1989) famous dancing figures that drew attention to the AIDS crisis, the figures I've drawn reflect not only my struggles with being raped, but also more generally the struggle to not be seen as a diseased, societal pariah as was the case growing up as a gay man in the 1980s. The tears of one of these figures help form the locked barrier that keeps me closeted. The other naked figure on the opposite side of the page depicts a person meditating. His actions help transform the judgmental daggers into a peace sign and hearts. It is my journey to mental wellness that freed me to be outside the self-hating closet. It was loving myself that opened me up to finding my life partner.

I have also chosen to use literary references, as I allude to Mary Renault's "Last of the Wine" (Renault, 1975) a historical novel that features two Greek lovers. To me the real heroes are not those who use violence and vengeance, but those who are able in the face of evil to use love. My second illustration (Figure 11.2) features a lone hand held mirror in a sea of white, and representing the height of a man standing.

The narration identifies this as the villain that tops them all. Inscribed on the handle of the mirror is an eye and the word "EGO." This connects the reader to the hidden theme in Figure 11.1. Barely noticeable, practically hidden in the sky, is my own eye. Eye appears twice in bold letters on the first page. A play on words, the "eye" is "I," the ego. Ultimately in my world the *monsters* and the *heroes* are one and the same. Gandhi, said it best, "The only devils running around are the ones in our own hearts, and that is where all our battles should be fought" (Attenborough, 1982). In the second drawing, I hold up the mirror to tap into that ego-driven passion, seeking to harness this energy, to help us become truly in love with ourselves. It is when we become so deeply connected to ourselves that we see and understand that we are greater than anything we can imagine. We are what Hinduism calls the Big Self, the Brahmin (Lorenzen, 2004). We become heroic.

Figure 11.2. EGO!
Source: Author.

RESEARCH, EDUCATION, AND EMPOWERMENT

Established boundaries of *common sense* create a particular power dynamic, one that fosters social death for the marginalized. Self-reflexive analysis breaks down this power dynamic. No longer ego-driven, the unmasked story reveals a much richer existence than one rendered by the so called "detached" observer. Coming out from underneath layers of protective armor lays bare a much more vulnerable and raw account, the naked truth, so to speak. The telling of the story becomes more authentic, creating space for the unheard, and freeing up previously suppressed existences.

As one can see in my comic illustration above, heteronormativity is a preoccupation of mine. Yet as Kumashiro asserts in *Definition of Anti-Oppressive*

Education, "There is not just one form of oppression ... certain ways of identifying or being identified—are normalized or privileged while other ways are disadvantaged or marginalized" (2000, n.p.). Anti-oppressive education seeks to challenge common sense in that, "it expects to be different, perhaps uncomfortable, and even controversial." It also seeks to liberate.

"Anti-oppressive education is premised on the notion that many traditional and commonsense ways of 'engaging' in education actually contribute to oppression in schools and society" (Kumashiro, 2000, n.p.). Because of this, I tend to err in favor of new ways of doing things in education. As a black, gay male living in poverty, I value the principles of spontaneity and improvisation. These skills have allowed me to navigate some challenging terrain. Living in the closet for three decades has taught me how to do things on the fly and in covert ways in order to protect myself. Using self-deprecating humor on the spot has often pre-empted and shielded me from danger.

Whether it's passing for white because of my generic name, or playing it straight and appearing wealthy, these things help me cope with immediate circumstances, but do little to challenge the system of injustice facing me and other marginalized peoples. Frantz Fanon (1961, p. 35), in *The Wretched of the Earth*, speaks about decolonization being "a process of complete disorder." This is not about tinkering with things but about wholesale change. As Kumashiro states, "ways of 'reforming' education actually mask the oppressions that need to be challenged" (2000, n.p.). As such, much of my educational philosophy revolves around "unmasking." I remember being told by a principal that "We didn't hire you to be a change agent," after I had come out of the closet on the job. I remember being grilled and excessively scrutinized by a Commission on Ministry in the southern USA for wanting to do joint youth group meetings between a black and a white church. My actions were jarring to the established order.

Whether it was shaving my head every day and donning all black wearing only a silver peace medallion or wearing a Mohawk hairstyle with hearts painted on my face, I have consistently challenged the "proper way" to present myself. Feeling voiceless in the run up to the Iraq war in 2003, I began painting peace signs on my face to give voice to a silenced perspective as a warmongering culture had drowned out all dissent. As Finlay asserts in, *Outing the Researcher: The Provenance, Process, and Practice of Reflexivity*, "voicing the unspoken can empower" (2002, p. 544). A Kenyan proverb also captures this well: "Until the lion has its own historian, the tale of the hunt will always glorify the hunter." My life's work has been centered around empowering myself and others to tell their stories.

One of the most important ways to challenge official stories is to take on the postmodern lens and critique this notion of the "detached" expert. In Finlay's 2012 *Outing the Researcher*, an example appears of a researcher using humor to "breach" a gap between a "detached researcher" and the subject. Humor, including sarcasm, becomes a way to break the established boundaries that enforce a particular power dynamic. My analysis of three memes for my Media Analysis Project demonstrated this.

Finlay states that researchers and educators "alter meaning, instead of delineating it" (2012, p. 531). Through this process, our backgrounds interact with the subject matter, but the lens through which I view the world does not innocuously describe any given context. The words I choose to speak, the analogies I make, the symbols I use in text and illustration do something other than communicate an *objective* reality; they present a unique and subjective picture. They shape, color, construct, and render an artistic interpretation of what I am experiencing.

Ellis, Adams, and Bochner's 2011 *Autoethnography: An Overview*, also challenges the superiority of objective accuracy. In it they examine the theme of being preoccupied with social justice versus having a "preoccupation with accuracy" (p. 11). In it they examine the theme of being preoccupied with social justice versus having a "preoccupation with accuracy" (Ellis et al., 2011, p. 11). This perspective captures my work as a black gay male educator living in poverty. I am constantly aware of how my identities invoke fear and curiosity in others, costing me to lose out on employment and other opportunities. These injustices have affected my survival chances and my quality of life. Often the supremacy of accurately following protocol has cost me dearly … financially, emotionally, and physically.

Coming from a family who was once considered the property of white slave owners, we never amassed any wealth or savings of any kind. Thus accurately following protocol has assigned us bad credit scores and given us high interest loans. Following the letter of so many laws has meant incredible hardship for many marginalized groups when what is needed is compassion and flexibility.

CONCLUDING THOUGHTS

One of the main themes that permeates this chapter is captured in a phrase from Finlay. "If we seek to be better learners and educators we must be willing to engage in "explicit, self-aware meta-analysis" (Finlay, 2012, p. 531). This practice of self-reflexivity brings honesty and authenticity to education. Doing this humbles us, sensitises us to others, and diminishes our ego. It reminds us that we are very much connected to everything and everyone.

This concept is very similar to the African philosophy of "Ubuntu": I am because we are. Therefore my existence is very much tied to everyone else's. As Martin Luther King, Jr. said in his *Letter From a Birmingham Jail*, "We are caught in an inescapable network of mutuality tied in a single garment of destiny" (King, 1963, n.p.). Living this way can be messy and defy easy categorization. Yet, Kumashiro (2000, n.p.) affirms that uncertainty and paradox are to be valued. I agree, and as such I live by the maxim my father told me: "You must learn to love the unpredictability of life." A life fully lived is a life lived in the in between space because liminal living liberates.

REFERENCES

Attenborough, R. (Producer & Director). (1982). *Ghandi* [Motion picture]. United States of America: Sony Movie Channel.

Ellis, C., Adams, T. E., & Bochner, A. P. (2011, January). *Autoethnography: An overview*. Forum: Qualitative Social Research. Retrieved from http://www.qualitative-research.net/index.php/fqs/article/view/1589/3095

Fanon, F. (1961). *Concerning violence from wretched of the earth*. Open Anthropology. Retrieved from https://openanthropology.org/fanonviolence.html

Finlay, L. (2012, April 4). *Outing the researcher*. Qualitative Health Research. Retrieved from https://blackboard.arcadia.edu/bbcswebdav/pid-1763657-dt-content-rid-2713604_1/courses/SUMMER2016.04.ED505B.OP1/Qual%20Health%20Res-2002Finlay-531-45%281%29.pdf

King, M. L. (1963). *Letter from a Birmingham Jail*. Dr. Wheeler of Carson Newman University. Retrieved from https://web.cn.edu/kwheeler/documents/Letter_Birmingham_Jail.pdf

Kumashiro, K. K. (2000). *Definition of anti-oppressive education*. Center for Anti-Oppressive Education. Retrieved from http://antioppressiveeducation.org/definition.html

Lorenzen, D. L. (2004). Introduction, in D. L. Lorenzen (Ed.), *Religious movements in South Asia 600–1800* (pp. 1–44), New Delhi, India: Oxford University.

Renault, M. (1975). *The last of the wine*. Retrieved from ftp://121.17.126.74/data1/ts01/english/novel/batch001/20100511205448837.pdf

CHAPTER TWELVE

Fear AND THE Unknown

Harrowing Experiences of LGBTQ Students in Higher Education

ERIC J. WEBER AND KARIN ANN LEWIS

INTRODUCTION

Earl Nightingale, an American motivational speaker of the 1950s, once said, "Whenever we're afraid, it's because we don't know enough. If we understood enough, we would never be afraid" (Joshua-Amadi, 2013, p. 10). The experiences of Lesbian, Gay, Bisexual, Transgender and Queer (LGBTQ) students attending colleges and universities, especially those in rural areas, are largely unknown. Historically, universities have failed to provide safe learning environments for LGBTQ students (Fanucce & Taub, 2010; Nelson & Krieger, 1997; Rankin, 2005, 2006; Walters & Hayes, 1998). In recent years across the United States, reports of harassment, assault, and high rates of suicide among LGBTQ college students continue to be all too common and further underscore the alarming lack of safe learning environments for this group of minority students. The recent unconscionable acts of violence towards and murder of innocent LGBTQ people in a nightclub in Orlando, Florida compelled the authors of this chapter to share some of the findings from a 2015 study in hopes of giving voice to LGBTQ college students (Weber, 2015).

Colleges and universities have a responsibility to provide and maintain a healthy, affirming—celebrating and supporting—and safe learning environment for all students; however, university faculty and administrators have little or no knowledge of LGBTQ students' experiences on campus. We do not know enough. The study referenced in this chapter endeavored to gain insight into the unknown perspectives and experiences of LGBTQ students on rural college campuses and give voice to this marginalized group.

Historically, society relies upon and continues to look to institutions of higher education for the knowledge required to make decisions in the interests of the common good, inform policy, and implement best practices for the benefit of all, which positions institutions of higher education to influence the public about issues related to LGBTQ individuals on a national level. In light of the Pulse nightclub massacre in Orlando, Florida, it is evident that leveraging the influence of higher education is more urgent and important than ever before, if we are ever to see a change for the common good at the national level.

This chapter provides a discussion of the stories LGBTQ college students shared during semi-structured, confidential interviews in a recent study. Fear and resiliency, themes that emerged from the interview data, offer a glimpse into the unknown experiences of LGBTQ college students as they navigate hostile campus climates and strive to find their place in higher education. As informative as the findings from the study are, the authors suggest that the most compelling insight from this study may very well be for us all to reflect on the unknown experiences of LGBTQ students who are not represented in the study.

RESEARCH BACKGROUND

This chapter is based on data collected in Weber's (2015) dissertation study. The following background information frames our discussion of the findings.

Purpose

The qualitative phenomenological study endeavoured to understand the lived experiences of LGBTQ students attending universities in rural, Bible Belt America—those areas with higher concentrations of fundamentalist Christian churches that take a literal interpretation of the Bible and a majority of the population with strong religious views. The findings from the study intend to make a contribution to the extant literature, as well as serve to assist leaders of institutions in promote healthy, affirming—celebrating and supporting—campus climates. The findings underscore the noted disconnect between a quality experience in higher education and what is actually experienced by LGBTQ students. Arguably, institutions could increase recruitment, retention, and graduation rates of this marginalized minority group, if LGBTQ students' needs are considered and addressed. Additionally, university campuses have the opportunity to lead by example and model social justice; institutions of higher education are well positioned to influence the public regarding the experiences and rights of LGBTQ individuals.

Review of the Literature

The literature review revealed that current experiences of LGBTQ students at most colleges and universities remain unknown. The current study demonstrates what Nelson and Krieger (1997) describe as a disconnect between the purpose of a postsecondary educational institution and what is actually experienced by students still exists today, especially for minorities like LGBTQ students: "Instead, personal growth is obstructed by violent attacks, disparaging remarks, hypocritical behaviors, and blatant discrimination from the majority; in this case, the heterosexual community (p. 79). The overall college experience is one designed to promote academic and personal growth to allow students to reach their full potential; however, this is not what students are actually experiencing" (Nelson & Krieger, 1997; Rankin, 2005; Walters & Hayes, 1998; Weber, 2015; Worthen, 2011).

The number of LGBTQ students attending postsecondary educational institutions is not clear; however, LGBTQ students exist on *every* campus. Yet many institutions fail to even acknowledge the existence of LGBTQ students on their campuses (Sanlo & Espinoza, 2012; Walters & Hayes, 1998), and LGBTQ students are marginalized on campuses regardless of occasional attention given towards equality (Rankin, 2005). Historically, the college experience of LGBTQ students has been fraught with negative experiences that hinder and at times completely prevent students from achieving their full academic and personal potential.

Methodology

The study included in-depth, semi-structured, confidential interviews with ten LGBTQ university students in rural, Bible Belt America, namely the states of Texas, Oklahoma, Arkansas, Louisiana, Kentucky, Tennessee, Mississippi, Alabama, West Virginia, Virginia, Maryland, Delaware, North Carolina, South Carolina, Georgia, and Florida.

Participant recruitment involved purposeful sampling facilitated through email by on campus gatekeepers with close connections to the LGBTQ student community. Thirteen students responded expressing interest in participating; however, three students declined an interview after agreeing to participate. One can only speculate, considering the stories the respondents who participated shared, that the level of fear and lack of trust these students felt prevented them from participating, even though they initially wanted to be part of the project. Participants identified as Lesbian, Gay, Bisexual, Transgender, or Queer and ranged from current registered freshman to recent alum from the years 2006–2015.

Findings about LGBTQ Student Victimization

Eight themes emerged from the data: influences from the region, factors related to campus climate, faculty awareness of LGBTQ student needs, residence hall experiences, institutional support, LGBTQ presence, LGBTQ student resiliency, and participant recommendations for their respective universities.

DOMINANT CHARACTERISTICS OF SUCCESSFUL LGBT STUDENTS

While all the findings from the study are critically important in working towards an understanding of the experiences of LGBTQ students, we selected the themes of fear and resiliency for discussion in this chapter.

Fear

From the findings, the theme of fear in the data is consistent with the literature: fear of the unknown, fear of personal safety; fear of discrimination; and fear of harassment (Fanucce & Taub, 2010; Nelson & Krieger, 1997; Rankin, 2005, 2006; Walters & Hayes, 1998). These fears impact virtually every aspect of the LGBTQ students' experiences in the study. Additionally, past feelings of fear, shame, and isolation seemed to carry over to college where the LGBTQ students expected more of the same, and there is little information to suggest an alternative reality for them (Rankin, 2005; Sanlo & Espinoza, 2012). For example, Palmer, a respondent in the study, explained that he expected to be bullied as a LGBTQ college student, based on his past personal experiences:

> I expected there to be some bullying because in high school, that's all I ever experienced was bullying … Growing up in grade school, middle school, and high school I was harassed all the time, just picked on and called names and stuff.

However, contrary to his trepidation and lingering fears, Palmer shared that, during his college experience, he did not encounter the kind of bullying he had endured in high school.

Some LGBTQ students chose to disguise their identities for fear that their LGBTQ identity would bring discrimination and ill treatment, or they simply did not know what might happen. Another respondent, Rosalind, stated, "I didn't want anybody to know … Feeling like everybody is judging you … it weighs on you and it breaks you down." In an effort to assimilate into a heteronormative campus while disguising their identities, these LGBTQ students even avoided fellow LGBTQ students, events, and anything that might expose them or lead people to question their identity. As Brad explained, "You do get a little bit nervous at the [LGBTQ] events when people are giving you very mean glances. That kind of makes me nervous sometimes."

Developing meaningful relationships with peers, a hallmark of the college experience, is nearly impossible, because LGBTQ students conceal fundamental aspects of their lives and themselves, making it difficult to make deep personal connections with others on campus. For example, Mark explained, "As an undergraduate student, I did not know what would happen if people knew I was gay. I was only open about my identity with a few select, inner-circle friends during that time.... I did not have many friends."

In addition to fear of discrimination and ill-treatment among their peers, and solely based on their identities as LGBTQ individuals, these students feared discrimination and unfair treatment by their instructors, an experience that impeded their ability to engage fully in academic learning experiences writ large. They feared that instructors would be harder on them or otherwise treat them differently, making academic success even more difficult. Rosalind's feelings were representative of the whole LGBTQ interview group:

> I felt like if they [faculty] knew [I was gay], then automatically they would be harder on me, and they would grade me harder, and they would do things, and it would make it worse for me, which would affect my grade.

Thus LGBTQ students go to great lengths to attempt to conceal their identity from their instructors in order to avoid potential discrimination or unequal treatment.

Fear of harassment and threats to their persona safety also caused the LGBTQ to avoid perfectly appropriate public displays of affection, such as holding hands with their significant others. These fears are rooted in past personal experiences of victimization or of having observed the malicious treatment of other LGBTQ students on campus. Vicki shared an example of how her lifestyle was circumscribed:

> I really don't like going out after dark just in general as a female for one. I feel awful saying that I feel less safe holding hands with her [my girlfriend] after dark, but I feel *way* less safe. I think that's [after dark] when, males especially, well straight males especially, they get a little bolder [at night]. The things that we've had said [to us] while walking after dark—that are yelled from across the street or yelled from cars—are obscene.

Liv described how other LGBTQ students she knew were afraid:

> I have other Lesbian friends that identify more masculine in their appearance, you know stereotypically. They have addressed and voiced to me how they feel uncomfortable walking around here on campus because of comments they get or looks. They're afraid of like, I don't know, being assaulted or something.

From the data, it became evident that the LGBTQ students' fear resulted in their not being afforded the same opportunities to express themselves with their partners as their non-LGBTQ peers; instead, they had to take precautionary measures, such as walking a safe distance away from their significant other to avoid drawing attention to the fact they were a couple and thus, avoiding harassment and safety issues.

While some LGBTQ students felt safe on their campuses most of the time, fear of personal harm and assaults remained a major concern for most others. The most severe safety issues facing LGBTQ students are physical and sexual assaults. Transgender students consistently described themselves as being easy targets for not only more frequent and severe harassment, but also as being more vulnerable to sexual assaults than other students. Alexus described sexual assaults she experienced as a transgender student:

> I've had three ... *three sexual* assaults on campus since I have been here—one my freshman, sophomore, and junior year. One [of the assailants] even mentioned, while the assault was going on, that he had noticed me before and how he could tell [I was Transgender] ... So, I do think that being Trans kind of made me vulnerable and basically put "victim" on my forehead, even though I do not see myself as that. I see myself as a survivor. I think I was an easy target.

Alexus' experience represents only one account of the sexual assaults experienced and described by the LGBTQ students in the study.

The threat of physical assault is a reality for LGBTQ students especially at the hands of heterosexual males, either due to homophobia or as a measure to enforce gender norms. Mark described his fear of heterosexual men:

> I am generally intimidated by men, although I cannot recall having any specific negative experiences. The intimidation I experience stems from an assumption that heterosexual men are likely to be homophobic, harassing, and violent towards LGBTQ individuals, especially Gay men. This intimidation led me to avoid certain areas on campus where groups of male students, like fraternities, would congregate.

In addition, heterosexual males may become violent towards Lesbians, when sexual advances are rejected, again due to homophobia, as a way to enforce gender norms, or to otherwise defend their own masculinity. Rosalind described her perspective about safety related to heterosexual males:

> So, you know, if you get a super fem [feminine], super attractive woman that, you know, says, "I'm gay." then she's got a higher risk of a straight man getting angry and, you know, getting violent just because she won't sleep with him.

These representative excerpts from the LGBTQ student interviews clearly illuminate how the students' negative experiences through high school and anticipation of ongoing victimization—theirs of some else's—have resulted in pervasive feeling of fear. Remarkably, and in spite of their fears, these LGBTQ students persevered and enjoyed some level of academic and personal success during their college careers. They personify resiliency: "the ability to overcome adversity and challenges, manage stress, and thrive in their personal ... lives" (Penn Resilience Training, 2016, n.p.).

Resiliency

Some LGBTQ students seem to be more resilient than others in that they are better able to succeed despite negative experiences (Wimberly, Wilkinson, & Pearson, 2015), and all of our respondents displayed some level of resiliency, persistence, and academic success in spite of their negative experiences. Although it is unclear how the students cultivated resiliency in such challenging campus climates, it is clear that the students that we interviewed were survivors who persevered in the face of adversity and exhibited grit (Duckworth, 2016).

Cyndi, Palmer, and Alexus exuded a high level of confidence. As Cyndi explained, "... I have a lot of confidence in thinking if anyone says anything to me, I can take them down." Similarly, Palmer demonstrated resilience and grit when he stated that he could turn any situation around: "I feel like I can take over the situation if something were to happen and turn it back around for my benefit." Alexus had experienced so much adversity as a Transgender student, but still exhibited grit and resilience: "I've been very outspoken about things.... I've been an activist pretty much since I've been on campus."

Some of the LGBTQ students interviewed developed coping strategies to avoid negativity, turn the tables in their favour, and force acceptance within heteronormativity. Ultimately, they persevered and succeeded, like Brad who stated:

> I've found if you are kind of in their face about it, you don't give them the chance to say anything negative or be negative—they get so flustered they can't do anything and they just kind of take it.

Rosalind explained that she had not been strong when first coming to her institution, but that her negative experiences had made her more resilient:

> It doesn't bother me now when they look at me and they roll their eyes, and give me the sideways glance. That doesn't bother me anymore because it happened [at this university] so much. I've learned to just kind of let it roll off my back, but starting out here when it happened, it bothered me.

Hanna's experiences also brought her to the point of not caring what other people thought about her as an LGBTQ individual:

> I stopped caring about what everybody thought by this point in my life, everybody, every single person in my life. ... I got to the point where [thinking], "You love me for all of me

or you don't really love me at all, and if you don't love me for everything that I am, then I really don't need you." ... just a lot of years of negativity or judgement or telling what you should or shouldn't do. I guess I just hit my fed up point and ended it.

Future research on grit and how LGBTQ students develop and cultivate resiliency is warranted. The evidence of resiliency among these LGBTQ students may explain why they were willing to step forward and share their stories about their experiences within unwelcoming and often hostile campus cultures. Perhaps due to their grit and resiliency, these 10 courageous LGBTQ individuals agreed to participate in the study.

This brings to our attention the concern about those who may not be as resilient and may not have felt safe enough to come forward and share their experiences. Alternatively, perhaps only resilient LGBTQ students persist and remain on campus. The attrition rate of LGBTQ students remains untracked. It is this unknown, the experiences of LGBTQ students who are not represented, the silent voices, that may be the most compelling concern for campus leaders and policy makers.

DISCUSSION

What might be considered the most intriguing and compelling aspect of this study—identification of the missing data—may be what future researchers need to explore. Apparently, all of the LGBTQ students interviewed exhibited resiliency, in spite of their negative experiences. Perhaps the voices and experiences of less resilient LGBTQ students are not included in this study for various reasons even more poignant and even more compelling than those of the student who are. Maybe these missing students failed to receive an invitation to participate because they did not have an existing rapport with the gatekeepers used to recruit participants. Perhaps fear prevented them from participating, fear of identifying themselves to the researcher and fear that confidentiality would not be maintained. Perhaps they are not out and, in some cases, have not accepted their own identity as LGBTQ.

Possibly too, perhaps less resilient LGBTQ students simply do not exist on campus, because they have already left the university or did not make it to campus in the first place. In any case, we do not know what the experiences are for LGBTQ students who withdraw, transfer, or otherwise do not persist at their university. At face value, the data depicts a collective story of LGBTQ students wrought with fear that is overcome by grit and resiliency and affords them some level of academic and personal success. However, one can assume that the experiences of those less resilient LGBTQ students would tell of different, possibly more frightening, tragic experiences. We are listening to the voices of these students in the silence of the data to give them the consideration they deserve, because their unknown experiences also matter.

FINAL THOUGHTS

As leaders in higher education, we are morally and ethically obligated to address the fears expressed by LGBTQ students and to work earnestly towards the development and support of educational environments that are safe and affirming for this minority group. Institutions of higher education have, not only the ability, but also the responsibility to be change agents, to be catalysts for positive social change. The University of Pennsylvania's Positive Psychology Center research studies of Positive Psychology, Resiliency, and Grit, and the Center's professional development training (Penn Resilience Training, 2016) demonstrate how to cultivate resiliency. We have a moral imperative to create campus climates that are affirming for all students, to foster resilience, and to model the implementation of social justice we need to thrive as a society.

Society writ large still relies upon institutions of higher education for thought leadership and the knowledge necessary to make decisions for the common good. This puts us in a strong position to influence public consciousness of the affairs and rights of LGBTQ individuals within the broader communities that house our colleges and universities. A spreading wild-fire of LGBTQ inclusion can ignite from the sparks created by institutions of higher education. Furthermore, this fire can influence far reaching and enduring societal change so that our campuses become environments that demand the safety and affirmation of LGBTQ individuals and that spread that wherever LGBTQ students go at the completion of their college careers.

Research, such as the constant monitoring and reporting of the lived experiences of LGBTQ students, will continue to inform the decisions that affect all students and must be undertaken if we ever hope to *understand enough*. The disconnect noted in the literature about what a college experience should be and what is actually experienced by LGBTQ students will be addressed as more research contributes to this discussion.

REFERENCES

Duckworth, A. (2016). Angela Duckworth. Retrieved August 26, 2016 from http://angeladuckworth.com/research/

Fanucce, M. L., & Taub, D. J. (2010). The relationship of homonegativity to LGBT students' and non-LGBT students' perceptions of residence hall climate. *The Journal of College and University Student Housing, 36*(2), 24–41.

Joshua-Amadi, M. (2013). Shatter your self-doubt: Simple strategies for developing confidence to live the dream you deserve. Bloomington, IN: Author House.

Nelson, E. S., & Krieger, S. L. (1997). Changes in attitudes toward homosexuality in college students. *Journal of Homosexuality, 33*(2), 63–81. doi:10.1300/J082v33n02_04

Penn Resilience Training. (2016). Retrieved August 26, 2016 from https://ppc.sas.upenn.edu/services/penn-resilience-training

Rankin, S. R. (2005). Campus climates for sexual minorities. *New Directions for Student Services, 2005*(111), 17–23. doi:10.1002/ss.170

Rankin, S. R. (2006). LGBTQA students on campus: Is higher education making the grade? *Journal of Gay & Lesbian Issues in Education, 3*(2–3), 111–117. doi:10.1300/J367v03n02_11

Sanlo, R., & Espinoza, L. (2012). Risk and retention: Are LGBTQ students staying in your community college? *Community College Journal of Research and Practice, 36*, 475–481.

Walters, A. S., & Hayes, D. M. (1998). Homophobia within schools: Challenging the culturally sanctioned dismissal of gay students and colleagues. *Journal of Homosexuality, 35*(2), 1–23. doi:10.1300/J082v35n02_01

Weber, E. J. (2015). *Experiences of LGBTQ students attending a university in rural, Bible belt America* (Doctoral dissertation). Retrieved from http://libproxy.eku.edu/login?url=http://search.proquest.com/docview/1736122681?accountid=10628

Wimberly, G. L., Wilkinson, L., & Pearson, J. (2015). LGBTQI student achievement and educational attainment. In G. Wimberly (Ed.), *LGBTQ issues in education: Advancing a research agenda* (pp. 121–139). Washington, DC: American Educational Research Association.

Worthen, M. G. F. (2011). College student experiences with an LGBTQ ally training program: a mixed methods study at a university in the southern United States. *Journal of LGBT Youth, 8*(4), 332–377. doi:10.1080/19361653.2011.608024

PART FOUR

Contrasting Examples of Leadership Training for LGBTQ+ Inclusiveness

CHAPTER THIRTEEN

Preparing Social Justice Leaders TO Deconstruct Heterosexual Privilege

KAREN (KARIE) K. HUCHTING, JILL BICKETT,
AND EMILY S. FISHER

INTRODUCTION

Imagine for a moment that you are the principal of a progressive public elementary school. A group of fifth grade students approaches you to ask if you would approve of a book to be included in the school library; the story involves a young boy kissing another boy. What do you do? Now imagine that you are a seventh grade teacher and one day in class a student yells across the room to another student, "That's so gay!" What do you do? Lastly, imagine for a moment that you are the principal of a private religious elementary school and a same-sex couple meets with you to discuss enrolling their child in your school. What do you do?

These are actual experiences shared by graduates from the educational leadership for social justice (LSJ) preparation program at Loyola Marymount University, located in Los Angeles, California. From these stories, and others we have heard from our graduates, we were challenged to take a deeper look at how our educational leadership preparation program is preparing school leaders to deconstruct heterosexual privilege and respond to the needs of all students and families.

CONTEXT

Our educational leadership preparation program, founded in 2004, is a three-year doctoral (Ed.D.) program. Candidates must possess a master's degree to be admitted and most are working full-time. Our motto is to train school leaders to "lead from any chair" (Zander & Zander, 2000, p. 66) and as such, our candidates are school principals, teachers, counselors, and superintendents, and they work across the educational spectrum in traditional public, charter, Catholic, private, and non-profit sectors. Candidates take all of their courses together as a cohort, which allows the diversity of their contextual experiences to deepen their knowledge and expand their perspectives. Additionally, our educational leadership preparation program is rooted in the mission of the University—the Jesuit and Marymount traditions, specifically—which, define social justice as *challenging the status quo*. We pride ourselves on infusing social justice and leadership into every course and experience for our candidates, and candidates are trained to acknowledge and deconstruct privilege.

Yet, with the ongoing and recent violent events towards the lesbian, gay, bisexual, transgender, intersex, and queer (LGBTIQ) community, we are forced to pause and reflect on the extent to which our educational leadership preparation program actually trains school leaders to deconstruct heterosexual privilege. As such, we reanalyzed the data we gather each year from exit interviews with graduates in order to examine this issue. As O'Malley and Capper (2015) remind us, those of us working to train educational leaders must begin to "[fracture] the center of the social justice discourse that typically focuses on questions of race/ethnicity and socioeconomic status" (p. 292), and prioritize our discussion about training school leaders to serve students and families who identify as LGBTIQ.

STATEMENT OF THE PROBLEM

There is a critical need to prioritize training for school leaders to work with and advocate for the LGBTIQ community in schools. The literature is clear: these students experience a hostile school climate and lack trust in their school leaders (Kosciw, Greytak, Giga, Villenas, & Danischewski, 2016). And they have good reason to not trust their school leaders (Kosciw et al., 2016); these leaders have received very little training in their educational leadership preparation programs (Mattheis, Perey, & Royaltey-Quandt, 2015).

Hostile School Climate

School leaders who subscribe to social justice leadership must understand school experiences for youth who identify as LGBTIQ. It is clear from national school climate surveys that a significant number of LGBTIQ youth experience a hostile school environment, including verbal and physical harassment and physical assault (Kosciw et al., 2016; Olsen, Kann, Vivolo-Kantor, Kinchen, & McManus, 2014).

As Kozik-Rosabal (2000) reminds us, these experiences occur to students who are "out" as well as students who are perceived to be outside of the heterosexual norm (as cited in Fisher & Kennedy, 2012). These experiences are related to lower academic achievement and educational aspirations; and higher levels of depression, substance abuse, and suicide attempts (Espelage, Aragon, Birkett, & Koenig, 2008; Kosciw et al., 2016; Olsen et al., 2014). And, outside of the school context, because LGBTIQ people are often disenfranchised, they negotiate homophobia and discrimination by creating defined public "safe spaces" where they congregate hoping to find respite from epithets and other derogatory labels (Blumenfield, 2010). However, in the case of the Pulse tragedy, the defined safe space became a target for violence, and the ultimate homophobic act, murderous violence against the LGBTIQ community. Such events further send the message to our LGBTIQ students that they are unsafe.

Lack of Trust

These hostile school conditions for LGBTIQ students are not new; for close to two decades, researchers have documented the persistent failure of schools to address the needs of LGBTIQ youth (see Harris, 1997; Human Rights Watch, 2001; Rofes, 1989; among others as cited in Koschoreck & Slattery, 2010). Several alarming statistics may explain why LGBTIQ youth often lack trust in school personnel to ensure their safety at school: Over a half (56.2%) of LGBTIQ students have heard their teachers and other school staff make homophobic comments; the majority (57.6%) of students who experience harassment do not report it to school officials because they do not believe that any action or consequence will result; and, in fact, over half (63.5%) of the students who did report incidents to school personnel report that nothing was done in response (Kosciw et al., 2016).

Koschoreck and Slattery (2010) outline several of the fears expressed by school leaders related to this issue, such as the discomfort in discussing sexual orientation, the belief that "sexuality" is a parental responsibility and not appropriate for school curriculum, or the fear that the school leader might become a target of harassment or lose her/his job if s/he gets involved. Such silence and lack of action make school leaders complicit in the creation of the hostile school climate for LGBTIQ youth. Beyond fear and silence, however, we must examine how school leaders are trained to address the needs of LGBTIQ youth in their schools.

Lack of Training

Literature on how educational leadership preparation programs address issues of gender and sexual minority identity is very limited; however, O'Malley and Capper (2015) recently published a study of faculty perceptions on how principals are trained to lead their schools via social justice leadership with a focus on equitable leadership for gender and sexual minorities. Faculty in the study represented a national sample and their perceptions of educational leadership preparation program training indicated that issues pertaining to gender and sexual minority identities were limited to only one faculty member or one course to address such issues. As such, training for educational leaders to advocate for LGBTIQ students does not appear to be an integrated approach across preparation programs, even those that purport to form social justice school leaders. These findings were supported by recent research presented at the 2015 annual meeting of the American Educational Research Association (AERA), which discussed developing a network across campuses in a university system to support LGBTIQ students in graduate preparation programs (Mattheis, Perey, & Royaltey-Quandt, 2015).

Analyzing data from students and faculty in educational leadership preparation programs within the same university system, the authors concluded that explicit heteronormative expectations exist in the university setting. The authors mentioned that if university faculty are unaware of the issues surrounding gender and sexual minority identities, they may inadvertently reinforce assumptions about the LGBTIQ community and contradict the leadership social justice training. It is clear that an integrated, systematic approach in leadership preparation programs is needed to train both university faculty and program candidates.

Knowing that K–12 schools produce inherently unequal educational outcomes (Black & Murtadha, 2007), that schools remain "contested sites of social struggle" (O'Malley & Capper, 2015, p. 291), and that school conditions for youth who identify as LGBTIQ are hostile (Kosciw et al., 2016), there is a clear need for social justice leadership (Marshall & Oliva, 2006) that includes issues of gender and sexual minority identities and heterosexual privilege. In order for school leaders to become the change agents necessary to transform inequitable systems, they must receive a broad and deep understanding of social justice in their leadership preparation programs, yet training for leaders to address issues related to gender and sexual minorities appears peripheral at best.

A CALL TO ACTION

To address the limited training educational leaders receive to advocate for youth who identify as LGBTIQ, we listen to our own candidates' experiences and echo the call to action asserted by O'Malley and Capper (2015) that educational leadership preparation programs must embed training for school leaders in an integrated way. To begin this important work, LSJ preparation programs benefit from a framework defining the characteristics of preparing an educational leader for social justice (Capper, Theoharis, & Sebastian, 2006).

A Framework for LSJ Programs

Capper, Theoharis, and Sebastian (2006) conducted an extensive review of the literature on social justice leadership to create their framework for preparing educational leaders for social justice. In addition to searching the literature broadly, they also intentionally included literature on sexual orientation and leadership when creating their framework. At the core of their educational leadership for social justice framework is creating a climate of "emotional safety for risk taking" (p. 212). Capper and colleagues assert that full engagement in an LSJ preparation program requires the intentional development of classroom and program conditions for students to feel a sense of security; this sense of security then allows students to take risks toward social justice ends.

Listening to the stories of graduates from our LSJ preparation program, we heard this same sentiment echoed. Graduates unanimously agreed that the cohort model of the program provided a deep sense of community and support, and a space for dialogue with other educators working in various educational contexts. This diversity both challenged and encouraged candidates to continue the struggle of being a leader for social justice in schools. However, graduates also indicated that our LSJ program could do a better job of establishing a safe space for all candidates to be authentic, especially as it relates to sexual and gender orientations. For example, one candidate, who identifies as gay, shared, "I don't feel like in the [program orientation] that there was a clear definitive statement about [the program's] openness or receptivity … to sexual orientation." As a gay male in an LSJ program, he did not feel safe to express his authentic self because the program was silent about the issue. He continued to share ways in which the program might further create a safe environment, which is at the core of Capper et al.'s (2006) framework for preparing educational leaders for social justice:

> In terms of having conversations with colleagues in a group setting, there wasn't any group norming about what's confidential, what should we be willing to share. It's interesting because in one way that's not a typical thing to expect in an academic setting necessarily but [know] that each one of us goes back to our realities where that is an issue.

As such, our LSJ program can improve by being explicit early on in the program, that candidates of all gender and sexual identities are welcome. Furthermore, professors can continue this inclusive message by establishing norms of confidentiality within their classroom discussions, so that candidates can feel safe to be authentic and not jeopardize professional experiences outside of the program. Moreover, when asked how the program integrated issues related to heterosexual privilege, one candidate shared:

> It all depended on the professor really … and when we talk about marginalized groups or historically marginalized groups, there definitely was an absence discussing anything

close to sexuality unless the professor explicitly said something. [male graduate, elementary school principal]

Other graduates who identify along the LGBTIQ spectrum shared that when the topic was not explicitly covered, they often felt like the "representative" of an entire group of people, which was a lonely and exhausting burden. Such feedback supports the need for our LSJ program to begin an integrative approach to explicitly address issues of heterosexual privilege across professors, curricula, course syllabi, and program materials. Such efforts are likely to create a safer environment where more candidates feel welcomed.

Framework Dimensions

With a safe environment at the foundation, Capper, Theoharis, and Sebastian (2006) highlight and define the key concepts for training educational leaders for social justice. These concepts include both student-centered and program-focused dimensions.

Horizontal dimension. Along the horizontal, student-centered dimension of their framework, Capper et al. (2006) discuss the knowledge, skills, and dispositions that leaders for social justice must possess. Knowledge refers to the need for school leaders to know and understand "evidence-based practices to create equitable schools" (p. 213) and the authors list examples, including knowing about the ill effects of tracking and pullout programs; and having a specific knowledge base of language acquisition, disability, and reading/math instruction and curriculum. In addition to this knowledge, school leaders for social justice must have the ability, or skills, to put their knowledge into practice. Examples include the ability to establish a service delivery team, to use data, and to lead conversations about equity and school improvement. Finally, the authors define the dispositions that educational leaders for social justice must possess as a critical consciousness within their belief systems and values, specifically listing examples such as an understanding of power dynamics and forms of privilege.

Vertical dimension. Along the vertical, program-focused dimension of the framework (Capper, Theoharis, & Sebastian, 2006) are the actual curriculum, pedagogy, and assessment components of LSJ preparation programs. First, leaders for social justice must be exposed to curriculum, or specific content areas, in their preparation programs in order to deepen their knowledge and to build skills. Capper et al. (2006) included examples such as learning about the stages of language acquisition or details related to special education. Pedagogy refers to how faculty teach adult learners and examples included case studies and reflective journaling.

Finally, assessment was discussed in terms of measuring learning outcomes at both the course and program level in order to have a sense of how candidates are transforming their consciousness and building their skills to lead through the lens of social justice. Capper and colleagues (2006) noted that they could not locate literature from LSJ programs related to assessing leadership knowledge and skills for social justice.

Applying the framework. Capper and colleagues noted that most articles they reviewed to create their framework for preparing educational leaders for social justice, discussed what "school leaders should be able to do, rather than what university faculty should do to prepare school leaders" (Capper et al., 2006, p. 216). Additionally, none of the examples listed by Capper et al. (2006) included specific ways in which the framework might be applied to deconstructing heterosexual privilege and advocating for the LGBTIQ community in their schools. As such, there is still work to be done to apply the framework to inform LSJ preparation programs. However, by applying the Capper et al. (2006) framework, we can begin to identify the knowledge, skills, and dispositions (horizontal dimension) that LSJ candidates should possess and the curriculum, pedagogy, and assessment (vertical dimension) that LSJ programs must offer to address the needs of LGBTIQ students.

Knowledge. In order to deconstruct heterosexual privilege, leadership programs must include curriculum about how schools contribute to heteronormative oppression (see Koschoreck & Slattery, 2010). Educators must learn about the formal and informal ways that heterosexual privilege is communicated, and the laws and policies which have been implemented to maintain the status quo in which heterosexuals and cisgender individuals have power and status. They must know how to develop anti-homophobic policies, and they must be trained to train others in an awareness of heteronormativity.

Leadership programs must also include curriculum which addresses how to become change agents in this arena. Programs must ask candidates to consider types of professional development, and opportunities for student support and curriculum, taking their understanding of homophobic oppression from theory to practice (Koschoreck & Slattery, 2010). And this cannot be done in a single class. The lens of deconstructing heterosexual privilege must be omnipresent, and accounted for in every course. Further, programs should do a heterosexism audit, where each course is analyzed for its content in relationship to deconstructing heterosexual privilege, and a comprehensive and articulated plan should be considered across all curricula.

Skills. Candidates must also possess the skills to find and address school data about the negative outcomes LGBTIQ youth experience in schools and they must have the ability to lead difficult conversations on behalf of this community. One graduate of our LSJ program shared with us an experience in her middle school classroom:

Someone said "that's so gay" and I said, "alright let's stop. What did you mean by that?" And the student said, "it means happy". And I said, "that's not the context in which you used it". So I called on [another student] and she said, "I guess it's a put-down". So I said, "what if people started to say 'that's so Filipino' or 'that's so Mexican?' Would you like that?" And they all said, "no". I said, "gay people don't like it either".

The graduate continued to share that because of this moment in her classroom back in 2006, each year she now has "the big talk" with her students about derogatory comments toward people who identify as LGBTIQ. During "the big talk" she shares her personal story about her gay cousin who was murdered in a hate crime in San Francisco. She challenges her students to think about the impact of their words:

> Do you think those guys who killed him just woke up and said, "I'm going to kill someone today?" Well they didn't do that. It starts by name calling. Then bullies. Then assault. But you know, I'm not saying everyone who is a name caller will grow up to be a murderer but you certainly give your energy and permission to those who do. Now, where do you want your energy to go?

Unless educators intervene, as did the teacher in the example, students will continue to experience a culture that rejects the LGBTIQ population, and accepts taunting and bullying as the norm.

There are other ways, however, that heteronormative oppressions occur, besides ignoring homophobic remarks. Denying that homophobia exists; assuming that all students and parents are heterosexual; disallowing gay/straight alliances designed to provide support for LGBTIQ students and their allies; and failing to include literature in the curriculum or in the library that addresses relevant and appropriate information about LGBTIQ communities and experiences (Koschoreck & Slattery, 2010) were several examples from the literature that resonated with the candidates with whom we spoke. Unless and until educational leadership programs teach to the need of recognizing and resisting heteronormativity in all its forms, social justice cannot be achieved for the LGBTIQ community.

Disposition. Candidates must possess a critical consciousness, which we believe occurs through engagement with others about their personal journeys of oppression in order to build empathy. Our LSJ program is intentionally designed as a cohort model in order to deepen candidates' perspectives about others and educational contexts. Graduates were unanimous in their response that our program exposes them to issues of privilege, and they further confirmed that they are encouraged to deconstruct privilege, though we learned that heterosexual privilege is less uniformly discussed than that of race or ethnicity. As Carbado (2010) asserts, "Racism requires white privilege. Homophobia requires heterosexual privilege" (p. 394). Much like Peggy MacIntosh's (1990) treatise "White Privilege: Unpacking the Invisible Knapsack," Devon Carbado's (2010) "Heterosexual Privileges: A List" details the myriad ways that heterosexuals daily benefit from their positionality, most times without being conscious of this privilege. For example, heterosexuality is always affirmed as healthy and normal in the media, husbands and wives can comfortably express affection in any setting without fear of harassment, children of heterosexual parents do not have to explain why their parents are of different genders, and no one has ever tried to "cure" a heterosexual's chosen orientation.

This list goes on, but a brief detail is enough to illustrate the work that must be done with educators so that they can understand the natural bias with which they may lead, and the education that must take place so that they can justly interact with the LGBTIQ population in their classrooms and their communities. Leadership programs, including ours, must do a better job of explicitly assisting with deconstructing heterosexual privilege, digging deep into the heteronormative cultural landscape, and resisting complacence in allowing heterosexual privilege to remain unnamed and un-interrogated.

Curriculum. Applying this vertical dimension to the preparation of educational leaders to deconstruct heterosexual privilege, we assert that candidates must have knowledge about sexual identity and gender development and an understanding that the structure of social institutions, including schools, institutionalizes homophobia. Despite laws and policies in place that aim to protect LGBTIQ students, "homophobia is still what people can expect" (Mayo, 2009, p. 262). Even in states with inclusive anti-bullying policies that protect students based on sexual orientation and gender identity, teachers may be prohibited from including positive representations of gays and lesbians in their curriculum (Mayo, 2009). Thus, an awareness of the silencing of issues around the institutionalization of homophobia, evidenced by a tolerance that dares not speak its name in curricula, is something that educators must be trained to recognize and act upon. Their leadership program is the place where this consciousness should be raised. As this example illustrates, it is a far more complicated landscape for educational preparation programs than a simple review of anti-bullying laws can address.

Thus, in addition to university faculty in educational leadership programs being aware of issues surrounding gender and sexual minority identities, and resisting embedded heteronormative expectations in university settings (Mattheis, Perey, & Royaltey-Quandt, 2015), programs must do the deep work of understanding how to integrate the true positionality of LGBTIQ students in our schools, by deconstructing heterosexual privilege, the insidious nature of homophobia, and how together these impact educational opportunity for all students.

Pedagogy. In our LSJ program, we are heavily influenced by our Jesuit and Marymount traditions that encourage reflective practice. Loughran (2002) suggests that reflection helps practitioners better understand what they know and do as they develop their knowledge of practice through rethinking their own ways of being and doing as practitioners. In light of this, adult learners must first be made aware of their own positionality around heteronormativity, and spend time reflecting and situating themselves in relation to the concept. Candidates in our program report that they have appreciated the reflective approach, and made great strides in uncovering their privilege, though many admit it was a difficult and rigorous process. One graduate commented that the program required an "introspective lens" and that it was a "transformative experience—changing the trajectory of my career, but also the trajectory of my consciousness." Thus, while all faculty embed reflection to prompt candidates to consider how they lead for social justice, our candidates remind us that faculty also need to reflect and "model authenticity" and be open about their own identities. Graduates shared that when faculty are open, they become a source of strength where the candidates feel permitted to do the same.

Another important method for adult pedagogy is the exposure to qualitative research and the use of the case study (Capper et al., 2006), which allows LGBTIQ student voices to be heard. Educators reluctant to confront issues of homophobia must see firsthand the impact of this silence. And educators who may question the validity of programs to help LGBTIQ youth, or the need for naming homophobia on their campuses, must read about youth who have been impacted by harassment, and schools which created safe places for LGBTIQ youth to thrive. Cosier (2009) details "two schools that make a difference for queer kids" (p. 292) in persuasive narrative vignettes, which include the voices of LGBTIQ students. Cosier (2009) reveals how alternative schools created spaces for kids that did not fit into the rigid social structures of traditional schools. This is a small example of the type of pedagogy, and the type of material that must be in the curriculum for leaders learning about justice for LGBTIQ students.

Assessment. LSJ preparation programs need to continually assess course learning outcomes and program goals. Ongoing assessment provides an avenue for continuous improvement and also assists with a timely response to the critical need for educators to advocate for their students who identify as LGBTIQ. Assessing LSJ programs related to deconstructing heterosexual privilege is important especially in light of O'Malley and Capper's (2015) recent finding that LSJ programs are not integrating such training in systematic ways. In our program, rooted in the Jesuit tradition of *contemplatives in action*, our candidates are encouraged to upset the status quo and pursue justice despite the odds. But assessing how candidates do this is a very complicated endeavor. In our program, several layers of assessments occur, many on an annual basis. Candidates are required to reflect on their personal progress in the program as part of their first benchmark, after completion of their first year. Candidates are also required to complete a formal exit interview after their completion in the program. Much of the data included in this chapter comes from these discussions.

Lastly, recent scholarship on our LSJ program (Huchting & Bickett, 2013) included field research where graduates' supervisors were interviewed to determine how and to what degree candidates had built their skills for implementing social justice over the course of the program. All three of these assessment endeavors have given us a clearer picture of where we are and where we need to be in order to prepare our educators for leadership towards social justice.

RECOMMENDATIONS

The framework by Capper et al. (2006) provides a way forward for LSJ programs to initiate change in how school leaders are trained to deconstruct heterosexual privilege and advocate for their LGBTIQ students and families. Such changes must include preparing school leaders with knowledge and skills to dismantle the status quo. Additionally, LSJ programs need to examine their own structures to ensure that they are not reinforcing dominant heteronormative biases.

The Change Process

The framework by Capper and colleagues (2006) outlines the dimensions required by LSJ programs to prepare educational leaders for social justice. These align with our LSJ program's definition of social justice as preparing leaders to challenge the status quo. At the core of their framework is providing a foundation of emotional safety, which acknowledges that being an educational leader for social justice requires risk. To be change agents in their educational communities, future leaders must have knowledge and skills, as well as the dispositional fortitude to withstand resistance. In preparing educational leaders for social justice to advocate for LGBTIQ communities in their schools, this resistance is very likely, given our pervasive heteronormative culture. As such, those of us working to train not just any educational leader, but leaders *for social justice* must begin to change the way we prepare candidates.

From our review of the literature, we assert that this change process requires a parallel approach. On one level, LSJ programs must train future school leaders to advocate for LGBTIQ communities in their schools. This work means that LSJ programs must provide information about gender and sexual minority identities to improve candidates' knowledge, develop their skills to meet the needs of the students they serve in PK–12 contexts, and challenge them to reflect on these issues in a meaningful manner that impacts their professional dispositions. Yet, in order for these future leaders to learn how to do this work in their own school contexts, simultaneously, LSJ programs need to be cognizant of their own culture. Faculty need to interrogate personal biases and university policies in order to project a culture of acceptance for all aspects of candidates' identities. If University faculty do not recognize their own biases or the issues surrounding gender and sexual minority identities, they may inadvertently contradict the social justice training they are attempting (Mattheis, Perey, & Royaltey-Quandt, 2015).

This work is not easy. It requires faculty to be comfortable with potential discomfort, to be open to dialogue with their candidates, and to be willing to change. To that end, we review literature and listen to our own candidates to co-construct recommendations. These recommendations align to the parallel approach we envision to begin the change process.

What School Leaders Need to Know, Be, and Do

Given the dearth of literature about *how* educational leadership preparation programs can train candidates to deconstruct heterosexual privilege (O'Malley & Capper, 2015), in addition to applying Capper et al.'s (2006) framework for preparing educational leaders for social justice, we borrow from literature informing practices and professional development at the PK-12 level to identify topics that are critical to incorporate into preparation programs to promote the knowledge, skills, and disposition that educational leaders need to enact systemic changes to ensure that LGBTIQ students receive equitable treatment and are able to learn, and even flourish, in a safe school environment.

For instance, Koschoreck and Slattery (2010) offer four systematic domains for PK-12 schools to implement an integrated model of inclusion: inclusive policies, professional development, inclusive curriculum, and supportive student organizations. As these four topics are reiterated across the literature on improving school climate for LGBTIQ students (see Fisher & Kennedy, 2012; Kosciw et al., 2016), they will be briefly outlined here. It should be clear that school leaders are not only in direct contact with students and families; they must lead the other adults on their school campuses.

Inclusive policies. Educational leaders are in a prime position to ensure that LGBTIQ-inclusive anti-bullying policies are in place, i.e., those that specifically include actual or perceived sexual orientation and gender identity/gender expression among the protected categories (Fisher & Kennedy, 2012; Kull, Kosciw, & Greytak, 2015). Research suggests that students who attend schools with inclusive policies report hearing fewer homophobic and transphobic comments and saw greater intervention by school staff when anti-LGBTIQ comments were made (Kosciw et al., 2016). Further, these policies provide a concrete framework for all other efforts to make schools safer and more support of all types of student diversity (Espelage & Rao, 2013).

Professional development. Educational leaders can make sure that all school staff understand anti-bullying policies and have a basic understanding of how to better meet the needs of LGBTIQ students by providing in-service professional development (Fisher & Kennedy, 2012; Whitman, 2013). In fact, it may be beneficial for preparation programs to have doctoral students research and develop different key aspects of this type of in-service training, leading to a final project that puts the different pieces together to create a more complete series of professional development modules that leaders can bring to their districts and/or schools. Whitman (2013) suggests that school staff should know appropriate language and terminology; understand sexual orientation and gender identity development; know current issues impacting LGBTIQ individuals; develop greater awareness of personal biases and misconceptions; and practice concrete skills to respond to bullying and advocate for LGBTIQ students.

Inclusive curriculum. "Inclusive curriculum validates the existence of an often invisible population, reinforcing the value of LGBTQ individuals themselves and sending a strong message to LGBTQ students about their worth" (Greytak & Kosciw, 2013, p. 157). Students attending schools with inclusive curriculum report feeling safer at school and having better attendance (Kosciw et al., 2016), and educational leaders are in a prime position both to help develop this curriculum and to support teachers who might experience resistance from parents and other stakeholders for integrating LGBTIQ topics into their existing curriculum.

Supportive student organizations. Educational leaders must understand that under the Equal Access Act of 1984, schools have to allow a gay-straight alliance or similar organization to meet on campus if they allow any other noncurricular student group to meet (Orr & Komosa-Hawkins, 2013). More importantly, however, students attending schools with this type of supportive organization reported lower levels of victimization and greater feelings of safety at school (Kosciw et al., 2016; Marx & Hensman Kettrey, 2016).

What LSJ Programs Need to Teach, Model, and Ensure

Not only do educators themselves need to know what to do and how to behave in their own schools and contexts, in order to properly serve and protect the LGBTIQ population, programs which instruct these future leaders need to reconsider how they approach the teaching of these candidates, so that the instructional space in universities models the attitude and provides the tools that educators will need to resist the dominant heteronormativity in social institutions. Based on our conversations from students, and from the literature we have reviewed, we have developed a set of recommendations for LSJ programs to help them enhance their sensitivity to and inclusion of issues related to the LGBTIQ population.

A culture of inclusivity. Programs must create a culture of inclusivity from the very beginning of the candidate's experience. First, in the initial moments of the program—whether during orientation or in the first classes—candidates must know that the program culture is inclusive. Faculty must speak the words of welcome to all candidates, and not assume that there are no LGBTIQ candidates who may need to be addressed. LGBTIQ candidates in University programs, especially in a Catholic University such as Loyola Marymount University, must hear these words of welcome. Faculty cannot be silent about inclusion. There must be intentionality, and openness in resisting the heteronormative culture, and one way to do this is to acknowledge that all candidates belong. In addition, programs must acknowledge that safe spaces do not exist uniformly outside of the University context. Where candidates may feel safe to be their authentic selves in a small classroom, with like-minded colleagues, such will not be the case, perhaps in their work place, or their community. Thus, norms around confidentiality, and the privacy of LGBTIQ candidates must be discussed early in the program.

One of our candidates reported to us that though he felt accepted and welcomed in his cohort, he was reluctant to share too much about issues around his LGBTIQ community because he did not know where that information would be shared. Thus, a "safe space" must mean not only being able to be one's authentic self without retribution in the classroom, but it must also establish the expectation of confidentiality so that sharing sensitive information will not be cavalierly revealed outside the University context, which may negatively impact employment or future opportunities because of the homophobic stigma in our society (Mayo, 2009).

Opportunities for candidates to practice strategies to handle the resistance they may encounter outside of their LSJ program are also critical to truly prepare future school leaders for social justice.

Inclusivity also demands ongoing reflection and an interrogation of personal biases (Loughran, 2002), in particular on the part of the faculty, so as to modify practice to meet the needs of LGBTIQ students. Faculty must know and understand the societal bias that exists against the LGBTIQ population, and they must ensure that none of that bias seeps into their own positionality. For example, language is an important tool which can unconsciously exclude LGBTIQ candidates. Always referring to committed partners as husband and wife, or assuming heterosexual norms in relationships, though perhaps no ill intention is meant, suggests a lack of awareness and sensitivity which LGBTIQ candidates may interpret as exclusionary or unwelcoming. If necessary, university faculty should participate in professional development reflections which can increase cultural awareness around these issues.

A culture of authenticity. While candidates must be welcomed as their authentic selves, faculty must also consider the impact of their own authenticity on program candidates. When university faculty can say who they are, and be open about their own positionality, candidates feel more confident that their authenticity will be honored and nurtured. Our candidates described hearing and seeing faculty as their true selves as promoting confidence and strength to become advocates for their LGBTIQ community. While it would never be appropriate for faculty to discuss personal sexual content in an educational leadership preparation program, faculty can be authentic about how they define their own family dynamic, thus representing and providing an array of definitions of "family" for candidates to see.

A culture of introspection. Both individuals and programs must be introspective, and unafraid to confront the challenges that arise in meeting the needs of the LGBTIQ population. Programs must look inward and discover where and when issues of heteronormativity are included in the curriculum. Though our program has a strong focus on social justice, candidates reported that educational issues related to the LGBTIQ population were confined to one or two courses.

Programs must intentionally include content related to serving this population, and they must do the hard work of looking deeply into each course and each program experience to determine the extent to which candidates are being exposed to this important social justice issue. Addressing LGBTIQ issues cannot be left to chance, nor can there be the assumption that because a program is focused on social justice, that this suffices as umbrella content that will broadly, though not specifically instruct about education and the LGBTIQ student population.

A culture of connectivity. LGBTIQ candidates in educational preparation programs must feel that the University that sponsors their program is also supportive of them and their endeavors. Programs should be overt about offering networking opportunities across campus to LGBTIQ groups, faculty, and social events. Seeing themselves in events and opportunities across campus will allow candidates to feel fully embraced, and encourage them to become their best selves. Furthermore, dealing daily with heteronormativity is a burden that many do not have to face. If LGBTIQ leadership candidates need help as they come to terms with this, and the ways in which they must lead their school population to resist this heavy oppression, it is the responsibility of the preparation program to point candidates in a direction where they can seek support, because classroom experiences may simply not be enough to meet this need.

Taken together, a variety of cultures must be nurtured for an educational leadership preparation program to be successful in serving both the candidates and the students that they lead. A culture of inclusivity, authenticity, introspection, and connectivity should be fostered so that all programs can meet the needs of the leaders they are forming, and the students that they are called to serve.

CONCLUSION

Given the hostile school climate and lack of trust our LGBTIQ youth have in school leaders, we return to our opening scenarios and ask: What would you do? Would you allow the book with a young boy kissing another boy to be included in the elementary school library? Would you address the derogatory "that's so gay" comment made by the student in your class? Would you work with a same-sex couple to enroll their child in your school?

Our LSJ graduates answered "yes" to each of these questions and from their courageous demonstration of what it means to be an educational leader for social justice, we, as faculty of an educational leadership preparation program, are learning from them and are challenged to do the same within our LSJ program. Like the principal of the elementary school, when upon realizing that only stories of heterosexual content were available in the school library, decided to include the book the children asked for, we also must include readings within our doctoral program curriculum that shape candidates' knowledge and understanding of students who identify as LGBTIQ. Similar to our graduate who addressed the "that's so gay" comment in her class, we must model how to have difficult conversations in our own classrooms by creating norms of acceptance and respect.

We must utilize pedagogical techniques that develop facilitation skills in our candidates, including reflective exercises to assist school leaders in finding their own voice. Finally, like our graduate who worked against the norm of his religious school community to enroll a child of a same-sex couple, we must cultivate a critical consciousness in school leaders to address institutional policies that contribute to the hegemony of heteronormativity in schools and we must examine our own program's institutional policies and practices to disrupt the status quo that exists in higher education as well.

REFERENCES

Black, W. R., & Murtadha, K. (2007). Toward a signature pedagogy in educational leadership preparation and program assessment. *Journal of Research on Leadership Education, 2*(1), 1–29.

Blumenfeld, W. J. (2010). How homophobia hurts everyone. In M. Adams, W. J. Blumenfeld, C. Castaneda, H. Hackman, M. Peters, & X. Zuniga (Eds.), *Readings for Diversity and Social Justice* (pp. 376–385). New York, NY: Routledge.

Capper, C. A., Theoharis, G., & Sebastian, J. (2006). Toward a framework for preparing educational leaders for social justice. *International Journal of Educational Administration, 44*(3), 209–224.

Carbado, D. W. (2010). Privilege. In M. Adams, W. J. Blumenfeld, C. Castaneda, H. Hackman, M. Peters, & X. Zuniga (Eds.), *Readings for diversity and social justice* (pp. 393–399). New York, NY: Routledge.

Cosier, K. (2009). Creating safe schools for queer youth. In W. Ayers, T. Quinn, & D. Stovall (Eds.), *Handbook of social justice in education* (pp. 285–303). New York, NY: Routledge.

Espelage, D. L., Aragon, S. R., Birkett, M., & Koenig, B. W. (2008). Homophobic teasing, psychological outcomes, and sexual orientation among high school students: What influence do parents and schools have? *School Psychology Review, 37*(2), 202–216.

Espelage, D. L., & Rao, M. A. (2013). Safe schools: Prevention and intervention for bullying and harassment. In E. S. Fisher & K. Komosa-Hawkins (Eds.), *Creating safe and supportive learning environments: A guide for working with lesbian, gay, bisexual, transgender, and questioning youth and families* (pp. 140–155). New York, NY: Routledge.

Fisher, E. S., & Kennedy, K. S. (2012). *Responsive school practices to support lesbian, gay, bisexual, transgender, and questioning students and families.* New York, NY: Routledge.

Greytak, E. A. & Kosciw, J. G. (2013). Responsive classroom curriculum for lesbian, gay, bisexual, transgender, and questioning students. In E. S. Fisher & K. Komosa-Hawkins (Eds.), *Creating safe and supportive learning environments: A guide for working with lesbian, gay, bisexual, transgender, and questioning youth and families* (pp. 156–174). New York, NY: Routledge.

Harris, M. B. (1997). *School experiences of gay and lesbian youth: The invisible minority.* New York, NY: Harrington Park Press.

Huchting, K. & Bickett, J. (2013). Inspired to lead: Two years of evaluation data from a Jesuit Ed.D. program for educational leadership in social justice. *Jesuit Higher Education: A Journal, 2*(2), 28–40.

Human Rights Watch. (2001). Hatred in the hallways: Violence and discrimination against lesbian, gay, bisexual, and transgender students in U.S. schools. New York, NY: Author.

Koschoreck, J. W., & Slattery, P. (2010). Meeting all students' needs: Transforming the unjust normativity of heterosexism. In C. Marshall & M. Oliva (Eds.), *Leadership for social justice: Making revolutions in education* (2nd ed., pp. 156–174). Boston, MA: Pearson.

Kosciw, J. G., Greytak, E. A., Giga, N. M., Villenas, C., & Danischewski, D. J. (2016). *2015 national school climate survey: The experiences of lesbian, gay, bisexual and transgender youth in our nation's schools.* New York, NY: GLSEN.

Kozik-Rosabal, G. (2000). "Well, we haven't noticed anything bad going on", said the principal: Parents speak about their gay families and schools. *Education & Urban Society, 32*(3), 368–389.

Kull, R. M., Kosciw, J. G., & Greytak, E. A. (2015*). From statehouse to schoolhouse: Anti-bullying policy efforts in U.S. states and school districts.* New York, NY: GLSEN.

Loughran, J. J. (2002). Effective reflective practice: In search of meaning in learning about teaching. *Journal of Teacher Education, 53*(1), 33–43.

Marshall, C., & Oliva, M. (2006). *Leadership for social justice: Making revolutions in education.* Boston, MA: Pearson.

Marx, R. A., & Hensman Kettrey, H. (2016). Gay-straight alliances are associated with lower levels of school-based victimization of LGBTQ+ youth: A systematic review and meta-analysis. *Journal of Youth and Adolescence, 45,* 1269–1282.

Mattheis, A., Perey, D., and Royaltey-Quandt, V. (2015, April). *Queering the Ed.D.: Developing advocacy leadership for LGBTQ students and studies across a university system.* Paper presented at Annual Meeting of the American Educational Research Association, Chicago, IL.

Mayo, C. (2009). The tolerance that dare not speak its name. In A. Darder, M. P. Baltodano, & R. D. Torres (Eds.), *The critical pedagogy reader* (pp. 262–273). New York, NY: Routledge.

McIntosh, P. (1990). White privilege: Unpacking the invisible knapsack. *Independent School, 49,* 31–36.

Olsen, E. O. M., Kann, L., Vivolo-Kantor, A., Kinchen, S., & McManus, T. (2014). School violence and bullying among sexual minority high school students, 2009–2011. *Journal of Adolescent Health, 55*(3), 432–438.

O'Malley, M. P., & Capper, C. A. (2015). A measure of the quality of educational leadership preparation programs for social justice: Integrating LGBTIQ identities into principal preparation. *Educational Administration Quarterly, 51*(2), 290–330.

Orr, A., & Komosa-Hawkins, K. (2013). Law, policy, and ethics: What school professionals need to know. In E. S. Fisher & K. Komosa-Hawkins (Eds.), *Creating safe and supportive learning environments: A guide for working with lesbian, gay, bisexual, transgender, and questioning youth and families* (pp. 156–174). New York, NY: Routledge.

Rofes, E. (1989). Opening up the classroom closet: Responding to the educational needs of gay and lesbian youth. *Harvard Educational Review, 59*(4), 444–454.

Whitman, J. S. (2013). Training school professionals to work with lesbian, gay, bisexual, transgender, and questioning students and parents. In E. S. Fisher & K. Komosa-Hawkins (Eds.), *Creating safe and supportive learning environments: A guide for working with lesbian, gay, bisexual, transgender, and questioning youth and families* (pp. 123–139). New York, NY: Routledge.

Zander, R. S., & Zander, B. (2000). *The art of possibility.* Boston, MA: Harvard Business School Press.

CHAPTER FOURTEEN

Increasing Gender AND Identity Competency Among Student Affairs Professionals

ANGELA CLARK-TAYLOR, KAITLIN LEGG, CARISSA CARDENAS, AND RACHAEL REHAGE

INTRODUCTION

The ways in which higher education student affairs (HESA) degree programs prepare students to work with diverse students is a prevalent and important area of scholarship within higher education research (Herdlein, Riefler, & Mrowka, 2013). Although the 2015 professional competencies of the National Association of Student Personnel Administrators (NASPA) and the American College Personnel Association (ACPA) include sexual orientation and gender identity, there is little research (Flowers, 2003) on how to best prepare student affairs professionals to work with students who inhabit "minoritized identities of sexuality and gender" (MIoSG) (Vaccaro, Russell, & Koob, 2015). We use the MIoSG acronym because, as new gender and sexual identities continue to come to light, the LGBTQ acronym (lesbian, gay, bisexual, transgender, and questioning) excludes and normalizes groups of people in ways that are inauthentic to all gender and sexual identities. Furthermore, and in part because of this research gap, these competencies are not formally taught in HESA programs.

With the rise of out students with MIoSG and the continued and escalating violence towards this community, it is increasingly important that HESA degree programs prepare future student affairs professionals to support students with MIoSG (Rivers, 2015). Colleges and universities are sites for transforming or transmitting cultural values and norms. We believe that an inclusive HESA graduate program understands the identity and needs of students, staff, and faculty with

MIoSG. Including this basic knowledge of campus communities with MIoSG could create a deeper understanding of inclusive curriculum that includes multiple identities and cultures. Queer knowledge can challenge cultures of hate by examining the connections and intersections among heterosexism, gender oppression, homophobia, sexism, classism, ableism, and racism in institutions of higher education. In addition, we argue that the inclusion of queer bodies of knowledge, which seek to deconstruct binary categories can expand our understanding of injustices as they have historically developed in higher education.

PREPARING STUDENT AFFAIRS PROFESSIONALS TO WORK WITH STUDENTS WITH MIOSG

This study seeks to begin filling the gap in research concerning the preparation of future student affairs professionals in regards to their ability to support and affirm MIoSG students through coursework in HESA programs. To accomplish this goal, we have conducted a mixed method data-gathering project of HESA programs affiliated with NASPA and ACPA professional organizations. We utilized the institutional websites of NASPA and ACPA affiliated HESA program's to gather available data on the curriculum, program requirements, course titles and descriptions, syllabi, and faculty research and teaching interests of each institution. Though findings show that there are some excellent examples of programs that do include coursework on MIoSG students, the overall formal integration of students with MIoSG into the HESA curriculum is sparse.

In this chapter we will summarize the current research on HESA programs preparing student affairs professionals to work with students with MIoSG. We will discuss the findings of our study to provide insight into the important trends in the HESA curriculum. Finally, we will offer strategies for HESA programs to better support the development of student affairs professionals' knowledge of students with MIoSG by provide lessons learned from a HESA course on students with MIoSG and a post-graduate professional development workshop for student affairs professionals that attempts to fill the knowledge gap.

There are many factors to consider in a culturally competent, social justice-oriented approach to student affairs. For this study, we are interested in understanding how higher education professionals are prepared to work with students with MIoSG. Preparation includes providing theoretical and practical knowledge that helps student affairs staff to serve students effectively by advancing meaningful change within oppressive power and policy systems. In addition, we must support HESA students in navigating their own identities (marginalized or dominant) while doing their work. To understand the current research being done in this area, we examined a variety of literature about student affairs competency areas, diversity and multicultural education, and MIoSG-specific training within HESA programs. The literature covers three major themes: (1) addressing diversity through multicultural education; (2) filling the gaps with MIoSG specific research and training; and (3) professional development and continued learning.

ADDRESSING DIVERSITY THROUGH MULTICULTURAL EDUCATION

Over the past 15 years, HESA programs have been implementing substantial changes in their curriculum to enhance student skills and knowledge in multicultural and diversity issues, with most programs reporting some sort of diversity requirement within formal coursework (Flowers, 2003). Yet, current attempts at integrated multicultural education curricula vary in topics presented, and usually exclude MIoSG. With the diversification of the student body, student affairs administrators play a critical role in mediating minoritized and dominant groups (Poynter & Washington, 2005). They must be prepared to engage in conversations and community building across multiple identities, including but not limited to gender, sex, sexual orientation, race, ethnicity, ability, and socioeconomic status. HESA faculty and staffs with lower reported multicultural competence are less likely to facilitate their own programs or create campus-specific programs and services. HESA faculty and staff members who report addressing diversity in their programs also demonstrate higher levels of multicultural competence (Wilson, 2015).

The strength of graduate students and new professionals in multicultural competence can be attributed to a variety of factors, such as training by faculty with an explicit commitment to social justice and who have integrated it across the curriculum (Edwards, Loftin, Nance, Riser, & Smith, 2014). Other elements include faculty members' personal belief systems, the compatibility of those various systems with a faculty (Martin & Dagostino-Kalniz, 2015), and their own identification within a minoritized identity group (Pope & Mueller, 2005).

Within the HESA classroom, the establishment of trust and openness is critical. It is especially critical to break down resistance and dispel discomfort in dialogue across identities and difference (Edwards et al., 2014; Kelly & Gayles, 2010). Even with the increase in diversity and multicultural curriculum, it is unclear if these programs are preparing students with the skills they need to provide interventions, counsel diverse students, apply identity development theories, and provide adequate programs and resources (Gayles & Kelly, 2007; Renn & Jessup, 2008).

Due to inconsistencies in training and competency-based learning outcomes (Herdlein et al., 2013), higher education professionals frequently acquire advocacy skills to address the issues that minoritized students face outside of their graduate school preparatory programs (Harrison, 2014). Some professionals learn these skills in undergraduate coursework in an interdisciplinary program such as feminist and queer studies, ethnic studies, and international studies instead of in the formal HESA curriculum. Prior experience and background in the nonprofit or government/public sectors may also inform these skills, though this too should not replace the formal instruction of MIoSG affirming strategies with the HESA classroom.

FILLING THE GAPS: MIOSG RESEARCH AND TRAINING

Renn (2015) identifies three key areas of current research for students with MIoSG in higher education: visibility, campus climate, and changing constructions of LGBTQ identities. The primary focus of this research has been on student development, with little work to explore how the ability to affirm and support students with MIoSG appears in HESA programs. While the literature clearly shows a jump in multicultural and diversity education programs, there is little to no evidence of a meaningful increase in MIoSG specific curriculum. Yet, addressing or ignoring MIoSG in the HESA classroom continues to have a significant impact on current and future students. The victimization, harassment, and invisibility of students with MIoSG impact their involvement, motivation, emotional well-being, and meaning making abilities in the classroom and throughout the campus (Renn, 1998; Vaccaro et al., 2015).

Student affairs professionals have the responsibility to promote holistic development for all students, and play an important role in helping students with MIoSG make meaning of their identity with resources, integrated curriculum, interpersonal opportunities, as role models, and through meaningful opportunities for self-reflection (Engelken, 1998). Additionally, faculty members report the need for support from student affairs professionals to navigate identity differences, student diversity, classroom management, and allyship in the classroom, but student affairs professionals are not being formally taught how to meet this need within their HESA programs (Garcia, Hoelscher, & Farmer, 2005). Though over a decade has passed since this study was published little change has been made on this front.

Some graduate students and faculty are already incorporating MIoSG in their courses. These individuals tend to be part of the communities with MIoSG themselves or have family or friends who are, yet they lack formal training on how to include this material in their work (Jaekel, 2016). In addition, these topics may be addressed as a single reading or a week of readings within a larger diversity course. Not surprisingly, graduate students report that they do not feel prepared to confront heterosexism and homophobia in learning environments (McCabe & Robinson, 2008).

While there has been little evidence to show an increase in MIoSG-specific training and coursework there are some resources and models to support new curriculum development. HESA faculty can draw from interdisciplinary fields such as gender and women's studies, queer theory, and LGBTQ studies programs (Renn, 2015). Additionally, faculty have been successful at introducing MIoSG in the classroom through popular culture and media (Cawthon, 2004). Pulling from the MIoSG inclusive legacy of LGBTQ and queer studies informs our thinking in many ways. It breaks the silence, validates identities, and provides safer environments for self-disclosure, experiential learning, and the exploration of identities and beliefs in a supportive, affirming environment (Chesnut, 1998).

As well, MIoSG identities can and have been integrated into the curriculum across a variety of topics, including coursework on law, human development theory, counseling, and career planning (Talbot & Viento, 2005), but these achievements should not serve as the only formal instruction on the topic. Given the current sociopolitical landscape of MIoSG on and off campus, student affairs professionals must be prepared to navigate campus politics and student experiences around policy, climate, safety, self-identification, visibility, and inclusion (Sanlo, 2002).

Some student affairs professionals are gaining training and skills to support students with MIoSG after their formal training through self-sought training to learn about inclusion, interventions, and identities after a negative situation has already occurred on their campus (Gannon-Rittenhouse, 2015). Formal coursework needs to be added to stop student affairs professionals from having to seek out additional training to develop introductory competencies once a MIoSG student has been victimized or further marginalized on their campus. Stand-alone survey courses should be presented as an introduction to MIoSG and experiences and provide these basic competencies and skills for all HESA students.

PROFESSIONAL DEVELOPMENT AND CONTINUED LEARNING

Within studies regarding both multicultural education and MIoSG specific learning, it is clear that the context for applying skills can vary across institutions and internal settings. Additional formal training and continued education are important supplements to HESA programs (Pope & Reynolds, 1997). Therefore, bridges from skill acquisition to critical awareness for action must be articulated explicitly through real world examples within the training and learning environment (Wernick, 2012). Opt-in, peer-led training programs and certifications such as "Safe Space" and "Safe Zone" are offered at campuses across the country and provide staff and faculty with supplemental training in awareness, knowledge, and skills to address students with MIoSG.

Harrison (2014) found that professionals supplemented their advocacy skills by developing specific knowledge of their institution's campus politics and informal networks of power to advocate more effectively. Advocacy and social justice or identity-based allyship are also institutionally specific (Ryan, Broad, Walsh, & Nutter, 2013). Professional learning or reading groups, also called knowledge communities, allow for colleagues to connect, challenge and support themselves, and receive feedback (ACPA & NASPA, 2015).

While advocacy skills are generally not taught in graduate programs, they are necessary for managing learning environments around issues of diversity, particularly when interpersonal conflict occurs (Garcia et al., 2005). Learning communities and reading groups among professionals may deepen understanding, allow space for critical self-analysis, and contribute to a collaborative, problem-solving community (Ness, George, Turner, & Bolgatz, 2010). These types of supplemental activates are important, but should not replace the formal instruction of these skills in the HESA classroom.

RESEARCH METHODOLOGY

The data in this study was gathered and analysed using a mixed method approach. Creswell and Plano Clark (2011) define mixed method research as an approach to research that includes at least one quantitative technique and one qualitative technique. This is true of this study, but in addition we approached mixed methods research as Greene (2007) describes as a way to enrich our findings with greater meaning by sharing both the statistical information and narrative information. The combination of this approach can be seen within consensual qualitative research (CQR) approach (Heppner, Kivlighan, & Wampold, 1992) to constructing our variables. The following two sections explain our data collection and analysis in greater detail.

Data Collection

Data was gathered from HESA programs affiliated with ACPA and NASPA using a mixed method approach. Some institutional barriers were discovered during data collection including the need to have an accurate and up-to-date website and program documents. The need to include students with MIoSG support skills in HESA programs is rapidly changing and thus may have been added to the formal program, but not updated on the website. Department curriculum, course offerings, and faculty research interests could be drastically different over subsequent years, but not updated on the universities website. In addition the use of adjuncts, graduate students, and visiting faculty for specialized courses limits the availability of what is on the web as contingent faculty are more transient and their work is rarely available within programmatic and market materials.

Upon completion, data was gathered on a total of 357 programs at 197 colleges and universities across the United States. 130 of these programs were terminal or doctoral degree granting programs and 227 were master's degree programs. 1.1% of the institutions were affiliated with ACPA only, 61.9% with NASPA members only and 37% were both ACPA and NASPA affiliated. 1.1% of these programs included a required course explicitly on MIoSG students and 19.3% of programs included MIoSG students as a piece of a required course. 5% of these programs included an elective course explicitly on students with MIoSG and 6.7% of programs included it as a piece of an elective course on students with MIoSG. 18.8% of programs had full-time faculty with research or teaching interest on MIoSG students.

Data Analysis

The research team conducted a website analysis of available data on the curriculum, program requirements, course titles and descriptions, academic handbooks, syllabi, and faculty research and teaching interests of each institution. Each program was coded for coursework on students with MIoSG, including: required coursework that is explicitly on students with MIoSG, required coursework that includes MIoSG students, elective coursework that is explicitly on students with MIoSG, elective coursework that includes MIoSG students, program faculty that have listed a research interest in MIoSG students, and the programs affiliation with NASPA, ACPA, or both.

In addition to investigating webpages and available documents, keywords used to search the website and program documents included LGBT, GLBT, LGBTQ, queer, sexuality, sexual orientation, gender, gender identity, transgender, lesbian, gay, and bisexual. Keywords were selected based on keywords in the MIoSG literature in higher education and student affairs. Selection criteria for the institutions and programs included being an accredited institution of higher education in the United States, and a member of NASPA or ACPA, and or being represented on either of these institutions graduate school programs databases. All website materials were coded for the same themes and all codes were reviewed by multiple research team members.

Quantitative tools were used to describe and analyse the data, while a qualitative approach was used to analyse and interpret results reflected in the study. We were open to discovering relationships, concepts, and ideas about our topic. The consensual qualitative research (CQR) approach (Heppner et al., 1992) was compatible with our philosophy and approach "... in that it relies on team members using unconstrained methods of coming to consensus though open dialogue"

(p. 522). Such an approach allowed us to not only to drive a hypothesis informed study, but we were additionally guided by the research questions to look at the qualitative nature of much of the data. Using a mixed method approach with both quantitative and qualitative data analysis enhanced the quality of the data gathered in this study and the analysis.

Results

We attempted to analyse the relationships between variables including: required coursework that is explicitly on students with MIoSG; required coursework that includes students with MIoSG; elective coursework that is explicitly on students with MIoSG; elective coursework that includes students with MIoSG and their affiliations with particular professional organizations and the NASPA region, but there were not enough counts within variables for a reliable measure. This was also true of the correlation between faculty interest and course offerings with the exceptions of faculty interest in MIoSG and having students with MIoSG students as part of a required class.

We used a Chi-square test for independence and found 16.2% of schools without faculty offered a required course with part of the curriculum dedicated to students with MIoSG compared with 32.8% of institutions that do have interested faculty. There was a significant relationship between faculty with teaching or research interests in MIoSG and including MIoSG in required HESA courses. X^2 (1, n = 357) = 9.65, p < .002. Cramer's V was used to determine the effect size was small but significant at .164 with a p value of .002.

Limitations

There were several limitations to this study. Institutions that are not currently members of NASPA or ACPA were not reviewed; this could potentially limit our overall understanding of HESA programs. Some institutional barriers include the need to have an accurate and up-to-date website and program documents, which could limit the accuracy of this study. The need to include students with MIoSG support skills in HESA programs is rapidly changing and thus may have been added to the formal program, but not updated on the website. Department curriculum, course offerings, and faculty research interests could be drastically different over subsequent years, but not updated on the universities website. In addition the use of adjuncts, graduate students, and visiting faculty for specialized courses limits the availability of what is on the web as contingent faculty are more transient and their work is rarely available within programmatic and market materials.

EXPANDING THE HESA CURRICULUM

Currently, educational opportunities for student affairs graduate students to learn about students with MIoSG is sparse. Most diversity and multicultural classes touch on a variety of identities and cultures, but not students with MIoSG. When MIoSG students were included, due to the many identities and cultures these courses covered, only 1–2 weeks were spent on readings or class discussion. Yet, we know that MIoSG identities are complex, nuanced, and ever expanding. To gain provide meaningful and useful education about students with MIoSG, HESA graduate students need time to not only learn basic terminology but also to grasp the culture, identity development, and experiential knowledge about the multiple communities within MIoSG students. In doing so, these future professionals will be more empowered to discuss, affirm, and act on behalf of a students with MIoSG on their campus.

Though it should not replace the need to require formal education in HESA programs to support students with MIoSG, the implementation of supplemental education can help to create a climate that can support formal classes within the HESA program. One informal way to ensure that students gain some knowledge on how to work with students with MIoSG is by having guest speakers. Some faculty may feel as if they are not able to teach this information properly and for that reason choose not to discuss it at all. Guest speakers ensure that students receive information prior to going out in the field. Having educational events that involve guest speakers can ensure forward movement in formal education around this topic. These events can be open to everyone and co-sponsored. Extra credit can be offered to students along with book stipends and conference funding for faculty to prepare them to teach on the needs of students with MIoSG. Another way to provide students with the information they need to best assist students with MIoSG could be through a Safe Space training. Trainings allow for students and faculty to commit an afternoon to begin to develop knowledge on the best ways to successfully serve students with MIoSG.

While these suggestions for improving student affairs programs can be easily incorporated, it is important to do so with caution. While it may be simple to have a guest speaker come in to one day of class it is not different then having one day of class lecture. No one can be expected to truly grasp learned material on one day of lecture, especially when this may be the first time learning it. They equally cannot be expected to be fully prepared to support and affirm students with MIoSG from one guest speaker.

Faculty support is crucial to creating an environment on campus and within HESA programs that is inclusive of students with MIoSG. Finding few faculty members had a background in students with MIoSG gave indication to what the educational atmosphere may feel like for students and faculty with MIoSG. Most faculty members that listed diversity as an area of interest stated that they researched or taught on women's issues, race, or ethnicity compared with the 18.8% of faculty that explicitly stated populations with MIoSG. Faculty members educating student affairs professionals in HESA programs can help to begin this movement by starting the conversation in class. They should challenge themselves to move away from the subject matter expert model and towards a model where faculty and students alike are learning and evolving with the topic. This provides more expansive opportunities to build a learning community within and among student affairs graduate students. Student affairs professionals should emerge from HESA programs feeling comfortable and inspired to access resources and speak about and with students with MIoSG in different campus settings.

There is clear and evident room for improvement in HESA programs regarding students with MIoSG. In order to ensure that student affair professionals are knowledgeable, capable, and empowered to work with the increasing population of students with MIoSG on campus, they must have the proper tools. Well-meaning professionals may be hesitant to speak about students with MIoSG because they are not experts on the frequently evolving perspectives and terminology among students with MIoSG. Students do not need to be experts to educate, advocate, or affirm, but they do need skills to begin the conversation and ability to access resources. It is our recommendation that HESA programs consider including a course on MIoSG students that include an understanding of sex, gender, sexuality, and sexual orientation across heterosexual and cisgender identities to queer and gender nonconforming identities. Identities of sexuality and gender are not exclusive to minoritized communities, but include all individuals and intersect with multiple identities.

POSTGRADUATE PROFESSIONAL DEVELOPMENT FOR STUDENT AFFAIRS PERSONNEL

Disparate and inconsistent training of higher education professionals presents challenges on campus, particularly in light of the national tragedies, tumult, and conflict related to minoritized identities. Though it should not replace the need to require formal education in HESA programs to support students with MIoSG, the implementation of professional development education can help to create a climate that can support and affirm students with MIoSG. Student affairs staff at the University of North Florida have proactively confronted this challenge by providing a cultural competency curriculum. The training program consists of an introductory course, six identity-based trainings, and a capstone course.

Staff members are introduced to concepts such as implicit bias, privilege, oppression, and allyship. The goal is to increase knowledge, awareness and skills that will make professionals more self-aware, increase critical thinking and inquiry, and more comfortable with the concept of social justice as a framework to approach their work. The six identity based trainings include one course specifically on sexual orientation, gender identity, and gender expression. The courses provide knowledge, awareness, and skills that move beyond vocabulary in order to dig into both theoretical concepts and case studies. Staff members are encouraged to take into consideration the intersections of multiple minoritized identities and leave each course with an action plan.

Training and continued conversations about social justice, power, privilege and oppression are necessary—even for well-educated people—to keep these issues front and center and move the conversation from an informal environment to the development of meaningful formal education that helps support and affirm students with MIoSG. Staff members who complete the program sometimes create informal learning communities in which they share e-mails with links to videos, articles, and other publications that are thought provoking, difficult, and important. Within this self-constructed knowledge community, staff members build trust and support so that they can challenge each other and grow. Training is not an end point, but instead facilitates opportunities to start a conversation, plant a seed, and help staff develop and grow slowly over time.

CONCLUSION

We are unable to answer all the questions raised both within the current literature and within our study. What we attempted to do in this study is begin to develop a general knowledge of how HESA programs currently represent curricular requirements and opportunities on their program websites and the documents available there. While students and HESA professionals may be informed that they will work with MIoSG students, very few of them are actually being prepared to do so in a formal educational setting. The prevalent practice of lumping MIoSG under multicultural competencies created a compelling and unsettling question for the nature of how HESA programs prepare students to serve communities with MIoSG.

The data collected in this study gives insight into the college campus atmosphere and a lack of inclusion for students and professionals with MIoSG. Supplemental trainings and events are useful platforms to move toward a formal curriculum that equips HESA programs to meaningfully train graduate student to become professionals that support and affirm students with MIoSG, but should not be relied upon as the dominant or permanent model. Upon completing a HESA program, student affairs professionals should have a basic foundations of difference, identity formation, and community development. Multicultural competencies should provide graduate students with the ability to understand major concepts on the construction of race, ethnicity, sexuality, gender, ability, and all other axes of identity.

REFERENCES

ACPA: College Student Educators International & NASPA: Student Affairs in Higher Education. (2015). *ACPA/NASPA professional competency areas for student affairs educators*. Washington, DC: Authors. Retrieved from https://www.naspa.org/images/uploads/main/ACPA_NASPA_Professional_Competencies_FINAL.pdf

Cawthon, T. W. (2004). Using entertainment media to inform student affairs teaching and practice related to sexual orientation. *New Directions for Student Services, 2004*(108), 7–47.

Chesnut, S. (1998). Queering the curriculum or what's Walt Whitman got to do with it. In R. L. Sanlo (Ed.), *Working with lesbian, gay, bisexual, and transgender college students: A Handbook for faculty and administrators* (pp. 221–230). Westport, CT: Greenwood.

Creswell, J. W., & Plano Clark, V. L. (2011). *Designing and conducting mixed methods research* (2nd ed.). Thousand Oaks, CA: Sage.

Edwards, K. T., Loftin, J. K., Nance, A. D., Riser, S., & Smith, Y. (2014). Learning to transform: Implications for centering social justice in a student affairs program. *College Student Affairs Journal, 32*(1), 1–17.

Engelken, L. C. (1998). Making meaning: Providing tools for an integrated identity. In R. L. Sanlo (Ed.), *Working with lesbian, gay, bisexual and transgender students: A handbook for faculty and administrators* (pp. 23–30). Westport, CT: Greenwood.

Flowers, L. A. (2003) National study of diversity requirements in student affairs graduate programs, *NASPA Journal, 40*(4), 72–82.

Gannon-Rittenhouse, E. M. (2015). *Heteronormativity and its effect on school belonging: A narrative inquiry of recent gender and sexuality diverse graduates* (Doctoral dissertation). Retrieved from ProQuest. Drexel University, Philadelphia, PA. (3731237)

Garcia, J. E., Hoelscher, K. J., & Farmer, V. L. (2005). Diversity flashpoints: Understanding difficult interpersonal situations grounded in identity difference. *Innovative Higher Education, 29*(4), 275–289. doi:10.1007/s10755-005-2862-9

Gayles, J. G., & Kelly, B. T. (2007). Experiences with diversity in the curriculum: Implications for graduate programs and student affairs practice. *NASPA Journal, 44*(1), 193–208.

Greene, J. C. (2007). *Mixed methods in social inquiry*. San Francisco, CA: Jossey-Bass.

Harrison, L. M. (2014). How student affairs professionals learn to advocate: A phenomenological study. *Journal of College & Character, 15*(3), 165–176. doi:10.1515/jcc-2014-0020

Heppner, P. P., Kivlighan, D. M., & Wampold, B. E. (1992). Major research designs. In C. Verduin (Ed.), *Research design in counseling* (pp. 115–165). Pacific Grove, CA: BrooksCole.

Herdlein, R., Riefler, L., & Mrowka, K. (2013). An integrative literature review of student affairs competencies: A meta-analysis. *Journal of Student Affairs Research and Practice, 50*(3), 250–269. doi:10.1515/jsarp-2013-0019

Jaekel, K. S. (2016). Innovations in teaching: How novice teaching assistants include LGBTQ topics in the writing classroom. *Journal of Effective Teaching, 16*(1), 89–101.

Kelly, B. T., & Gayles, J. G. (2010). Resistance to racial/ethnic dialog in graduate preparation programs: Implications for developing multicultural competence. *College Student Affairs Journal, 29*(1), 75–85.

Martin, R. J., & Dagostino-Kalniz, V. (2015). Living outside their heads: Assessing the efficacy of a multicultural course on the attitudes of graduate students in teacher education. *Journal of Cultural Diversity, 22*(2), 43–49.

McCabe, P. C., & Rubinson, F. (2008). Committing to social justice: The behavioral intention of school psychology and education trainees to advocate for lesbian, gay, bisexual, and transgendered youth. *School Psychology Review, 37*(4), 469–486.

Ness, M. K., George, M.A., Turner K. H., & Bolgatz, J. (2010). The growth of higher educators for social justice: Collaborative professional development in higher education. *InSight: A Journal of Scholarly Teaching, 5*, 88–105.

Pope, R. L., & Mueller, J. A. (2005). Faculty and curriculum: Examining multicultural competence inclusion. *Journal of College Student Development, 46*(6), 679–688. Baltimore, MA: John Hopkins University Press. doi:10.1353/csd.2005.0065

Pope, R. L., & Reynolds, A. L. (1997). Student affairs core competencies: Integrating multicultural awareness, knowledge, and skills. *Journal of College Student Development, 38*(3), 266–77.

Poynter, K. J., & Washington, J. (2005). Multiple identities: Creating community on campus for LGBT students. *New Directions for Student Services, 2005*(111), 41–47.

Renn, K. A. (1998). Lesbian, gay, bisexual, and transgender students in the college classroom. In R. L. Sanlo (Ed.), *Working with LGBT college students: A handbook for faculty and administrators* (pp. 231–238). Westport, CT: Greenwood.

Renn, K. A. (2015). Higher education. In G.L. Wimberly (Ed.), *LGBTQ issues in education: Advancing a research agenda* (pp. 141–160). Washington, D.C.: American Educational Research Association.

Renn, K. A., & Jessup-Anger, E. R. (2008). Preparing new professionals: Lessons for graduate preparation programs from the national study of new professionals in student affairs. *Journal of College Student Development, 49*(4), 319–335.

Rivers, I. (2015). Homophobic and transphobic bullying in universities. In H. Cowie (Ed.), *Bullying among university students: Cross-national perspectives* (pp. 48–60). New York, NY: Routledge.

Ryan, M., Broad, K. L., Walsh, C. F., & Nutter, K. L. (2013). Professional allies: The storying of allies to LGBTQ students on a college campus. *Journal of Homosexuality, 60*, 83–104. doi:10.1080.00 918369.2013.735942

Sanlo, R. (2002). Scholarship in student affairs: Thinking outside the triangle, or Tabasco on cantaloupe. *NASPA Journal, 39*(2), 166–180.

Talbot, D. M., & Viento, W. L. E. (2005). Incorporating LGBT issues into student affairs graduate education. *New Directions for Student Services, 2005*(111), 75–80.

Vaccaro, A., Russell, E. I., & Koob, R. M. (2015). Students with minoritized identities of sexuality and gender in campus contexts: An emergent model. *New Directions for Student Services, 2015*(152), 25–39.

Wernick, L. J. (2012). Leveraging privilege: Organizing young people with wealth to support social justice. *Social Service Review, 86*(2), 323–345.

Wilson, A. B. (2015). Examining the role of multicultural competence in leadership program design. *Journal of Leadership Education, 14*(1), 1–13. doi:1012806/V14/I1/R1

PART FIVE

Moving Forward

Inclusive LGBTQ+ Policy Implementation

CHAPTER FIFTEEN

George Washington University

One Campus Takes Comprehensive Action Against Hate Crimes

CAROL A. KOCHHAR-BRYANT

INTRODUCTION

Our communities across the nation are experiencing growing inequities in access to resources. Hispanic/Latinos, African Americans, people living in poverty, people with disabilities, youth, seniors, immigrants, and LGBT communities face barriers when trying to access health, employment, housing and other services. These inequities further marginalize diverse communities. All communities are responsible for the safety and quality of life of all residents, and to ensure that they can participate fully in social, economic, political, and cultural life. Consider a few jarring examples on the impact of discrimination because they support the urgent call to attend to this human rights agenda.

1. The LGBT community is at a higher risk for suicide because they lack peer support and face harassment, mental health conditions and substance abuse. For LGBT people aged 10–24, suicide is one of the leading causes of death. LGBT individuals are four times more likely and questioning youth are three times more likely to attempt suicide, experience suicidal thoughts or engage in self-harm than straight people. Between 38 and 65% of transgender individuals experience suicidal ideation (Grant, Mottet, & Tanis, 2012; Kann et al., 2015; National Alliance on Mental Illness, 2016).
2. The LGBT community reports higher rates of drug, alcohol and tobacco use than that of straight people. Major factors that contribute to substance

use by LGBT people include prejudice, discrimination, lack of cultural competency in the health care system and lack of peer support (Institute of Medicine of the National Academies, 2011).
3. An estimated 20–30% of LGBTQ people abuse substances, compared to about 9% of the general population (National Alliance on Mental Illness, 2016).
4. Recent statistics from the Federal Bureau of Investigation (FBI) and the National Coalition of Anti- Violence Programs (NCAVP) show that crimes against LGBT people remain a serious problem. According to the FBI, 19% of hate crimes in 2012 included some form of sexual orientation bias, 40 while a separate report found 26% of transgender people experienced physical assault because they were transgender (Grant et al., 2012).
5. One in five hate crimes committed in the U.S. in 2013 were due to bias based on the victim's sexual orientation, and for the first time, gender identity has been added as a separate bias category (FBI, 2015).
6. Though LGBT people are included in the federal hate crimes law, fewer than half of states have passing or expanding laws which aim to protect LGBT individuals from bullying in schools or discrimination in employment, housing and public accommodations like restaurants and stores (Gates, 2014).
7. A recent survey found that 56% of lesbian, gay, and bisexual respondents and 70% of transgender or gender-nonconforming respondents had been discriminated against in a healthcare setting (Gates, 2014; Lambda Legal, 2010).
8. LGBT people are disproportionately likely to be homeless, as are LGBT youth. An estimated 20% to 40% of homeless youth in the United States identify as LGBT or believe they may be LGBT43 compared to an estimated 5% to 7% of youth who identify as LGBT (Cray, Miller, & Durso, 2013).
9. Forty-three percent (43%) maintained most of their family bonds, while 57% experienced significant family rejection (Ryan, Huebner, Diaz, & Sanchez, 2009).
10. In the face of extensive institutional discrimination, family acceptance had a protective effect against many threats to well-being including health risks such as HIV infection and suicide. Families were more likely to remain together and provide support for transgender and gender non-conforming family members than stereotypes suggest (Grant et al., 2012, Report of the National Transgender Discrimination Survey).
11. A welcoming family is crucial to the health and well-being of LGBT youth. Unfortunately, research shows that up to 30% of families reject their children when they learn they are LGBT.

According to the *National Transgender Discrimination Survey*,

> It is part of social and legal convention in the United States to discriminate against, ridicule, and abuse transgender and gender non-conforming people within foundational institutions such as the family, schools, the workplace and health care settings, every day.... Nearly every system and institution in the United States, both large and small, from local to national, is implicated by this data. (Grant et al., 2012, p. 8)

There are no federal protections for LGBT civil rights. Fewer than a third of all U.S. states have laws protecting people from discrimination based on sexual orientation, and only a handful prohibit discrimination based on a person's gender identity or expression. While LGBT Americans continue to face discrimination in matters of employment, housing, public accommodation, and on college campuses, substantial progress has been made in recent years.

RECENT ADVANCES IN CAMPUS POLICY FOR LGBT INDIVIDUALS

One year ago (2016), Democrats introduced the Equality Act to add LGBT Americans to our civil rights law, however, Congress has still not taken action. However, the LGBT community has made historic gains in the fight for equality in recent years, most notably the Supreme Court's decision on June 26, 2015, to legalize nationwide same-sex marriage. There have been several federal recent policy advances that reduce discrimination for LGBT individuals, including the following:

12. In March 2016, the Obama Administration appointed the first transgender White House LGBTQ Liaison.
13. In April 2016, the White House Office of Personnel Management revised the definition of spouse in its Family and Medical Leave Act (FMLA) regulations to permit Federal employees with same-sex spouses to use FMLA leave in the same manner as those with opposite-sex spouses.
14. In May 2016, the Department of Education issued new guidance for school districts to ensure that transgender students will be treated with dignity in public and federally funded schools, including having equal access to sex-segregated facilities, such as restrooms and locker rooms that are consistent with their gender identity.
15. In May 2016, the Department of Health and Human Services (HHS) Office for Civil Rights implemented a regulation that provides explicit protections from discrimination on the basis of sex stereotyping—including for lesbian, gay, and bisexual people—and gender identity in healthcare and

insurance under the provisions of Section 1557 of the Affordable Care Act (ACA).
16. In June 2016, the Pentagon lifted their ban on transgender people serving openly in the U.S. military.
17. In June 2016, the Department of Labor (DOL) published requirements that prohibit discrimination by federal contractors against workers on the basis of gender identity or sex stereotyping. (Grant et al., 2012).

On the employment front, 22 states and the District of Columbia protect workers from employment discrimination based on sexual orientation (and all but three on the basis of gender identity), and most Fortune 500 companies already have non-discrimination policies in place that protect LGBT workers (U.S. Department of Labor, 2014). It is also an area of special emphasis, given the reality that according to the 2011 National Transgender Discrimination Survey, nearly half of transgender workers report having been fired, or not hired or promoted, because of discrimination (Grant et al., 2012).

ECONOMIC DEVELOPMENT, WORKFORCE DEVELOPMENT AND INCLUSION

The United Nations community generally recognizes three categories of human rights: economic, social and political. Economic rights include the right to work, to change jobs, to relocate and to advocate for safe working conditions and fair wages. Just as with other minority populations, making workplaces accessible and inclusive for LGBT workers is an important emerging issue—and one that aligns with the broader mission of the Department of Labor to open doors of opportunity to all workers. However, no federal law explicitly provides these protections, leaving many workers vulnerable to possible discrimination and harassment on the job. Also, in a majority of states, there are no clear state laws protecting residents and visitors from anti-LGBT discrimination in employment, housing and business services.

Education is the key to national development, and academic institutions have long played a central role in human resource and talent development. Improving conditions for individuals who have experienced chronic discrimination requires strategic investment in the preparation of workers which is grounded in the assumption that broader educational and economic opportunity will bring social stability and self-determination for these individuals. Therefore, the goal of promoting access to post-secondary education is central to the goals of broader economic growth within communities and states.

The current conditions for LGBT individuals throughout the nation require a continued commitment from academic institutions and employers to assist with educational development for all. In the arena of employment discrimination and economic insecurity, the following findings from the *Report of the National Transgender Discrimination Survey* (Grant et al., 2012) and Sears and Mallory (2015) of the Williams Institute are important:

18. Studies show that anywhere from 15% to 43% of gay people have experienced some form of discrimination and harassment at the workplace. Moreover, a staggering 90% of transgender workers report some form of harassment or mistreatment on the job. These workplace abuses pose a real and immediate threat to the economic security of gay and transgender workers.
19. Double the rate of unemployment: Survey respondents experienced unemployment at twice the rate of the general population at the time of the survey, with rates for people of color up to four times the national unemployment rate.
20. Ninety percent (90%) of those surveyed reported experiencing harassment, mistreatment or discrimination on the job or took actions like hiding who they are to avoid it.
21. Forty-seven percent (47%) said they had experienced an adverse job outcome, such as being fired, not hired or denied a promotion because of being transgender or gender non-conforming.
22. Over one-quarter (26%) reported that they had lost a job because they were transgender or gender non-conforming and 50% were harassed.
23. Large majorities attempted to avoid discrimination by hiding their gender or gender transition (71%) or delaying their gender transition (57%).
24. The clear majority (78%) of those who transitioned from one gender to the other reported that they felt more comfortable at work and their job performance improved, despite high levels of mistreatment.
25. Respondents who were currently unemployed experienced debilitating negative outcomes, including nearly double the rate of working in the underground economy (such as the sex trade or selling drugs), twice the homelessness, 85% more incarceration, and more negative health outcomes, such as more than double the HIV infection rate and nearly double the rate of current drinking or drug misuse to cope with mistreatment, compared to those who were employed.
26. Respondents who had lost a job due to bias also experienced ruinous consequences such as four times the rate of homelessness, 70% more current drinking or misuse of drugs to cope with mistreatment, 85% more incarceration, more than double the rate working in the underground economy, and more than double the HIV infection rate, compared to those who did not lose a job due to bias

So how can the university make its case to lawmakers who seem deeply sceptical? Is this a matter of talent development and work-force preparation, as it is with other minorities in higher education—African Americans, Hispanic/Latinos, women, and people with disabilities?

CAMPUSES WORK TO PROMOTE EQUITY: AGAINST SOME ODDS

A campus community has the same responsibility as other institutions—as students should not be responsible for their safety and inclusion. There are no easy answers for how to achieve greater equity and inclusion in a campus community.

There are about 250 LGBT resource centers on campuses across the country (Rego-Craft, 2014). At many of those institutions, the centers play a significant role in campus life. They provide programs and resources for lesbian, gay, bisexual, and transgender students and employees, as well as training for the broader campus community. And in the aftermath of tragedies like the mass shooting last month at a gay nightclub in Orlando, Fla., the centers have taken on crucial support roles. Area colleges released statements of condolence, provided counseling services, organized blood drives, and planned memorials. A statement from John C. Hitt, president of the University of Central Florida, emphasized support for those who identify as lesbian, gay, bisexual, transgender, or queer, saying, "I tell our LGBTQ students, faculty, staff, and alumni this: You are not alone. Your university stands with you" (Hitt, 2016).

Recently, however, these resource centers are threatened by limited financial resources, disbelief that inequities exist, lack of political will and uncertainty about the best approaches. Despite recent advances in federal protections, the struggle for LGBTQ equality is far from over, as many states push forward laws legitimizing discrimination. Anti-LGBT arguments are being recast as faith-based ones, protecting people whose faith denies the existence of LGBT people and who argue that being gay is a matter of "life choice". In other words, gay people could change their behavior if they wanted to. This argument has been used to support many kinds of discriminatory practices and policies. However, scientists are increasingly finding evidence that sexual orientation is largely determined by genetics, not choice.

A recent ground-breaking study details how 800 gay participants shared notable patterns in specific regions of the human genome (Sanders et al., 2015). The study involved a genome-wide linkage scan on 409 independent pairs of homosexual brothers (908 analysed individuals in 384 families), by far the largest study of its kind to date. Results support the existence of genes on chromosome 8 and chromosome Xq28 which influence development of male sexual orientation

(Sanders et al., 2015). These findings do not persuade those who claim that: (1) homosexuality cannot be a Constitutional right, because all our rights come from God (Bryan Fischer, Focal Point Radio, July 28, 2016); (2) there is a homosexual agenda; and (3) that empowerment of LGBT individuals requires that society accept, celebrate and support those with different sexual identities, as we did with gender equality.

On the positive side, there are now 18 states plus Washington, DC that have explicit protections from discrimination for the LGBT population. However, the Human Rights Campaign (2016) has been tracking more than 200 anti-LGBT bills introduced in 2015 in 32 states across the country, an increase from previous years. The largest number of these anti-LGBT bills were aimed at authorizing individuals, businesses and taxpayer-funded agencies to cite religion as a reason to refuse goods or services to LGBT people.

Other anti-LGBT bills seek to restrict access to bathrooms by transgender people and to eliminate the ability of local governments to protect LGBT residents and visitors. For example, current and former students involved in the University of Tennessee at Knoxville's Pride Center discuss how it can continue its programming for LGBT students in the 2016–2017 academic year since a new state law is defunding it (Brown, 2016a). Republican state lawmakers stripped $436,000 from the university's Office for Diversity and Inclusion for a year, diverting the funds and forcing the office to close for the 2016–2017 academic year (Zamudio-Suarez, 2016). Furthermore, a committee of the Tennessee House of Representatives plans to investigate how the state's public colleges spend funds earmarked for diversity (Brown, 2016b). Other states such as Georgia, North Carolina and Mississippi, are promoting so-called *religious freedom bills* which allow businesses to deny services to gay and lesbian couples by citing religious principles. Such bills are criticized as discriminatory against gays, lesbians and transgendered people and are being perceived as the latest attempts by conservative lawmakers to stop the stride toward equality that the LGBT community has made in recent years.

The American Association of University Women reported that more than 70% of LGBT students encounter sexual harassment at college (Hill & Silva, 2009). Incidents such as the following are common on campuses across the United States:

27. A heterosexual student at GW University was beaten after another heterosexual student mistook him for being gay … the victim was transported to GW Hospital with significant head trauma, including bleeding in his brain (Anand, 2011).
28. A student was assaulted as he walked past the 925 Apartments. The student's assailants reportedly said, "You guys are faggots and queers", as they punched the student until he fell to the ground. Once he rose, they

repeated the action until he collapsed a second time, after which they fled (Grover, 2015).
29. A member of the GW University Police Department said he was assaulted three times over three years. One instance was a sexual assault but he never reported the crimes to authorities, a decision he now says he regrets (Peligri, 2014).

These incidents have propelled the George Washington University to face its challenges with LGBT hate crimes on campus and to respond swiftly. In the heart of Washington DC, GW is among the most politically active campuses in the nation, so if it can happen here, it can happen anywhere. Gay students are very concerned that it is occurring not only in the surrounding community but right on campus. They believe that solutions require a shared responsibility and that LGBT students must raise their awareness about "microaggressions" and must speak up when confronted with intolerance (Grover, 2015; Mullins, 2013).

CAMPUS RESPONSES TO DISCRIMINATION AND HATE CRIMES

"The academy" is a broad term, typically invoked to represent everyone engaged in higher education (Stead, 2015). It has a responsibility as a central agent in contributing to social cohesion by raising student and faculty awareness of the impacts of discrimination. In his briefing to the Geneva-based Human Rights Council, United Nations Special Rapporteur Mutuma Ruteere (2013) commented that education has a central role in creating new values and attitudes, and in providing important tools for addressing deep-rooted discrimination, the legacy of historical injustices, and contemporary forms of racism. He stated:

> The essential role of education, particularly when targeted at youth, in promoting and enhancing democratic values, tolerance, mutual respect and understanding, inclusion, intercultural harmony, and universal respect for human rights and fundamental freedoms, as well as in countering the rise of extremist political parties, movements and groups. (Ruteere, 2013, unpaginated)

Over the past decade, GW continues to transform its culture into one that better fosters diversity and inclusion. In the words of GW president Steven Knapp:

> We must do more than explore and discuss … colleges and universities could achieve excellence only if they embrace the talents, experience, and contributions of students from all backgrounds. "Indeed," I added, "our democracy as a whole can thrive only if the doors of educational opportunity at all levels are fully and visibly open to members of all the communities that make up the fabric of our nation". (Knapp, 2016)

GW has become a champion and a leader in anti-discrimination action on campus.

Policy Changes at GW

Several academic and policy changes were needed to signal a campaign of inclusiveness and anti-discrimination on campus. This campus-wide initiative included the establishment of a new Office of Diversity and Inclusion, mandatory faculty training, Law School admissions modifications, new support services, and several academic innovations described below.

GW Office of diversity and inclusion. In 2010, GW President Steven Knapp announced a new initiative to promote diversity and inclusion within and beyond the university community. A key component of that initiative was the creation of the President's Council on Diversity and Inclusion, a group of university community members including staff, faculty, and students that was charged by President Knapp to generate ideas and formulate recommendations for increasing the university's effectiveness in reaching out to persons of all backgrounds. This initiative was followed by an Office of Diversity and Inclusion.

Faculty and Student Mandatory Training. In 2016 faculty were required to complete an online learning module, *Preventing Sexual Harassment and Discrimination*. The primary goal of this course is to enable faculty to identify prohibited harassing behaviors, including sexual harassment. Faculty are viewed as essential force in helping the institution maintain an environment free from harassment, discrimination, and intimidation. Incoming George Washington University students also participated in a new mandatory training program, *Sexual Assault Prevention and Response Training*, part of the university's comprehensive strategy to prevent campus sexual assault and to respond effectively to the issue. Over the summer of 2015, incoming freshmen and graduate students were required to complete *Think About It*, a self-guided online training module that examines the interconnected issues students face, including substance abuse, the spectrum of sexual violence, Title IX rights and responsibilities, healthy relationships and bystander intervention. Upon completion of *Think About It*, students were required to sign up for mandatory in-person training sessions during Welcome Week and discuss these issues with peers and facilitators during the weeks that followed (Steinhardt, 2015).

New law school admissions questions. GW will join only four top 20 law schools to add LGBT status to its applications (voluntary) by tracking the number of gay and transgender applicants to establish better support services and pair students with alumni and mentors. LGBT applicants would be encouraged to apply knowing that GW would be a supportive place for them to be and a good fit (Sette, 2013). The idea was presented to the law school administrators in the fall of 2015, comparing the school's application with that of its peer schools, such as Boston University, University of Pennsylvania and University of Washington, which include the LGBT option for applicants.

Academic Innovation

Intellectual and behavioral norms that affect campus climate are set by faculty as are interventions that lead to sustainable learning about race and LGBT issues. Institutions of higher education that aspire to value the histories and experiences of all students must involve faculty as well as students (Vega, 2014). Some campuses offer course work through African American studies, Native American studies, and Arab American Studies, as well as History departments, and more recently LGBT studies. Such curricular diversity can increase intergroup understanding and communication and reduce racial prejudice (Denson & Chang, 2009).

For students and faculty in the Academy, exploring latent prejudice should be as integral a part of academic development as core content and field experience. The gradual accumulation of prejudice during a childhood and over a lifetime is in part what defines a marginalized experience, making explanation and communication with someone who does not share this identity particularly difficult. Because micro-aggressions go largely unnoticed by those who commit them, Sue recommends that we use education to end micro-aggression (Sue, 2010, 2015). Students and faculty need opportunities to explore themselves as racial-cultural beings, to uncover their unconscious biases, and to learn that these biases can hurt those around them.

For example, in light of the Ferguson, Ohio police shootings, at one large urban university, as well as the recent Orlando nightclub massacre, student groups are beginning to address race and LGBT relations on campus. At GW more than 20 student organizations have come together to address police discrimination, promote dialog, and improve communication between officers and students. Issues they are concerned with include anti-profiling, behavior profiling, ethics, and use of force. Students petitioned for a website to report incidents of discrimination.

What part can faculty play directly to reduce such instances of racism in the academic settings? It is important that faculty carefully examine their courses and curriculum to ensure that they advance equity as learning goals for students, threshing out aspects that perpetuate inequities. Being *equity-minded* involves inventorying the contradictions between the ideals of democratic education and the social, institutional, and individual practices that contribute to persistent inequities in college outcomes among different racial and ethnic groups, socioeconomic classes, and sexually oriented groups. Equity-minded faculty are aware of the sociohistorical context of exclusionary practices and discrimination in higher education and the effect of power asymmetries on opportunities and outcomes for students of color and students of low socioeconomic status (Witham, Malcom-Piqueux, Dowd, & Bensimon, 2015). Being equity-minded also involves being conscious of the ways that higher education—through its practices, policies, expectations, and unspoken rules—places responsibility for student success on the groups that have experienced marginalization, rather than on the shared responsibility of the individuals and institutions whose responsibility it is to remedy that marginalization. Witham et al. (2015) outlined that equity-minded practices are created through the following:

> willingness to look at student outcomes disaggregated by race and ethnicity as well as socioeconomic status;
> recognition that individual students are not responsible for the unequal outcomes of groups that have historically experienced discrimination and marginalization in the United States;
> sensitivity and respect for the aspirations and struggles of students who are not well served by the current educational system;
> belief in the fairness of allocating additional college resources to students who have greater needs due to the systemic shortcomings of our educational system in providing for them;
> recognition that the elimination of structural racism in institutions of higher education requires intentional critical examination of the structures, policies, practices, norms, and values believed to be race neutral (Lawrence & Keleher, 2004; Quiroz-Martinez, HoSang, & Villarosa, 2004; itham, Malcom-Piqueux, Dowd, & Bensimon, 2015).
> Understanding that the broader term, diversity, is meant to represent all perspectives from groups that have traditionally been excluded from or insufficiently examined in the curriculum (at all levels—department, program, course) (Bennett, 2008).

Such equity-minded practices work well with the infusion of diversity content at the course level and this can involve several entry points, such as:

> Course description and objectives that reflect diversity: How does the discipline help prepare students to live and work in today's multicultural democracy and interdependent world?
> Content integration that includes multiculturalism: What issues of diversity, social justice, and civic engagement are infused in my course curriculum and how?
> Instructional resources and materials: How inclusive are my selected materials?
> Faculty and student worldviews and learning styles: How do student and faculty worldviews, learning styles, and teaching strategies match, and how are my students' learning styles accommodated?
> Assessment diversification: How do assessment activities accommodate my students' learning styles?
> Faculty and student worldviews and learning styles: How do student and faculty worldviews, learning styles, and teaching strategies match, and how are my students' learning styles accommodated?

In these ways, faculty can advance equity by crafting instructional objectives and learning goals that challenge students to identify how society works to perpetuate inequities.

Many professors are content experts in multicultural settings and, as such, they can and should play a central role in engineering and integrating pedagogical tools that intervene against institutional discrimination. Effective intervention requires a transformation process that involves:

> making the *invisible* visible by exposing micro-aggressions;
> reflecting upon one's own cultural experiences and prejudices;
> recognizing the impact of cumulative micro-aggressions on the individual;
> identifying the effects of collective micro-aggressions on groups of individuals;
> developing a commitment to change one's own behavior; and
> providing leadership for others.

Women's, Gender, and Sexuality Studies Program

Since its inception in 1972, GW's Women's, Gender, and Sexuality Studies Program (WGSS) has offered an interdisciplinary program with an undergraduate major and minor as well as several graduate degrees. The curriculum brings together scholarship on women in the humanities, social sciences, and natural sciences. Students in WGSS courses are encouraged to explore traditional and current issues in gender and social justice studies and to critically challenge inequity and inequality. The curriculum offers courses that examine the world from diverse vantage points—gender, race, age, class, sexuality, ethnicity, nationality, etc.—and encourages students to explore and voice varying points of view, from a multidisciplinary vantage point. The program provides students unique access to resources and internship opportunities in Washington, DC.

Many WGSS graduates go on to professional and graduate schools in law, humanities, social sciences, and other fields. They secure jobs in both the private and public sector, in business, law, government, public interest and social service organizations, the arts, and elsewhere. Expertise in women's issues, along with other academic and professional skills, is valued by a spectrum of organizations.

Undergraduate Women's Studies Minor. At the undergraduate level, a Women's Studies minor was introduced in 1989. A major and two five-year Masters and Bachelor's programs were added in 2000. LGBT became a minor in 2011. The Women's Studies Program became the Women's, Gender, and Sexuality Studies Program in Fall 2016.

LGBT and Sexuality Studies Minor. The LGBT and Sexuality Studies Minor is housed in and administered by the Women's Studies Program. The minor draws on the work of a significant community of faculty working in various parts of LGBT and Sexuality Studies scholarship. The minor offers students an opportunity to consider key social and academic issues through the critical lens of LGBT and Sexuality theory and applied research. This minor is in keeping with the mission of the Women's Studies program: an interdisciplinary program dedicated to research, teaching, and practice on gender as it intersects with race, class, age, ethnicity, sexual orientation, religion, and other socially important categories.

A minor in LGBT & Sexuality Studies helps students bring questions to the surface about gender roles, sex and sexuality, health and wellbeing, economic and political development, war and peace, and the list goes on. In all of these, both old and emergent questions concerning LGBT populations and individuals, and sexuality more broadly, play a key part. The LGBT and Sexuality Studies minor prepares students to go on to professional and graduate schools in law, humanities, social sciences, and other fields, and to pursue careers in both private and public sectors, including business, law, government, public interest and social service organization.

Support Services

In keeping with GW's collaboration with student leadership, three additions to our traditional support services have been set up to better serve our LGBT community. Details of the LGBT resource center, the "GW PAL" smartphone app, and the social media network to share *microagressions* are described here.

Creation of an LGBT Resource Center. The George Washington University (GW) Lesbian, Gay, Bisexual and Transgender (LGBT) Resource Center celebrates and supports sexual and gender diversity and inclusion by providing comprehensive educational, support, and advocacy services. These services include training, special events, and mentoring designed to empower LGBT students, faculty, and staff to achieve academic excellence, embrace personal wellness, and pursue professional success.

Reporting Crimes by Smartphone. The GW Office of Safety and Security and Division of Information Technology have introduced a new mobile safety application for our University called "GW PAL", or the Personal Alarm Locator. When installed and opened on either an iOS or Android smartphone, this app acts as a mobile silent alarm. Students can press the *Help* button during any emergency on campus, and quickly communicate to the GW Police Department with their phone number, GPS location and a short text message. Users are also able to send crime tips via GW PAL, along with photos or videos if desired. Tips can be sent from any location on or off campus. Other features include a shortcut to your smartphone flashlight, and a quick dial link for local taxi companies.

Social Media Network to Share Microagressions. GW's website for reporting sexual violence and Title IX violations on campus, "Haven", has a user-friendly update after students advocated for a new site. The aim is to allow users to quickly access information about their options—whether related to seeking care after an assault, accessing help through the university or community, or getting involved in prevention efforts. The updated website's homepage now offers links to emergency and non-emergency contact information.

CLOSING

GW intends to strengthen and accelerate efforts to make sure we realize the promise to be a community of scholars in which the interests, contributions, and aspirations of all our students, faculty, and staff are recognized, respected, and given the fullest possible scope (Knapp, 2016). But the true measure of our commitment and success is not just the work that we do within the classroom and in the campus community, but rather is through the graduates who carry their commitment to justice out into the world that they will impact.

Universities solve the challenges that cross cultural borders; build cultural and political understanding; and model environments that promote dialogue, debate. As leaders of our organizations we are all grappling to find a path forward that is respectful, equitable, and just. At the same time, we each recognize that these difficult and delicate issues require us to draw upon our skill, our empathy, and our courage. We must all continue learning together.

REFERENCES

Anand, P. (2011, March 10). MPD labels Ivory Tower assault a hate crime. *GW Hatchet*. Retrieved from http://files2.gwhatchet.com/a/pdfs/20110310.pdf

Bennett, J. M. (2008). Transformative training: Designing programs for culture learning. In M. A. Moodian (Ed.), *Contemporary leadership and intercultural competence: Understanding and utilizing cultural diversity to build successful organizations* (pp. 99–110). Thousand Oaks, CA: Sage.

Brown, S. (2016a, July 15). Can University of Tennessee students keep a staple of LGBT life afloat? *Chronicle of Higher Education*. Retrieved August 14, 2016 from http://chronicle.com/article/Can-U-of-Tennessee-Students/237138

Brown, S. (2016b, February, 17). Under fire from lawmakers, a flagship tries to explain why diversity matters. *Chronicle of Higher Education*. Retrieved from http://www.chronicle.com/article/Under-Fire-From-Lawmakers-a/235332

Cray, A., Miller, K., & Durso, L. (2013). *Seeking shelter: The experiences and unmet needs of LGBT homeless youth*. Retrieved from Center for American Progress website: https://www.americanprogress.org/wp-content/uploads/2013/09/LGBTHomelessYouth.pdf

Denson, N., & Chang, M. J. (2009). Racial diversity matters: The impact of diversity-related student engagement and institutional context. *American Educational Research Journal, 46*(2), 322–353.

Federal Bureau of Investigation. (2015). *Preliminary semiannual uniform crime report*. Hate Crimes Statistics Report. Uniform Crime Reporting Program. Washington, DC: U.S. Government Printing Office. Retrieved from https://ucr.fbi.gov/crime-in-the-u.s/2015/preliminary-semiannual-uniform-crime-report-januaryjune-2015/home

Fischer, B. (2016). It is not possible for homosexual behavior to be a constitutional or moral or ethical or legal right. July 28, 2016, 11:05 am. *Focal Point Radio*. Tupelo, MS: American Family Radio.

Gates, G. J. (2014, August 25). LGBT Americans report lower well-being. *Gallup well-being*. Washington, DC: Gallup, Inc. Retrieved from http://www.gallup.com/poll/175418/lgbt-americans-report-lower.aspx

Grant, J. M., Mottet, L. A., & Tanis, J. (2012). *Injustice at every turn: A report of the national transgender discrimination survey*. Washington, DC: National Center for Transgender Equality and National Gay and Lesbian Task Force. Retrieved from http://www.thetaskforce.org/static_html/downloads/reports/reports/ntds_full.pdf

Grover, D. (2015, October 1). Opinion: Students should speak up to prevent hate crimes. *GW Hatchet*. Retrieved from http://www.gwhatchet.com/2015/10/01/dan-grover-students-should-speak-up-to-prevent-hate-crimes/

Hill, C., & Silva, E. (2009). *Drawing the line: Sexual harassment on campus*. American Association of University Women Educational Foundation. Washington, DC Retrieved from ERIC database (ED489850).

Hitt, J. (2016, June 12). President Hitt: UCF stands with Orlando against terror. *College and Campus News*. University of Central Florida. Retrieved from http://today.ucf.edu/ucf-stands-with-orlando-against-terror/

The Human Rights Campaign. (2016). *Preview 2016. Pro-equality and anti-LGBT state and local legislation*. Retrieved from http://hrc-assets.s3-website-us-east-1.amazonaws.com//files/assets/resources/2016_Legislative-Doc.pdf

Institute of Medicine of the National Academies. (2011, March 31). *The health of lesbian, gay, bisexual, and transgender people: Building a foundation for better understanding*. Report No. RA564.9.H65H44 2011. Washington, DC: National Academies Press.

Kann L., Olsen E. O., McManus, T., Harris, W.A., Shanklin, S.L., Flint, K.H., ... Zaza, S. (2015, August 12). Sexual identity, sex or sexual contacts, and health-related behaviors among students in grades 9–12—United States and selected sites, 2015. *Morbidity and Mortality Weekly Report: Surveillance Summaries, 65*(9), 1–202. Centers for Disease Control. doi:10.15585/mmwr.ss6509a1

Knapp, S. (2016, July 12). Message from President Knapp. *GW Today*, p. 1. Retrieved from https://gwtoday.gwu.edu/message-president-knapp

Lambda Legal. (2010). *When health care isn't caring: Lambda legal's survey of discrimination against LGBT people and people with HIV*. New York, NY: Lambda Legal. Retrieved from http://data.lambdalegal.org/publications/downloads/whcic-report_when-health-care-isnt-caring.pdf

Lawrence, K., & Keleher, T. (2004). Chronic disparity: Strong and pervasive evidence of racial inequalities: Poverty outcomes and structural racism. In Race and Public Policy Conference. University of California, Berkeley, CA.

Mullins, D. (2013, October 30). In epidemic of campus sex crimes, LGBT cases often neglected. *Aljazeera America*. Retrieved from http://america.aljazeera.com/articles/2013/10/30/sexual-assault-ahiddenissueamonglbgtcommunity.html

National Alliance on Mental Illness. (2016). *How do mental health conditions affect the LGBTQ community?* Alexandria, VA: NAMI. Retrieved from http://www.nami.org/Find-Support/LGBTQ

Peligri, J. (2014, October 22). GWU police officer regrets not reporting hate crimes. *Washington Blade*. Retrieved from http://www.washingtonblade.com/2014/10/22/gwu-police-officer-regrets-reporting-hate-crimes/

Quiroz-Martínez, J., HoSang, D., & Villarosa, L. (2004). *Changing the rules of the game: Youth development & structural racism*. Washington, DC: Philanthropic Initiative for Racial Equity.

Rego-Craft, Z. (2014). *Suggested best practices for supporting trans students.* New York, NY: Consortium of Higher Education. Retrieved from https://lgbtcampus.memberclicks.net/assets/trans%20student%20inclusion%20.pdf

Ruteere, M. (2013, June 14). *Quality education can help prevent racism and xenophobia.* Remarks by the Special Rapporteur. Retrieved from the United Nations Human Rights Council (Geneva) website: http://www.un.org/apps/news/story.asp?NewsID=45174#.VMuDDmUo6Ul

Ryan, C., Huebner, D., Diaz, R. M., & Sanchez, J. (2009, January). Family rejection as a predictor of negative health outcomes in white and Latino lesbian, gay, and bisexual young adults. *Pediatrics, 123*(1), 346–352.

Sanders, A. R., Martin, E. R., Beecham, G.W., Guo, S., Dawood, K., Rieger, G., … Bailey, J. M. (2015). Genome-wide scan demonstrates significant linkage for male sexual orientation. *Psychological Medicine, 45*(7), 1379–1388. doi:10.1017/S0033291714002451

Sears, B., & Mallory, C. (2015 October). *Gender identity and sexual orientation discrimination in the workplace: A practical guide.* Arlington, VA: The Williams Institute. Retrieved from http://williamsinstitute.law.ucla.edu/research/workplace/gender-identity-and-sexual-orientation-discrimination-in-the-workplace-a-practical-guide/

Sette, M. (2013, February 4). New question considered for LGBT law applicants. *GW Hatchet.* Washington, DC: The George Washington University.

Sheridan, V. (2015, April 27). For tough topics like race, students share experiences on social media. *GW Hatchet.* Washington, DC: The George Washington University.

Stead, V. (2015). A call to action. In V. Stead (Ed.), *The Education Doctorate (Ed.D.): Issues of access, diversity, social justice, and community leadership* (pp. 1–3). (Equity in Higher Education Theory, Policy, and Praxis). Oxford: Peter Lang.

Steinhardt, R. (2015, October 21). New sexual assault prevention and response training wraps up. *GW Today.* Washington, DC: The George Washington University.

Sue, D. W. (2010). *Microaggressions in everyday life: Race, gender, and sexual orientation.* Hoboken, NJ: John Wiley & Sons.

Sue, D. W. (2015). *Race talk and the conspiracy of silence: Understanding and facilitating difficult dialogues on race.* Hoboken, NJ: Wiley.

Supiano, B. (2016, June 14). Orlando's colleges offer solace in the wake of tragedy. *Chronicle of Higher Education.* Retrieved from http://www.chronicle.com/article/orlandos-colleges-offer/236792

U.S. Department of Justice. (2001). *Hate crimes on campus: The problems and efforts to confront it* (Report No. NCJ 187249). Center for the Prevention of Hate Violence. University of Southern Maine. Retrieved from https://www.ncjrs.gov/pdffiles1/bja/187249.pdf

U.S Department of Labor. (2014). *Advancing LGBT workplace rights.* Retrieved from https://www.dol.gov/asp/policy-development/lgbt-report.pdf

Vega, T. (2014, February 25). Colorblind notion aside, colleges grapple with racial tension. *The New York Times.* Retrieved from http://www.nytimes.com/2014/02/25/us/colorblind-notion-aside-colleges-grapple-with-racial-tension.html?_r=0

Witham, K., Malcom-Piqueux, L. E., Dowd, A. C., & Bensimon, E. M. (2015). *America's unmet promise: The imperative for equity in higher education.* Washington, DC: Association of American Colleges and Universities.

Zamudio-Suarez, F. (2016, May 20). Bill diverting funds from University of Tennessee. Diversity office becomes law. *Chronicle of Higher Education.* Retrieved from http://chronicle.com/blogs/ticker/bill-diverting-funds-from-u-of-tenn-diversity-office-becomes-law/111517

CHAPTER SIXTEEN

Beyond Safe Zones

Disruptive Strategies Towards LGBTQ Inclusion on Campus

PIETRO A. SASSO AND LAUREL PUCHNER

INTRODUCTION

The term LGBTQ refers to a range of gender and sexual minorities. Widespread calls for LGBTQ tolerance and inclusion on college campuses within the last biennium have led to a lot of progress in recent years in efforts to be inclusive of LGBTQ students, faculty, and staff. However, the reputation of higher education as slow to embrace change is based in reality, and while the lived experiences and narratives of LGBTQ students are often represented on today's campuses, this representation tends to be limited in scope and manner. Institutions need to work harder to support, embrace, and give voice to students who identify within the queer spectrum.

One reason for the limited effects of efforts to meet the needs of LGBTQ students is that these efforts tend to be limited to climate surveys and Safe Zone-type programs. While LGBTQ climate surveys and Safe Zone programs have made major contributions to the creation of safe spaces in colleges and to improvements in campus climates, such efforts generally do not achieve the outcomes necessary to fully address inclusion and equity. Recent years have seen a significant increase in the number of students who come to college with knowledge of their non-normative gender identity and/or sexual orientation (Kosciw, Greytak, Diaz, & Bartkiewicz, 2010; Macgillivray, 2007), and LGBTQ youth are currently less likely than in the past to feel compelled to hide their identities (Beemyn & Rankin, 2011).

However, while students feel more open and able to exercise their right to freedom of identity and expression, college and universities have simply authored additional layers of neoliberal policy that seek to inculcate or cocoon LGBTQ students with awareness weeks or other related programming to promote tolerance, rather than inclusion and acceptance. Instead of providing direct support for LGBTQ populations, SafeZone and inclusive policies speak to the shadow support of LGBTQ students, but this is merely a curtain. Beyond this veil is a historically underserved and marginalized subpopulation with distinctive developmental and identity needs.

In this chapter we begin with an overview of what research says about LGBTQ experiences on college campuses, followed by a description of typical approaches to LGBTQ inclusion on campuses, along with their shortcomings. We end with a discussion of ways for colleges and universities to address inclusivity that go beyond the traditional Safe Zone and campus climate-based approaches.

UNIVERSITY-RELATED CHALLENGES FOR LGBTQ INDIVIDUALS

Heterosexual and cis*gender (non-transgender) students have become more supportive of their LGBTQ peers in recent years. In 2011 the Higher Education Research Institute (2011) reported that two-thirds of first-year undergraduate students reported supporting same-sex marriage and more than three-fourths of respondents believed that gay men and women should be able to adopt children (Higher Education Research Institute, 2011). This marks a tremendous adjustment over a 30 year period, though it is far from sufficient.

Discrimination and Heterosexism

Research suggests that despite this positive trend toward openness and awareness of LGBTQ rights, LGBTQ students, staff, and faculty still must navigate heterosexist (the assumption that everyone is and/or should be heterosexual and that there are only two genders) and discriminatory environments. Rankin, Weber, Blumenfeld, and Frazer (2010) conducted one of the first national studies of campus climate, involving more than 5,000 LGBTQ students, staff, and faculty. As part of their extensive set of findings, they found that one-quarter of LGBTQ respondents and one-third of trans-identified respondents had experienced harassment or violence on their college campus because of their sexual or gender identity. They also found that 44% of gay male students, 52% of bisexual and lesbian students, 55% of transfeminine students, and 65% of transmasculine students did not come out at times because of a fear of negative reprisal or evaluation.

As can be seen in the aforementioned statistics, transgender students experience more discrimination and oppression than cis*gender gay and heterosexual students. This is corroborated by a study conducted by the National Center for Transgender Equality (NCTE) which found that harassment among transgender and gender non-conforming students was so severe that it led almost one-sixth of respondents to leave their schools (Grant, Mottet, & Tanis, 2011).

Other domains within higher education that are of particular concern are athletics and Greek life (Rankin & Merson, 2012; Rankin et al., 2011). One study of five Division I institutions found significant levels of heterosexist and homophobic attitudes held by student athletes, coaches, and athletic administrators (Wolf-Wendel, Toma, & Morphew, 2001). The study examined attitudes towards a variety of types of diversity and it was noted by the researchers that, "questions about sexual orientation brought about the most highly charged responses" (Wolf-Wendel et al., 2001, p. 467). Many study participants denied that LGBTQ individuals were members of their teams or expressed negative reactions to the idea of having LGBTQ team members. Research on fraternities and sororities show more positive experiences for fraternity members in recent years than in the past, but still find harassment as part of the Greek experience for LGBTQ students (Rankin, 2007; Rankin, Weber, & Hesp, 2013).

Heterosexism and homophobia are also problems in classrooms and other academic spaces. *Explicit marginalization* occurs when students receive overt or direct homophobic messages. An example might be a classroom where a nursing faculty member explicitly states that "gay health issues" will not be address in the course because that is for another professor to discuss (Connolly, 2000; DeSurra & Church, 1994). Importantly, a classroom climate does not have to be overtly hostile to affect learning. An accumulation of subtle forms of marginalization, including the presence of microaggressions, can create what is sometimes called a *chilly* classroom climate and can have a profound negative impact on learning (Ambrose, Bridges, DiPietro, Lovett, & Norman, 2010; Hall & Sandler, 1984).

Exposure to subtle and indirect homophobic messages is sometimes called *implicit marginalization*, such as when, for example, a faculty member in an introductory public health course states that all gay health related concerns will be addressed through an overview of the HIV/AIDS epidemic. Other examples include heterosexist language (for example, use of language that assumes that all males have female romantic partners) and an absence of classroom discussion of or acknowledgement of non-normative sexual and gender identities.

Chilly climates exist partly because addressing gender and sexuality still present significant challenges for faculty and students in the shared space of the collegiate classroom, either when LGBTQ issues are the intended focus within a course or when they arise in the midst of unrelated course dialogue. This leads to classroom environments in which LGBTQ college students are often afraid to disclose their sexual and gender identity, and often feel "invisible" and "silenced" as they realize their experiences are not reflected in coursework or classroom dialogue (Ellsworth, 1989; Evans, 2000; Gortmaker & Brown, 2006; Lopez & Chims, 1993; Rankin, 2003; Renn, 2000).

Mental and Physical Health

Social environments that are heterosexist and characterized by negative attitudes, prejudice, and discrimination have significant negative implications for identity development and for the mental and physical health of LGBTQ populations (DiPlacido, 1998; Reed, Prado, Matsumoto, & Amaro, 2010; Silverschanz, Cortina, Konik, & Magley, 2007; Waldo, Hessen-McInnis, & D'Augelli, 1998; Woodford, Krentzman, & Gattis, 2012). Making matters worse, an unwelcoming campus environment acts as a barrier to supportive resources and support-seeking behaviors (D'Augelli & Rose, 1990).

One adverse mental health outcome resulting from the increased levels of psychological distress placed on LGBTQ individuals is alcohol and drug use/abuse (Cabaj, 2000; Flowers & Buston, 2001; Weber, 2008). Binge drinking has been found to be more prevalent among LGBTQ college students than their heterosexual peers (DeBord, Wood, Sher, & Good, 1998), and LGBTQ college students who experience and witness incivility and hostility are more likely to use drugs and alcohol than those who do not (McCabe, Bostwick, Hughes, West, & Boyd, 2010; Weber, 2008; Woodford et al., 2012)

Foremost in the minds of most higher education professionals is the significant risk of suicidality, particularly among gay men and specifically related to levels of depression (Wolf-Wendel et al., 2001). LGBTQ students have been found to be more depressed, isolated, and lonely compared to heterosexual students (Westefeld, Maples, Buford, & Taylor, 2001). Results from the National Longitudinal Study of Adolescent Health (NLSAH) suggest that LGBTQ adolescents were at an increased risk for depressive symptoms and suicidality compared to their heterosexual peers due to victimization (Galliher, Rostosky, & Hughes, 2004; Russell & Joyner, 2001; Silenzio, Pena, Duberstein, Cerel, & Knox, 2007).

TYPICAL UNIVERSITY APPROACHES TO CREATION OF AN INCLUSIVE INSTITUTION

The lack of continued examination of best practices beyond probing for perceptions of feeling supported by LGBTQ students or grassroots coalition networks lead by dedicated faculty and staff, continues to hamper efforts to institutionalize equity. The two main approaches to creating more positive and safe environments on college campuses are climate surveys and safe zone/safe space efforts. While a campus climate survey is often used to inform safe zone programming, these efforts are simply exiguous.

Campus Climate Evaluation

Campus climate, or the extent to which people feel respected, valued, and included on campus, matters for student learning, and the extent to which a climate is positive varies according to group. For example, a climate can be more positive for men than for women (Ballard, Bartle, & Masquesmay, 2008). The idea of positive versus negative campus climates arose in the early 1980s and was applied to race and gender as well as sexual orientation (Renn, 2010). LGBTQ campus climate research soon followed, with the goals of increasing visibility of LGBTQ students and sending a message that LGBTQ students deserved a good education like all other students. This research along with research on lesbian, gay, and bisexual student identities and experiences throughout the 1990s helped spur the inclusion of sexual orientation and gender identity in higher education anti-discrimination policies and the development of LGBTQ programming on the part of student affairs personnel (Renn, 2010). Such research has continued into the 2000s (c.f., Brown, Clarke, Gortmaker, & Robinson-Keilig, 2004; Ellis, 2009), and includes the 2010 State of Higher Education for Lesbian, Gay, Bisexual and Transgender People, referred to earlier, which provided results of a large and comprehensive multi-institutional study of campus climate for LGBTQ students (Rankin et al., 2010).

In 2003, the Council for the Advancement of Standards in Higher Education published a set of standards for policies and practices related to meeting the needs of LGBTQ students on college campuses (Council for the Advancement of Standards in Higher Education, 2003; Lipka, 2011). Then in 2007, Campus Pride, a non-profit LGBTQ advocacy group, created the Campus Pride Index. This index is a similar set of national standards for identifying an LGBTQ-friendly campus, and comes in the form of a tool that colleges and universities can use for self-assessment of policies, practices, and programs related to LGBTQ student inclusion (https:www.campusprideindex.org).

The tool contains 54 questions that fit into eight different factors pertaining to issues such as LGBTQ policy inclusion, LGBTQ campus safety, academic life, housing, and other areas. Questions include items asking, for example, whether the institution has an LGBTQ alumni group and whether they offer students the option of being matched with an LGBTQ-friendly roommate (Lipka, 2011). Based on the results an institution receives a zero to five star score.

Safe Zone Programs

One common means of remediating negative campus climates for LGBTQ students is the development of safe spaces or implementation of a Safe Zone program. Safe Zone programs are focused on developing allies who want to aid in stopping oppression of LGBTQ individuals (Ballard et al., 2008; Finkel, Storaasli, Bandele, & Schaefer, 2003). Sometimes run by professional staff, sometimes by faculty and sometimes by student groups, these predominantly university-based programs usually offer LGBTQ awareness training and stickers with a symbol indicating a positive LGBTQ stance for allies to post in their workspaces signaling the presence of a "safe zone" for LGBTQ individuals (Poynter & Tubbs, 2008).

Other common elements of these programs are a training manual, social events, and objects, such as pens, t-shirts, and key chains that are identified through symbols or writing as being affiliated with the Safe Zone program (Poynter & Tubbs, 2008). Sometimes Safe Zones offer the stickers to anyone who wants them, and other times stickers are contingent on participation in a training session (Ballard et al., 2008). In any case the focus is on public identification of such allies so that LGBTQ youth recognize the presence of allies and to encourage others on campus to become allies (Poynter & Tubbs, 2008).

Safe Zone programs and campus climate surveys and indexes have helped bring about significant positive changes to the college experiences of LGBTQ students, though the effect has been greater for lesbian, gay, and bisexual students than for transgender students (Ballard et al., 2008; Renn, 2010). Many higher education institutions have instituted policy changes, allotted money, and developed LGBTQ resource centers. However, some educators point to limitations to these approaches. The Campus Climate Index "measures services, not sensitivities" (Council for the Advancement of Standards in Higher Education, 2003; Lipka, 2011), and at some institutions it is completed by administrators whose focus is more on improving the image of the institution as opposed to the actual climate. On a practical level, policies only work when problems are brought to the level of a grievance, and are not helpful for every day, mundane types of climate problems (Ellis, 2009).

Safe Zone trainings are usually voluntary, which means there is a tendency for such programs to "preach to the choir," so to speak, without reaching the students, faculty, and staff who are most in need of awareness and sensitivity training (Ellis, 2009). The fact that so many who attend Safe Zone trainings already have a relatively high level of awareness might explain why one study found that 63% of faculty and staff who had attended training reported that their attitude had not changed and participants in general reported that their knowledge increased by a very small amount only (Ballard et al., 2008).

Research demonstrates that microaggressions, such as use of the expression "that's so gay," have a large impact on the experience of LGBTQ individuals, and may be relatively immune to Safe Zone training, especially since research indicates that use of this expression is not necessarily associated with strong anti-gay beliefs or feelings (Woodford, Howell, Kulick, & Silverschanz, 2013). Questionable, as well, is whether Safe Zone programs actually provide safe spaces: a majority of students in one study reported that they did not feel any safer near an office with a Safe Zone sticker than they did in other campus sites, and some had seen vandalized stickers (Ballard et al., 2008).

Beyond the Common Focus

In the context of research, Renn (2010) has called for a need to move "beyond the common focus on creating transfriendly facilities, locker rooms, and residence halls" (p. 136). Ellis (2009) calls for focusing more on non-LGBTQ students who are causing the problems, less on attitudinal change, and more on the wider social context. As alluded to earlier, higher education, like K-12 schools, is structured around heterosexism (Mayo, 2014; Renn, 2010). Renn calls for queering the structural assumptions around which higher education is organized, by changing how gender, sexuality, and identity are conceptualized and how these conceptualizations are embedded in institutional structures. This cannot be done via climate studies, climate indexes, or policy change.

The limitations of Safe Zone programs and climate surveys are especially clear when it comes to genderism and oppression of transgender individuals. The Campus Pride Climate Index (2016) is relatively inclusive of trans-identified needs, but actual change to meet the needs of transgender students has been slow. Only in the last few years have some institutions allowed students to use preferred names and pronouns on student records (Landecker, 2016). Some efforts, including Safe Zone trainings, often use the LGBTQ moniker, with that T included, even though they actually only address LGBTQ issues (Marine & Catalano, 2015).

More importantly, the dominant view of biological sex as unchangeable and dichotomous holds extreme social importance, meaning that the disruption caused by the existence and/or presence of transgender individuals is strong, leading to more overt hostile discrimination than that experienced by cis*gender LGBTQ individuals (Marine & Catalano, 2015). Genderism, or "cultural enforcement of a rigid masculine/feminine gender binary," is pervasive (Nicolazzo, 2016, 539). One can include sexual identity in the anti-discrimination policy of an institution, but "genderism and transphobia … are omnipresent forms of violence that continually reify the gender binary through social discourses and practices" (Nicolazzo, 2016, p. 540).

BEYOND CAMPUS CLIMATE AND SAFE ZONES: STRATEGIES AND IMPLICATIONS FOR PRACTICE

Safe Zone and Campus Climate approaches have helped to improve the college experience of LGBTQ students in important ways. For example, many colleges and universities have developed more inclusive policies (e.g., equal opportunity statements, extending same-sex benefits to partners) and/or created resources (e.g., LGBTQ centers, health care for transitioning transgender students) (Biegel & Kuehl, 2010; Rankin et al., 2010; Zemsky & Sanlo, 2005). However, higher education institutions still have significant capacity for improvement, especially in terms of systemic change. We have divided our suggested approaches to campus change into three interrelated categories. The first set of changes involves facilitating the typical Safe Zone and campus climate approaches better. This means filling in certain important gaps in programming geared toward addressing LGBTQ students' needs, especially with respect to trans-identified students. The second approach is to focus on intersectionality by decreasing class, racial, and all forms of segregation and marginalization on campuses. The third is focusing on transforming campus structures to breakdown gender and sexuality binaries—in other words, "queering higher education" (Renn, 2010, p. 132).

Filling in the Climate and Safety Gaps

Campus Climate and Safe Zone approaches fill important needs, but are typically limited in scope. One important area of need that is commonly not addressed is student help with the coming out process and its aftermath (Stewart & Howard-Hamilton, 2015). College is often an awakening for students in terms of sexual and gender identity, and the presence of openly gay role models (residence hall and student affairs staff, faculty) and a generally supportive environment can be very helpful (Evans & Broido, 1999). Further, declaring that one is different from the norm, in terms of gender or sexuality, is an initial step in the coming out process, but the challenges go beyond that. For example, as part of their identity development, LGBTQ students begin to recognize that dominant life scripts will not work for them, and many will need help in reframing life goals and relationship goal, especially with regard to informing parents and other relatives and friends that the traditional nuclear family option is not part considered within their life goals (Stewart & Howard-Hamilton, 2015). Public celebration of romantic relationships is more difficult, including small tasks like finding an appropriate Valentine's Day card (Stewart & Howard-Hamilton, 2015).

Choosing a major and committing to a career path may be more daunting for the LGBTQ student (Tomlinson & Fassinger, 2003), and some LGBTQ students who experience a negative campus climate may be fearful of using campus resources such as academic advising or the career center (Tomlinson & Fassinger, 2003). Thus, universities need to make efforts to create the perception that academic advising and other campus resources are LGBTQ-friendly. And in addition to intentionally and openly hiring LGBTQ student affairs professionals, institutions should provide professional development for faculty and staff in the area of LGBTQ support.

Another common gap in LGBTQ programming is provision of sexuality information specifically tailored to LGBTQ individuals, including transgender students (Mayo, 2014). Obviously any course that addresses sexuality should critically analyze the sexuality information it is providing and make sure it is providing information for all students. However, because not everyone takes courses that include sexuality and because sexuality needs of heterosexual cis*gender individuals are much more likely to be provided through general societal means, specific programming efforts need to be made for providing sexuality education and information for LGBTQ students (Mayo, 2014).

The final gap in typical Safe Zone approaches that we will highlight is attention to transmasculine and transfeminine issues. Transgender oppression tends to be more overt than LGBTQ oppression, but attention to trans-oppression and to transgender awareness is much lower than attention to LGBTQ oppression. As indicated earlier, one reason for this is the strength of genderism (belief in a strict separation between genders and in dichotomous genders) and transphobia (Marine & Catalano, 2015; Nicolazzo, 2016). Trans individuals disrupt the male-female binary and the traditionally accepted triadic connection between gender roles, gender identity, and biological sex. Biological sex, even more than sexual orientation or gender roles, is falsely considered discrete and unchangeable. The gender binary is socially extremely important, and the disruption to this binary brought by transgender individuals leads to extreme fear, hatred, and discomfort on the part of the public (Marine & Catalano, 2015; Nicolazzo, 2016). Another reason less attention is paid is because the numbers of transgender students are lower than the numbers of LGBTQ students. Thus, compared to LGBTQ issues, the literature is limited, though this is improving.

The Campus Climate Index, for example, does include quite a few criteria related to meeting the needs of transgender individuals. However, athletics and classrooms are not adequately addressed by such criteria (Beemyn & Rankin, 2016). Safe Zone-provided LGBTQ awareness training, as indicated earlier, often fails to include information about transgender challenges, and this information is needed to counteract commonly held false beliefs about transgender individuals. For example, many believe that being transgender necessarily means moving from one discrete gender to another, with the end goal of becoming the other gender through surgery, even though trans identity includes many more options than that (Park, 2016).

Counseling and health services preparedness for transgender issues for students is often lacking, and residence halls often handle trans issues on a case by case basis without intentionality, which leads to individuals experiencing microaggressions and feelings of exclusion. It is found that staff bungle their way through the process of getting students the services they need and a lack of support and active hostility were described as factors that discouraged "coming out" (Evans & Broido, 1999; Marine & Catalano, 2015). Even in LGBTQ majors there are few courses on transgender issues compared to those on LGBTQ issues, and a lack of transgender instructors. Institutions need to hire transgender faculty and encourage and support more research and study advocating for transgender causes (Park, 2016).

Intersectionality

The second category of approaches to improving college life for LGBTQ individuals involves attending to other oppressions, for several reasons and in several different ways (Mayo, 2014). In discussing school settings, but no less applicable to post-secondary, Mayo (2014) points out that classism, racism, sexism, and ableism affect the experiences of LGBTQ individuals because they overlap with the experience of being queer for many and thus have an important impact on their experiences (Mayo, 2014; Stewart & Howard-Hamilton, 2015). Thinking about intersectionality, or the ways that individuals are shaped by multiple identities, is essential.

The discrimination experienced by someone who is gay and African American and female, for example, cannot be understood in additive terms of homophobia plus racism plus sexism, because the intersection of different identities creates a completely different experience. For example, homophobia is different for a woman than for a man, and sexism is different for a lesbian than for a heterosexual woman; LGBTQ students of color experience more violence than white LGBTQ students (Mayo, 2014). Additionally, negative campus climate might make a lesbian's identity more salient, which then may lead her to be fearful of using campus resources such as academic advising or the career center (Tomlinson & Fassinger, 2003).

Also, experiencing the practice of oppression does not mean that one understands other forms. LGBTQ students of color sometimes do not attend programs aimed at LGBTQ students because of racism of white LGBTQ students. So, to improve the lives of LGBTQ students, LGBTQ programming needs to integrate education about racism, ableism, classism, sexism into Safe Zone and other campus programming. Paying attention to intersectionality also includes desegregating the institution through anti-sexist initiatives such as hiring more male secretaries, more female electrical engineering and computer science faculty members, and additional faculty of color in general.

Queering Higher Education

The third category of approaches for meeting the needs of LGBTQ students, faculty, and staff on college campuses involves what Renn (2010) calls *queering higher education*. Queer theory is a set of approaches to thinking about sexuality and gender that question normative assumptions (Stewart & Howard-Hamilton, 2015). For example, queer theory sees sexuality, gender, and gender expression as fluid as opposed to fixed, and gender identity as a process rather than a noun. Queer theory also challenges assumptions about normality and questions labels (Stewart & Howard-Hamilton, 2015).

Queering higher education involves shifting the way we look at gender and sexuality and identity, and moving away from normative binaries in terms of students, leaders, organizations, governance, policies, and teaching. It also means creating structures that look at gender as process, that do not pit one gender against the other, and that minimize the distinction between and among genders (Mayo, 2014; Renn, 2010). Renn argues further that this breaking down of binaries should move beyond issues directly related to LGBTQ individuals (male-female, gay-straight, transgender, cis*gender) and extend to breaking down multiple normative binaries, such as instructor-student, administrator-faculty, research-practice, and others.

One important area for disrupting heteronormativity is the curriculum. Providing more courses related to queer studies is helpful, but queering the institution requires going much farther and paying attention to the fact that virtually all curricula are built on dominant ideas about gender and gender identity and sexual orientation, with LGBTQ issues tending to be simply an add-on in certain subjects (Mayo, 2014). One of many ways to disrupt the dominant discourse is discussion of the social construction of gender and of gender as process (Mayo, 2014; Renn, 2010). Another is "critical interrogation of masculinity" (Woodford et al., 2013, p. 431), focused on decreasing male student discomfort around gender noncomformity; this discomfort, of course, is derived from reactions males have received all of their lives for deviating from gender norms.

Another potential mode of disruption is via discussion of intersex people (those who have both male and female genital, gonadal, and/or chromosomal sex traits). People who are intersex disrupt binary thinking about sex in many of the same ways that transgender individuals do. In one interesting study Davis, Dewey, and Murphy (2016) show how medical providers who treat intersex people and those who serve trans people generally do not perceive it possible that a healthy gender identity could exist in a gender variant person, and that in the process of trying to make people conform to society's expectations of the alignment between biology and identity, they pathologize "bodily variance" (495).

Encouraging disruptions of sexuality among faculty and staff is yet another strategy. Speaking in terms of K-12 education, Mayo suggests that "heterosexual teachers ... queer themselves" (p. 71), by which she means all instructors need to create disruptions in heteronormative and gendernormative schema. Small disruptions include referring to gay women and their wives, and using nonheterosexist language. Getting heterosexual teachers to queer themselves also involves getting instructors to think about their sexuality as a part of their pedagogy—heterosexual teachers tend to embody straightness, and in doing so they are reinforcing heteronormativity to students (Mayo, 2014, p. 29).

Disruptions to heteronormativity need to occur outside of the regular classroom as well. Safe Zone awareness trainings, as with much LGBTQ programming, tend to use what Mayo calls "anti-bias" pedagogies, dealing with harassment and bias, and not with deeper disruptions of heteronormativity. The trouble with anti-bias pedagogies is that it makes it seem like individual acts of bias are the problem as opposed to the entire system of oppression. This type of approach also reinforces differences between LGBTQ individuals and others, instead of working to erode the binaries and binary thinking (Mayo, 2014). Returning to some of the issues discussed pertaining to intersectionality, above, institutions also need to keep in mind that LGBTQ individuals, although in some cases more critical about binaries than cis*gender straight people, generally do not themselves know a lot about the problematic nature of binaries and heteronormativity (Mayo, 2014).

Another important aspect of queering the college curriculum entails focusing on what Mayo (2014) refers to as "queer relationalities." These are the ways in which homophobia, heterosexism, genderism, sexism, heteronormativity and transphobia negatively affect everyone's experiences in ways seldom recognized, such that the experience of oppression is shared more than most realize. We are all disadvantaged in many ways by living in a culture that simplifies masculinity, femininity, gender, and sexuality, and highlighting and discussing these is a good way to break down barriers between categories such as gay-straight-transgender-cis*gender. One way in which shared oppression occurs is with cis*gender, straight, family members of gay and transgender individuals.

Another instance occurs when our heterosexual children are victims of homophobic bullying. Third, a lot of "heterosexual" social interaction is infused with same-sex desire and with worries about homophobia and transphobia, such that "Heteronormativity is as fractured and riddled with anxiety as any other dominant social formation" (Mayo, 2014, p. 48). Essentially, we all transgress norms, and everyone at some point is a victim of dominant messages about sexuality and gender, as gender normative social policing leads to negative experiences for all. Experiences are of course generally much worse for those who do not conform to dominant norms, but it is important to identify, recognize, and discuss how negative these norms are for all.

As part of an effort to queer relationalities, educators should help everyone question their own current desires, and to ask the question of to what extent the dominant and limiting messages about gender and sexuality that we grew up with have influenced and altered them (Mayo, 2014). One specific aspect of heteronormativity that queering relationalities reveals, for example, is the double standard around sexualization (Mayo, 2014). Many people mistakenly believe that talking about LGBTQ issues means talking about sex, which often makes them uncomfortable.

What needs attention is how much of gendernormative social life is also about sexuality, even though it is not recognized as such, because sexualisation is often recognized only in non-normative contexts. A prime example of sexualizing something that is not sexual occurs when some worry that if transgender individuals are allowed to use certain bathrooms they will engage in unwarranted sexual encounters with others. Conversely, within the gendernormative realm, others often do not see sexuality when it is present. So, for example, few question whether it is appropriate to hold events such as proms or fraternity parties, even though the probability for sexual assault or unwanted sexual advances are quite high with such events (Mayo, 2014). This presents a double standard of "sexualization of space" for trans students (Tillapaugh, 2016).

CONCLUSION

In this chapter we have provided a variety of strategies for going beyond typical current approaches to meeting the needs of LGBTQ students, faculty, and staff in higher education. These approaches are not exhaustive, and some are easier to implement than others, given current societal structures. Importantly, working on these strategies involves recognizing, accepting, and addressing an inherent tension between disrupting and dissolving binaries, necessary for systemic and structural change, while at the same time working within these socially real binaries.

In other words, we need to focus on differences between the triadic social constructs of gender, sex, and sexualities in order to address certain problems, even as we attempt to eliminate the binary thinking that creates the dichotomies to begin with. For example, to counteract homophobia, we need to provide safe spaces for members of oppressed groups, which involves segregation, even as we try to have inclusive dialogues showing how genderism and homophobia impact everyone. Also, as indicated earlier, to counter sexism, institutions should hire more male secretaries and more female computer scientists, even though doing so places a genderist focus on the distinction between male and female. The hope is that coming at the problem from both ends might eventually lead to a meeting in the middle, whereby sexism is gradually diminished as distinctions between genders are gradually eroded. Power structures and the political forces that accompany them may never allow this ideal to be reached. A lot of progress has been made in the last half-century, and that should make us optimistic about continuing the fight.

REFERENCES

Ambrose, S. A., Bridges, M. W., DiPietro, M., Lovett, M. C., & Norman, M. K. (2010). *How learning works: Seven research-based principles for smart teaching.* San Francisco, CA: John Wiley & Sons.

Ballard, S. L., Bartle, E., & Masequesmay, G. (2008). Finding queer allies: The impact of ally training and safe zone stickers on campus climate. *Online Submission.*

Beemyn, G., & Rankin, S. (2011). *Lives of transgender people.* New York, NY: Columbia University Press.

Beemyn, G., & Rankin, S. R. (2016). Creating a gender-inclusive campus. In Martinez-San Miguel, Y. & Tobias, S. (Eds.), *Trans studies* (pp. 21–32). Rutgers, NJ: Rutgers University Press.

Biegel, S., & Kuehl, S. J. (2010). *Safe at school: Addressing the school environment and LGBT safety through policy and legislation.* A Report of the Great Lakes Center for Education Research and Practice, the National Education Policy Center, and the Williams Institute in the UCLA Law School. Retrieved from http://greatlakescenter.org, http://nepc.colorado.edu, and http://www.law.ucla.edu/williamsinstitute

Brown, R. D., Clarke, B., Gortmaker, V., & Robinson-Keilig, R. (2004). Assessing the campus climate for gay, lesbian, bisexual, and transgender (GLBT) students using a multiple perspectives approach. *Journal of College Student Development, 45*(1), 8–26.

Cabaj, R. P. (2000). Substance abuse, internalized homophobia, and gay men and lesbians: Psychodynamic issues and clinical implications. *Journal of Gay & Lesbian Psychotherapy, 3*(3–4), 5–24.

Campus Pride Index. (2016, November). Retrieved from https://www.campusprideindex.org/

Connolly, M. (2000). Issues for lesbian, gay, and bisexual students in traditional college classrooms. In V. Wall & N. J. Evans (Eds.), *Toward acceptance: Sexual orientation issues on campus* (pp. 109–130). Lanham, MD: University Press of America.

Council for the Advancement of Standards in Higher Education. (2003). *CAS professional standards for higher education* (5th ed.). Washington, DC: Author.

D'Augelli, A. R., & Rose, M. L. (1990). Homophobia in a university community: Attitudes and experiences of heterosexual freshman. *Journal of College Student Development, 31,* 484–491.

Davis, G., Dewey, J. M., & Murphy, E. L. (2016). Giving sex: Deconstructing intersex and trans medicalization practices. *Gender and Society, 30*(3), 490–514. doi:10.1177/0891243215602102

DeBord, K. A., Wood, P. K., Sher, K. J., & Good, G. E. (1998). The relevance of sexual orientation to substance abuse and psychological distress among college students. *Journal of College Student Development, 39*(2), 157–168.

Desurra, C. J., & Church, K.A. (1994, Nov.). *Unlocking the classroom closet: Privileging the marginalized voices of Gay/Lesbian college students.* Paper presented at the Annual Meeting of the Speech Communication Association (80th), New Orleans, LA.

DiPlacido, J. (1998). Minority stress among lesbians, gay men, and bisexuals: A consequence of heterosexism, homophobia, and stigmatization. In G. Herek (Ed.), *Stigma and Sexual Orientation* (pp. 138–159). Thousand Oaks, CA: Sage.

Ellis, S. J. (2009). Diversity and inclusivity at university: A survey of the experiences of Lesbian, Gay, Bisexual and Trans (LGBT) students in the UK. *Higher Education, 57,* 723–739. doi:10.1007/s10734-008-9172-y

Ellsworth, E. (1989). Why doesn't this feel empowering? Working through the repressive myths of critical pedagogy. *Harvard Educational Review, 59*, 297–324.

Evans, N. J. (2000). Creating a positive learning environment for gay, lesbian, and bisexual students. *New directions for teaching and learning, 2000*(82), 81–87.

Evans, N., & Broido, E. (1999). Coming out in college residence halls: Negotiation, meaning making, challenges, supports. *Journal of College Student Development, 40*, 658–668.

Finkel, M. J., Storaasli, R. D., Bandele, A., & Schaefer, V. (2003). Diversity training in graduate school: An exploratory evaluation of the Safe Zone project. *Professional Psychology: Research and Practice, 34*(5), 555–561.

Flowers, P., & Buston, K. (2001). "I was terrified of being different": Exploring gay men's accounts of growing-up in a heterosexist society. *Journal of Adolescence, 24*(1), 51–65.

Galliher, R. V., Rostosky, S. S., & Hughes, H. K. (2004). School belonging, self-esteem, and depressive symptoms in adolescents: An examination of sex, sexual attraction status, and urbanicity. *Journal of Youth and Adolescence, 33*(3), 235–245.

Gortmaker, V., & Brown, R. (2006). Out of the closet: Differences in perceptions and experiences among out lesbian and gay students. *College Student Journal, 40*, 606–619.

Grant, J. M., Mottet, L. A., & Tanis, J. (2011). Injustice at every turn: A report of the national transgender discrimination survey. Washington, DC: National Center for Transgender Equality and National Gay and Lesbian Task Force.

Hall, R. M., & Sandler, B. R. (1984). *Out of the classroom: A chilly campus climate for women?* A Guide from the Association of American Colleges Project on the Status and Education of Women. Washington, DC.

Higher Education Research Institute. (2011) Diverse learning environments: Assessing and creating conditions for student success. Retrieved August 15, 2010 from http://heri.ucla.edu/dle/index.php

Kosciw, J., Greytak, E., Diaz, E., & Bartkiewicz, M. (2010). The 2009 national school climate survey: The experiences of lesbian, gay, bisexual and transgender youth in our nation's schools. New York, NY: Gay, Lesbian and Straight Education Network.

Landecker, H. (2016). The week. *The Chronicle of Higher Education, 62*(41), A4.

Lipka, S. (2011). For gay students, more room on campuses. (Cover story). *The Chronicle of Higher Education, 57*(57), A1–A6.

Lopez, G., & Chims, N. (1993). Classroom concerns of gay and lesbian students: The invisible minority. *College Teaching, 41*(3), 97–103.

Macgillivray, I. K. (2007). Gay-straight alliances: A handbook for students, educators, and parents. New York, NY: Harrington Park Press.

Marine, S. B., & Catalano, D. C. J. (2015). Engaging trans* students on college and university campuses. In S. J. Quaye & S. R. Harper (Eds.), *Student engagement in higher education* (pp. 135–148). New York, NY: Routledge.

Mayo, C. (2014). *LGBTQ youth and education: Policies and practices*. New York, NY: Teachers College Press.

McCabe, S. E., Bostwick, W. B., Hughes, T. L., West, B. T., & Boyd, C. J. (2010). The relationship between discrimination and substance use disorders among lesbian, gay, and bisexual adults in the United States. *American Journal of Public Health, 100*(10), 1946–1952.

Nicolazzo, Z. (2016). "Just Go In Looking Good": The resilience, resistance, and kinship-building of trans* college students. *Journal of College Student Development, 57*(5), 538–556.

Park, P. (2016). Transgendering the academy: Insuring transgender inclusion in higher education. In Y. Martínez-San Miguel & S. Tobias (Eds.), *Trans studies: The challenge to hetero/homo normativities* (pp. 33–43). Rutgers, NJ: Rutgers University.

Poynter, K. J., & Tubbs, N. J. (2008). Safe zones. *Journal of LGBT Youth, 5*(1), 121–132.
Rankin, S. (2003). Campus climate for gay, lesbian, bisexual, and transgendered people: A national perspective. New York, NY: National Gay and Lesbian Task Force Policy Institute.
Rankin, S. (2007). Experiences of gay men in fraternities: From 1960 to 2007. Charlotte, NC: Lambda 10 Project.
Rankin, S., & Merson, D. (2012). *LGBTQ college athlete national report*. Charlotte, NC: Campus Pride.
Rankin, S., Merson, D., Sorgen, C., McHale, I., Loya, K., & Oseguera, L. (2011). *Student-Athlete Climate Study (SACS) final report*. University Park, PA: The Pennsylvania State University.
Rankin, S., Weber, G., Blumenfeld, W., & Frazer, S. (2010). *2010 State of higher education for lesbian, gay, bisexual & transgender people*. Charlotte, NC: Campus Pride.
Rankin, S., Weber, G., & Hesp, G. (2013). Experiences and perceptions of gay and bisexual fraternity members from 1960 to 2007: A cohort analysis. *Journal of College Student Development, 14*(5), 12–27.
Reed, E., Prado, G., Matsumoto, A., & Amaro, H. (2010). Alcohol and drug use and related consequences among gay, lesbian and bisexual college students: Role of experiencing violence, feeling safe on campus, and perceived stress. *Addictive Behaviors, 35*(2), 168–171.
Renn, K. A. (2000). Including all voices in the classroom: Teaching lesbian, gay, and bisexual students. *College Teaching, 48*, 129–135.
Renn, K. A. (2010). LGBTQ and queer research in higher education: The state and status of the field. *Educational Researcher, 39*(2), 10.
Russell, S. T., & Joyner, K. (2001). Adolescent sexual orientation and suicide risk: Evidence from a national study. *American Journal of Public Health, 91*(8), 1276–1281.
Silenzio, V. M., Pena, J. B., Duberstein, P. R., Cerel, J., & Knox, K. L. (2007). Sexual orientation and risk factors for suicidal ideation and suicide attempts among adolescents and young adults. *American Journal of Public Health, 97*(11), 2017–2019.
Silverschanz, P., Cortina, L., Konik, J., & Magley, V. (2007). Slurs, snubs, and queer jokes: Incidence and impact of heterosexist harassment in academia. *Sex Roles, 58*, 179–191.
Stewart, D., & Howard-Hamilton, M. F. (2015). Engaging lesbian, gay, bisexual students on college campuses. In S. J. Quaye & S. R. Harper (Eds.), *Student engagement in higher education* (pp. 121–134). New York, NY: Routledge.
Tillapaugh, D. W. (2016). Understanding sexual minority male students' meaning-making about their multiple identities: An exploratory study. *Canadian Journal of Higher Education, 46*(1), 91–108.
Tomlinson, M. J., & Fassinger, R. E. (2003). Career development, lesbian identity development, and campus climate among lesbian college students. *Journal of College Student Development, 44*(6), 845–860.
Waldo, C., Hessen-McInnis, M., & D'Augelli, A. R. (1998). Antecedents and consequences of victimization of lesbian, gay, and bisexual young people: A structural model comparing rural university and urban samples. *American Journal of Community Psychology, 26*(2), 307–334.
Weber, G. N. (2008). Using to numb the pain: Substance abuse and abuse among lesbian, gay, and bisexual individuals. *Journal of Mental Health Counseling, 30*, 31–48.
Westefeld, J. S., Maples, M. R., Buford, B., & Taylor, S. (2001). Gay, lesbian, and bisexual college students: The relationship between sexual orientation and depression, loneliness, and suicide. *Journal of College Student Psychotherapy, 15*(3), 71–82.
Wolf-Wendel, L., Toma, J. D., & Morphew, C. (2001). How much difference is too much difference? Perceptions of gay men and lesbians in intercollegiate athletics. *Journal of College Student Development, 42*(5), 465–479.

Woodford, M. R., Howell, M. L., Kulick, A., & Silverschanz, P. (2013). "That's So Gay!": Heterosexual male undergraduates and the perpetuation of sexual orientation microagressions on campus. *Journal of Interpersonal Violence, 28*(2), 416–435. doi:10.1177/0886260512454719

Woodford, M. R., Howell, M. L., Silverschanz, P., & Yu, L. (2012). "That's So Gay!": Examining the covariates of hearing this expression among gay, lesbian, and bisexual college students. *Journal of American College Health, 60*(6), 429–434.

Woodford, M. R., Krentzman, A. R., & Gattis, M. N. (2012). Alcohol and drug use among sexual minority college students and their heterosexual counterparts: The effects of experiencing and witnessing incivility and hostility on campus. *Substance Abuse and Rehabilitation, 3*, 11–23.

Zemsky, B., & Sanlo, R. L. (2005). Do policies matter? *New Directions for Student Services, 2005*(111), 7–15.

CHAPTER SEVENTEEN

Supporting Queer Survivors of Sexual Assault on Campus

NICOLE BEDERA AND KRISTJANE NORDMEYER

INTRODUCTION

During college, Ashley felt as if she had found her community in her campus' LGBT organization. As she told us:

> I felt like college was a really, really safe and welcoming place for me for the most part ... I had really found my niche of people. My main group was the LGBT club on campus and I just felt like they really got me. It was the first time in my life that I remember feeling like I could be my whole self with people and not worry about being judged.

Before long, Ashley had taken a leadership role in the club. She organized events and tried to help new members find the same comfort in the group that she had.

Ashley prioritized inclusion highly, even for members of the club she didn't necessarily like. One of those members was Hannah. Hannah had a tendency to be physically touchy with other members of the club and Ashley often felt as if Hannah disregarded her boundaries. Despite this discomfort, Ashley still regularly invited Hannah to events that she thought would interest her and made a point to smooth out difficulties in their relationship to protect the dynamic of the group. Ashley made no exception for an out-of-town conference that she thought Hannah would enjoy, even though they would need to share a hotel room. Hannah eagerly agreed to join the group and used her proximity to Ashley on the trip to make repeated sexual advances on her. At one point, Ashley woke up to Hannah trying to remove her bra and whispering her intentions to have sex with Ashley.

Once they returned from the trip, Hannah continued to badger Ashley about starting a romantic relationship. After repeated requests from Hannah, Ashley agreed to let Hannah come over so Ashley could make it clear that she had no romantic interest in her and so that they could establish firm boundaries in their relationship that would allow them both to comfortably stay in the same LGBT club. During this conversation, Hannah continued to pressure Ashley into sexual contact, including questioning the legitimacy of Ashley's pansexuality for refusing the advances of a transgender person. When Ashley continued to turn her down, Hannah raped her.

After the sexual assault, Ashley felt torn. She knew that she didn't want to see Hannah again, but she also wanted to keep her rape quiet. Ashley turned to a mentor on campus for advice, but the mentor neglected to mention that she had an obligation to report any act of sexual violence shared with her. Without Ashley's knowledge, their conversation became a preliminary investigation during which her mentor probed for details about the incident.

In this way, Ashley was forced into reporting her sexual assault to the campus authorities and her rape quickly became public. Because so many of her friends were involved with social justice organizations on campus, the lines between personal conversations and official evidence for the investigation became blurred. Ashley also felt forced to disclose her sexual assault to people who she would have otherwise not told, including her girlfriend who served on the student judiciary board that determined the legitimacy of sexual assault complaints. Despite her desire for privacy, her sexual assault had turned into a rumor among students and staff in social justice organizations.

In all of this turmoil, Ashley tried to advocate for herself. She knew that she didn't want to see Hannah anymore, so she asked leaders in the LGBT club to ensure they would never be in the same space. In response, Ashley was accused of violating the principles of inclusion that the club espoused and *she* was the one who stopped receiving invitations to events. Ashley internalized her exclusion. She felt that her critics were right in accusing her of trying to exclude a transgender person from one of the few spaces truly safe for them and so she didn't fight very hard for her space in the LGBT club. In contrast, Hannah ardently defended her right to the club and access to the people in it, even after admitting to the members of the club that she had raped Ashley. At times, Hannah resorted to coercive measures like threatening to commit suicide if people in the club distanced themselves from her. By the end of the school year, Hannah still had a stronghold in the club and Ashley only had one friend from the club left. To Ashley, her eviction from the LGBTQ community on campus and loss of her close friendships with other queer people was just as painful as the rape itself.

ACADEMIC SCHOLARSHIP ON LGBTQ SEXUAL VICTIMIZATION

Ashley is one of the respondents in an ongoing interview study on queer cisgender women's experiences with sexual violence in college. Sexual victimization rates among queer college women are alarmingly high (Cantor et al., 2015; Johnson, Matthew, & Napper, 2016; Krebs, Lindquist, Warner, Fisher, & Martin, 2007). In comparison to heterosexual women, lesbian and bisexual women are significantly more likely to be sexually assaulted both before and during college (Martin, Fisher, Warner, Krebs, & Lindquist, 2011). Despite its prevalence, both LGBTQ resource centers and victim advocacy offices commonly overlook the unique challenges faced by queer sexual assault victims in college, leaving them without the support they need for recovery.

The impact of this institutional blind spot is likely quite severe. Although there is little research on the effect of sexual trauma on LGBTQ college students, the academic literature on queer survivors of adult sexual trauma indicates that recovery from sexual maltreatment is especially arduous for LGBTQ women (Balsam, 2002). Studies directly comparing heterosexual sexual assault survivors with lesbian and bisexual survivors have found that both groups experience similar psychological distress as the result of sexual violence, including depression, daily stress, and increased alcohol use (Descamps, Rothblum, Bradford, Bradford, & Ryan, 2000). However, lesbian and bisexual survivors of sexual abuse may be particularly likely to struggle with eating disorders, anxiety disorders, and suicidal ideation, as indicated by comparative research on child sexual assault survivors (Roberts & Sorensen, 1999). Even the basic safety needs of queer survivors may not be met. Researchers have found that bisexual women are particularly likely to experience revictimization in comparison to heterosexual and lesbian survivors (Hequembourg, Livingston, & Parks, 2013). These disparities are likely intensified in part because queer survivors feel unwelcome in the communities that typically support LGBTQ people and sexual assault victims since few groups give ample attention to the intersection of queer and survivor identities (Balsam, 2002).

In the college environment, the stakes may be particularly high for queer survivors. At some schools, institutional policies that prohibit same-sex relationships have led to the expulsion of queer victims (see for example, Alberty, 2016). Hostile college environments may further traumatize survivors who remain on campus, many of whom are recently displaced from the support networks of their hometowns. While there is little research on LGBTQ survivors of college sexual assault, there is reason to believe that queer survivors face unique challenges in the college setting that will impact their recoveries.

Our study seeks to better understand the sexual violence perpetrated against lesbian, bisexual, and queer cisgender women on campus and the unique needs of these survivors. We interviewed lesbian, bisexual, and queer cisgender women who considered themselves college sexual assault survivors. To recruit respondents, we contacted organizations in a mountain west state that worked with either the LGBTQ community or survivors of sexual violence. Both the parameters of our study and our recruitment techniques require participants in our study to recognize their sexual assaults as acts of violence, feel secure in a queer identity, and be willing to share both of these marginalized identities with a team of researchers. For these reasons, our sample may be somewhat unique and will not contain the experiences of sexual violence victims or LGBTQ people who have not yet come to understand these respective identities. We also expanded our study from the original organizations and respondents using a snowball sampling method. Respondents received a $40 gift card for their participation. The study is ongoing.

During open-ended interviews, we asked respondents to recount their experiences with sexual violence, including a description of their college victimization(s), reflection on how their assault(s) affected them and their relationships to others, and discussion of any connection between their sexual assault(s) and their sexual identity. To maximize the respondents' control of the interviews and ability to recount traumatic experiences, they received the interview guide ahead of time. Throughout our discussion of the data from this study, we use pseudonyms to protect our respondents' confidentiality. We have also made small edits in our respondents' direct quotes for clarity such as removing filler words like "um" and "like."

In line with the emphasis of this volume, we focused our analysis on the treatment of queer sexual assault survivors by campus LGBTQ organizations and prominent members of campus LGBTQ communities. While there is a need for additional work on curbing sexual violence perpetrated against members of the LGBTQ community and advocating for LGBTQ survivors across campus, many of our respondents reported more immediately needing the support of their queer peers and mentors due to the intersectional nature of their sexual victimizations. Central to securing the safety and comfort of queer sexual assault survivors on campus is maintaining LGBTQ organizations and communities as safe spaces. For these reasons, we write with collegiate LGBTQ organizations in mind.

QUEER WOMEN'S EXPERIENCES

Like Ashley, most of the women in our sample felt that their sexual assaults were inextricably linked to their sexual identities. In many cases, they believed their sexual assaults were motivated by their sexual orientation.

Harm Caused by Student Members of the LGBTQ Campus Community

Most commonly, the women in our sample were informed by their assailants who commented on their sexual orientations in some way. For example, Ashley's rapist tried to coerce her into sex through suggesting a "real" pansexual person would never refuse sex with a transgender person. Another respondent's rapist confessed during criminal sentencing that he had targeted her because he had never had sex with a lesbian and thought it would be an exciting challenge. For these respondents, their sexual assaults were not merely acts of gender-based violence, but also hate crimes. To recover, they needed the support of people who understood both types of victimization.

Every respondent mentioned that the intersection of these two types of violence terrified them. They didn't just feel vulnerable due to their gender, but also because of their sexual orientations. One respondent, Zoe, told us in great detail about how after being sexually assaulted multiple times, she worried many people interpreted her bisexuality as consent to taboo sexual encounters. She said:

> The downfall to being a queer woman and an attractive queer woman ... is that there is this hot bi girl thing, like, "She's kinky." They strip me of my sexuality and instead make [me] this hot kinky thing. Like fetishized, like sexualized ... like [because] I'm bi, I must be into crazier shit or I must be willing to do more stuff ... I hate telling people that I'm bi because men think it's an attention thing where I'm trying to turn them on.

After her sexual assaults, Zoe feared disclosing her sexual orientation because she found her bisexuality so closely tied to men's expressions of entitlement to sexual contact with her. Even people who may have a positive reaction to her bisexuality felt threatening since they may have other veiled sexual intentions and have little or no regard for her consent. Zoe's sexual assaults introduced her to another way that bisexual women could be terrorized, even by people who appeared accepting or celebratory of queer sexual identities.

After a sexual assault, fear of both LGBT hate crimes and gender-based violence intensified if the respondent's assailant also belonged to the LGBTQ community. Ashley described the way her rapist's transgender identity made her feel particularly betrayed and weary of the community that once felt like her safe haven:

> Part of the reason why it felt so betraying that [Hannah] had done this to me is that I felt really safe with women—and at the time she identified as a woman and appeared to me as a woman [although she came out as trans soon afterward]. After the sexual assault, I felt myself really pulling away from masculine women and from masculine trans people and trans men and also just men.... It's been tricky because even my current partner, who is trans sometimes has similar colors to Hannah.

Previously, Ashley had felt comfortable and even protected by transgender people and cisgender women, but after her assault, she began to doubt the safety of both communities. While Ashley previously would have relied on the LGBTQ community for safety from someone who targeted her on the basis of her sexual orientation, her rapist's transgender identity compelled her to distance herself and wonder if anywhere or anyone was truly safe.

In some cases, these fears alone led the women in our study to withdraw from LGBTQ spaces on campus, but more commonly they leaned on LGBTQ resources only to feel retraumatized in some way. Often, respondents noted how their sexual assaults led them to question or adjust their sexual identities in a way that many of their queer friends contested. Even though this reaction is common among young lesbian and bisexual sexual assault survivors (Robohm, Litzenberger, & Pearlman, 2003), the women in this study reported feeling afraid of judgment for playing into a stereotype that queer women were simply damaged from previous sexual assaults that made them fear or hate men. They needed the support of queer communities as they explored their sexual identities as both survivors and queer women, but found many of their friends unsupportive of the process because they considered the associated stereotypes problematic and potentially stigmatizing for LGBTQ people.

Conversely, many respondents reported that their sexual assaults led queer friends to question their sexual orientations and the legitimacy of their victimization. For example, one respondent, Sydney, told us about how her girlfriend had spread a rumor in their queer social circle that her sexual assault had actually been regrettable drunken sexual experimentation and infidelity. In her words:

> A few months later, [my girlfriend] told everyone that it was like, "Yeah, [Sydney] got drunk at a party and, like, had a bad experience with a guy and then, like, came home and tried to make everyone feel bad for her about it like it was some sexual assault." She went out of her way to tell people that it was my fault.

Like many college students, Sydney's girlfriend blamed Sydney for her sexual assault and suggested it may have been consensual. However, Sydney's girlfriend also insinuated that in addition to questioning the legitimacy of her sexual assault, Sydney's sexual orientation should face scrutiny. This forced Sydney to defend her identification with the LGBTQ community before she could receive any support from her queer friends to heal from her sexual assault. At the time of our interview, Sydney still struggled to find queer friends who she felt comfortable talking to about her recovery. Furthermore, whether the women in our sample maintained or modified their sexual identities following their sexual assaults, they felt their queer allies on campus no longer trusted their judgment and sought to make decisions about their sexual orientations for them.

Often the treatment of queer survivors did not seem intentionally malicious, but instead reflected how ill equipped LGBTQ organizations on campus were to address the needs of sexual assault survivors. Ashley's story provides a salient example of mistreatment by her university's LGBT club. She had looked to the LGBT club for support after being sexually assaulted by a transgender rapist, craving confirmation that she could be safe in queer spaces and worried that sharing details of her sexual assault with people outside of the LGBTQ community would lead to the stigmatization of transgender people as sexually violent. However, her rapist's association with the LGBT club made her anxious. To feel comfortable using the LGBT club as a resource, Ashley sought reassurance that she would not be forced to share space with her rapist. Ashley's request presented the LGBT club leadership with a difficult decision. They wanted their club to be a safe space, but they also believed deeply in creating an inclusive atmosphere for all queer-identified people. To remove Ashley's rapist from the club would clearly violate the latter principle.

In the absence of knowledge about how to deal with the sexually traumatized or the behaviors of perpetrators, the club never considered that Ashley's rapist might sexually assault someone else in the club or that her mere presence could be too distressful for Ashley to remain a member. Instead, they assumed that an apology would suffice to remedy the harm caused and then struggled to understand why Ashley still questioned the club's policy of universal inclusion. In the end, the club failed to keep Ashley safe and, as a result, subtly and perhaps unintentionally pushed her out of the club during a time when she most needed a queer support network.

Harmed Caused by College Staff Members

Thus far, we have discussed harm caused to queer sexual assault survivors by other students who play a predominant role in LGBTQ organizations on campus. However, some of our respondents also reported negligence by staff that may shed light on the culture of maltreatment among students, including those who worked in LGBTQ organizations. Again, Ashley's experience provides a clear example. Before turning to the student-led LGBT club for assistance, Ashley reached out for guidance from a mentor employed by the university. The mentor encouraged Ashley to share details of her sexual assault without informing Ashley that she would be mandated to report everything she divulged and without consideration for the toll that could take on Ashley's life.

As a result, Ashley was forced into an exhausting investigation and, because she had revealed the identity of her rapist as well as the sexual assault's connection to an official event of the LGBT club, she was unable to keep her sexual assault private. The investigation led many in the LGBT club to learn intimate details of Ashley's sexual assault from campus administrators, which then sparked debates and rumors that pressured Ashley to disclose even more information.

While Ashley was the one most affected by these actions, she wasn't the one who chose to involve all of these people; an administrator on campus had made that decision for her. This senior college official's actions modeled two specific harms: (1) how to remove a sexual assault survivor's autonomy, and (2) how to place decisions about how she should proceed after her victimization exclusively in the hands of those with organizational authority.

RECOMMENDATIONS FOR SUPPORTING QUEER SURVIVORS

Two substantial and equally important recommendations underpin the ways in which support can be made accessible to queer survivors. First, it is essential to take advantage of opportunities to work with anti-violence experts. Second, care must be taken to create safe LGBTQ spaces for survivors.

Collaborating with Anti-Violence Experts

LGBTQ resources on campus need to be prepared to address the needs of survivors because sexual violence affects a huge segment of the LGBTQ student population. LGBTQ organizations must recognize sexual violence as a common aspect of the queer experience and as one of the most pervasive forms of hate crimes perpetrated against queer communities. Just as LGBTQ organizations insist that their affiliates become educated about more visible experiences that frequently affect the queer community like bullying, workplace discrimination, and homelessness, LGBTQ organizations should seek out and distribute information on sexual violence that occurs within the LGBTQ community.

Both staff and students affiliated with LGBTQ organizations on campus should be held to a higher standard of inclusion and sensitivity toward the needs of survivors. The organizations need to collaborate with other campus and community groups already experienced with the needs of sexual assault survivors. Senior campus administration should also lend an ear to survivors who come forward with their experiences, allowing students themselves to call out harmful practices and set an agenda for improvement.

Collaboration with sexual violence prevention groups would have certainly offered the survivors in our study a reprieve from some of the common mistakes made by college administrators. Returning to Ashley's story as an example, her mentor's treatment of the mandatory reporting requirement for university faculty and staff exemplifies inexperience with victim-centered approaches to sexual assault response that retraumatized Ashley and further removed her life events from her control. Ashley's mentor interpreted the university's mandatory reporting requirement as a demand that she begin conducting a preliminary investigation by asking probing questions to fully understand the story. As a result, the report of Ashley's rape began with a momentum she could not stop before she even knew a report would exist.

A more common practice among campus victim advocates is to interrupt a student who has begun to disclose a sexual assault and make them aware of the repercussions of seeking advice from a mandatory reporter. A student can then ask for advice from a mandatory reporter on how to respond to a hypothetical sexual assault without feeling forced into an investigation. Even if the student wishes to go on, advocates do not seek extensive information from victims. Instead, they seek and report the minimum amount of information possible and allow the victim to control their own narrative during investigation. These techniques empower victims to make a decision about whether or not to report their sexual assault rather than forcing them into a time-intensive and often quite public investigation. Even if staff affiliated with LGBTQ organizations on campus are sympathetic to the difficulties faced by sexual assault survivors, they would certainly benefit from receiving best practices in sexual assault prevention and response from campus and community experts.

Making LGBTQ Spaces Safe for Survivors

There are some structural barriers faced by sexual assault survivors that are unique to LGBTQ spaces and that will require the discretion of queer leaders. For example, securing the safety and comfort of sexual violence victims can be particularly complex when two students have legitimate reasons for wishing to inhabit the same queer space on campus. In Ashley's case, she and her assailant were both active members of the university's LGBT club and both looked to the club and its members for support after the sexual assault. To ban Ashley's rapist from the club would violate principles of inclusion central to most LGBTQ organizations, but to allow her to remain affiliated with the club effectively excluded Ashley and potentially placed other members of the club at risk of sexual violence (Lisak & Miller, 2002). To truly protect survivors—and those not yet victimized, but who regularly come into contact with known sexual assailants—LGBTQ organizations must revise their policies on inclusivity to ban or limit rapists' involvement in safe spaces.

These approaches must be fair to all members of marginalized sexual and gender identities, but also victim-centered. For example, allowing a rapist to access individual resources available to the LGBTQ community like counseling or advocacy services, but precluding them from participating in community events could be a compromise between LGBTQ inclusion and ensuring the safety of sexual assault survivors. In scenarios like this one, it is crucial that those working within LGBTQ organizations use a trauma-informed approach to making decisions that pertain specifically to their spaces on campus.

Securing the safety and comfort of sexual assault survivors obviously extends beyond minimizing the continued pain caused by perpetrators. Campus LGBTQ organizations must also put ample consideration into easing the burden of victims by creating environments that are understanding and respectful of their experiences. In our sample, we most commonly saw this principle violated by members of the queer community who questioned the legitimacy of a survivor's sexual assault allegations or discouraged survivors from exploring the way their sexual identities may have changed after their sexual assaults. These microaggressions went largely unchallenged by the queer community and pressured survivors into silence and isolation after their assaults, especially about topics that they most wanted to address with other queer people. Like microaggressions aimed at the queer community, microaggressions perpetrated against sexual assault survivors should not be tolerated in LGBTQ spaces.

CONCLUSION

While our work is in its preliminary stages and there is very little research on queer sexual violence victims, the scholarship that does exist emphasizes the importance of taking a proactive approach to support survivors. Queer survivors deserve safe spaces on campus, especially among LGBTQ organizations and communities. Through collaboration with sexual violence prevention organizations and empowerment of the survivors that share their stories, campus LGBTQ organizations can become a safe haven instead of yet another space of retraumatization.

REFERENCES

Alberty, E. (2016, August 16). Students: BYU Honor Code leaves LGBT victims of sexual assault vulnerable and alone. *The Salt Lake Tribune.*

Balsam, K. F. (2002). Traumatic victimization in the lives of lesbian and bisexual women: A contextual approach. *Journal of Lesbian Studies, 7*(1), 1–14.

Cantor, D., Fisher, B., Chibnall, S., Townsend, R., Lee, H., Bruce, C., & Thomas, G. (2015). Report on the AAU campus climate survey on sexual assault and sexual misconduct. *The Association of American Universities.* Washington, DC: Association of American Universities.

Descamps, M. J., Rothblum, E., Bradford, E., Bradford, J. & Ryan, C. (2000). Mental health impact of sexual abuse, rape, intimate partner violence, and hate crimes in the National Health Care Survey. *Journal of Gay & Lesbian Social Services, 11*(1), 27–55.

Hequembourg, A. L., Livingston, J. A., & Parks, K. A. (2013). Sexual victimization and associated risks among lesbian and bisexual women. *Violence Against Women, 19*(5), 634–657.

Johnson, L. M., Matthew, T. L., & Napper, S. L. (2016). Sexual orientation and sexual assault victimization among US college students. *Social Science Journal, 53*(2), 174–183.

Krebs, C. P., Lindquist, C. H., Warner, T. D., Fisher, B. S., & Martin, S. L. (2007). *The campus sexual assault (CSA) study.* Washington, DC: U.S. Department of Justice.

Lisak, D., & Miller, P. M. (2002). Repeat rape and multiple offending among undetected rapists. *Violence and Victims, 17*(1), 73–84.

Martin, S. L., Fisher, B. S., Warner, T. D., Krebs, C. P., & Lindquist, C. H. (2011). Women's sexual orientation and their experiences of sexual assault before and during university. *Women's Health Issues, 21*(3), 199–205.

Roberts, S. J., & Sorensen, L. (1999). Prevalence of childhood sexual abuse and related sequelae in a lesbian population. *Journal of the Gay and Lesbian Medical Association, 3*(1), 11–19.

Robohm, J. S., Litzenberger, B. W., & Pearlman, L. A. (2003). Sexual abuse in lesbian and bisexual young women: Associations with emotional/behavioral difficulties, feelings about sexuality, and the "coming out" process. *Journal of Lesbian Studies, 7*(4), 31–47.

CHAPTER EIGHTEEN

Stories OF LGBTQ+ Hate, Fear, Hope, AND Love IN THE University OF Hawai'i System

Twenty Years of the Marriage Equality Movement

RAE WATANABE, TARA O'NEILL, AND CAMARON MIYAMOTO

INTRODUCTION

In 1993, the Hawai'i Supreme Court's ruling in *Baehr v. Lewin* became the first to state that excluding same-sex couples from marriage is discrimination. This ruling launched the freedom to marry movement (Lambda Legal, 2016). Within the United States, the *Baehr v. Lewin* ruling served as a catalyst for the Congressional passage of the Defense of Marriage Act (DOMA) in 1996 (Sant'Ambrogio & Law, 2010). In Hawai'i, the 1993 ruling resulted in ugly fights, which led to passage of the first state constitutional amendment targeting gay relationships (Lambda Legal, 2016). Deitrich (1994) ponders the overall lessons of *Baehr v. Lewin;* however, the lessons in Hawai'i are more specific. This chapter focuses on the impact the struggle for marriage equality has had on the social climate of the University of Hawai'i's (UH) system with specific focus on two of the system's ten campuses, University of Hawai'i at Mānoa (UHM) and Leeward Community College (LCC).

This chapter is divided into four sections. In an effort to set context for the evolving and devolving social climate in Hawai'i and subsequently on campuses within the UH system, section one provides background about the *Baehr v. Lewin* ruling and the resulting growth in public opposition to LBTQ relationships and same-sex marriage beginning in 1993. As part of this discussion, we explore the impact of *mainland/continental* group (i.e., Human Rights Campaign, the Christian Coalition and other religious groups) involvement in the Hawai'i marriage debates. In the next two sections, we engage in a narrative approach toward the practice of "critical humanism" (Plummer, 2005) by sharing stories that explore the impact of Hawai'i's shifting social climate on two of the university system's campuses and the reaction from UH students, faculty and administration.

Section two focuses on the flagship campus of UH Mānoa (UHM) from the experiential lens of Camaron Miyamoto (third author), the director of the Mānoa-based LGBTQ+ Center. Section three focuses on Leeward Community College (Leeward CC) from the experiential lens of Rae Watanabe (lead author), long-time faculty member and campus LGBTQ advocate. The fourth and final section evaluates where the UH is as a system in 2016 and ponders future direction.

COMMUNITY AND CAMPUS IMPACT OF *BAEHR V. LEWIN*

On May 5, 1993, the Hawai'i Supreme Court decided *Baehr v. Lewin*, the same-sex marriage case. The court held that the State's denial of same-sex marriage ran afoul of both the Equal Protection Clause and the Equal Rights Amendment (ERA) of the Hawai'i State Constitution—both of which include "sex" as a protected class. A sea change was at hand. The world had turned; the very ground beneath our feet had shifted (Morris, 2015, p. 3).

The 1993 *Baehr v. Lewin* case transformed the UH system's ten campuses. As schools are microcosms of the larger communities they serve, the campuses have reflected the conflicts, challenges and changes in Hawai'i's larger community over the 20- year effort for marriage equality (Kosciw, Greytak, Bartkiewicz, Boesen, & Palmer, 2012). For example, prior to 1993, blatant homophobia was rare. Instead, silent tolerance of LGBTQ people was common among Hawai'i's families and the UH campuses. By contrast, *Baehr v. Lewin* catalysed organized opposition to same-sex marriage, many homophobic actions and reactions, and attempts in the UH System to create more welcoming spaces.

When Hawai'i became the focal point for the legalization of same-sex marriage, the national forces for and against same-sex marriage organized and, some might say, invaded Hawai'i. Unfortunately, the pro same-sex marriage forces had little understanding of Hawai'i, its rich history and its diverse population. In 1990, Caucasians made up only 369,616 out of a total of 1,108, 229 people in Hawai'i. Other substantial populations included the Japanese at 247,486, the Filipinos at 168,682, and the Native Hawaiians at 138,742 (Bureau of the Census, 2011). All of these groups, as well as other smaller ones, made up the cultural tapestry of Hawai'i with its varying values. One value that they shared, however, being an island population with limited physical space, was respecting everyone's right to privacy (Krauss, 2002) or creating mental space. In addition, as explained by Morris (2015):

> Although same-sex marriage seemed foreign to many in 1993, it should not have. Hawaiian tradition was rife with stories of same-sex love, same-sex partners, and bisexuality. Even so, it became necessary post-*Baehr* for us to bring this information to light, to flesh it out and reify it for a new generation from whom years of colonial homophobia had hidden it, and to "put feathers on our words" as proof of the ancient "Hawaiianness" and continuous "indigeneity" of these things. (p. 4)

Due to both *local style* and Hawaiian cultural roots, it was common in Hawai'i, prior to 1993, to have Gay and Lesbian family members who were welcome in their families, but almost no one openly identified as Gay or Lesbian. The same-sex marriage fight would change that. The main forces for same-sex marriage were led by the Human Rights Campaign (HRC), self-described as "America's largest civil rights organization working to achieve lesbian, gay, bisexual, transgender and queer equality" (http://www.hrc.org/). These representatives did not understand the culture of Hawai'i, nor its impact on local people's values.

HRC called a meeting at Ward Warehouse of "local leaders" of Hawai'i. The criteria for determining "local leaders" remain unclear; however, Ku'umeaaloha Gomes, a Native Hawaiian and LGBTQ activist, was invited to attend. Over the years, Gomes would play many central roles in the UH system's work toward LGBTQ campus safety and representation serving as an organizer for many community groups, as well as the Chair of the UH President's Commission on the Status of LGBTI Equality (Section 4 for the history of the UH President's Commission on the Status of LGBTI Equality). Gomes attended HRC's first meeting at Ward Warehouse, and reported that, "representatives from HRC explained how 'we' would legalize same-sex marriage by focusing on it as a constitutional issue." In particular, they promoted the beauty of the full faith and credit clause of the Equal Rights Amendment and how once same-sex marriage was legal in one state, said clause would "guarantee" legalization nationwide.

HRC did not ask "local leaders" for their opinion on whether or not they thought this would be an effective strategy. Gomes explained:

> There was no interest in knowing how Native Hawaiians culturally talked about sexuality, which was actually on a spectrum in what we call *'moe aku, moe mai'* the recognition of sleeping here and there, meaning with men or with women. I walked away from that entire experience feeling like we Hawaiians were silenced and being put into the American LGBT box, in spite of that not being our experience. (personal communication, September 8, 2016)

From the beginning and with little regard for "local" culture, especially the host culture, HRC's approach was very much "from the head" and very public in a place where "heart" and respecting others' privacy mattered more. The right to privacy is so sacrosanct in Hawai'i that "invasion of privacy" is a crime (Privacy Protections, 2015).

Like HRC, the forces behind the first wave of federal and state anti-same-sex-marriage also believed that, "Hawai'i was on the cusp of legalizing same-sex marriage—and, perhaps more importantly, the belief that this would mean same-sex marriage was effectively everywhere" (Grossman, 2013, p. 2). For example, Senator Trent Lott from Mississippi argued that if:

> [S]uch a decision affected only Hawai'i, we could leave it to the residents of Hawai'i to either live with the consequences or exercise their political rights to change things. But a court decision would not be limited to just one State. It would raise threatening possibilities in other States because of [the Full Faith and Credit Clause]. (Grossman, 2013, p. 2)

Local and national anti-same-sex marriage forces converged on Hawai'i. As explained by Hull (2015), the leading organization supporting the 1998 anti-same-sex marriage constitutional amendment was "Save Traditional Marriage '98' (STM), a nominally secular group that received heavy support from both the Catholic Church and the Church of Latter Day Saints ... other groups included the Alliance for Traditional Marriage, Hawai'i Family Forum and Hawai'i's Future Today" (p. 214). The Alliance for Traditional Marriage seemed a more grassroots organization under the leadership of local businessman Mike Gabbard.

Their approach was to build fear and dread of same-sex marriage among Hawai'i's people. This Alliance morphed into a powerful local PAC under the leadership of Co-Chairs Diane Ho Kurtz (then Executive vice president, Hawai'i Biotechnology Group Inc.) and Bill Paul (former chairman of the Hawai'i Chamber of Commerce and the Hawai'i Visitors Bureau) and Rev. Marc Alexander (then Vice chairman of Hawai'i's Future Today and future Vicar General of Hawai'i's Catholic Church). Locally, the PAC generated significant funds. Just one $100 per plate dinner at the Hyatt Regency Waikiki was paired with a $125 business seminar, featuring Stephen Covey (best-selling author of *The 7 Habits of Highly Effective People* and *The 7 Habits of Highly Effective Families*), and was expected to raise $40,000–$50,000 (Yuen, 1997).

Because of the believed potential national significance, Hawai'i was also invaded by "Christian" forces. High-ranking officials from the Christian Coalition and Pat Robertson's American Center for Law and Justice came to Hawai'i. Mirroring HRC's actions, they called a private meeting of about 25 religious leaders. There, they taught the religious leaders to walk the fine line between legally registering their congregants to vote and encouraging them to be "active citizens" and illegally using the pulpit to decry same-sex marriage. The Christian forces also taught the Hawai'i pastors, priest and rabbis that they were still free to express their personal opinions (Yuen, 1998). The religious leaders did this at every turn and became crucial in the battle against same-sex marriage as they turned their congregants against the idea of inclusion.

Having armed themselves with national funds and fear, the forces against same-sex marriage created the most anti-gay atmosphere Hawai'i had ever seen. Anti-gay commercials, inciting fear about what LGBTQ people were teaching children, flooded Hawai'i's television airwaves while the pro same-sex marriage commercials insisted it was a constitutional issue. The pro-same sex marriage forces did use emotion to argue that denying LGBTQ people the right to marry was just like denying Japanese Americans' rights during World War II (Hawai'i gives, 1998). While Hawai'i's people understood and condemned what happened in World War II, the plight of children was more powerful.

This battle raged in Hawai'i for five years and as a result, in 1998, after some failed attempts of the legislature in amending the marriage statute to prohibit same-sex marriage, the electorate approved a ballot initiative called Amendment 2 to the State Constitution, which provided: "The legislature shall have the power to reserve marriage to opposite-sex couples" (Morris, 2015). Hawai'i voters approved the amendment by a vote of 69.2–28.6% (Hawai'i Office of Elections, 1998), and the state legislature exercised its power to ban same-sex marriage until the passage of the Hawai'i Marriage Equality Act of 2013 (Grossman, 2013). Between the time of 1993 *Baehr v. Lewin* ruling and the legislature's passage of the marriage equality act is 20 years of vitriolic religious and political advocacy against same-sex marriage and the LGBTQ community in Hawai'i. As the state and its people worked their way through the adoption of "a new status, called 'reciprocal beneficiaries,' which enabled same-sex couples to register for limited mutual rights" (Grossman, 2013, p. 3) in 1997, to the 1998 constitutional amendment vote, to the adoption of "civil unions" in 2011 and finally marriage equality in 2013, the social atmosphere created in relation to the LGBTQ community would have positive and negative effects on the UH System.

IMPACT ON THE FLAGSHIP CAMPUS, UNIVERSITY OF HAWAI'I AT MĀNOA

The University of Hawai'i at Mānoa (UHM), the flagship campus of the UH System, played a significant role in the emergence of marriage equality for both Hawai'i and the United States. Ninia Baehr, at the time of the filing of the legal case *Baehr v. Lewin* was the Director of the Women's Center at the University of Hawai'i at Mānoa. Consequently, UH Mānoa was not immune from the increasingly homophobic climate that infused the 1990's in Hawai'i. To help ensure that the University of Hawai'i would uphold its commitment to diversity and non-discrimination, administrators Dr. Doris Ching and Dr. Amy Agbayani established the UH Task Force on Sexual Orientation. One of the key projects that started in 1994 was the Safe Zone Training program for LGBTQ people and their allies.

However, two forms of LGBTQ hate erupted on the UH Mānoa campus, and they were effectively addressed by members of the campus community. The first relates to Native Hawai'ian communities and the discourse that emerged around LGBTQ issues, sovereignty and marriage equality. The second has two parts and is specific to the Department of Athletics at UH Mānoa and homophobic statements that made national news.

Na Mamo O Hawai'i was founded by Ku'umeaaloa Gomes, Director of Kua'ana Native Hawai'ian Student Services, and named by Puakea Nogelmeir, Professor of Hawai'ian Language at UH Mānoa. The mamo blossom in Hawai'i is a rare yellow flower that has the strength to grow in a lava flow. This unique flower symbolizes LGBTQ Native Hawaiian populations and the members of Na Mamo O Hawai'i. The synergy of this organization was fueled by campus-community praxis. Many members were LGBTQ Kanaka Maoli students, faculty and staff at UHM; a larger part were members of the LGBTQ Native Hawai'ian community; and a significant part of the membership were LGBTQ non-Native Hawai'ian allies. According to Gomes, "What made us unique was we were creating visibility and voice for LGBTQ Native Hawaiians in the Sovereignty and Independence Movements and in the discourse around same-gender marriage" (personal communication, September 15, 2016).

In a story from the magazine *Island Lifestyle* (Resilient resistance, 1996, p.17), founding members explained that their organization was dedicated to sovereignty, independence and LGBTQ equality as well as to help offer a critique of the issue of same-gender marriage in Hawai'i. Central to this critique is the role of using tourism to and the commodification of native people to "sell" marriage to the state legislature and other lobbying efforts. Further, "we have never had a real discussion about same-gender marriage. The assumption is that we all agree with marriage as an institution, despite the fact that traditionally, marriage is about private property, and about benefits derived from employment" (Resilient Resistance, 1996, p. 17).

Just as Na Mamo O Hawai'i played a key role in offering a critique of the mainstream LGBTQ lobbying efforts for same-gender marriage, this organization spearheaded discourse on Hawai'ian sovereignty and LGBTQ Native Hawai'ians. There was heated debate on Kauai when some religiously-affiliated Native Hawai'ian leaders asserted that the push for same gender marriage was an abhorrence to righteousness and what is "pono" or "just" in Hawai'i. They used the Hawai'i state motto, which are the words of King Kamehameha III: "Ua Mau Ke Ea O Ka 'Āina I Ka Pono" or "the life/breath/sovereignty of the land is perpetuated righteousness" to claim that moving toward marriage equality would defy what was righteous or pono for the sovereignty of Hawai'i. The very existence and works of Na Mamo O

Hawai'i provided a counter narrative that helped to reinterpret and reclaim what in the Hawaiian language was "pono"—what was and is righteousness. Oppression is what is in opposition to that which is righteous or pono.

For 77 years, the rainbow was the righteous logo of UHM athletic teams. A story, told orally as is Native Hawaiian tradition, tells of a game at then Honolulu Stadium where UHM was losing—badly. Then, a rainbow appeared in the sky and the UHM football team began catching up. UHM won that game! Ever since, the rainbow was UHM's proud logo.

The same-sex marriage battle would change that, too. In 2000, then Athletic Director Hugh Yoshida "acknowledged the decision to change the logo stemmed, in part, from concerns about how the rainbow has become a symbol of gay pride and acceptance" (Rainbow Comments, 2000). Even though administrative meetings, which included members of the President's Commission on LGBTI Equality, were held at UHM, Yoshida apologized for his comment and nothing more really changed. UHM "Rainbows" became the "Warriors"; the rainbow logo was replaced by an "H" with jagged edges on either vertical sides, suggesting a Native Hawaiian weapon. Coincidentally, the rainbow logo, which many still loved, was brought back as "retro" in 2013, the same year that same-sex marriage became law in Hawai'i (Reardon, 2013). Today, UHM uses both logos.

A far more public problem in UHM Athletics unfolded in 2009 as the fight for legal recognition of same-sex marriage and eruptions of LGBTQ+ hate continued. UH Mānoa Head Football Coach Greg McMackin issued an insensitive and homophobic comment at a Western Athletic Conference press conference. McMackin said that Notre Dame University's football team does a "little faggot dance" as part of their pre-game ritual as he demonstrated the dance for reporters who laughed (Tsai, 2009). Some sports people dismissed his words as "talking trash" and being "part of the game." But for many LGBTQ people and their allies, McMackin's slur was no laughing matter. McMackin's attempt to emasculate the Notre Dame players as not as strong as the University of Hawai'i Warriors, who intimidate their opponents with the culturally appropriated Maori "haka" or chant, would become an education for him.

Coach McMackin's "education" included a 30-day suspension without pay as well as a "voluntary" 7% pay cut. At the time, McMackin's salary was $1.1 million per year. The suspension cost him about $169,000 while the pay cut cost him $77,000 (Asato, 2009). Insulting LGBTQ people was no longer remotely acceptable at UHM—this was now crystal clear. In fact, Coach McMackin made his comments in Salt Lake City in the afternoon, and by that evening Miyamoto received a call on his (Miyamoto's) cell phone from the Coach *at the instruction of the Chancellor*. Over the next several days, there were symbolic meetings, press conferences (where the Coach tearfully apologized to the LGBTQ community), and agreements to unify UHM's campus community.

Then UH Mānoa Chancellor, Virginia Hinshaw, symbolically asserted that all members of our community are valued; both the coach, and all members of the lesbian, gay, bisexual, and transgender community. She stressed the dedication to work and sacrifice and the pain that was felt personally by Coach McMackin while also highlighting the need to address potential harm to the University campus climate and well-being of LGBTQ students.

The Coach's pay cut was not his only *lesson*. Chancellor Hinshaw determined that one of the desired outcomes to denote progressive action would be to have Coach McMackin record a public service announcement stating that homophobia is wrong, he had learned from his mistake, and that we must challenge others when we hear anti-gay comments. The agreement between all parties concluded that a public service announcement would be created and distributed to local television stations or news media (Shapiro, 2009). There were not any stipulations that the University would pay for time, issue a press release, or advocate for the public service announcement to actually air on television or radio. Unfortunately, the public service announcements never aired on local media.

However, Coach McMackin was mandated to attend a student meeting and apologize to the LGBTQ and ally students in the room. While the single conversation didn't heal all wounds, The LGBTQ+ Center at the University of Hawai'i at Mānoa continues to move forward, advocating and supporting students regardless of gender identity/expression or sexual orientation. In fact, Camaron Miyamoto just offered a mandated training to all coaches and athletics staff on September 12, 2016.

IMPACT ON LEEWARD COMMUNITY COLLEGE

The effects on the UH System were not limited to the flagship campus. In 1994, at Leeward CC in Pearl City, Hawai'i, the late Joan Souza (then a counselor on campus) sought out, then brand new Instructor of English and one of the few openly LGBTQ faculty members, Rae Watanabe (lead author of this chapter). Souza was a straight ally and crusader with one thing in mind—protect LGBTQ students, faculty and staff from the onslaught of negativity they were being exposed to off-campus. Souza's status as a straight ally and her irrepressible personality were crucial. She could say things that Watanabe (educated by the born-again Southern Baptists and born and raised in Hawai'i) wouldn't or couldn't say, especially to Souza's fellow counselors, many of whom were very religious. Together, Souza and Watanabe started the first LGBTQ student group at Leeward. In order to get started, they got lunch bags and put colorful notes on the outside that asked, "Who says there's no such thing as a free lunch?" Inside the bag was an invitation to LGBTQ students and their allies to come to an actual free lunch, which

Souza and Watanabe funded from their own pockets. During student orientation in 1995, they stood at a heavily trafficked area on campus and offered the lunch bags. Most students took it, completely amused by the question and the mystery of whatever was in the bag. A few gave it back when they saw it was a lunch for LGBTQ students and their allies, but the more common response was, "Oh, I need to give this to [insert name here]," and they would promise to pass it on to their LGBTQ friends.

Souza contributed too many things to mention here, but her greatest contribution was adopting the Safe Zone program in 1994. She was a voracious reader and saw that Rutgers University had a program that trained volunteers to have a sign designating them as "safe" to talk to about LGBTQ issues. This created actual zones of trained faculty and staff offices as well as students, wherever they were, for LGBTQ students to approach for help. All of the trained volunteers were not expected to be counselors; they were resource people with lists of places that an LGBTQ student could go to for help.

Souza, however, noted that the workbook was "not local," and she asked Watanabe for help in rewriting the booklet. Together one summer, they revised the booklet by changing words that seemed too confrontational, by adding a list of Hawai'i resources and by adding an entire page of the Native Hawaiian definition of "mahu," which is often translated as "homosexual" or "hermaphrodite" but in Hawai'i is usually used for MTF transgender people. This special page was written by Kumu Hinaleimoana Wong, who has since become very well known for the documentary of her life, *A Place in the Middle*. ("Kumu" is a Native Hawaiian title that means "teacher" and it denotes utmost respect for the teacher.) The Safe Zone program was successful at Leeward CC, so it was quickly adopted by the UH System as Miyamoto pointed out in the previous section.

As the anti-Gay rhetoric heated up off-campus, a very negative event occurred at Leeward Community College (Leeward CC). Anti-gay graffiti began popping up all over campus in the Spring of 1998 and Safe Zone flyers were defaced as well as torn down. The Leeward CC security guards as well as the faculty and staff labored to find the perpetrators of these crimes. When security finally caught Richard Rudd and Carl Hill, the Honolulu Police Department were familiar with them. According to the police, Rudd and Hill had been performing anti-gay graffiti in different locations since 1994, the year after *Baehr v. Lewin* was filed. Furthermore, Hawai'i was one of only thirteen states that did not have hate crime legislation at the time. If it had, Rudd and Hill would've already served a prison sentence (U.S. Department of Justice, 1996).

However, the Leeward CC response from faculty and staff was impressive. Then, Provost Barbara Polk took her Safe Zone sign and put it inside her office glass, making it impossible to deface her poster. She also provided support and encouragement at every turn. In response to the actions of Rudd and Hill, Polk and

Souza, by now the Chair of the UH Task Force on Sexual Orientation, encouraged Watanabe to submit a report to the Student Conduct Committee, detailing the costs of Rudd's and Hill's actions. There were physical costs, such as the cost of aqua blasting graffiti off of concrete or of the labor in scraping graffiti off of tile, as well as the multiple costs of replacing Safe Zone posters.

There were also emotional costs, such as the mental anguish of any LGBTQ faculty, staff, or student at Leeward CC and even of those who loved someone LGBTQ. After seeing some of the graffiti, one student said to Watanabe, "I feel like someone hit me in the stomach. Someone very, very close to me in my family is a lesbian. I'm scared of what these guys would do to her...." Such mental effects are not to be dismissed. How do LGBTQ students focus on studying and LGBTQ faculty and staff focus on working if they feel unsafe? Additionally, the mental effects can be long-lasting. Herek, Gillis and Cogan (1999) found that even five years after a hate crime, victims show signs of psychological distress, including depression, stress and anger.

Lisa Anderson and Martin Shapiro, then two Leeward CC faculty members, began to mobilize. Anderson and Shapiro suggested to Souza and Watanabe that the Hawaiian name of the LGBTQ student group be changed to Gay Straight Alliance because of the instant name recognition. At first, Watanabe was hesitant to change the group's Hawaiian name to the GSA because she thought of the GSA as strictly for K-12 schools and she worried about further damage to the host culture, but Anderson's and Shapiro's argument of instant name recognition won her over. Meetings of the newly dubbed GSA at Leeward CC were so well-attended that one of them was moved outside, so that attendees could sit in a large circle under a shade tree.

The stage was now set for another possible negative event. On Coming Out Day in 1999, the GSA decided to show the movie *The Wedding Banquet*. It was to be an enjoyable social event. However, the Catholic Club heard about this event and in typical "telephone" fashion, the GSA was now hosting an actual Gay wedding on campus! The Alliance for Traditional Marriage mobilized to help Leeward CC's Catholic Club.

On that day, when Watanabe turned onto Ala Ike Street (the street that abuts campus), two rows of the Alliance for Traditional Marriage flags on either side of the street greeted her. At first, she was afraid. Having survived anti-LGBTQ confrontations, she took precautions and didn't park where she usually parked, walked across campus, and discovered an Alliance table in front of the cafeteria. As she walked and regained her composure, she remembered an old Japanese saying, "Every crisis is an opportunity." Within an hour of arriving on campus, Jonathan Wong, a Leeward CC counselor and the faculty advisor for the Catholic Club, came to her office. He seemed very upset yet chose his words carefully as he paced and tried to learn about the impending Gay wedding. When Watanabe realized what the confusion was, she burst into laughter, which relaxed Wong immediately.

She explained the misunderstanding. Wong laughed, they exchanged pleasantries and went on with their day. However, the Japanese saying proved true. The media had already been called to campus by the Alliance, so Watanabe used it as an opportunity to plug Coming Out Day. That evening, anyone in Hawai'i watching television news, learned what Coming Out Day was and that Leeward CC had one.

More positive events began to unfold at Leeward CC. Anderson also asked Watanabe if she had ever heard of the *Love Makes a Family* traveling art exhibit. She had but Watanabe was never a big dreamer; she was mostly a survivor. Anderson then proposed writing a grant to bring the exhibit to Hawai'i. In 2000, Anderson and Watanabe won a grant to bring said exhibit to Hawai'i. The exhibit, which was shown at Leeward CC's Library as well as at UH-Hilo in 2001, generated a lot of excitement among the campuses' population, for few had ever seen happy pictures of LGBTQ families (personal communication, September 11, 2016).

By 2010, all of Leeward CC counselors had been *highly encouraged* to take the Safe Zone training and most of them had, even the most anti-LGBTQ and religious among them. Today at Leeward CC, the Safe Zone is often included in New Employee Orientation and is mandatory for all students who participate in Student Government. The former was made possible by long-time LGBTQ ally Cindy Martin, Staff Development Coordinator; the latter was made possible by Lexer Chou, Student Life Coordinator, strong LGBTQ ally and now Co-Chair of the Commission on LGBTQ+ Equality.

CURRENT LGBTQ CAMPUS CLIMATE WITHIN THE UH SYSTEM

Made evident from the sampling of experiences shared in sections two and three of this chapter, the social challenges and successes of the same-sex marriage debate in Hawai'i over 20 years had both community and policy impacts on the UH System as a whole. Though often catalysed by negative events, such as the slandering of the campus LGBTQ community by an athletic director or hates crimes in the form of vandalism and hate speech, the UH system as a whole has attempted to meet these challenges by creating policies, community actions and safe spaces that allow for LGBTQ students, faculty and staff to thrive.

One of the most meaningful institutional outcomes of the political and social tensions created on the UH system's campuses over decades of the state's animated marriage equality debate was the transformation of the "UH Systemwide Task Force on Sexual Orientation" to "The President's Commission on the Status of LGBTI Equality." The task force was created in the early 1990's as a temporary and immediate system response to issues of LGBTQ student safety resulting from the social tensions generated by the impending 1998 constitutional amendment campaign and vote. In 1999, this temporary task force was permanently adopted by the office of the UH System President and renamed "The President's Commission on the Status of LGBTI Equality." The commission consists of two faculty, staff and/or student members from each of the 10 campuses appointed by the President of the University (Office of the President, 2016). The new President's Commission focused their attention on developing and supporting GSA organizations on all of the system's campuses, increasing Safe Zone trainings and the number of faculty who identified as Safe Zone trainers and/or designated their offices and/or classrooms as "safe spaces," and providing the president's office policy recommendations and feedback.

In 2014, the President's Commission on the Status of LGBTI Equality wanted to investigate what the outcome of their years of work had been. To do so, they conducted a "Campus Climate Assessment" on each of the 10 UH System campuses (see Figure 18.1.) Using a survey developed by Campus Pride Index, the "leading national non-profit organization for student leaders and campus groups working to create safer, more LGBTQ-friendly learning environments at colleges and universities" (Campus Pride Index, 2016).

The survey is a "virtual tool for assisting campuses in learning ways to improve their LGBTQ campus life and ultimately share the educational experience to be more inclusive, welcoming and respectful of LGBTQ and ally people" (Campus Pride Index, 2016). Measured factors and categories of questions included: LGBT Policy Inclusion, Support & Institutional Commitment, Academic Life, Student Life, Housing and Residence Life, Campus Safety, Counseling & Health, and Recruitment & Retention Efforts. Scores were reported on a scale of 0–5 stars with 5 being the highest. Overall system results are shown in Table 18.1 which appears at the end of the chapter.

The results of this survey (see Table 18.1, below) indicated that the UH System had made significant positive improvements in the safety and educational experiences of LGBTQ students and their allies. Each of the 10 campuses had active GSA programs, Safe Zone training was taking place on all campuses with three campus (Mānoa, Leeward CC, & Kapiolani CC) developing substantial "Safe Zone Tool Boxes" that had enabled the exponential growth of the program.

Table 18.1. Campus Pride Index 2014 Survey Results.

Policy Inclusion	4.5
Support and Institutional Commitment	5
Academic Life	4.5
Student Life	5
Housing and Residence Life	4.5
Campus Safety	5
Counseling & Health	4.5
Recruitment & Retention Efforts	4

These efforts had clearly had impact but there was still room to improve. For example, the 4.5 Academic Life score was the result of students reporting that they did not see LGBTQ content and/or ideas explicitly addressed in their academic course work.

This feedback prompted the commission to review the course catalogues of each campus and evaluate the present LGBTQ topic courses. The result was very few (i.e., 2–3 on the Mānoa campus and none on others). While the system received a perfect score in the Campus Safety category, some respondents reported that not having access to unisex bathrooms negatively impacted their campus experience. In addition, while respondents report feeling safe overall on the System's campuses, the lower score in Recruitment & Retention Efforts is, in part, in relation to the recruitment and retention of openly LGBTQ faculty and staff, of which there are still exceptionally few in the UH System.

CONCLUSION

Review of the survey findings and impact of the commission's early work revealed the need for expanding the thinking of the role of the commission and people for whom it seeks to give voice within the UH System. As such, in the Fall of 2015, the commission formally changed its name to "UH Commission on Lesbian, Gay, Bisexual, Transgender and Queer+ (LGBTQ+) Equality" and adopted an amended vision statement which reads:

> The University of Hawaiʻi Commission on Lesbian, Gay, Bisexual, Transgender, and Queer+ (LGBTQ+) Equality is committed to fostering a shared responsibility for inclusiveness, equality, respect, and social justice throughout the UH System. To better serve our campus communities, we want to ensure that all members of our UH campuses are aware of rights and resources available to them. (Office of the President, 2016)

The new name and expanded vision of the commission has enabled the organization to work at the intersectionality of LGBTQ issues, a Title IX gender perspective, and a Native Hawaiʻian identity lens, among others. For example, the commission is currently working with the system to advocate Title IX resource and policy development with an LGBTQ inclusiveness lens and LGBTQ+ "preferred name" policies and procedures that also support student and faculty's Native Hawaiʻian identity expression. While there is still much work to do, the UH system typifies the evolutionary political process and has come a long way in 20 years with respect to the recognition and support of LGBTQ rights. However, like most social evolutionally processes, efforts to support equity and social justice within the system will require continued advancement.

UH Commission on the Status of LGBTI Equality Survey

LGBT Policy Inclusion	Yes	No	N/A
1. Does your campus prohibit discrimination based on sexual orientation by including the words "sexual orientation" in its primary non-discrimination statement or Equal Employment Opportunity policy?			
2. Does your campus include sexual orientation in public written statements about diversity and multiculturalism?			
3. Does your campus prohibit discrimination based on gender identity or gender expression by including the words "gender identity" or "gender identity or expression" in its primary non-discrimination statement or Equal Employment Opportunity policy?			
4. Does your campus include gender identity/expression in public written statements about diversity and multiculturalism?			
5. Does your campus offer health insurance coverage to employees' same-sex partners?			
6. If Yes, does your campus "gross up" wages for employees who enroll for same-sex partner health benefits to cover the added tax burden from the imputed value of the benefit that appears as income for the employee?			
7. If No, does your campus offer cash compensation to employees to purchase their own health insurance for same-sex partners?			
8. What other benefits does your campus offer equally to both opposite-sex spouses of employees as well as same-sex partners of employees? Please indicate your response accurately on what your campus offers.			
a. Dental			
b. Vision			
c. Spouse/partner's dependent medical coverage			
d. Sick or bereavement leave			
e. Supplemental life insurance for the spouse/partner			
f. Relocation/Travel assistance			
g. Tuition Remission for spouse/partner/dependents			
h. Survivor benefits for the spouse/partner in the event of employee's death			
i. Retiree health care benefits			
j. Employee discounts			
k. Use of campus facilities/privileges for spouse/partner/family			
l. Child-care services for spouse/partner family			
9. Does your campus include LGBT issues and concerns and, or representations of LGBT people in the following:			
Grievance procedures			
Housing guidelines			
Admission application materials			
Health-care forms			
Alumni materials/publications			

Originally from the LGBT-Friendly Campus Climate Index
http://www.campusprideindex.org/

Revised 1.17.14 mj

UH Commission on the Status of LGBTI Equality Survey

10. Does your campus have inclusive methods for transgender students to self-identify their gender identity/expression on standard forms for the following:			
Application for Admission			
Application/Designation for Housing			
Student Health Forms			
11. Does your campus have an accessible, simple process for students to change their name and gender identity on university records and documents?			
LGBT Support & Institutional Commitment	**Yes**	**No**	**N/A**
1. Does your campus have a full-time professional staff member who is employed to support LGBT students and increase campus awareness of LGBT concerns/issues as 50% or more of the individual's job description?			
1a. If No, does your campus have at least one graduate staff person who is employed to support LGBT students and increase campus awareness of LGBT concerns/issues as 50% or more of the individual's job description?			
2. Does your campus have an LGBT concerns office or an LGBT student resource center (i.e. an institutionally funded space specifically for LGBT, gender and sexuality education and/or support services)?			
2b. If No, does your campus have another office or resource center that deals actively with and comprises LGBT issues and concerns (e.g. Women's Center, Multicultural Center)?			
3. Does your campus have a Safe Zone, Safe Space and, or Ally program (i.e. an ongoing network of visible people on campus who identify openly as allies/advocates for LGBT people and concerns)?			
4. Does your campus have a standing advisory committee that deals with LGBT issues similar to other standing committees on ethnic minority/multicultural issues that advises the administration on constituent group issues and concerns?			
5. Do senior administrators (e.g. chancellor, president, vice-president, academic deans) actively demonstrate inclusive use of the words "sexual orientation" and/ or "lesbian, gay, bisexual" when discussing community, multicultural and/or diversity issues on campus?			
6. Do senior administrators (e.g. chancellor, president, vice-president, academic deans) actively demonstrate inclusive use of the words "gender identity/expression" and/or "transgender" when discussing community, multicultural and/or diversity issues on campus?			
7. Does your campus have a LGBT alumni group within the existing alumni organization?			
8. Does your campus provide gender-neutral/single occupancy restroom facilities in administrative and academic buildings?			
LGBT Academic Life	**Yes**	**No**	**N/A**

Originally from the LGBT-Friendly Campus Climate Index
http://www.campusprideindex.org/

Revised 1.17.14 mj

UH Commission on the Status of LGBTI Equality Survey

1. Does your campus have LGBT-specific courses offered through various academic departments and programs?			
2. Does your campus have a LGBT studies program that offers a one or a combination of the following:			
Academic Major			
If so, Name of Degree Major:			
Academic Minor			
If so, Name of Academic Minor:			
Academic Concentration			
If so, Name of Academic Concentration:			
Academic Certificate			
If so, Name of Academic Certificate:			
3. Does your campus integrate LGBT issues into existing courses when appropriate?			
4. Does your campus have a significant number of LGB-inclusive books and periodicals on sexual orientation topics in the campus library/libraries?			
5. Does your campus have a significant number of transgender-inclusive books and periodicals on gender identity/expression topics in the campus library/libraries?			
6. Does your campus include sexual orientation issues in new faculty/staff programs and training opportunities?			
7. Does your campus include gender identity/expression issues in new faculty/staff programs and training opportunities?			
LGBT Student Life	**Yes**	**No**	**N/A**
1. Does your campus regularly offer activities and events to increase awareness of the experiences and concerns of lesbians, gay men, and bisexuals?			
2. Does your campus regularly offer activities and events to increase awareness of the experiences and concerns of transgender people?			
3. Does your campus regularly hold social events specifically for LGBT students?			
4. Does your campus have a college/university-recognized organization for LGBT students and allies?			
5. Does your campus have any student organizations that primarily serve the needs of underrepresented and/or multicultural LGBT populations (e.g. LGBT Latinos/Latinas, international LGBT students, LGBT students with disabilities)?			
6. Does your campus have any student organizations that primarily serve the social and/or recreational needs of LGBT students (e.g. gay social fraternity, lesbian volleyball club, gay coed lacrosse club)?			
7. Does your campus have any academically-focused LGBT student organizations (e.g. LGBT Medical Association, LGBT Public Relations Organization, Out Lawyers Association)?			

Originally from the LGBT-Friendly Campus Climate Index
http://www.campusprideindex.org/

Revised 1.17.14 mj

UH Commission on the Status of LGBTI Equality Survey

8. Does your campus have any student organizations that primarily serve the religious/spiritual needs of LGBT students (e.g. Unity Fellowship for Students, Gays for Christ, LGBT Muslims)?			
LGBT Housing & Residence Life	Yes	No	N/A
1. Does your campus offer LGBT students a way to be matched with a LGBT-friendly roommate in applying for campus housing?			
2. Does your campus enable transgender students to be housed in keeping with their gender identity/expression?			
3. Does your campus provide a LGBT theme housing option or a LGBT/Ally living-learning community program?			
4. Does your campus offer students with non-student same-sex partners the opportunity to live together in family housing equally to those married opposite-sex couples in the same situation?			
5. Does your campus allow residence life staff with same-sex partners who are not affiliated with the college/university to live together in a residence hall on an equal basis with married opposite-sex couples?			
6. Does your campus offer gender-neutral/single occupancy restrooms in campus housing?			
7. Does your campus offer individual showers in campus housing to protect the privacy of transgender students?			
8. Does your campus provide on-going training on LGBT issues and concerns for residence life professional and student staff at all levels?			
LGBT Campus Safety	Yes	No	N/A
1. Does your campus have a clear and visible procedure for reporting LGBT-related bias incidents and hate crimes?			
2. Does your campus have a bias incident and hate crime reporting system for LGBT concerns that includes the following:			
Bias Incident Team			
Methods for supporting the victim			
Outreach for prevention of future incidents			
Protocol for reporting hate crimes and bias incidents			
3. Does your campus public safety office do outreach to LGBT people and meet with LGBT student leaders/organizations?			
4. Does your campus provide training for public safety officers on sexual orientation issues and concerns and/or anti-gay violence?			
5. Does your campus provide training for public safety officers on gender identity/expression issues and concerns and/or anti-transgender violence?			
LGBT Counseling & Health	Yes	No	N/A
1. Does your campus offer support groups for LGBT individuals in the process of coming out and for other LGBT issues/concerns?			
2. Does your campus offer individual counseling for students that is sensitive and affirming for (supportive) LGBT issues/concerns?			

Originally from the LGBT-Friendly Campus Climate Index
http://www.campusprideindex.org/

Revised 1.17.14 mj

UH Commission on the Status of LGBTI Equality Survey

	Yes	No	N/A
3. Does your campus provide training for health-center staff to increase their sensitivity to the special health care needs of LGBT individuals?			
4. Does your campus actively distribute condoms and LGBT-inclusive information on HIV/STD/STI services and resources?			
5. Does your campus enable transitioning transsexual students to have their hormone replacement therapy covered by insurance?			
LGBT Recruitment & Retention Efforts	**Yes**	**No**	**N/A**
1. Does your campus actively seek to recruit and retain LGBT students, similar to other targeted populations (e.g. ethnic/multicultural students, athletes, international students)?			
2. Does your campus have any scholarships specifically for LGBT students and LGBT allies?			
3. Does your campus include sexual orientation issues in new student orientation programs?			
4. Does your campus include gender identity/expression issues in new student orientation programs?			
5. Does your campus have a Lavender or Rainbow Graduation (i.e. a special graduation ceremony for LGBT students and allies)?			
6. Does your campus have a LGBT mentoring program to welcome and assist LGBT students in transitioning to academic and college life?			
7. Does your campus participate in an LGBT admissions fair to do outreach to prospective LGBT college students?			

Completed by

Campus Name

Originally from the LGBT-Friendly Campus Climate Index
http://www.campusprideindex.org/

Revised 1.17.14 mj

Figure 18.1. UH Commission on the Status of LGBTI Equality Survey.

REFERENCES

Asato, B. (2009, August 1). UH coach McMackin suspended, takes pay cut. *Honolulu Advertiser.* Retrieved from http://search.proquest.com/docview/415085162?accountid=86187

Campus Pride Index. (2016). About Us. Retrieved from https://www.campusprideindex.org/menu/aboutus

Deitrich, J. (1994). The lessons of the law: Same-sex marriage and Baehr v. Lewin. *Marquette Law Review, 78*(1), 121–152.

General Election. (1998). Hawai'i Office of Elections, November 3, 1998, Retrieved from http://elections.hawaii.gov/resources/revision-and-amendment-of-the-hawaii-state-constitution

Grossman, J. L. (2013). Hawai'i Comes Full Circle on Same-Sex Marriage. *Verdict.*

Hawai'i Gives Legislature the Power to Ban Same-sex Marriage. (1998, November 3). Retrieved from http://www.cnn.com/ALLPOLITICS/stories/1998/11/04/same.sex.ballot/

Herek, G. M., Gillis, J. R., & Cogan, J. C. (1999). Psychological sequelae of hate crime victimization among lesbian, gay, and bisexual adults. *Journal of Consulting and Clinical Psychology, 67*(6), 945–951.

Hull, K. E. (2006). Same-sex marriage: The cultural politics of love and law. New York, NY: Cambridge University Press.

Kosciw, J. G., Greytak, E. A., Bartkiewicz, M. J., Boesen, M. J., & Palmer, N. A. (2012). The 2011 national school climate survey: The experiences of lesbian, gay, bisexual and transgender youth in our nation's schools. *Gay, Lesbian and Straight Education Network (GLSEN).* 121 West 27th Street Suite 804, New York, NY 10001.

Krauss, B. (2002, May 1). Our Honolulu. *Honolulu Advertiser.* Retrieved from http://the.honoluluadvertiser.com/article/2002/May/01/ln/ln60abob.html

Lambda Legal (2016). Beahr v Miike. Retrieved from http://www.lambdalegal.org/in-court/cases/baehr-v-miike

Morris, R. J. (2015). Implications of Hawai'i same-sex marriage for policy, practice, & culture. *Asian Pacific American Law Journal, 20*(1), 1–24.

Office of the President. (2016). UH Commission on Lesbian, Gay, Bisexual, Transgender and Queer+ (LGBTQ+) Equality. Retrieved from https://www.Hawai'i.edu/offices/op/lgbti/index.html

Plummer, K. (2005). Critical humanism and queer theory. *The Sage Handbook of Qualitative Research, 3*, 357–373.

Privacy protections in state constitutions. (2015, March 12). Retrieved from http://www.ncsl.org/research/telecommunications-and-information-technology/privacy-protections-in-state-constitutions.aspx

Rainbow comments upset gay activists. (2000, July 28). *Honolulu Star-Bulletin.* Retrieved from http://search.proquest.com/docview/412296893?accountid=86187

Reardon, D. (2013, November 15). The 'H' takes a week off as rainbows go retro. *Honolulu Star-Advertiser.* Retrieved from http://search.proquest.com/docview/1458712409?accountid=86187

Resilient resistance: the activism of Ku umeaaloha Gomes. (1996, October). *Island Lifestyle*, pp. 16–18.

Sant'Ambrogio, M. D., & Law, S. A. (2010). *Baehr v. Lewin* and the long road to marriage equality. *U. Haw. L. Rev., 33*, 705.

Shapiro, D. (2009, August 05). UH learns lessons from past PR fiascos. *Honolulu Advertiser.* Retrieved from http://search.proquest.com/docview/415016758?accountid=86187

Tsai, S. (2009, July 31). UH weighs response to McMackin's slur. *Honolulu Advertiser.* Retrieved from http://search.proquest.com/docview/414935061?accountid=86187

U.S. Department of Justice. (1996). *Hate Crimes Statistics* [Data file]. Retrieved from https://ucr.fbi.gov/hate-crime/1996

United States. Bureau of the Census. (2011). The Population of Hawai'i by Race/Ethnicity [Data file]. Retrieved from http://www.ohadatabook.com/T01-03-11u.pdf

Yuen, M. (1997, November 12). New isle PAC hopes to derail gay marriages. *Honolulu Star-Bulletin*. Retrieved from http://search.proquest.com/docview/412249601?accountid=86187

Yuen, M. (1998, June 19). Christian soldiers pour in for same- sex battle. *Honolulu Star-Bulletin*. Retrieved from http://search.proquest.com/docview/412270491?accountid=86187

PART SIX

Reaching Out

Transformative LGBTQ+ Curriculum and Pedagogy

CHAPTER NINETEEN

Creating an Inclusive Learning Environment for LGBT Students on College Campuses

CLAYTON R. ALFORD

INTRODUCTION

All colleges should develop academic environments that discourage discrimination against students and faculty who identify themselves as lesbian, gay, bisexual, or transgender (LGBT). Burney (2012) documents many instances of harassment and discrimination against LGBT students because of their sexual orientation. Institutions of higher education should expand their curriculums to include courses on LGBT culture and sexual diversity. They should urgently fund centers focused on making LGBTQ faculty and students safe, comfortable, and welcome throughout the campus. Such centers would welcome all students and faculty, regardless of their sexual identity. This chapter will examine strategies colleges could use to create learning environments that welcome faculty and students of all sexual identities and preferences.

HISTORICAL BACKGROUND

Linde, Lemonik, and Mikaila (2015) discussed the United Nations adoption of the Universal Declaration of Human Rights in 1948 as a pledge to provide social justice. This chapter will explore LGBT rights as Human Rights. Only recently and reluctantly, have colleges begun to address these rights after landmark Supreme Court opinions on marriage equality.

Despite the Human Rights platform, Fowler's (2015) interview with Shane Windmeyer on his "Campus Pride" organization revealed that a quarter of gay college students met forms of harassment and discrimination every day on campus. Fowler found only about 13% of colleges listed sexual orientation as a category of their non-discrimination statement and only seven percent of college institutions included gender identity.

In 1987, researchers and organizations converged to establish networks that engaged in LGBT research including conferences and seminars (Jones, 2013). The trend also moved away from viewing non-heterosexuals as deviants and sexual nonconformists. College educators embraced sexualities research during the 1990s and the trend continues into the 21st century.

According to Orlov and Allen (2014), many LGBT faculty members avoid revealing their sexual orientation for fear of reprisals from colleagues and college administrators. All faculty members deserve the same right to reveal or hide their sexual orientation or identity. Tyson (as cited in Orlov & Allen, 2014) used the term heterosexism. Tyson's followers believed heterosexuality was the only suitable form of sexual orientation. This approach implied that all other forms of sexual identity were deviant.

Some LGBT students might develop a feeling of inferiority and, ostracism from other students because their sexual identity does not align readily with heterosexism. Dermer, Smith, and Barto (2010) asserted supporters of LGBT rights needed to understand the societal, individual, and rational forces that negatively influence LGBT students. Educators who support inclusiveness of LGBT students might face bigotry and homophobia. Dermer et al. suggested the derogatory term homophobia originated as a way to marginalize this minority group.

Similarly, Ball, Buist, and Woods (2014) suggested the word Queer deserved the same recognition as lesbian, gay, bisexual, and transgender and used the acronym LGBTQ. Some criminologists believe the term queer deserves recognition in criminology and other fields of academia. Ball et al. suggested criminologists improve their interaction with people who identify as LGBTQ and conduct research into social and criminal injustices experienced by them. These researchers further suggest criminologists define queer criminology as diverse methods, reflections, and perspectives on how those who consider themselves LGBTQ view their sexuality within society.

Current queer criminology research focuses too much on deviance and injustice for those identified as LBGTQ and largely ignores education and economic opportunities. Other organizations in educational research actively promote matters about the LBGTQ community. Ball et al. (2014) claimed criminologists fell behind in LGBTQ research and called for more research into this community. Criminologists should expand their role in educational inclusion for postsecondary LGBTQ students.

Jones (2013) added the term intersex to gay, lesbian, bisexual, transgender, and queer (GLBTIQ) to comprise research in sex education methodology. Regardless of the acronym, students who see their sexuality as different face discrimination in college campuses. One persistent problem involves bullying of students who identify their sexual orientation as different from heterosexual. Jones stated college educators believed education was a major factor in combatting bullying on college campuses. The bullied student is a recent phenomenon in social science and education research (Jones, 2013).

Further investigation of LGBT research revealed the acronym of LGBTQQIA to represent lesbian, gay, bisexual, transgender, queer, questioning, intersex, and allies (Steinmetz, 2014). The research literature contains little on intersex people. This group deserves further investigation for the general populace to understand them through an objective lens. According to Steinmetz, intersex suggests a misalignment at birth and the chromosomes do not typically match in the usual manner.

MAINTAINING A SAFE ENVIRONMENT FOR LGBT STUDENTS

Institutions of higher learning should do more than pay lip service to LGBT-related antidiscrimination and antiharassment policies. All students have the basic right to feel secure; college administrators must develop effective programs that provide all students with a safe environment. According to Burney (2012), a college or school is one of the places where hate crimes are prevalent. Some might suggest college authorities have failed to make the safety of all students a sufficiently high priority.

Still others advised educators to create curriculums that integrate LGBT content for K-12 schools. Veceillo (2012) suggested educators develop more diverse and up-to-date curriculums to accommodate LGBT students. The FAIR Education Act of California of 2011 (FAIR) required school districts to provide accurate, fair, inclusive, and respectful accounts of people with disabilities and people who identify as LGBT. FAIR also required social studies and history curriculums to include LGBT programs. School districts in other states could benefit from including LGBT programs into their curriculums and embracing inclusion.

Signing FAIR into law-triggered controversy (Veceillo, 2012). People did not know how the act would affect K–12 students and the curriculum. Veceillo (2012) proposed including LGBT content in California's social studies and history content standards. California introduced more gay-themed books into the school curriculum. FAIR did not make wholesale changes to the curriculum, which already included mandatory provision for ethnic diversity (Willis, 2011).

FAIR helped education stakeholders include LGBT subject matter in the California school curriculum. Despite California requiring all school districts to have LGBT material in their curriculum, DeWitt (2015) found many school districts in other states were very reluctant to follow the same path. The Anti-Defamation League (ADL) called for bringing LGBT topics into school curriculum (ADL, 2015). Nevertheless, introducing such subjects into the K–12 school curriculums continues to spark contentious debates and controversy.

DeWitt (2015) identified three reasons for a reluctance for many school districts to implement LGBT topics in the curriculum. He mentioned unsupportive administrators and parental pushback, as many parents do not want their children exposed to such matters. The final reason DeWitt listed was school stakeholders did not know where to start coverage of LGBT material. People often fear the unknown and unfamiliar.

Therefore, it is with this background that many LGBT students enter college with little or no exposure in their K–12 Schools to satisfactory coverage of their sexual identity. Colleges have the unenviable task of creating a curriculum that accepts students from diverse backgrounds. At the same time, they must develop programs and curriculums of substance that handle the diversity of sexual identity and orientation as comprehensively as the diversity of race, creed, and ethnicity.

Fordham University, in New York City, chronicled what they considered successful LGBT college programs (DiPietro, 2012). The report presented by Fordham provides resource material for college educators concerned with creating diverse programs. Fordham University's Center for Ethics Education hosted productive discussions on creating LGBTQ inclusive learning experiences that offered attendees valuable resources.

Kennesaw State University classified their resources as General GLBTIQ Teaching Resources. DiPietro (2012), of Kennesaw State University, identified seven principles necessary to creating successful LGBT-inclusive classrooms. She felt students (a) prior knowledge could help or hinder them in learning about diversity as knowledge from prior experiences can shape new information and discover if students become receptive to it. Other areas involved (b) organization, (c) motivation, (d) mastery, (e) goal-directed practice with feedback, (f) students' current level of development, and (g) monitoring learning approaches. DiPietro believes learners connect information to the pathways developed by their lived experiences. She postulated students' motivation is a sustaining force in receiving new information.

DiPietro (2012) suggested mastery required students to develop competent skills and learning how to apply the information they learned and students needed appropriate feedback to improve their learning outcomes. Students' current intellectual, social, and emotional ability influenced how those from stigmatized groups developed their self-image. The Kennesaw State University Professor claimed students needed to become self-directed learners able to oversee and adjust their approaches to learning. The principles developed by DiPietro could help everyone across the educational spectrum.

Haring-Smith (2012) described the benefits and challenges offered by the diversity of American culture and suggested institutions of higher learning reflected the American culture. She recognized the racial and gender improvements at colleges. Many educators believe in diversity and embrace cultural differences. Haring-Smith commented on invisible diversity and encouraged colleges to reflect and provide equal access and opportunity to students and faculty of all races, cultures, and genders. She suggested their economic and social differences did not prevent them from succeeding in an accepting educational environment.

LGBTQ CAMPUS CLIMATE

Blumenfeld (2012) found LGBTQ people now are recognizing their sexual identities earlier than in the past and readily accepting their non-heterosexual status. One thinks that colleges remain bastions of liberalism where ideas flow freely and everyone welcomes diversity.

Tolerance and Bigotry Often Coexist on Campus

Unfortunately, for many LGBTQ student, a campus climate can remain difficult and unsafe, according to Blumenfeld (2012). Gay, Lesbian, Straight Education Network (GLSEN), as cited by Blumenfeld, noted prevalent bullying and harassment in K-12 schools of such students by peers, faculty and staff. This often alienated students and stakeholders.

The idea of safety applies not only to LGBT students, but also to LGBT faculty members. Smith, Wright, Reilly, and Esposito (2008) addressed the idea of safety concerns for such faculty on college campuses. These educators suggested that such faculty needed a sense of personal security to provide best instructional services to learners. They referenced research that suggested educators who felt safe had higher levels of productivity and professional efficacy.

DiPietro (2012) believes a resolution to this disconnect can come with integrating disciplines by devoting scrutiny to their content. Students connect to a discipline when they see the discipline as having relevance in their lives. Personal reflection, awareness of self, and self-monitoring offer critical implications for closeted LGBT students, according to DiPietro. Educators, who offer a nurturing climate, could allow more reflection and introspection of students to share their true feelings without their instructor or peers judging them.

Students' views of a classroom environment where they do not feel welcomed present challenges to college educators. The subjectivity of students can influence their opinions. Kalatskaya (2016) believed the meaning of learning becomes lost when students fail to see a connection to real-life events. She promoted personal meaning in learning. Consequently, learning differs at different stages of age development (Kalatskaya, 2016). Education needs to have relevance for learners, LGBT college students often feel disaffected from the curriculum.

This becomes disturbing to LGBT students when they suspect that heterosexuals view them as invisible, with no rights or feelings. Bilodeau and Renn (2005) found many student affairs professionals believed they needed to grasp how such learners developed their sexual identities before implementing programs for this group. Some student affairs personnel and other college staffers might have little knowledge of LGBT concerns. A collaborative effort becomes useful when creating programs to accommodate LGBT students' needs on college campuses.

Colleges can benefit from the valuable expertise of scholars who have a personal narrative that shares their experiences about identifying with the LGBT community. If non-heterosexual faculty did not feel threatened by revealing their identity, perhaps they would share more about their feelings of sexual identification. Orlov and Allen (2014) believed the perceived backlash levelled against non-heterosexual faculty members becomes a burden. LGBT faculty members must weigh their choices carefully before acknowledging sexual identities that might jeopardize their employment and livelihood.

Cullen (2007) identified many examples of heterosexual privilege not granted to members of the non-heterosexual community. A heterosexual privilege checklist revealed that heterosexuals did not fear if those close to them found out about their sexual preferences, they would not suffer social or economic reprisals (Heterosexual Privilege Checklist, n.d.) The checklist contained a list 40 examples of heterosexual privileges including the lack of fear in revealing sexual orientation to family, friends, and co-workers. The heterosexual privilege checklist originated from research on white privilege by McIntosh (1990), where McIntosh provided a list of 50 types of advantages whites had over nonwhites in America.

Within this framework, college education stakeholders (faculty, students, administrators, trustees, staff, and security personnel) will need substantial training on the sensitivity of the LGBT community and to reduce or remove heterosexual privilege. The advantages of heterosexual privileges become evident when one reads the checklist. Heterosexuality's pervasive sense of normality leads to labeling any divergence as deviant.

Later, members of the LGBT community have to overcome the insidious labeling and defamation by members of the heterosexual college community. Cullen (2007) implied some in the heterosexual community believe that LGBT members do not have the right to exist. Many members in both communities struggle to coexist peacefully. Coexistence between both groups can occur when each group recognizes the differences and works to develop harmonious relationships.

Like all students, LGBT students can experience negative, passive, or neutral attitudes toward learning. Rarely is the student active because of external forces out of the student's control, according to Kalatskaya (2016). The current trend in education calls for educators to remind advanced learners to take charge of their own learning. However, students of any orientation could channel their intellectual curiosity elsewhere, if they believe the curriculum has little connection to them.

Innovative Learning for LGBT Students

Students feel involved with learning when they form or develop a connection with learning. An innovative instructor will find a way to reach his or her students and share resources of topical interests with them. According to Kalatskaya (2016), innovative learning characteristics focus on recognizing students' own meaning of learning. The pride, dignity confidence in achievement, and intellectual initiative contribute to students' subjectivity level (Kalatskaya, 2016). An important duty of college instructors involves the ability to help students set up practical goals that go beyond the prescribed college curriculum. Smith et al. (2008) concluded innovation in schools with support for LGBT faculty and students saw a positive correlation between teacher efficacy and student achievement.

Schools have developed innovative programs to support student diversity and Smith et al. (2008) believed additional factors such as shared-decision making, self-confidence, and collegial relationships between school personnel all contribute to school innovation. Austin (1990) explained factors such as race, class, and gender all affect the views of individuals. The existence of college diversity suggests that many in the academic community do not view events through a heterosexual lens.

Thus, LGBT faculty and students' opinions often conflict and do not align with those views held by the heterosexual community. Thinkers steeped in the European tradition suggest divergent dialog and diversity of ideas exists side-by-side because of the collegial bonds traditionally held by members of the academic community. The strength of collegiality, according to Austin (1990), motivates faculty members who have often rated it far more relevant than higher salaries as long as the atmosphere allows for autonomy (Austin, 1990).

The spirit of collegiality should allow LGBT faculty members to feel less ostracized and able to express their identities. Smith et al. (2008) claimed most educational professionals wanted conditions for such students to improve. However, according to Smith et al., educators have only begun in this century to look at improving conditions for LGBT faculty. More research would provide information on the struggles LGBT faculty members face in the college community.

The climate for LGBT faculty members on college campuses evolved with the climate of society (Smith et al., 2008). Nevertheless, conflict can arise when diverse cultures mingle, such as LGBT culture and the dominant heterosexual culture when they converge and ideas of the academy sometimes collide. Austin (1990) asserted American colleges changed because of changing views held by the public who, over time, have become more tolerant about such concerns. Colleges do not always keep pace with the cultural trends and norms of society on students, faculty, and other staff members who identify themselves as non-heterosexual.

Smith et al. (2008) also examined heteronormativity and gender role polarization as problems in the workplace environment. This research team kept a vague and ambiguous definition of heteronormativity. Eldis (2016) pointed out practitioners and policymakers vigorously try to impose heteronormative exclusions and inequalities that often adhere to the status quo. Eldis is a website that strives to promote equity in the workplace environment. The website proclaims it provides information on international development concerns and remains dedicated to improving conditions for people in the workplace.

Some educators believe that too much emphasis on political correctness deprives many colleges of character and meaning. Treadgold (2016). This dichotomy presents challenges to colleges that encourage equality, diversity, liberalism, and sustainability they justifiably argue against elitism, racism, sexism, and heteronormativity (Treadgold, 2016). One could argue the origins of heteronormativity need further examination instead of wholesale revocation of the theory. Many college students might have little or no knowledge of this paternalistic system that clearly defines gender roles in culture. Treadgold prefers that colleges highlight academic freedom more so than inclusion and diversity.

Enson (2015) believed far too little progress developed in removing heteronormativity in both education and healthcare. Enson defined heteronormativity as a form of severe institutionalized norms that inflicts negative effects on the livelihood of LGBTQ citizens and causes non-heterosexuals to reflect negatively on themselves. Gender mandates that males and females adhere to prescribed norms, which can result in labeling as an outcast anyone who adopts a variation from these prescribed roles.

According to Enson (2015), gender is a socially built patriarchal system that influences society. Society demands citizens subscribe to certain behaviors that match the stereotypical conduct of a person's gender. Individuals who resist the dictates of society run the risk of having the label of deviant ascribed to them, or the dominant culture may ostracize them. Enson speculated that pervasive and stereotypical gender norms contributed substantially to the increased heterosexual dominance and heteronormativity. Essentially and inseparably, gender and culture link and unify in dictating the behaviors of males and females, as defined by their birth certificates.

THE ACADEMY AND LIBRARY CENSORSHIP OF LGBT CONCERNS

The culture of the academy implies that good work and deeds result from like-minded individuals who assemble at the academy to promote positive change and universal improvement for everyone. Austin (1990) pointed out the culture of the academy implied the institution needed a mission and goals to sustain the institution. Leadership style, curriculum, academic standards, faculty characteristics, student-body composition, and location define a college's culture (Austin, 1990). The mission defines the institution where one works or studies.

Tensions arise when cultures clash and diversity becomes a footnote or talking point. Austin (1990) claimed the meeting of different cultures from faculty and students can lead to conflict. She offered some suggestions to help colleges improve their diversity. Austin advised institutional leaders to help faculty members to understand the differences in their respective fields and review how cultural values influence the opinions of faculty members. Austin stressed the importance of the academy outlining institutional priorities; the academy should celebrate institutional values and put in place a clear reward and evaluation system.

Therefore, the research into LGBT concerns merits a similar importance or priority as any other department or division conducting research funded through the university. Antell, Strothmann, and Downey (2013), in their research, found some librarians employed self-censorship about LGBT-themed resources. These librarians implied some in the library science field do not want to deal with controversial issues and do a form of self-censorship. Libraries house all types of objectionable reading material that some might find insensitive and offensive.

Librarians, like researchers, have inherent biases; however, censorship at university libraries needs further inspection. A researcher might admit to holding a particular bias and under scrutiny, another investigator can detect researcher bias. However, concerns arise when a librarian removes a book from the shelf through selective inspection. Antell et al. (2013) suggested that most libraries did not have LGBT collections of high quality. Library censorship exits in red states and blue states and in both urban and rural areas, as stated by Antell and her colleagues. Library censorship does not gather the attention it needs.

Sawyer, Sasso, Gandara, Weaver, and Jackson (2015) discussed Sheltered Instruction Observation Protocol (SIOP) and LGBT attitudes to an inclusive workplace agenda. In such a workplace, employees regardless of sexual orientation feel comfortable and secure. SIOP actively supports LGBT members to engage in scholarly research. Some of SIOP research might bridge the research-to-practice gap.

Out and Equal, an American not-for profit organization whose supporters encourage workplace equality, encourages high quality practitioner research. This organization, which supports LGBT concerns, holds a summit each year devoted to the needs of diversity in employment, and offers a forum for such members to network. At the summit, Out and Equal advised greater engagement and cooperation with SIOP and members of the LGBT community (Sawyer et al., 2015).

STRATEGIES TO IMPROVE CONDITIONS OF LGBT FACULTY AND STUDENTS

Colleges grapple with strategies to improve conditions of LGBT faculty and students. Fowler (2015) stated it made economic sense for colleges to reach out to all potential students in today's buyers' market and explain ways they accept students from all communities. Students have a choice where to attend college and students might lean toward attending institutions with records of encouraging diversity. Fowler also believed more students, regardless of their sexual identity, want to attend colleges noted for their tolerant atmosphere.

Even so, Fowler (2015) pointed out that not all colleges have embraced diversity, particularly regarding sexual identity. She mentioned Campus Pride still held relevance for helping LGBT students adjust to college education. Campus Pride works with historically black colleges and universities (HBCUs) to help faculty, administrators, and students function on campus (Fowler, 2015). Minority groups often benefit from allies. Fowler believed heterosexual allies often act as advocates for LGBT students. However, she warned breaking the cycle of invisibility needed more LGBT people from all socioeconomic statuses standing up for their rights.

Windmeyer (2012) challenged college faculty, staff, and administrators to shed their ambivalence towards LGBT rights as they have the responsibility for the safety of such students on campuses. Colleges should recognize and cure campus discrimination and harassment of LGBT students and faculty. The harassment of LGBT students remains high and protections low, according to Windmeyer. He called for accountability by college administrators for the safety of all such students.

Enson (2015) believed those in education and in the healthcare field could do more to correct biases inflicted against LGBT students and faculty. She cited the 2012 Stonewall report's recommendations that schools take an active part in preventing homophobic bullying. Some would argue that educators fail to act aggressively against bullying of LGBT faculty and students. It will take a widespread and far-reaching effort by all members of the academic community to combat discrimination against LGBT members.

This might mean working with librarians on college campuses to avoid the self-censorship of banning LGBT-themed books and academic material. Antell et al. (2013) claimed librarians have discretionary power to self-censor material they might find objectionable, including selections of LGBT material. The notion that colleges involve freethinking and intellectual growth suggests their libraries should encourage and promote scholarly and academic debate.

CONCLUSION

Social justice as an idea and theme filters through most colleges. Social change can originate from grass-roots efforts and receive approval from members of the entrenched intellectual college community. As for gender roles, members of the LGBT community have opposed the notion that one's sexual identity must align with the heterosexual majority's. Some academy members prefer colleges to avoid encouraging or endorsing LGBT rights. Some academy members believe colleges should keep a neutral posture toward LGBT rights. They view as controversial and challenging even talking about such topics. Recent backlashes against members of the LGBT community caused some academicians to reevaluate views on heteronormativity.

REFERENCES

Antell, K., Strothmann, M., & Downey, J. (2013). Self-censorship in selection of LGBT themed materials. *Reference & User Service Quarterly, 53*(2), 104–107.

Anti-Defamation League. (2015). The time is now: Bringing LGBT topics into the classroom. Retrieved July 12, 2016 from http://blog.adl.org/education/the-time-is-now-bringing-lgbt-topics-into-the-classroom?utm_source=rss&utm_medium=rss&utm_campaign=the-time-is-now-bringing-lgbt-topics-into-the-classroom

Austin, A. (1990). Faculty cultures, faculty values. *New Directions for Institutional Research, 68*, 74. Retrieved July 31, 2016 from http://studentlife.uci.edu/leadership/admin_intern/documents/FacultyCultures.pdf

Ball, M., Buist, C. L., & Woods, J. B. (2014). Introduction to the special issue on queer/ing criminology: New directions and frameworks. *Critical Criminology, 22*, 1–4. doi:10.1007/s10612-013-9231-2

Bilodeau, B. L., & Renn, K. A. (2005). Analysis of LGBT identity development models and implications for practice. *New Directions for Student Services, 111*(Fall). Retrieved July 24, 2016 from https://msu.edu/~renn/BilodeauRennNDSS.pdf

Blumenfeld, W. (2012). LGBTQ campus climate: The good and the still very bad. *Diversity & Democracy, 15*(1). Retrieved July 18, 2016 from http://www.diversityweb.org/DiversityDemocracy/vol15no1/report.cfm

Burney, M. (2012). Diverse-convergence: Diversity and inclusion. *Chronicle of Higher Education, 3*(16), 50–53.

Cullen, M. (2007). Examples of heterosexual privilege. In *Teaching for Diversity and Social Justice* (2nd ed.).. Retrieved July 26, 2016 from http://www.mauracullen.com/wp-content/uploads/2010/11/Examples-of-Heterosexual-Privilege.pdf

Dermer, S. B., Smith, S. D., & Barto, K. K. (2010). Identifying and correctly labeling sexual practice, discrimination and oppression. *Journal of Counseling & Development, 88*(Summer), 325–331. Retrieved July 10, 2016 from EBSCOhost database.

DeWitt, P. (2015). 3 reasons why many schools won't offer LGBT curriculum. Retrieved July 12, 2016 from http://blogs.edweek.org/edweek/finding_common_ground/2015/07/3_reasons_why_many_schools_wont_offer_LGBT_curriculum.html

DiPietro, M. (2012). Applying the seven learning principles to creating LGBT-inclusive education. *Association of American Colleges & Universities, 15*(1). Retrieved July 17, 2016 from https://www.aacu.org/publications-research/periodicals/applying-seven-learning-principles-creating-lgbt-incl

Eldis. (2016). Why does heteronormativity matter? Retrieved August 3, 2016 from http://www.eldis.org/go/topics/resource-guides/gender/keyissues/heteronormativity/why-does-heteronorm

Enson, S. (2015). Causes and consequences of heteronormativity in healthcare and education. *British Journal of Nursing, 10*(2), 73–78.

The FAIR Education Act. (2011). Retrieved July 11, 2016 from http://www.faireducationact.com/about-fair/

Fowler, N. (2015). An interview with Shane Windmeyer. *INSIGHT into Diversity, 82*(3), 28–29.

Haring-Smith, T. (2012) Broadening our definition of diversity. *Association of American Colleges & Universities, 98*(2), Retrieved July 17, 2016 from https://www.aacu.org/publications-research/periodicals/broadening-our-definition-diversity

Heterosexual privilege checklist. (n.d.). Retrieved July 26, 2016 from http://www.sap.mit.edu/content/pdf/heterosexual_privilege.pdf

Jones, T. (2013). How sex education research methodologies frame GLBTIQ students. *Sex Education, 13*(6), 687–701, doi:10.1080/14681811.2013.806262

Kalatskaya, N. N. (2016). Personal meanings of learning in the process of formation of students' subjectivity. *International Journal of Environmental & Science Education, 11*(5), 685–692. doi:10.12973/ijese.2016.341a

Linde, R., Lemonik, A., & Mikaila, M. (2015). Teaching progress: A critique of the grand narrative of human rights as pedagogy for marginalized students. *Reading Teacher, 103*, 26–36.

McIntosh, P. (1990). White privilege: Unpacking the invisible knapsack. Retrieved July 28, 2016 from https://www.deanza.edu/faculty/lewisjulie/White%20Priviledge%20Unpacking%20the%20Invisible%20Knapsack.pdf

Orlov, J. M., & Allen, K. R. (2014). Being who I am: Effective teaching, learning, student support, and societal change through LGBT faculty freedom. *Journal of Homosexuality, 61*, 1025–1052. doi:10.1080/00918369.2014.870850

Sawyer, K., Sasso, T., Grandara, D., Weaver, J., & Jackson, M. (2015). From the SIOP LGBT committee: Bringing research into practice: SLOP's engagement with out and equal. *The Industrial-Organizational Psychologist, 52*(3), 173–175.

Smith, N. J., Wright, N., Reilly, C., & Esposito, J. (2008). A national study of LGBT educators' perceptions of their workplace climate. American Educational Research Association. *New York*. Retrieved July 31, 2016 from http://files.eric.ed.gov/fulltext/ED501252.pdf

Steinmetz, K. (2014). This is what intersex mean. *Time Magazine*. Retrieved July 11, 2016 from http://www.isna.org/faq/history

Treadgold, W. (2016). The university we need. *Commentary, 141*(2), 27–32. Retrieved August 3, 2016 from http://web.a.ebscohost.com.contentproxy.phoenix.edu/ehost/pdfviewer/pdfviewer?vid=4&sid=8e481da7-7109-4f2f-b46b-87f968171f16%40sessionmgr4007&hid=4212

Veceillo, S. (2012). Enacting FAIR education: Approaches to integrating LGBT content in the K-12 curriculum. *Multicultural Perspectives, 14*(3), 169–174.

Willis, J. (2011). The FAIR Education Act: Intertwining history and tolerance in California schools. *Harvard Law and Policy Review.* Retrieved July 11, 2016 from http://harvardlpr.com/2011/04/19/the-fair-education-act-intertwining-history-and-tolerance-in-california-schools/

Windmeyer, S. (2012). Invisible students, missing programs and policies: Taking responsibility for safety and academic success of the LGBR population. *University Business, 15*(6), 25–25.

CHAPTER TWENTY

Transgender/Gender Non-Binary Inclusion IN Higher Education Courses

BRANDON L. BECK, KATHERINE LEWIS, AND SUSAN M. CROTEAU

INTRODUCTION

Student discrimination and harassment is unfortunately commonplace on college campuses. In particular, gender diverse and sexual minority students are marginalized at high rates. Curricular intervention is needed to overcome the marginalization and to support the students who are part of these underrepresented communities.

Transgender is the "T" in the often-heard acronym LGBT. Meaning "beyond" or "on the other side of" gender, it typically refers to people who identify or express their gender in a way that does not align with socially normed expectations for their birth sex. The term LGBT stands for Lesbian/Gay/Bisexual/Transgender and is an overly-simplistic way of grouping a wide variety of sexual and gender minorities into a single community. Sometimes the acronym changes from LGBT to LGBT+ to LGBTQI or LGBTQIA or a variety of other acronyms that have varying degrees of popularity or ease of use. In most cases, the "Q" stands for queer or questioning, the "I" for Intersex, and the "A" for Asexual, Aromantic, Agender, or Ally. In any of these variations, many identities are still not represented by a letter in the acronym, and the acronym is still confined by Western English-speaking cultural standards. In this study, researchers will use the acronym LGBTQIA to be as inclusive as possible while still working within the bounds of current English linguistic practices (Beck, 2014, p. 2).

Within the classification discourse, Fassinger and Areseneau (2007) notably reported:

> Sexual minorities—typically classified into the four categories of lesbian, gay, bisexual, and transgender (LGBT) people—face common struggles with societal oppression related to their sexual minority status, and they therefore face similar difficulties in developing positive individual identities and healthy communities within that context of oppression. The increasingly frequent addition of "T" to "LGB" speaks to the public—and professional—conflation of all sexual minority concerns under a shared umbrella of invisibility, isolation, and discrimination. However, there are particular dimensions of experience that differentiate these four sexual minority groups in important ways, shaping group-specific trajectories for the development and enactment of identity. (Chapter 1, Section 1, para. 1)

The point here is that each piece of the LGBTQIA umbrella is important individually and that individuals within each piece are important as well. Researchers, influenced by their own experiences and worldviews, may seek to deconstruct the "T" piece of the LGBTQIA umbrella. Indeed, some take issue with the use of the "umbrella" metaphor altogether.

We advocate using the umbrella metaphor with caution. Umbrella terms tend to group disparate people together in a limiting fashion; however, they also give language and voice to marginalized people and help to form alliances across differences in ways that can generate political action. Although some individuals identify with a particular group, we should be careful not to place people into categories without their consent. As the blogger Kristen Stewart (2014) noted,

> … umbrella terms can create an "us-them mentality … eras[ing] our individuality by lumping everyone who is not cisgender and heterosexual into one big group of 'other.' [sic] On the other hand, [they can create] unity and community and power in numbers." (n.p.)

In sum, while it may be beneficial to include transgender/gender non-binary individuals under the LGBTQIA umbrella for the purposes of enhancing their solidarity with other marginalized groups, it is vital that we recognize the factors that disproportionately impact members of that group. It is to those factors that we now turn.

Transgender/gender non-binary students are more marginalized than their cisgender peers, especially on school campuses (Beemyn, Curtis, Davis, & Tubbs, 2005; Beemyn & Rankin, 2016). According to Greytak, Kosciw, and Diaz (2009), one-third of transgender/gender non-binary students heard school staff make homophobic remarks, sexist remarks, and negative comments about someone's gender expression over the course of one year. In addition, these students face high levels of harassment and bullying within educational institutions (Rands, 2009). Transgender/gender non-binary individuals face marginalization outside educational institutions as well. For members of this group, murder is an everyday possibility, especially for community members who are also persons of color. From January to July of 2016, 15 known murders of transgender/gender non-binary women of color occurred in the United States (Collins, 2016).

Often, LGBTQIA inclusion strategies are discussed in higher education settings, but the "T" remains invisible and silent. Educational scholars, however, have recommended making both curricular and pedagogical changes, such as offering gender-complex education, in efforts to support transgender/gender non-binary students (Rands, 2009). We, the authors, support these recommendations that will allow the "T" to be both seen and heard.

After interviewing transgender/gender non-binary students about their experiences, we discovered several ways in which these students are marginalized by faculty; in response, we presented curricular and pedagogical tools (developed from the student interview data) to faculty at the Multicultural Curriculum Transformation and Research Institute (MCTRI), a week-long workshop focused on best practices for broadening and enriching the curriculum by re-envisioning goals, content, teaching strategies, assessment, and classroom interactions with a multicultural lens. After the workshop, we analyzed participant/authors' autoethnographic reflections and informal data from interviews with selected workshop participants in order to develop strategies and suggestions for continued improvement of the workshop model.

THEORETICAL FRAMEWORK

In working toward LGBTQIA inclusion in higher education settings, we utilize concepts of critical curriculum and pedagogy to explore possible strategies for such inclusion at the classroom level. This lens challenges educators to deconstruct and critique social structures, especially those that lead to the oppression of historically marginalized groups (Pishghadam & Naji Meidani, 2012).

According to Page (2016), "Principles of critical pedagogy and critical multicultural education (which includes attention to sexual orientation and gender identity) embrace transforming curriculum, increasing educational equity, and preparing students to live in a diverse society" (p. 116). Furthermore, Pinar and Bowers (1992) contend that, "most educational theorists who have envisioned using the educational process to support social reform could be said to exhibit a 'critical perspective'" (p. 163). Critical pedagogy and curriculum, then, is about focusing on issues of equity and access while transforming the how and what of teaching, relevant to the educational goals of social reform.

Despite critical theory's focus on addressing issues of social injustice, some have taken issue with the way in which this framework conceptualizes diversity.

Critical curriculum and pedagogy scholars Giroux and McLaren (1989) posit that "cultural difference has been treated as a deficit" (p. xxiv). In their view,

> A curriculum policy must be put forth that argues for the importance of drawing upon the cultural resources that students bring to schools as a basis for developing new skills and engaging existing knowledge claims. This concept suggests advocating curriculum policies and modes of pedagogy that both confirm and critically engage the knowledge and experience through which students give meaning to their lives. (p. xxiv)

In this way, Giroux and McLaren suggest that diversity enhances curricular and pedagogical experiences and should be capitalized upon whenever possible.

Through this critical, social reform-oriented lens, we conducted a qualitative study of their work with the MCTRI. Ultimately, the researchers aim to learn more about how transgender/gender non-binary students might inform development of faculty training around issues of their own experiences and how faculty could then apply those strategies and knowledges presented at these workshops. The feedback and information gathered will be used to improve the workshop from year-to-year.

PREPARING FOR PROFESSIONAL DEVELOPMENT

Prior to planning and executing the workshop for transgender/gender non-binary inclusion in higher education classrooms, the researchers interviewed transgender/gender non-binary college students. Interviews with transgender/gender non-binary students showed that students most want faculty to recognize them as students first. Transgender/gender non-binary students reported in interviews and personal conversations that they often have a legal name on the rosters that doesn't match the name they go by and that they have chosen pronouns that they have to disclose to let faculty and friends know about their gender identity, resulting in a continuous self-outing process in classrooms. Students expressed that they want faculty members to be aware of this and to be able to support this process without further outing them by making statements about their identity status or by misgendering them by calling the legal roster even after they've been asked to use a chosen name and pronoun.

Students indicated that faculty members who do the best at respecting them as transgender/gender non-binary students are the ones who include transgender/gender non-binary topics in their classes without expecting students from this community to take on the role of teacher. These students also encouraged us to remind faculty that all students are unique and that everyone has a gender. Transgender/gender non-binary students are encouraging faculty to embrace the concept of gender diversity and the gender spectrum and are interested in seeing classes that include curriculum that recognizes this concept.

Overall, students helped us determine that faculty who called on transgender/gender non-binary students currently enrolled in the class to be the voice for their already marginalized community, often outing them in the process, need to rethink the way they acknowledge and access the identities of their students. Furthermore, some faculty refused to use chosen names and pronouns, while others taught transgender/gender non-binary topics in ways that do not reflect the real-lived experiences of transgender/gender non-binary students. Guided by these student experiences and perspectives, we built a professional development workshop centered on identity work, critical awareness and reflection activities, storytelling, and allyship as a process of building relationships.

IMPLEMENTING PROFESSIONAL DEVELOPMENT

Successful professional development is a complex and strategic process. In this section, we discuss the complexity of individual identity and the importance of critical awareness and reflection.

Identity Work

One of our guiding philosophies in our work in leading this course transformation institute is that in order for a faculty member to work with students of diverse identities and to be respectful of diverse identities, the faculty member must be able to do some personal identity work. As facilitators, we have engaged in our own identity work and are continually conversing with each other and reflecting on our own concepts of power and privilege and of how our identity pieces make us who we are and how they influence our teaching. In order to lead into deeper discussions of how to create inclusive and transformative classes for transgender/gender non-binary students, we first facilitated some identity reflection activities with our participants to begin a process of identity development and thought. These exercises helped the participants explore the benefits of individualizing their curricula. Implicit in this exploration is the notion that critical pedagogy demands an awareness that people are individuals whose identity may not be expressed in ways that reflect common stereotypes about the community to which they belong.

The first awareness activity that we took the participants through was the "snowflake activity." At the outset, every participant is given a blank piece of paper. Vague directions are given (close your eyes, fold the paper in half, fold the paper in half again, tear off the lower right hand corner, turn the paper over, tear off the current right hand corner, unfold the paper, open your eyes and hold your paper up and look around the room). Discussion with the group follows the activity based on guided questions such as "How did this activity make you feel?" "What was difficult about this activity?" "What were your first thoughts when you saw the other participants' snowflakes?" "How do these snowflakes represent the people with whom we interact in our classes?" "What elements of a diverse society can we see metaphorically in this activity?"

Faculty members who were part of the MCTRI expressed fears about this activity. They said things such as, "I was worried that I wasn't doing the right thing." "I thought that mine wasn't going to be like everyone else's." They related this to diversity in that not all their students are the same, and some of their students repeatedly come to class worried about how they will be perceived.

The second activity, called "Cross the Line", is designed to explore concepts of power and privilege for the purpose of encouraging critical thinking about the experiences of diverse populations. During this activity, a set of identity statements is read aloud. Participants are asked to step forward (thereby "crossing the line") when a statement applies to them. While this activity is commonly used in diversity and cultural competence workshops, we have adapted it to our purposes by directly relating the statements to the topics of gender identity and expression, and university teaching. After the activity is complete, we conduct a discussion about power and privilege, and talk about how reflecting on our own positions in the social hierarchy helps us prepare to lead others as they reflect on their own situatedness.

Critical Awareness and Reflection

The next step in our facilitation involves the presentation of statistics related to transgender/gender non-binary college students. These statistics come from a major research report (Greytak, Kosciw, & Diaz, 2009) and responses from our own interviews with students. We then lead a discussion of these marginalizing conditions (e.g., violence, suicide, the usage of names and pronouns), as well as ways in which colleges can be inclusive of these students as proposed by (Beemyn et al., 2005; Beemyn & Rankin, 2016).

Storytelling. Wright and Sandlin (2009) posit that "Individual life experiences, beliefs, morals, ethics, political choices, and personal philosophies—our identities— are filtered through the images, commentary, and artful editing of the forces that operate through popular culture" (p. 135). Wright (2007) indicates that popular culture and media are powerful teaching tools and their effects have lasting impact on learners. Wright's philosophy thus encourages us to share personal stories and explore portrayals of transgender/gender non-binary people in popular culture. To these ends, our lead author tells his own story of being transgender, while the other two authors share their experiences of allyship with the transgender/gender non-binary community, allowing time for participants to ask questions about those experiences. We then engage in discussions about how members of this community are portrayed in entertainment and the media. Many of our participants have questions about Caitlyn Jenner and characters on such cable television shows as *Orange is the New Black* and *Transparent*, and the lead author is then able to compare his real life experiences to these pop culture images.

Our lead researcher, in telling his story, talks about having been a transgender student and of now being a transgender faculty member and of advising the transgender student group at our university. He grew up in and around our university because of the way the town and university interact with each other and because his parents both work at the university—his dad as a professor and his mom as an academic advisor. He knew from a very young age that he wanted to be a professor. He never dreamed it would be at Texas State, but when he finished his PhD and the job opportunity was available, he thought coming back to San Marcos might be nice.

Given the fabulous world of Facebook, all of his high school friends knew that he had transitioned, and the people who recruited him to work at Texas State had known him his whole life because they knew his parents, so he was already out as a transgender man to them as well. He couldn't imagine a better way to begin his career as a professor, knowing that he wanted to be able to be open about his transgender identity and journey and to work a research agenda around transgender/gender non-binary inclusion in schools and practice activism while fulfilling his academic duties.

Our co-authors tell their stories of learning the lifelong process of allyship. During our first year of doctoral studies, we attended several allies trainings and learned about the campus climate for transgender/gender non-binary students. Intrigued, we contacted Dr. Beck and formed a research collaborative. Through this collaborative, we have expanded our knowledge of what it means to be an ally and are continually learning and growing in allyship with the transgender/gender non-binary community. We are both involved in several campus groups and committees that focus on this community's needs, and actively work to address such needs on our campus. We have also conducted research on transgender/gender non-binary inclusion in K-12 and higher education, and present our findings at research conferences for the purpose of expanding knowledge of the issue among educators and educational leaders.

Allyship. The other two researchers discussed allyship as a process of building relationships within gender diverse communities. After sharing their background stories about becoming involved in transgender/gender non-binary-inclusive research, in general, and in the MCTRI, in particular, the researchers discussed the importance of speaking *with* and not *for* communities. They also talked about the necessity of respecting an individual's *first person authority* (Bettcher, 2009). MacDonald (2013) sums up *first person authority* (FPA) nicely by explaining that a person's "self-identifications trump your assumptions" (p. 138). Disrespecting the *first person authority* of a transgender individual is, according to Bettcher (2009), an act of transphobia.

The message to those engaged in the process of allyship, then, is to make deliberate efforts to be guided by an ethical principle of transgender authority over transgender experience. The two authors then followed up with a list of suggestions for appropriate and inappropriate actions to take and words to use when engaging in the lifelong process of allyship. Workshop participants then responded to and discussed these suggestions.

EVALUATING PROFESSIONAL DEVELOPMENT: INTERVIEWS WITH FACULTY MEMBERS

After interviewing several faculty members who attended the workshop, we found that participants were motivated to attend based on the desire to help students develop inclusive and affirming attitudes. Faculty participants aimed to learn methods, strategies, attitudes, and skills conducive to helping their students develop cultural sensitivity and empathy for others. They were also interested in improving the curriculum in their courses that focused on topics of transgender/gender non-binary people and social structures.

One participant said he learned about the personal experiences of transgender/gender non-binary people "in a world where binary is the prevailing assumption." He pointed to the importance of using more inclusive pronouns, sharing that he frequently used the phrase "he or she" in class with the intention of being inclusive of all students. He went on to describe a non-binary student who challenged him on this pronoun usage, and helped him to see that he was "actually excluding them [the non-binary student] and other non-binary people." One participant admitted that before MCTRI he did not teach about transgender/gender non-binary people at all, although he did "gesture at the fact that some people do not identify with traditional gender roles."

Other participants used the interaction in MCTRI as an opportunity to explore lessons they were already teaching and to problematize and deconstruct the ways in which they approach transgender/gender non-binary topics in their courses. One participant talked about how she fears teaching gender and sexuality in her course because she doesn't feel that she'll ever know as much as someone who has lived the experience. We talked about the role of the ally and the importance of using the resources available in order to talk about difficult topics, including listening to student ideas without putting students on the spot.

In another positive development, a participant stated that the MCTRI session will enable him to "engage [transgender/gender non-binary students] with more understanding and sensitivity and perhaps a greater awareness of preconceptions that would have been invisible previously." He also stated that he has become more aware of typical practices which could make such students uncomfortable or place them in danger, specifically mentioning "taking attendance by calling people's first names on the attendance sheet and inadvertently outing someone." Another participant described his new approach to teaching about transgender/gender non-binary people in the following ways:

> Now, I spend a whole class session or two talking about the social construction of gender and trans-issues, instead of just gesturing at some of the biases and flawed assumptions people standardly make about gender. In the process of preparing for this, I have learned a ton about gender and biological sex as well. So I think the process has led me to develop much more nuanced categories and a much more fine grained understanding of these issues.

After the MCTRI was over, multiple participants followed up with us in order to have extended conversations about their curriculum and lessons on transgender/gender non-binary topics, as well as ways that they can serve as allies and promote understanding and inclusion in their classrooms. These follow-up conversations help us to see the value of our work and to continue to reflect on the ways in which we talk about personal transgender/gender non-binary experience, allyship, and curricular transformation.

CONCLUSION

As Giroux and McLaren (1989) suggest, diversity enhances curricular and pedagogical experiences and should be capitalized upon whenever possible. As we, the authors, reflect on our experiences in facilitating course transformation, we recognize that valuing diversity is vital to the transformation process. We will, therefore, continue to explore the individual experiences of students and faculty using a critical pedagogy approach.

Future implications for our work include using feedback to provide more concrete ways to transform curricula. Our own growth and development in areas of supporting social reform through a critical perspective must continue to expand from the identity development, narrative exploration, and allyship development to include hands-on curriculum development and examples of work that we do in our own classes that includes such techniques as messaging on the syllabus, articles incorporated in class discussions, modeling of class discussions on topics of transgender/gender non-binary topics, and resources to support such discussions in a variety of curricular fields. In thinking about how we continue to improve the work that we do, we must consider First Person Authority (FPA), as well. While we already take into consideration the FPA of transgender/gender non-binary people, we must expand to take into account the FPA of participants, as well. To this end, we plan on pre-surveying participants to determine their knowledge of and current use of transgender/gender non-binary topics in their course.

In conclusion, we believe that exploring the design and facilitation of a faculty development workshop on transgender/gender non-binary inclusion can assist other educational leaders in creating a campus climate that is more affirming for and inclusive of transgender/gender non-binary students. This involves several stages: Listening to transgender/gender non-binary students, engaging with faculty members committed to course transformation, continually assessing the facilitation based on participant feedback is key to understanding what is best for helping faculty create inclusive environments for transgender/gender non-binary students—creating a place of peace and justice for all students to have the best learning opportunities possible.

REFERENCES

Beck, B. L. (2014). *Trans/forming educational leadership: Retrospectives of transgender persons as public intellectuals in school contexts*. (Doctoral dissertation). Retrieved from Texas State Alkek Library. https://digital.library.txstate.edu/handle/10877/5245

Beemyn, B., Curtis, B., Davis, M., & Tubbs, N. J. (2005). Transgender issues on college campuses. *New Directions for Student Services, 111*, 49–60.

Beemyn, G., & Rankin, S. R. (2016). Creating a gender-inclusive campus. In Y. Martínez-San Miguel & S. Tobias (Eds.), *Trans studies: The challenge to hetero/homo normativities* (pp. 21–32). New Brunswick, NJ: Rutgers University Press.

Bettcher, T. M. (2009). Trans identities and first person authority. In L. Shrage (Ed.), *You've changed: Sex reassignment and personal identity*. Oxford: Oxford University Press.

Collins, S. (2016). Deeniqua Dodds becomes the 15th transgender person to be killed in 2016. *Vibe*. Retrieved July 15, 2016 from http://www.vibe.com/2016/07/deeniqua-dodds-transgender-woman-killed/

Ellsworth, E. (1989). Why doesn't this feel empowering? Working through the repressive myths of critical pedagogy. *Harvard Educational Review, 59*(3), 297–325.

Fassinger, R. E., & Areseneau, J. R. (2007). "I'd rather get wet than be under that umbrella": Differentiating the experiences and identities of lesbian, gay, bisexual, and transgender people. In K. J. Bieschke, R. M. Perez, & K. A. DeBord (Eds.), *Handbook of counseling and psychotherapy with lesbian, gay, bisexual, and transgender clients* (2nd ed.). Washington, DC: American Psychological Association.

Giroux, H. A., & McLaren, P. (1989). Schooling, cultural politics, and the struggle for democracy. *Critical pedagogy, the state, and cultural struggle*. New York, NY: SUNY Press.

Greytak, E. A., Kosciw, J. G., & Diaz, E. M. (2009). *Harsh realities*. New York, NY: GLSEN.

MacDonald, J. (2013). An autoethnography of queer transmasculine femme incoherence and the ethics of trans research. *40th Anniversary of Studies in Symbolic Interaction, 40*, 129–152.

Page, M. L. (2016). *LGBTQ inclusion as an outcome of critical pedagogy*. Retrieved from http://libproxy.txstate.edu/login?url=http://search.ebscohost.com/login.aspx?direct=true&db=eue&AN=114185912&site=ehost-live

Pinar, W., & Bowers, C. (1992). Politics of curriculum: Origins, controversies, and significance of critical perspectives. *Review of Research in Education, 18*, 163–190. Retrieved from http://www.jstor.org/stable/1167299

Pishghadam, R., & Naji Meidani, E. (2012). A critical look into critical pedagogy. *Journal for Critical Education Policy Studies (JCEPS), 10*(2), 464–484. Retrieved from http://libproxy.txstate.edu/login?url=http://search.ebscohost.com/login.aspx?direct=true&db=eue&AN=88941568&site=ehost-live

Rands, K. E. (2009). Considering transgender people in education: A gender-complex approach. *Journal of Teacher Education, 60*(4), 419–431.

Stewart, K. (2014). Talk the talk: Umbrella terms. Gaelick [E-zine]. Retrieved from www.gaelick.com

Wright, R. R. (2007). The Avengers, public pedagogy, and the development of British women's consciousness. *New Directions for Adult and Continuing Education, 115*, 63–72.

Wright, R. R., & Sandlin, J. A. (2009). Cult TV, hip hop, shape-shifters, and vampire slayers: A review of the literature at the intersection of adult education and popular culture. *Adult Education Quarterly, 59*(2), 118–141.

CHAPTER TWENTY-ONE

"How Do You Ally?"

Redefining the Language We Use in Ally Education

LAURA D. GENTNER AND KRISTEN ALTENAU KEEN

INTRODUCTION

In the days following the mass shooting at Orlando's Pulse nightclub on June 12, 2016 that resulted in 49 people's deaths and 53 people's injuries, social media feeds were filled with articles on how to be an ally for the LGBTQ+ community in the wake of such a tragedy. While vigils were held across the country in solidarity with the LGBTQ+ community (and the Latinx community to a lesser degree), the country engaged in conversations about prejudice, xenophobia, causes of and responses to violence, hate crimes versus terrorism, privileged, oppressed, and intersecting identities, access to firearms, and mental health. These conversations took place in the context of a larger national discourse including police shootings of black people, transphobic restrictions on public restroom use, and racially, socio-economically, and ideologically charged political primaries.

Calls for social justice are more fervent. The national discourse continues to react to increases in visible violence connected to systems of oppression. Identities are being understood in more intricate, nuanced, and overlapping ways.

As the pendulum swings toward awareness of social justice issues, there is an equal and opposite reaction when those with long-held privileges resist losing them. The traditional lines between oppressed people and their allies are blurred. A new concept of allyship is critical to address the increasing cultural capacity for understanding complex systems of oppression and their effect on intersecting identities. This chapter proposes shifting the traditional concept of "ally" as a noun and identity toward "ally" as a verb and action. The authors further suggest that higher education is an ideal setting in which to establish and promote this reconceptualization of allyship through unique educational opportunities like ally trainings and similar experiences designed to provide participants with the knowledge and skills to better ally with the LGBTQ+ community.

ALLY (N.): "ALLY" AS IDENTITY

Historically, "ally" has been defined as an identity, especially in relation to the LGBTQ+ community. The label was reserved for heterosexual, cisgender individuals who voiced support for members of the LGBTQ+ community. That support has taken many forms over the years, from setting aside fears to provide care for HIV/AIDS patients, to standing in solidarity with family members in pride protests and celebrations, to using seats at influential tables to further the cause of LGBTQ+ inclusivity, to simply telling LGBTQ+ people that they are welcome. The label of "ally" has even been included occasionally as an identity within acronyms for the LGBTQ+ community.

However, many have strong opinions as to whether individuals who are heterosexual and cisgender (denoting or relating to a person whose self-identity conforms with the gender that corresponds to their biological sex; not transgender), no matter how affirming as allies, can truly be a part of the LGBTQ+ community (Sansui, 2016), given the privilege they hold in relation to sexual orientation and gender identity. In addition, there is no litmus test for "ally" as an identity (Ji & Fujimoto, 2013), one only needs to claim the label. This creates significant inconsistency among expectations of ally behaviors and attitudes, as well as inconsistency about the perceived usefulness of allies for the benefit of the LGBTQ+ community. The result is a broad collection of criticisms of allies (McKenzie, 2015; Shaanmichael, 2013; Smith, n.d.; Utt, 2013) and lists of how to be a better ally, sometimes with conflicting messages (Dupere, 2016; Ingall, 2016; Maza, 2016; Reich, 2014).

While academic literature is largely silent on the benefits or disadvantages of "ally" as identity, the world of LGBTQ+ and social justice blogs is not silent, and the disadvantages tend to outweigh the advantages (McKenzie, 2015; Shaanmichael, 2013; SJWiki, n.d.; Smith, n.d.; Utt, 2013). The majority of bloggers who voice frustration with "ally" as identity do not offer an alternative. Indigenous Action Media (IAM) does offer "accomplices" as an alternative to allies in the context of decolonization and restoring indigenous identity, arguing that the definition of accomplice implies fully vested action (2014). While the implied action of "accomplice" is beneficial, it still has the potential pitfall of being considered an identity.

Ultimately, giving heterosexual, cisgender individuals the identity of "ally" further silences those with marginalized identities. The LGBTQ+ community is increasingly diverse as research on sexual orientation and gender identity expands and more identities are discovered and given attention. People with identities outside gay and lesbian (such as bisexual, transgender, asexual, pansexual, aromantic, genderfluid, agender, and others) experience erasure because of a lack of prominence, prevalence, and understanding. As an example, a Google search of the terms "erasure lgbt" returned results that focused almost exclusively on bi-erasure and trans-erasure, failing to address the erasure of the vast majority of LGBTQ+ identities that experience erasure. For those who struggle with erasure, the inclusion of ally as identity in acronyms or descriptions of the LGBTQ+ community magnifies experiences of erasure, prioritizing those with more privilege. Further, "ally" as a separate identity for heterosexual, cisgender people implies that members of the LGBTQ+ community are incapable of taking action or effecting change for themselves and others within the larger marginalized community.

Many college campuses utilize "ally" as an identity in their ally trainings, working to teach students how to be a strong ally to the LGBTQ+ community. As a result, "ally" as identity has given rise to research focused on heterosexual, cisgender allies and their experiences, motivations, and barriers, which is certainly helpful in ally training and education. However, these studies are generally based on limited, informal input from LGBTQ+ identifying people, such as the LGBT Ally Identity Measure (Jones, Brewster, & Jones, 2014), which not only excluded responses from non-heterosexual individuals, but also only consulted eight LGBTQ+ identifying individuals in the process of creating the instrument. By keeping the focus on the allies, rather than the needs of the marginalized population, heterosexual, cisgender people are given further privilege. In order to truly ally with the LGBTQ+ population, educators and heterosexual, cisgender people must prioritize the needs and desires of those who identify within the LGBTQ+ community.

ALLY (V.): "ALLY" AS ACTION

Empirical research studying allyship from the perspective of the marginalized population is scarce (Brown & Ostrove, 2013; Gentner, 2016). One small qualitative study (Gentner, 2016) sought insight from LGBTQ+ college students on what they wanted or needed in an ally. Students overwhelmingly expected particular actions and behaviors. Those actions fell into three categories: education (taking the initiative to learn more about different identities), personal support (listening and supporting friends as they come out and navigate oppression on a daily basis), and advocacy (fighting alongside members of the LGBTQ+ community to stand for equality). These findings align with recommended ally actions from LGBTQ+ support organizations like Gay, Lesbian & Straight Education Network (GLSEN) and PFLAG. This highlights the need to shift concepts of "ally" from identity to action, from noun to verb.

"Ally" as verb highlights the ability of all people within the LGBTQ+ community to take action and effect change. The LGBTQ+ community is often stereotyped as a monolithic population, rather than a community with not only diverse sexual orientations and gender identities, but also a wide range of other intersecting identities, such as race, ethnicity, socioeconomic status, religion, and ability. Crenshaw (1989) coined the term *intersectionality* to describe how people who hold multiple marginalized identities experience compounded oppression. Intersectionality is critical in understanding not only the complex diversity among the LGBTQ+ community, but also the ways in which privilege and marginalization play out among intersecting identities within the LGBTQ+ community (Anders & Devita, 2014). Using the erasure described in the above section as an example, "ally" as a verb honors the work of gay and lesbian members of the LGBTQ+ community in bringing attention to asexual, pansexual, or aromantic identities. Likewise, a black, cisgender lesbian woman can ally with trans women of color. To take the example of allyship beyond the LGBTQ+ community, LGBTQ+ identifying individuals can ally with those in poverty, Jews can ally with Muslims, and latinx individuals can ally with Native Americans, and vice versa. To ally, one need only take an action to support someone with a marginalized identity different than their own identity.

One significant contribution of the current literature on ally as identity has been the illumination of barriers existing for heterosexual, cisgender individuals. Ji and Fujimoto (2013) describe a few hesitations to ally identification:

> It is difficult for a person to determine if he or she has the requisite qualifications to perform the many supportive, educational, and advocacy roles the allies have. A person may have positive attitudes about LGBT issues, but not feel compelled to engage in LGBT activism. ... Moreover, openly identifying as an ally can leave a person vulnerable to negative reactions making it difficult for someone to be comfortable openly identifying oneself as an ally in all personal and professional settings. (p. 1696)

These barriers can significantly hinder some heterosexual, cisgender people from taking action to support the LGBTQ+ community. Yet many of these barriers to ally identity can be easily resolved by defining "ally" as taking action to support members of a group with which one does not identify. By redefining "ally" as a verb, the conversation shifts from "being an ally" (static statements of support or living up to a role) toward "to ally" (taking action to benefit the community).

One need not wait to cross a threshold of being enough of an ally in order to do something. Instead, anyone can ally by taking an action that benefits the LGBTQ+ community. This simple shift in language also implies the perpetual action needed to fight against daily social injustices directed toward the LGBTQ+ community. There is no stopping at owning an ally identity; it is all about action. The seemingly insurmountable task of dismantling systems of oppression and preventing others from having to experience the injustice of prejudice and violence is made manageable by breaking it down into specific actions, which can grow into habits, which make a difference when added together.

Shifting how people define a term requires a shift in culture, which is no small feat. Intentional, consistent, and cohesive language goes a long way in shifting the way a community understands and describes an espoused value (Manning & Bogdan Eaton, 1993). For instance, instead of asking people to describe *why* they ally, asking people to describe *how* they ally necessarily requires them to think about actions they take or have taken. Higher education professionals work daily with campus community members in the midst of shifting their ways of thinking and contemplating their own identities. Not only do "studies show that universities are an important place for cultivating LGBTQ acceptance" (Worthen, 2011, p. 335), but also that student affairs practitioners can play a significant role in shifting student cultures (Manning & Bogdan Eaton, 1993). Therefore higher education has an opportunity to be at the forefront of redefining "ally" as a verb.

ALLYSHIP (N.): REVITALIZING ALLY TRAININGS

There are many educational methods that college campuses can use to transform the term "ally" from a noun to a verb in student vernacular, thereby encouraging an allyship philosophy. While classroom and student organization presentations, campus wide events, and awareness campaigns are all valuable tools to communicate important messages to students, ally trainings provide a unique and powerful learning experience for undergraduate students on campuses across the country. These intentional trainings provide opportunity for exploration of the complexities of sexual orientation and gender identity, reflection on personal biases and beliefs, and contemplation of privilege and oppression existing throughout American culture. But in order to genuinely improve our campus climates and teach our students how to ally, we must move past our students only learning to critically think about these topics, and move toward them taking action against these injustices.

Through intentional learning outcomes, program design, and assessment, ally training programs can model learning environments void of heteronormativity and filled with examples of active inclusivity. One analysis of ally training learning outcomes focuses on important competencies, such as developing awareness of biases and heterosexual privilege, with no focus on continued action (Woodford, Kolb, Durocher-Radeka, & Javier, 2014). Popular lesson plans such as "Coming Out

Stars" (n.d.) are incredibly powerful, and can leave heterosexual, cisgender students feeling anger, frustration, and shock that their LGBTQ+ peers and friends experience oppression throughout their daily lives (Worthen, 2011).

This results in students seeking opportunities for activism that are unclear to them when they have already been given the title of "ally" by the training they have just attended, implying a completion of their learning. By transitioning ally trainings away from teaching students how to be an ally and toward how they can actively ally on a daily basis, students leave empowered and determined to do actions that will fight against oppression on their campuses. This new shift in thinking of "ally" as a verb aligns with previous educational efforts and philosophies, but calls the field to take another step forward by encouraging engaged and intentional critical thinking, leading to changes in students' behavioral choices.

Bystander intervention curricula are designed to create action and can be a guiding force in restructuring ally trainings to incorporate this new concept. In considering the impact of the Violence Against Women Act and Title IX on college campuses, there has been a significant increase in efforts made toward educating all students on skills needed for bystander intervention. We can draw from this framework and apply it to ally training design. If we look at homophobia and oppression as categories of power based personal violence that need to be stopped through intervention, we can use the sexual violence bystander intervention frameworks to guide our thinking in inspiring ally actions from our students.

For example, Green Dot (www.livethegreendot.com), a popular bystander intervention program that aims to shift social culture on college campuses, utilizes social psychology literature, bystander literature, and social diffusion theory to strategically train thought leaders on college campuses in recognizing warning signs to violence, understanding their barriers that may discourage them from intervening, and choosing the most appropriate action (despite their barriers) that will stop the moment of violence in a safe way. The program encourages campuses to strategically recruit and train popular opinion leaders, who are then trained to lead by example to improve their campus culture (Edwards, 2014; Rogers, 1983). By applying this philosophy to ally trainings, facilitators can utilize incredible intentionality to their practices before, during, and after ally trainings.

Intentional recruitment of participants encourages strategic thought as to who would most benefit from the education and who will lead social justice change on their own campus by influencing their peers and friends to get involved in fighting injustices toward the LGBTQ+ community. During the training, facilitators transition from focusing solely on reflection and knowledge increase, and shift conversation toward brainstorming strategic actions that students can do on their campus to actively fight against oppression. In following Green Dot philosophy, facilitators must understand that all members of their ally trainings, regardless of sexual orientation or gender identity, likely experience barriers to intervening in homophobic situations. By encouraging a student-led brainstorm in the training with realistic scenarios, facilitators prepare students to identify their potential barriers and help them create ideas for strategies they can use despite those barriers in allying with the LGBTQ+ community in their everyday interactions.

Facilitators can also create unique opportunities for participants who identify within the LGBTQ+ community to discover ways that they can ally with other members of the community (e.g. a gay white man allying with a lesbian woman of color, etc). Finally, by incorporating strategic assessment tools throughout the process, such as tracking participation, utilizing classroom assessment techniques during the training as immediate feedback in discussion (Angelo & Cross, 1993), and following up with participants to better understand their ally behaviors since training, facilitators will begin to have a strong sense of the effectiveness of the training in changing campus culture.

As campuses work to incorporate allyship as a core component of ally trainings, most activities and discussions most likely need not be deleted, but follow up discussions and processing in the training need simply to be modified to incorporate this new philosophy. By focusing on allyship as a key learning outcome of ally trainings, facilitators should continue to explore complexities of identities, privilege, oppression, and bias through creative lesson plans and curriculum development. To explore this additional question of allyship, facilitators need to ask an additional follow up question after each activity: "Now that you understand this further, what are you going to do about it to make our campus better?" Ideally, this discussion will lead student participants to brainstorm realistic options for themselves in how they can better ally with their LGBTQ+ peers.

CONCLUSION

Institutions of higher education are uniquely positioned to invite our students to think critically about issues of social justice, privilege, and oppression in hopes of preventing tragedies like the events that occurred at Pulse nightclub on June 12, 2016. While the term "ally" has historically been utilized as a noun, bestowed upon heterosexual, cisgender allies who support members of the LGBTQ+ community, a new movement is rising to shift "ally" into a verb. By challenging students to answer the question "how do you ally?", higher education professionals create an opportunity for all students to focus on their daily actions that either support the status quo, or fight against injustices toward the LGBTQ+ community.

Ally training programs create unique opportunities for higher education institutions to focus on culture change. By learning from successful programs like Green Dot, ally training facilitators can find opportunities for genuine campus culture change by utilizing popular opinion leaders as change agents across campus (Edwards, 2014). Ally training facilitators can encourage students to look past their barriers to intervention, and think creatively about how they can stop moments of homophobic, biphobic, and transphobic abuse against LGBTQ+ persons, and dismantle systems of LGBTQ+ oppression.

While ally trainings can help participants better understand LGBTQ+ identities and how each member of the campus community can advocate for them throughout the day, ally trainings alone cannot shift campus culture past tolerance without administrative support and resources (Ballard, Bartle, & Masequesmay, 2008). Ally trainings can provide critical education to members of a campus, but must be one component of a larger strategy, complementing other programming and education that takes place across campus. Through a comprehensive education strategy that approaches the complexities of allyship from many different levels, each college campus has the power to make our communities safer for all members of the LGBTQ+ community.

REFERENCES

Anders, A. D., & Devita, J. M. (2014). Intersectionality: A legacy from critical legal studies and critical race theory. In D. Mitchell Jr., C. Y. Simmons, & L. A. Greyerbiehl (Eds.), *Intersectionality & higher education: Theory, research, & praxis* (pp. 31–44). New York, NY: Peter Lang.

Angelo, T. A., & Cross, K. P. (1993). Classroom assessment techniques: A handbook for college teachers. San Francisco, CA: Jossey-Bass Publishers.

Ballard, S., Bartle, E., & Masequesmay, G. (2008). Finding queer allies: The impact of ally training and safe zone stickers on campus climate. *Online Submission*.

Brown, K. T., & Ostrove, J. M. (2013). What does it mean to be an ally? The perception of allies from the perspective of people of color. *Journal of Applied Social Psychology, 43*, 2211–2222.

Coming Out Stars Activity. (n.d.). Retrieved from https://lgbtteachingaids.files.wordpress.com/2012/03/coming-out-stars-activity.pdf

Crenshaw, K. (1989). Demarginalizing the intersection of race and sex: A black feminist critique of antidiscrimination doctrine, feminist theory and antiracist politics. *The University of Chicago Legal Forum, 140*, 139–167.

Dupere, K. (2016). 6 ways to be a better straight ally at Pride events. Retrieved from http://mashable.com/2016/06/24/lgbtq-pride-straight-allies/#wZOh20ajdOq9

Edwards, D. (2014). *gd 2.0: Green Dot College Strategy*. Green Dot, et cetera, Inc.

Gentner, L. D. (2016). What's Ein an ally? The effect on perceptions of campus climate by LGBTQ+ identifying students expectations of an experiences with LGBTQ+ allies (Masters' scholarly project).

Indigenous Action Media. (2014). Accomplices not allies: Abolishing the ally industrial complex. Retrieved from http://www.indigenousaction.org/accomplices-not-allies-abolishing-the-ally-industrial-complex/

Ingall, M. (2016). How to be a better ally. Retrieved from http://www.tabletmag.com/jewish-life-and-religion/206130/how-to-be-a-better-ally

Ji, P., & Fujimoto, K. (2013). Measuring heterosexual LGBT ally development: a Rasch analysis. *Journal of Homosexuality, 60*(12), 1695–1725.

Jones, K. N., Brewster, M. E., & Jones, J. A. (2014). The creation and validation of the LGBT ally identity measure. *Psychology of Sexual Orientation and Gender Diversity, 1*(2), 181–195.

Manning, K., & Bogdan Eaton, S. (1993). Loosening the ties that bind: Shaping student culture. In G. D. Kuh (Ed.), *Cultural perspectives in student affairs work* (pp. 95–109). Lanham, MD: American College Personnel Association.

Maza, C. (2016). Call yourself an LGBT ally? Here's how to actually be one. Retrieved from https://www.washingtonpost.com/news/soloish/wp/2016/06/09/call-yourself-an-lgbt-ally-heres-how-to-actually-be-one/

McKenzie, M. (2015). How to tell the difference between real solidarity and "Ally Theater". Retrieved from http://www.blackgirldangerous.org/2015/11/the-difference-between-real-solidarity-and-ally-theatre/

Reich, V. (2014). 10 tips for LGBT allies. Retrieved from http://www.villageq.com/10-tips-lgbt-allies/

Rogers, E. M. (1983). *Diffusion of innovations*. New York, NY: Free Press.

Sansui, V. (2016). Some people are pissed off with American apparel for using the term "Ally" on its pride bag. Retrieved from https://www.buzzfeed.com/victoriasanusi/some-people-are-pissed-off-with-american-apparel-for-using-t?utm_term=.duV767ey40#.viNbDb7ql0

Shaanmichael (2013). "Ally" is not an identity. Retrieved from https://theshaananigans.wordpress.com/2013/02/16/ally-is-not-an-identity/

SJWiki Ally. (n.d.). Retrieved August 30, 2016, from SJWiki: http://sjwiki.org/index.php?title=Ally&oldid=11174#.V8WTZCgrKUk

Smith, M. D. (n.d.). The case against "allies". Retrieved from http://feministing.com/2013/10/01/the-case-against-allies/

Utt, J. (2013). So you call yourself an ally: 10 things all 'Allies' need to know. Retrieved from http://everydayfeminism.com/2013/11/things-allies-need-to-know/

Woodford, M. R., Kolb, C. L., Durocher-Radeka, G., & Javier, G. (2014). Lesbian, gay, bisexual, and transgender ally training programs on campus: Current variations and future directions. *Research in Brief, 55*(3), 317–322.

Worthen, M. G. F. (2011). College student experiences with an LGBTQ ally training program: A mixed methods study at a university in the southern United States. *Journal of LGBT Youth, 8*, 332–377.

CHAPTER TWENTY-TWO

Utilizing Indigenous Pedagogies to Uproot Racism and LGBTQ+ Intolerance

A Student Affairs Perspective

CAMARON MIYAMOTO, DEAN HAMER, JOE WILSON, AND HINALEIMOANA WONG-KALU

THE KINGDOM OF HAWAI'I

Native Hawai'ian epistemologies may play an important role in supplanting the dominant oppressive narrative to counter acts of LGBTQ+ violence at the University of Hawai'i at Mānoa. The dominant oppressive narrative is a Western world view that assumes that Hawai'i is just like any of the other 50 states in America. That narrative ignores the reality that prior to 1898, Hawai'i was a sovereign nation yet to interface, or rather, be colonized by American imperial interests. In 1994, President Clinton offered an apology to the Hawai'ian people for the illegal overthrow of the Hawai'ian Kingdom by the United States. This nod from Washington D.C. acknowledges the on-going assertion that Hawai'i is not only unique in it's relation to America, but helps bring into focus the tenuous nature of statehood. To assume that Hawai'i peacefully or joyously transitioned into the imperial giant called the United States requires the assumption of historical, cultural and spiritual amnesia that is grounded in the violence of racist genocide.

So how, then can Hawai'i, a place with deep wounds of violence offer the healing solution to the modern day, dominant oppressive narrative that is at once racist, sexist and homophobic? This chapter will focus on two different modern eruptions of violence in Hawai'i that were fueled by a continued pattern of privilege, power, ignorance and hostility that comes from un-informed invasion. Both instances of racial and LGBTQ+ hate occurred at the University of Hawai'i at Mānoa or involved students in the matter that called for mediation by student affairs professionals. Both responses were grounded in indigenous, Native Hawai'ian epistemologies and a local sense of place rather than American and foreign influences.

Native Hawai'ian epistemologies are grounded in land, culture and self-determination—in the spiritual creation stories of the islands and the responsibilities and privileges that stem from them. Our kuleana (responsibility) to the land plays a central role. Land is a concrete example of the complexity that the United States has super-imposed over the Kingdom of Hawai'i. A significant part of the University of Hawai'i at Mānoa sits on a large plot of ceded lands from the crown, the Kingdom of Hawai'i. On January 4, 1893, Queen Lili'uokalani signed into law an act passed by the Hawai'ian Kingdom Legislature that established the Hawai'i Bureau of Agriculture and Forestry. This government bureau would become the foundation of what, in 1907, would become the College of Agriculture and Mechanical Arts, the forerunner of the University of Hawai'i at Mānoa.

Interestingly, the University of Hawai'i at Mānoa has a mission statement that adheres to the ideal of creating a "Hawai'ian sense of place." This is fitting given the history of the land and institution. But how does this compare to the present-day reality? How can an institution comprised of mainly settler-colonists create such a place? What is our kuleana, our responsibility and privilege as non-Native Hawai'ians to ensure that we honor the history and traditions of Hawai'i?

Let's start with a story; a history lesson that we can all learn from. Here is text from the film Kumu Hina that offers a fresh perspective on Hawai'ian history (Kumu Hina [Motion Picture], 2014):

> Before the coming of foreigners to our islands, we Hawai'ians lived in aloha, in harmony with the land and one another. Every person had their role in society, whether male, female, or māhū, those that embody the masculine and feminine traits that are in each and every one of us. Māhū were valued and respected as caretakers, healers, and teachers of ancient traditions who passed on sacred knowledge from one generation to the next, through hula, chant and other forms of wisdom.
>
> When American missionaries arrived in the 1800s, they were shocked and infuriated by these practices and did everything they could to abolish them. They condemned our hula and chant as immoral, they outlawed our language, and they imposed their religious strictures across our lands. But we Hawai'ians are a steadfast and resilient people. And so, despite over 200 years of colonization and oppression, we are still here.

The perspective is fresh because it brings into view those who heretofore have largely been excluded from history, those who Western culture now refers to as transgender. However this is neither accurate nor gives due value to the status and revered place māhū have, and continue to, hold in Hawai'i. According to Tuhiwai Smith, indigenous methodologies are more collective; people were valued for their contributions, not individual achievements and identities. As such, "Māhū were valued and respected as caretakers, healers, and teachers of ancient traditions who passed on sacred knowledge from one generation to the next, through hula, chant and other forms of wisdom" (Kumu Hina [Motion Picture], 2014).

This lack of respect and shock brought the creation of the foreign and pagan "other" that defied bipolar restriction of man and woman and Western cultural norms. The result was the commodification of human experience and genocide through the banning of the realm of māhū: in particular chant and hula. This experience reverberates through on-going contact with American society with the ways racist and LGBTQ+ hate becomes articulated in Hawai'i, including at the University of Hawai'i at Mānoa.

INDIGENOUS NARRATIVES OF PLACE AND VOICE

A significant instance of racist and LGBTQ+ hate on campus occurred in 2009, when an American church group called Bema ministries from San Francisco, California, came to the University of Hawai'i. Their ministry preaches a message of "Cry to God" and takes its in your face message across the county to various college campuses and venues such as the Super Bowl, and Mardi Gras. At UH Mānoa, the ministry targeted both LGBTQ+ people and Native Hawai'ians. LGBTQ+ people were derided as 'unnautural' and 'sinners' and Native Hawai'ians were described as 'immoral' or 'pagan' by the preachings of "Cry to God."

A mainland [American] U.S. Christian hate group calling itself Bema ministries turned up on the campus last week to preach, harass, photograph, and intimidate students at the Campus Center. … They showed upon the University of Hawai'i's Mānoa campus, screamed and shouted at students for a few hours on Wednesday, got kicked out because they didn't have a permit, and then returned with a permit issued by the university chancellor the next day.

The student code of conduct expressly forbids hate speech yet this non-student group came on campus and not only made anti-gay statements, but told Hawai'ian students that the sovereignty movement was idolatrous and evil, and told Buddhist students they would burn in hell. The main course of hate was reserved for UH Mānoa's gay, lesbian, bisexual, transgender and intersex students (activist blog, Queers United, 2009).

According to news reports, 500–600 students gathered in opposition to the hateful messages being shouted by the Bema Ministries on campus. The reactions by students were as diverse as the hate that was spewed against various populations: LGBTQ+ people, Native Hawai'ians, idol worshipers, Buddhists, and women. As covered in local press, blogs and media, one student was arrested for smashing a church member's camera. A majority of students showed their disapproval of the messages from Bema Ministries by booing and hissing. Others laughed and said "Who are you to judge? I am judged by God and that is not you!"

There was one powerful counter-protest to the hateful speech that was not reported in local or national news. Students responded with traditional Hawai'ian chant to drown out the American visitors. The chant is tied intrinsically to place, specifically a Native Hawai'ian sacred place with the chanting of sacred words. According to Frantz Fanon, "For a colonized people the most essential value ... is first and foremost the land: the land which will bring them bread and, above all, dignity" (1961, p. 44). In the documentary Kumu Hina, Kumu Hinaleimoana Wong proclaims: "Listen to my voice: Ai ke mumu keke na keke pahoehoe ke ... [wela iluna o Halemaʻumaʻu ke] When I was in high school I was teased and tormented for being too girlish—But I found refuge in being Hawai'ian, in being Kanaka Maoli" (Kumu Hina, 2014).

What stronger connection is there between sacred place and word than the traditional chant? Without the use of any microphones, the traditional chant drowned out the foreign ministry with the ease of unleashing a hurricane and the simplicity of speaking power to truth through the ancestors. As if it were the 1800s, this chant shocked and destabilized the foreign missionaries yet again. It is as if they were at once destabilized and unarmed to respond to the spiritual power of the Hawai'ian chant on Hawai'ian soil.

According to Hawai'i News Now, "This is the group's last protest in Hawai'i. While they have a strong stance against homosexuality, the group says their demonstration has nothing to do with the state's current consideration of a same-sex civil union bill" (Arab, 2009).

UNMASKING MARRIAGE (IN)EQUALITY BY ENGAGING NATIVE HAWAI'IAN EPISTEMOLOGIES

Foreign interests wash up onto the shores of Hawaiʻi and litter the airport tarmac when it comes to the past debate of marriage equality that continued from 1992 to 2013. The next section examines the struggle for marriage equality in Hawaiʻi to unmask the failure of the Western divide and conquer strategy which relies on the creation of the 'other' (Said, 1978), and false notions of 'traditional' family values. Linda Tuhiwai Smith (1999) uses an indigenous critique to challenge the Western paradigms that reinforce the "idea that history is constructed around binary categories" (p. 31); and "the idea that history is patriarchal" (p. 31).

In the 1990s, Hawaiʻi rose to the forefront of the marriage equality movement in the United States when a local circuit judge ruled that it is sex discrimination to deny individuals marriage on the basis of their genders. National attention came upon Hawaiʻi as a gay rights epicenter. With this came outside American political influences from family values coalitions and certain churches intent on retaining the "sanctity of marriage" as between a man and a woman. There was quick movement in the legislature to protect marriage as American-funded interested descended upon Hawai'i. The capitol became wrought with LGBTQ+ organizations and Pro-family organizations that both had their agendas to push for either marriage equality or the sanctity of marriage. The result was a constitutional convention that created the opportunity for a popular vote to change the Hawai'i State Constitution to define marriage as between one man and one woman.

The more holistic Hawai'ian cultural perspective on inclusion and respect for all offered ways forward in that fractious debate. Let us return to the reality and on-going legacy of māhū in Hawai'i. In Hawai'i, there is a special place between "man," or "kane" and "woman," or "wahine," This place is occupied by the "māhu"—those blessed with both aspects of male and female (Kumu Hina, 2014). Māhū play a pivotal role in countering Western paradigms of LGBTQ+ and racist hate. How then can this knowledge be shared with the University of Hawai'i community? This past summer of 2016, I collaborated with our New Student Orientation programs to ensure that all new students attending orientation would have the opportunity to refresh or enhance their knowledge base of the history of Hawai'i, the meaning of māhū, and create opportunities to learn through the knowledge base created by the Kumu Hina team.

This work can best be understood within the context of what Linda Tuhiwai-Smith describes as four major tides within the Indigenous Research Agenda that supplant the dominant Western paradigm. The tides ripple in waves like the sea, a giver of life, and "represent movement, change, process, life, inward and outward flows of ideas, healing, transformation and mobilization—represent processes" (Tuhiwai Smith, p. 120). "How can we work within a Western institution that largely privileges Western ways of knowing to reshape the minds and life-experiences of our new students? There are four major tides represented in the Indigenous Research Agenda: survival, recovery, development and self-determination" (Tuhiwai Smith, 1999, p. 121).

This section highlights the pivotal role māhū play in countering Western paradigms of hate and describes the development, implementation and assessment of curriculum for New Student Orientation at the University of Hawai'i i at Mānoa. Returning to the text of "The Meaning of Māhū" in the documentary Kumu Hina (2014), we can see how the language of the narrative mirrors the major tides of the Indigenous Research Agenda: survival, recovery, development and self-determination.

Survival was of the essence when foreign missionaries "were shocked and infuriated" by the valued māhū and "they condemned our hula and chant as immoral, they outlawed our language, and they imposed their religious strictures across our lands" (Kumu Hina, 2014). Recovery is continually recreated by the acknowledgement of māhū in Hawai'i and the significant role they carry. Development is demonstrated by the fact that ancient traditions persist. These traditions might have been forgotten from some of the common folks, but the Hawai'ian Renaissance of the 1970s and the current deepening of spiritual cultural reclamation is unwavering. Lastly, what better testament to the significance of self-determination than this statement from an animated clip "The Meaning of Māhū" in the documentary *Kumu Hina*:

> They condemned our hula and chant as immoral, they outlawed our language, and they inposed their religious strictures across our lands. But we Hawai'ians are a steadfast and resilient people. And so, despite over 200 years of colonization and oppression, we are still here. (Kumu Hina Project, 2015)

This animated clip was played for all students who attended New Student Orientation during Summer 2016, to popular approval in a session entitled "We All Live in the Same Pond" (Miyamoto, 2015).

At the opening of the session there is statement of the University Policy of Non-Discrimination, that includes among other protected categories, "race," "sex," "gender identity/expression" and "sexual orientation." Student Orientation leaders welcomed student participants back to the ballroom with the reminder that we have a policy of non-discrimination. While this is a Western legal way of looking at our responsibility, our kuleana, students are reminded also that we live in a shared ecosphere; we all live in the same pond and our actions impact one another. We have particular rights and privileges that come with coexistence in this pond.

This session evoked the imagery of a salt water pond, a Native Hawai'ian traditional way for cultivating fish using rock walls and the tides of the ocean. Fish would swim in and stay to feed in the safety of the rock walls. This is the epicenter of self-determination (Tuhiwai-Smith 121), where the ripples of survival, recovery and development meet and rest; in this case this center of self-determination is further protected by the foundation of the rock wall encircling the salt water pond. We live within the rock wall that is bounded by values of non-discrimination, respect, well-being, responsibility to describe the academic and economic interchange within the university. These rocks form the foundation for a strong fish pond that we are calling UH Mānoa. This is the pond we live, work and study in.

After viewing the animated clip, students are asked to work at their tables of about 10 students to describe what it is like in their particular fish pond, with each of the student participants being represented by a fish in that pond. Students are asked to describe who they are, where they come from, how do they describe their community and position within it. They write down key words on their construction paper fish. Each student shares with the group at their table in the ballroom before we debrief in the larger group to see what we have in common and identify what strengths we carry in our cultural, spiritual, sexual and racial differences. Through the combination of watching the prompt of the aninmated clip "The Meaning of Māhū" (Kumu Hina, 2014), and the group discussion that follows, students utilize critical thinking skills to reflect on the meaning of "māhū," the impact of American missionaries in the 1800s and the resiliance of Native Hawai'ians. The following are the stated learning outcomes:

- Participants will learn about gender diversity in Hawai'i
- Increase understanding of one's own values and respecting the values of others.
- Identify ways to practice the true meaning aloha and its true concept of love, honor, and respect

To close the session students share that our fishpond is UH Mānoa. It is a diverse and wide-ranging community. One thing that can hold us together is a culture of nurturance and respect. Our fishpond and the fact that our fish co-exist and thrive within its waters serve as a reminder that we should always celebrate who we are because of our mutual respect and individual contributions. We need to be secure in our own culture, sexuality, gender identity, race and ethnicity to stand strong next to others who face various forms of oppression. This is particularly true for those of us with various degrees of access to power and privilege in shifting interactions and solidly founded institutions that serve as barriers to freedom. Luckily, education does not have to be one of those institutions.

INDIGENOUS CULTURES: UPROOTING LGBT HATE FROM THE BASE

When the Bema ministries came to campus and marriage equality became a fractious debate, it is clear that strength and an oppositional voice was found through indigenous paradigms. Chant and role and tradition of the māhū in Hawai'i are too powerful a force to be ignored. In fact they are not only the past but future key to uprooting LGBTQ+ hate in Hawai'i from its very base.

As stated by Goodyear-Kāʻōopua, Hussey, and Wright (2014) "In the last two decades there has been a backlash against Hawai'ian movements" (p. 24). At the same time, there has been an increase of Hawai'ian movements for self-determination, land, culture and sovereignty on campus. When I scan my memory of protests and movements on campus I continue to see the prominence of māhū and LGBTQ+ Native Hawai'ians leading chant, hula, community organizing and protocol. Interestingly, the cultural hegemony perpetrated by American imperialism can be supplanted by the continual rebirth of indigenous culture; it is key to uprooting LGBTQ+ hate from its very base.

There was the first Mahele—that which divided Native Hawai'ian people from the land. In this case, there is growing resistance to the patenting of kalo (taro)—"Hāloa has become the symbol a second Māhele, now called the Mana Mahele" ("Kū'ē Mana Māhele" in Goodyear-Ka'ōpua et al., 334). This is the new realm, the territory of biocolonialism through the genetic modification of kalo by the University of Hawai'i. In fact, thousands of acres of land are used to test genetically modified growing. What is even more troublesome than the on-going genetic modifications, chemicals and experimentation is the fact that kalo, known as Hāloa is sacred to Native Hawai'ians. Kalo is sibling to the Native Hawai'ian people. It is their kuleana to care for this family member—not to own it or lay claim to it. Some say that is slavery. There is a mo'olelo, a teaching, that Hāloanakalaukapalili, the fist kalo, is the elder sibling of the Hawai'ian people. One activist says "They took our land; they took our kingdom; they took our confidence, our pride, eveverything. Now they like take our mana (lifeforce)" ("Kū'ē Mana Māhele" in Goodyear-Ka'ōpua et al., 334).

In 2005, there was a first attempt by the university to patent kalo, to take ownership and claim right to that particular plant. By 2006, protests of the university practices were starting to spread. In 2007, protests emerged on the university campus—many led or organized by LGBTQ+ Native Hawai'ians or māhū people. It's as if being in that "place in the middle" (Kumu Hina, 2014), creates valuable portals for seeing more than one point of view at once. Historically, māhū have been healers, caretakers, carriers of culture and knowledge. In the modern day this is being manifested by bridging the past through chant and hula; by opening protocol in ceremony and resistance.

In what ways does this create direct ways to challenge continued pattern of violence against the Native Hawai'ian body, spirit, and culture? In the earlier interface of the missionary "discovery" of the māhū in Hawai'i they sought to tame the practices of chant and hula and language through what was essentially part and parcel to genocide. During the debacle of the same-gender/marriage equality debates in Hawai'i i, local ways of viewing relationships became codified in Western law and māhū played significant roles in pointing out the historical hypocricy of American family values. Now the body politic of colonization again targets its violence on the Native Hawai'ian body, culture and spirit—just like it did in the 1800s with the "taming" of the māhū. Kalo and Hāloa are being held hostage spiritually. Now, rather than destabilizing the dominant Western narrative, māhū have the power to effectively define the dominant narrative on campus and in Hawai'i.

REFERENCES

Arab, Z. (2009, March 6). Student confrontation with anti-gay demonstrators leads to arrest at UH. *Hawai'i News Now*. Retrieved from http://www.hawai'inewsnow.com/story/9958192/student-confrontation-with-anti-gay-demonstrators-leads-to-arrest-at-uh

Fanon, F. (1961). *The wretched of the earth*. New York, NY: Grove Press.

Goodyear-Kaʻōpua, N., Hussey, I., & Wright, E. K. (Eds.). (2014). *A nation rising: Hawai'ian movements for life, land and sovereignty*. Durham, NC: Duke University Press.

Hamer, D., Wilson, J. (Producers and Directors), & Florez, C. (Co-producer). (2014). *Kumu hina: A place in the middle* [Motion Picture]. Nashville, TN: Qwaves Productions.

Kumu Hina Project. (2015, April 3). *The meaning of māhū* [Video file]. Retrieved from https://www.youtube.com/watch?v=2pCThN5y46Q

Miyamoto, C. (2015). *We all live in the same pond* (Training module). LGBTQ+ Center, University of Hawai'i at Mānoa.

Queers United. (2009, March 10). Anti-gay hate group allowed on U of Hawai'i campus [Web blog post]. Retrieved from http://queersunited.blogspot.com/2009/03/anti-gay-hate-group-allowed-on-u-hawai'i.html

Said, E. (1978). *Orientalism*. New York, NY: Pantheon.

Tuhiwai Smith, L. (1999). *Decolonizing methodologies: Research and indigenous peoples*. Dunnedin, New Zealand: University of Otago Press.

CHAPTER TWENTY-THREE

Dialogues ON Diversity

A Curricular Option to Promote LGBTQIA Inclusion on Campus

PAUL S. HENGESTEG

INTRODUCTION

From June 2015 to June 2016, the LGBTQIA community in the United States has experienced significant joys and losses. We have celebrated the Supreme Court's ruling on same-sex marriage and rejoiced Title IX's expansion of transgender inclusion. We have been frustrated by legislation limiting queer protections and we mourned the loss of 49 of our kin at the Pulse Nightclub massacre in Orlando, Florida—during Pride Month, no less. National events like these highlight the broad range of views regarding the LGBTQIA community, and yet, many times we do not see two sides in dialogue. College campuses are similar. As institutions, we say we value diversity, yet research indicates LGBTQIA inclusion at major universities across the nation, while present and measurable, is inconsistent (Mehra, Braquet, & Fielden, 2015). Furthermore, we fall short of providing students "opportunities to interact meaningfully with their peers across social differences" (Quaye, 2008, p. 41). This chapter provides a curricular example of creating intentional, meaningful environments for students to learn and engage about social identities, specifically within LGBTQIA spectra (Harper & Anontio, 2008).

Efforts to increase diversity on college campuses have taken many forms, and should be celebrated as ways to ensure the community of students, faculty, and staff on campus is, in fact, a representation of the local and global societies in which they are a part. Beyond the global connection, or perhaps more importantly, these efforts should continue so that LGBTQIA people feel welcomed and valued in the academy, and included as part of institutional diversity efforts.

A study of campus environments reveals what is valued within a community and how the people (administrators, faculty, students, and staff) within a campus culture promote respecting differences and similarities (Strange & Banning, 2001). Some campuses with a strong focus on social justice initiatives create a space where understanding one's self and others is commonplace. On the other hand, some campuses maintain the status quo by their inability to bring people together to explore systems of oppression. By not pro-actively celebrating the contributions of all people and failing to adapt equitable policies, these institutions are complicit in supporting racism, ageism, sexism, ableism, heterosexism, classism, and many other troubles our modern society faces. It is these sentiments that yield to the tragedies experienced in the United States in recent past that have further marginalized many people.

Harper and Antonio (2008) have identified four key areas of diversity that should be present on a modern college campus: structural, interactional, curricular, and co-curricular. When combined, they provide a holistic roadmap for creating diverse and inclusive campus environments. Structural diversity refers to the presence of diversity, or a numerical account of the makeup of the community in regards to certain groups or identities. Interactional diversity refers to the contact a person has with someone who is different. Curricular and co-curricular diversity refer to the experiences or knowledge gained either in the classroom or outside of it. These four areas of diversity are synergistic to each other; each are impacted by the others. The presence of one does not equate to the presence of the other.

Of particular importance to structural diversity as it relates to the LGBTQIA community, institutions are able to quantify the racial, ethnic, gender, religious, disability, and veteran populations on campus, but many campuses are not collecting data on queer identities. Without federal protections for non-hetero and non-cisgender identities, the drive for institutions to enumerate these identities is limited. Similarly, the *presence* of LGBTQIA students, faculty, and staff on campus does not mean *interactions* between them and those who are heterosexual or cisgender is positive or healthy, or even happening at all.

Scholar-practitioners have debated the impact of LGBT resource centers on college campuses (Patton, 2011; Renn, 2011), but agree that they have value and provide a sense of community to students (and also faculty and staff, but perhaps to a lesser extent) who identify within the queer spectra of gender identity, expression, or sexual orientation. These centers can be a home to advocacy, activism, support, as well as healing and discussion in response to national tragedy, such as the mass shooting at Pulse Nightclub in Orlando in June, 2016. Nonetheless, identity-based resource centers are only one ingredient in an inclusive campus environment, and only one place out of many available where learning takes place. Classrooms can also serve as a place of learning about LGBTQIA identities and experiences.

In the spirit of replacing LGBTQIA hate with respect and inclusion, a curricular focus undertaken at Iowa State University (ISU) is a one-credit undergraduate course called Dialogues on Diversity (DoD). What follows in this chapter is information about how the course serves as a conceptual foundation for those interested in developing a similar course on other campuses. Assessment data will provide some "lessons learned" and articulate the impact of this course for students. The intent is that the information in this chapter will assist other educators in creatively developing similar courses on their campuses, including ways to promote collaboration among academic and student affairs (Steffes & Keeling, 2006).

DIALOGUES ON DIVERSITY

Dialogues on Diversity (DOD), or "Dialogues" as the course is sometimes known, has been offered on the ISU campus for more than ten years. It is designed as a half-semester class, which means it meets seven times in the later part of the semester. Each section, with a maximum of 20 students, meets once per week for an hour and fifty minutes. The majority of students who take the course are first year students, although students from each class comprise enrolment for the 100-level course. Multiple sections of the course happen during the semester and are taught by a duo of trained facilitators, ranging from graduate students (both masters and doctoral level), student affairs professionals, and an occasional faculty member. Ideally, a new facilitator is paired with a veteran facilitator. The goals of this kind of pairing are to allow one person to have some experience with the course while the other becomes familiar, to encourage growth of teaching and facilitation skills with a potential mentor, and to meet people from different parts of the university. Each facilitator is compensated a modest fee for their time, which many use toward professional development or conference travel. Facilitators, rather than 'professors,' are used to create a more equal playing field between students and instructors in the conversation.

From a pedagogical standpoint, DoD is unique because it breaks away from the traditional narrative of professor vs. student where the person in the front of the room imparts knowledge on the students. Freire (2000) names this the banking model of education where an expert or authority deposits information into a learner like money into a checking account. A queering of this model disrupts what is considered to be normal, thereby allowing students to be reflective knowers, to be active participants in learning, to create their own answers (and more questions again), and to leave questions unanswered (Luhmann, 1998). While facilitators are responsible for grading course participation and assignments, the course hopes to create an environment of trusted peers in the classroom, so as to allow more open, honest dialogue to occur. The more students can perceive their facilitator as a contemporary leading a discussion, the better, another example of queering the traditional classroom.

Facilitators are provided with course content from the Course Coordinator so they are not required to create their own lesson plans or activities. However, facilitators are welcome to 'go off script' as their comfort and expertise allow. Classrooms have a full array of technological support as well as moveable furniture so as to create a physical space more conducive to large- and small-group dialogue and interaction (Strange & Banning, 2001).

A critical part of the course structure is the inclusion of gender identity and sexual orientation. Additional weeks cover course start-up and closing, as well as other socially constructed identities. Certainly, there is tremendous ground to cover in a short period of time for an introductory course. This constrained time period means many things for the course, including a difficulty to construct intersectional conversation because many students are talking about the identity-of-the-week for the first time. Nonetheless, Quaye (2008) reminds us that oftentimes, students are not given the opportunity to discuss matters of social justice in an *intentional* way (emphasis added), and because of this reality, diversity efforts are slow to proceed on many campuses. Assessment information later in this chapter will demonstrate student response to the creation of such environments.

DIALOGUES ON GENDER AND SEXUAL ORIENTATION

When discussing gender, students have responded overwhelmingly positively to the use of a gender Fishbowl activity. In the activity, the women of the group sit in a circle and are prompted through a discussion where the men observe and listen. After some time, the circles swap and the same questions are asked. Following this, the whole group is asked to process what they heard, what they learned, what surprised them, and how they will think or act differently with the new information they gained. For some students, this is the first opportunity to share frustrations about their own gender and have those concerns received by others.

There is one significant limitation of the Fishbowl activity, however. That is, it uses a gender binary (Lev, 2004, as cited in Evans, Forney, Guido, Patton, & Renn, 2010), and overlooks the transgender, agender, gender fluid, and non-binary communities. This limitation should be noted and considered for those who are looking to replicate a course such as this on their own campus. The intent, however, is for students to understand male privilege as oppressive to any other gender identity.

When the class discusses sexual orientations, the lesson plan suggests a few activity options. The team of facilitators may choose what fits best for their group of students. Current options include: viewing of the movie *Bridegroom* with discussion; an activity called "Coming Out Stars" where students are led through a virtual coming out process; or attending a student panel presentation on their own campus (called Speakers Bureau at ISU) about coming out and navigating the campus as an LGBTQIA-identified student.

A Speakers Bureau panel is a group of two to four students, graduate or undergraduate, who present to classes, Greek letter organizations, student organizations, or any other space that requests a panel. Each panel is unique in its composition because it relies on schedule availability of the panelists. The panel is accompanied by a moderator, who is a full-time staff member of the LGBT Student Services Center. The panel begins with basic ground rules, and then each panelist introduces themselves (usually including their pronouns) and shares their coming out story in five minutes of less. Once the stories are shared, the remaining time together is an open, honest, respectful, and frank question-and-answer period. Audience members are encouraged to ask questions based on anything on their minds—responses to stories, meanings of pronouns, curiosities, and so on. Informal feedback from faculty has been very positive, citing that students in the audience are genuinely moved by the stories of the panel.

In contrast to hearing stories from others, during Coming Out Stars, students are asked to identify five important aspects of their own lives, including friends, family, social groups, career goals, and support networks. While guided through the activity, depending upon the color of the star they randomly chose, they either kept the point of their star in-tact (representing a smooth coming out process), folded that point back (indicating that the person/group representing that point is still present, although damaged in some way as a result of coming out), or torn off (suggesting that coming out has resulting in an alienation that cuts them off from further interaction). At the conclusion of the activity, those with full stars, damaged stars, and no stars are asked to respond to that specific coming out process and what it is like to observe some people with full stars (privilege) versus tattered stars.

Regardless of the path chosen by the facilitators, students in the course are expected to engage in dialogue with peers about non-hetero identities. This dialogue includes understanding the power and privilege heterosexual students have, and how the dominant narrative of a "straight society" impacts themselves, their friends, their family members, and the campus culture.

ASSESSMENT METHODOLOGY

Assessment for DoD has recently been done in two major forms, both formative in nature so as to influence changes and improvements in the future (Fitzpatrick, Sanders, & Worthen, 2011). The assessment data referenced in this chapter come from the spring semester of 2016. One of the bodies of assessment data comes from the facilitators. A meeting was called at the end of the semester, which acts similar to a focus group (Cooper, 2009), because the facilitators serve as experts on putting the lesson plans into action, and are thereby able to respond to that experience, providing qualitative information to the Course Coordinator. It should be noted that the Course Coordinator *may* be a facilitator, although it is not a requirement. At ISU recently, there has been sufficient interest in the community to be facilitators that the Course Coordinator was not needed to teach as well.

The second body of assessment data comes from a census-wide electronic survey (Figure 23.1) administered to students registered for the course across all sections (Gansemer-Topf & Wohlgemuth, 2009). The survey was conducted via Qualtrics with an overall response rate of approximately 35%. All eight sections of the course were represented in the responses.

FINDINGS

Rich data comes from both processes. This section highlights data collected from the students and the facilitators. Students largely appreciate the intentional opportunity to discuss social justice topics, and specifically topics related to gender and sexual orientation. Many students wish the course's format could be extended. Facilitators also find benefits from being associated with the course. They are thankful for opportunities to engage with students in a way that may not be *the norm* for them, and note that student reflections improved over time. Facilitators also used a designated feedback meeting as a time to offer suggestions for the future.

From the Student Survey

The student survey asked several open-ended questions as well as questions with a five-point scale ranging from "Completely Agree" to "Completely Disagree." When asked which topics from the course students learned the most about, gender and sexuality were regularly cited. Gender and sexuality were also well-represented in the question that asked which topic students would prefer to have more time for discussion and understanding. (To be clear, topics of race and privilege were also present in these questions, but are not the primary focus of this chapter.) One interpretation of this phenomenon is that students are learning a lot in the course, and are curious to learn more, or are wishing the course offered more time to explore identity deeper. This supports Quaye's (2008) statement that intentionally-crated opportunities for this type of learning are critical for student engagement with social justice issues.

One student commented in their anonymous survey, "I really enjoyed the coming out star activity and then [the] activity where we discussed our genders (what we like/ don't like, our experiences, etc.)." Another student shared that the most meaningful activity for them was a, "[t]ie between the Fishbowl activity and watching the [ted] talks." When asked about a particular reading that was helpful for students, one member of a fraternity said the following. However, the student does reverse the gender of the person in the reading, as it was about a fraternity man, not a sorority woman:

> The article that stuck with me the most was the article about a girl coming out as gay to her sorority. As I am in a fraternity, I found the article memorable because it described the ideals that I currently find in my chapter. The accepting environment in our chapter was further realized ... soon after, one of our brothers officially came out to the entirety of the house with thundering applause and support.

Students were also asked to indicate their level of agreement to a series of twelve statements that complete the sentence, "As a result of this course,..." The results of some of those statements are illustrated in Figure 23.1. It is observable that a majority of students feel more confident and comfortable in dialogue about social identities, and sharing their perspectives in the classroom in general.

In addition, while the percentages are slightly lower compared to other statements, students indicate they have or will change their perceptions of those who are different from themselves. Finally, more than three-quarters of the students in the course would recommend the class to peers. Given the expedited time frame of the course, this is viewed by many at ISU as a victory in creating change on campus, and is part of the reasoning behind the desire to expand the course into the full semester in the future.

From the Facilitator Focus Group

The final meeting of the facilitation group seeks to find strengths and weaknesses of the readings, activities, assignments, dialogue, and course preparation. In the group discussion, facilitators can share what about the readings did not connect with students (e.g., it was too dense, or it did not seem relevant to our community). Conversely, if an aspect of the course made it easier for students to dialogue in the classroom, that feedback is brought forward. Moreover, facilitators are able to hear from each other about successes and pitfalls they experienced in their classrooms over the duration of the course. What worked well for some may have been "a miss" for others, and the group can speculate how or why that was the case and offer suggestions for next time.

Also during the final meeting of facilitators, they expressed their passion for the course and gratitude to engage with undergraduate students about issues of

Question: "As a result of this course, ..."	Completely Disagree	Disagree	Unsure	Agree	Completely Agree	% Agree (n) and Comp. Agree
... I feel more comfortable sharing my thoughts and opinions in class	1	1	5	24	12	43 83.7
... I feel more comfortable discussing my own social identities	1	1	5	22	14	43 83.7
... I feel more comfortable discussing social identities which I do not hold	1	1	6	18	17	43 81.4
... I have a better understanding of gender and gender issues	0	0	8	19	15	42 81.0
... I have a better understanding of sexual orientation and issues related to the LGBT community	1	1	5	21	14	42 85.7
... I will change (or already have changed) my perceptions of those who are different from me	3	2	9	12	16	42 66.7
... I will reconsider (or already have reconsidered) how my own dominant identities may impact others	3	1	7	19	12	42 73.8
I would recommend this course to my peers	1	2	5	15	19	42 81.0

Figure 23.1. Student Survey.

social justice, which they may not have the opportunity to do in their other roles within the university. They observed that students improved in the quality of their reflections through their reflective journal entries (a weekly assignment), and in general were quite successful in the course. Some noted that students in engineering courses were particularly enthusiastic to learn in the class, perhaps because of limited opportunities for learning about diversity in their home fields of study. According to registration data for the spring 2016 course, students from the College of Engineering at ISU comprised the highest percentage of students in the course, despite the course being housed in the College of Human Sciences.

From the Classroom Activities

Consistently, even more than the readings, results of both the facilitator focus group conversation and the student survey suggest that classroom activities such as the Fishbowl or the Coming Out Stars activity are a vitally important part of student learning about the socially-constructed identities of gender and sexual orientation. Facilitators also observed that a majority of students registered for the course to either fulfill a diversity requirement or to remain full time as a result of dropping a course. They suggested that a one-credit course is a way to do "covert social justice work" (personal communication, April 30, 2016) with students who are not sure, or may not care, what the course will be about.

The facilitators felt the course would benefit from more time. They suggested that by the time students come to college, they have absorbed many messages about social justice and marginalized identities which usually support or benefit dominant identities. "To unlearn biases and previously learned information takes considerably more time," (personal communication, April 30, 2016) one added.

Jones (2008) suggests that student resistance to learning about one's identities and privileges might be predictable, which is important for coursemers to remember. Exploring one's cultural dominance is not comfortable for many, and can cause feelings of resentment, confusion, denial, and defensiveness. This kind of resistance was observable in the student survey. Although negative comments were not made regarding gender or sexual orientation, student remarks were offered that suggest dialogues related to race and White privilege were not as well received.

Despite the presence of some student resistance, it is encouraging to see students seeking more opportunities for learning. Similar to the facilitators, students felt they could benefit from more time with the course. The following three comments suggest the course should be a full semester and worth more than one credit:

> "MAKE COURSE 3 CREDITS/ ALL SEMESTER [original use of capital letters]"
> "Make it a full semester course, maybe 2 cr? It seems like we're always out of time and never get to answer all the discussion questions."
> "[M]ake it 3 credits, and possible [to] get it required for all students."

THE FUTURE OF DIALOGUES ON DIVERSITY

If you believe the old adage that nothing is forever, you know there is always a chance for programming in higher education to be cut. There is, after all, cost associated with a course such as DoD to cover facilitator stipends and course materials. However, when compared to the costs of one-time speakers, who are undoubtedly excellent at their craft or research but do not remain on campus to continue dialogue about their message, a course like DoD can be very efficient at bringing groups of relative strangers together. Moreover, the group meets repeatedly for sustained engagement over time. The importance of continued dialogue cannot be underscored enough, as understanding and dismantling systems of dominance and oppression cannot be done in a single sitting.

This course, however, can be replicated on any college campus. In fact, it would be interesting to compare success and setbacks on various campus types. Does the course work better on a smaller, liberal arts campus because of its community nature? Or is a large research institution better because of a broader range of students and interests? Are comprehensive institutions, often with rich histories as teaching schools, set up to be better prepared because of their "generalist" nature (Hirt, 2006)? Regardless of institutional type, social justice educators exist on every campus to make the course customizable to their own environment—a resource that deserves to not be overlooked.

One professional expectation that exists in the student affairs field is collaboration with academic affairs (Steffes & Keeling, 2006). Historically, this practice has been tense and yielded mixed response. Nonetheless, a course such as DoD offers rich opportunity to narrow the perceived divide between these two institutional divisions. Wise course planning includes creating space for all to participate, and may not even require that a course like this be housed strictly in an academic space; what might a continuous student affairs course look like with similar goals?

As the Course Coordinator for this course for a year, two overarching considerations warrant mentioning here. One, an important structural lesson learned from comparing the two semesters, is the careful sequencing of course topics. When comparing the feedback of facilitators in the fall and in the spring, it seems that conversation was healthier and more robust in the classroom when gender and sexual orientation were placed prior to discussing race. This was that case for the spring because facilitators found that students were relatively non-responsive in the class until after conversations on race. While this phenomenon was not investigated closely, it may be because some students may have encountered people within the LGBTQIA community, and are more able to have conversation on the topics, and less so for those of a non-White race. Recall that for many students, discussing race may be a very new experience. If you are at a predominantly white institution (PWI), this may be important in your own planning. Second, be cognizant of tensions playing out on campus. What may seem obvious, or even painful, to marginalized students and their allies, may not be on the radar of students holding dominant identities and thus require contextualization for their understanding.

THE FUTURE OF DIALOGUES ON GENDER AND SEXUAL ORIENTATION

As evidenced above, students, for the most part, seem eager to learn about social justice topics. As institutions continue to promote diversity and inclusion in their strategic plans and unit goals, it is vital to promote LGBTQIA advocacy throughout those efforts as well. By limiting diversity work to only some identities (such as race or country of origin), colleges and universities are left with incomplete goals to include everyone. Moreover, curricular inclusion of non-cis and and non-straight people does not need to remain exclusively within the domain of gender, women, and sexuality studies. Creating dialogue around gender and orientation is the work of all educators, irrespective of any boundaries, and should be prioritized similarly to that of other diversity initiatives.

Although DoD will continue to include gender and sexual orientation in its curriculum, exactly *how* that is done remains to be seen. One of the greatest benefits the course such is its flexibility to respond to national trends, events, or tragedies such as the Pulse Massacre. If places of higher education are simply microcosms of society as a whole, and I believe they are, it behoves us as educators to be able to respond as needed and as appropriate to the ever-changing landscape of LGBTQIA people.

One idea worth considering in the future, which works particularly well if the course is not expanded to a full course, is focusing each section of the course on a specific topic, rather than taking the "smorgasbord" approach. Doing so will deepen the dialogues for each identity discussed, not just for the broader terms of gender and sexual orientation. This approach affords students the opportunity to take the same course three times, each time with a different topic, thereby enabling them to earn up to three separate credits.

As noted earlier in this chapter, those who identify within queer communities are not quantifiably counted by institutions the same way some other identities are. Without federal protections, doing so may create more risk than benefit. Therefore, one simple truth remains: purposefully providing more interaction and dialogue across the divides of orientation and gender expression will be vital to the success of comprehensive diversity initiatives on college campuses.

CONCLUSION

Recent national events highlight the need for college campuses to address LGBTQIA hate. Campus efforts toward diversity and social justice education take many forms, and a diverse portfolio of these efforts is suggested for any campus. Curricular diversity options (Harper & Antonio, 2008) should not be overlooked and intentional dialogues among peers should be championed (Quaye, 2008) in efforts to increase awareness of and sensitivity toward queer communities. Further, institutional type (Hirt, 2006) offers many opportunities for faculty and staff to make social justice education manageable and customizable on their own campus.

This chapter highlights the curricular diversity efforts undertaken at Iowa State University with positive results. Assessment data suggests that students appreciate the opportunity to engage in dialogues around sexual orientation and gender identity, as well as other socially constructed identities, and would like further opportunities to discuss the identities within LGBTQIA+ spectra. Campus leaders from student affairs and academic affairs should embrace the opportunity to think creatively about how a course like DoD might be a positive influence for student learning and change on their campus.

REFERENCES

Cooper, R. M. (2009). Planning for and implementing data collection. In John H. Schuh (Ed.), *Assessment methods for student affairs*. San Fracisco, CA: Jossey-Bass.

Evans, N. J., Forney, D. E., Guido, F. M., Patton, L. D., & Renn, K. A. (2010). *Student development in college: Theory, research, and practice* (2nd ed.). San Francisco, CA: Jossey-Bass.

Fitzpatrick, J. L., Sanders, J. R., & Worthen, B. R. (2011). *Course evaluation: Alternative approaches and practical guidelines*. Upper Saddle River, NJ: Pearson Education.

Freire, P. (2000, first published in 1971). *Pedagogy of the oppressed*. New York, NY: Bloomsbury Publishing.

Gansemer-Topf, A. M., & Wohlgemuth, D. A. (2009). Selecting, sampling, and soliciting subjects. In John H. Schuh (Ed.), *Assessment methods for student affairs*. San Francisco, CA: Jossey-Bass.

Harper, S. R., & Antonio, A. L. (2008). Not by accident: Intentionality in diversity, learning, and engagement. In S. R. Harper (Ed.), *Creating inclusive campus environments for cross-cultural learning and student engagement*. Washington, DC: National Association of Student Personnel Administrators (NASPA).

Hirt, J. B. (2006). *Where you work matters: Student affairs administration at different types of institutions*. Lanham, MD: University Press of America.

Jones, S. R. (2008). Student resistance to cross-cultural engagements: Annoying distraction or site for transformative learning? In S. R. Harper (Ed.), *Creating inclusive campus environments for cross-cultural learning and student engagement*. Washington, DC: Student Affairs Administrators in Higher Education (NASPA).

Luhmann, S. (1998). Queering/querying pedagogy? Or, Pedagogy is a pretty queer thing. In W. F. Pinar (Ed.), *Queer theory in education* (pp. 141–155). Mahwah, NJ: Lawrence Erlbaum Associates.

Mehra, B., Braquet, D., & Fielden, C. M. (2015). A website evaluation of the top twenty-five public universities in the United States to assess their support of lesbian, gay, bisexual, and transgender people. In J. C. Hawley (Ed.), *Expanding the circle: Creating an inclusive environment for LGBTQ students and studies*. Albany, NY: SUNY Press.

Patton, L. D. (2011). Promoting critical conversations about identity centers. In P. M. Magolda & M. B. Baxter Magolda (Eds.), *Contested issues in student affairs: Diverse perspectives and respectful dialogue*. Sterling, VA: Stylus Publishing.

Quaye, S. J., (2008). Student voice and sensemaking of multiculturalism on campus. In S. R. Harper (Ed.), *Creating inclusive campus environments for cross-cultural learning and student engagement*. Washington, DC: Student Affairs Administrators in Higher Education (NASPA).

Renn, K. A. (2011). Identity centers: An idea whose time has come ... and gone?. In P. M. Magolda & M. B. Baxter Magolda (Eds.), *Contested issues in student affairs: Diverse perspectives and respectful dialogue*. Sterling, VA: Stylus Publishing.

Steffes, J. & Keeling, R. P. (2006). Creating strategies for collaboration. In R. P. Keeling (Ed.), *Learning reconsidered 2: Implementing a campus-wide focus on the student experience* (pp. 69–74). Washington, DC: American College Personnel Association (ACPA), Association of College and University Housing Officers-International (ACUHO-I), Association of College Unions-International (ACUI), National Academic Advising Association (NACADA), National Association for Campus Activities (NACA), National Association of Student Personnel Administrators (NASPA), and National Intramural-Recreational Sports Association (NIRSA).

Strange, C. C., & Banning, J. H. (2001). *Educating by design: Creating campus learning environments that work*. San Francisco, CA: Jossey-Bass.

CHAPTER TWENTY-FOUR

Remember PULSE

LGBT Understanding and Learning Serves Everyone

PAMELA ROSS McCLAIN

INTRODUCTION

> PULSE
> Punched, pulverized, pushed to the ground
> Upsurge in violence against
> LGBTs abound
> Stabbed, strangled, shot, silenced by suicide. 49 died,
> Executed for living with pride.
> —PAMELA ROSS MCCLAIN

The PULSE acrostic poem above is written in remembrance of the Pulse Club goers whose lives were lost in Orlando, Florida as a result of a terrorist rampage. The hate-fuelled tragedy that occurred in Orlando sent shockwaves across the globe. The intense disgust precipitated by these indefensible acts of violence spanned far beyond the LGBT community. The poem illuminates the intolerable acts of violence perpetuated against Lesbian, Gay, Bi-sexual, and Transgender (LGBT) people has an impact far beyond the LGBT community.

The intense disgust precipitated by these indefensible acts of violence that occurred at PULSE forced the world to take notice. Despite the wide media coverage and public outcry in response to the Pulse Club travesty, it can be said that it is easier to be desensitized to catastrophic events that do not affect familiar faces. We must all intentionally resist the inclination to take a blind eye to the agony worn on faces that are unlike our own. Each Pulse victim bore the face of a human being and their loss of life should be ever present in the hearts and minds of all persons who value the universal sanctity of human life. Following is an alphabetical list of the Pulse Club causalities that collectively convey the numerical magnitude of the death toll represented by these individuals' names (ages):

> Stanley Almodovar III (23), Amanda Alvear (25), Oscar A. Aracena Montero (26), Rodolfo Ayala-Ayala (33) Antonio Davon Brown (29), Darryl Roman Burt II (29), Angel L. Candelario-Padro (28), Juan Chevez-Martinez (25), Luis Daniel Conde (39), Cory James, Connell (21), Tevin Eugene Crosby (25), Deonka Deidra Drayton (32), Simon Adrian Carrillo Fernandez (31), Leroy Valentin Fernandez (25), Mercedez Marisol Flores (26), Peter O. Gonzalez-Cruz (22), Juan Ramon Guerrero (22), Paul Terrell Henry (41), Frank Hernandez (27), Miguel Angel Honorato (30), Javier Jorge-Reyes (40), Jason Benjamin Josaphat (19), Eddie Jamoldroy Justice (30), Anthony Luis Laureanodisla (25), Christopher Andrew Leinonen (32), Alejandro Barrios Martinez (21), Brenda Lee Marquez McCool (49), Gilberto Ramon Silva Menendez (25), Kimberly Morris (37), Akyra Monet Murray (18), Luis Omar Ocasio-Capo (20), Geraldo A. Ortiz-Jimenez (25), Eric Ivan Ortiz-Rivera (36), Joel Rayon Paniagua (32), Jean Carlos Mendez Perez (35), Enrique L. Rios, Jr. (25), Jean C. Nives Rodriguez (27), Xavier Emmanuel Serrano Rosado (35), Christopher Joseph Sanfeli, (24), Yilmary Rodriguez Solivan (24), Edward Sotomayor Jr. (34), Shane Evan Tomlinson (33), Martin Benitez Torres (33), Jonathan Antonio Camuy Vega (24), Juan P. Rivera Velazquez (37), Luis S. Vielma (22), Franky Jimmy Dejesus Velazquez (50), Luis Daniel Wilson-Leon (37), and Jerald Arthur Wright (31). (The City of Orlando, 2016, June 12)

Viewing these names collectively is staggering. In disbelief, the world looked on in utter shock as the identities of the slain Pulse Club patrons were revealed, and gave witness to what happens when hate crimes targeted at any group are allowed to proliferate. When you put names and faces on the growing number of acts of harassment and hate crimes directed at the LGBT community, the need for a call to action becomes glaringly apparent. Yet heightened public awareness about LGBT issues should not be the isolated by-product of history-making hate crime rampages.

On any given day, there are more people who do not condone LGBT hate crimes than there are those who perpetuate hate crimes or believe that they are justifiable. One would hope that in the 21st century, those persons who harbour hate toward the LGBT community would be atypical and unrepresentative the masses. Nonetheless, even in the absence of overtly hateful thoughts and intentions, one can argue that ignorance or indifference toward LGBT issues creates a bigger space for a minuscule fraction of hate mongers to appear that they represent a larger population than they do in actuality. In others words, if one person commits acts of physical violence or verbal abuse by spewing hate-filled LGBT epithets while nine onlookers watch in silence and inaction, then the power of one takes on the momentum of ten. Dr. Martin Luther King, Jr. (1967) eloquently made this case when he stated, "We will have to repent in the generation not merely for the hateful words and actions of the bad people, but for the appalling silence of the good people." Vocal friends and allies who are willing to break their silence as a matter of social responsibility are imperative supporters of the LGBT community. It is not necessary that friends and allies see eye to eye on all LGBT issues but it is necessary to abandon the either/or mentality to take on a both/and approach in order to reach consensus thinking. We must acknowledge the intersectionality of diverse populations and value working cooperatively in a spirit of reciprocal respect and shared benefit. The both/and approach allows people of similar but differing thoughts and ideologies to collaborate to forge acceptable and mutually advantageous solutions (Roper, 2014).

I write this chapter from the perspective of a university faculty member who is a self-proclaimed friend and ally to the LGBT community, as well as an advocate for diversity and inclusion as a means to achieving institutional excellence for everyone.

PERPETRATORS UNLEASHED ON LGBTS = SENSELESS EVIL

There is no state in the United States of America without documented LGBT hate crimes. Consider the following as poignant snapshots of reported LGBT hate crimes:

> Matthew Wayne Shepard was a 21-year-old student, a slight and friendly poli-sci major at the University of Wyoming. On October 6, 1998, Shepard met Russell Henderson and Aaron McKinney at a bar in Laramie, Wyoming; the men offered to drive Shepard home. Instead they drove to a desolate rural area where they tortured Shepard, robbed him, and tied him to a fence and left him to die. He was discovered some 18 hours later by a bicyclist who thought Shepard was a scarecrow. According to media reports and the book *Illusive Shadows: Justice, Media, and Socially Significant American Trials*, his face was completely covered in blood, except where tears had washed the blood away. (Anderson,-Minshall, 2012, p. 5)

> Gwen Amber Rose Araujo ... went to a party bravely wearing a miniskirt for the first time, and she never came home. The 17-year-old Araujo was transgender, and after Paul Merel's girlfriend discovered and outed Araujo at a party both girls were attending, four men—Michael William Magidson, 22, Jose Antonio Merel, 22, Jaron Chase Nabors, 19, and Jason Cezares, 22—beat Araujo, slashed her face, hit her on the head with a shovel and a frying pan, strangled her, hog-tied her, wrapped her body in a sheet, and tossed her into the back of a pick-up truck. They drove her to a camp ground about 100 miles away in the Sierra foothills and dumped her body. (Anderson,-Minshall, 2012, p. 3)

> At 8:15 a.m. on February 12, Brandon McInerney, age 14, stormed into the computer lab of Oxnard, Calif.'s E.O. Green Junior High. Armed with a small caliber handgun, he shot 15-year-old Lawrence King twice in the head in front of a roomful of students. (Broverman, 2008, p. 1)

The question must be asked. What can be learned from these LGBT hate crimes? Two things can be learned, namely how to mobilize for change and how to shift from apathy to action in support of LGBT students. The need for this shift is urgent because hate crimes will not subside unless explicit, policy-driven principles are implemented at all institutional levels.

THE PULSE PRINCIPLE

My PULSE principle, Pro-LGBT Understanding and Learning and Serves Everyone is rooted in four themes. Theme one looks at the educational benefits to universities when higher education administrative leaders, faculty, staff, and students support LGBTs as allies. Theme two shares the transformative potential of pedagogies that provide pro-social and unbiased learning experiences for university students and their contextual communities at-large. Theme three offers an explanation of why *LGBT safe spaces* enhance the entire university community. Lastly, theme four inspects the nature of the hatred that is in the nucleus of hate crimes and proposes that unconditional inclusion is the only cure. The intentional reiteration of the PULSE acronym throughout these themes reflects an attempt to constructively preserve the memory of the Pulse Club victims through the application of proactive principles which hold potential to lessen the likelihood of future hate crimes and suggest ways to value LGBT diversity.

P.U.L.S.E. Theme 1: Proactive University Leadership Supports Equity for LBGTs

Given that the charge to lead in higher education is not a responsibility to be taken lightly, Chancellors, Presidents, Provosts, and the like are placed in key leadership positions that shape the future of their institutions as well as that of the world at-large. Larry D. Roper makes the case:

> As the diversity of college campuses continues to grow the multiplicity of personal and educational needs students bring will expand as well. We have seen in recent years that the increased enrolment of groups such as returning veterans, international students, students with disabilities, transgender students, homeless and food insecure students, and undocumented students, among others—have pressed campus leaders to reconsider the adequacy of programs and services. (2014, p. 207)

Determining the adequacy of resources is never a simple task but it is a necessary one. Given the proper strategic resources, student diversity can be a unifying strength in universities led by culturally aware and inclusive leaders. It can also be a divisive weakness if university leaders are not consciously responsive to the cultural needs of their entire university community.

Like the larger communities in which they are embedded, college communities may include people who hold entrenched, unchallenged, and biased perspectives, individuals or groups who commit inexcusable acts of intimidation that range from bomb threats to verbal and physical assaults. College campuses are unfortunately not immune to hate crimes. These incidents can occur in any region of the nation and at any type of higher education learning institution. The United States Department of Justice, Office of Justice Programs, (2001, October) authored the Bureau of Justice Assistance Monograph entitled, *Hate Crimes on Campus: The Problem and Efforts to Confront It*. This report provides compelling evidence that educational institutions are not impervious to hate crimes and that proactive measures must be taken to assure the safety and well-being of all university students, staff, faculty, administrators, community partners, visitors, and affiliates.

When proactive policies and practices are put into place, the chance for social acceptance and positive interpersonal interactions amongst all increases. University leaders are in vital positions to assure that university learning systems excel by embracing the full spectrum of diversity that exists within them.

P.U.L.S.E. Theme 2: Pedagogies to Unlearn LGBT Stereotypical Expectations

Universities have a long history of incubating the intelligentsia who are among the world's most vital natural resources, that of an enlightened workforce. These institutions are simultaneously charged with inducting college students into *the world that is* while at the same time inspiring them to be pioneers who can create *a world anew* with possibilities not yet imagined.

Higher education campuses function as microcosms of our larger global society and encompass its vast diversity. Eclectic groups comprised of different races, creeds, colors, socioeconomic statuses, abilities, gender identities, affectional orientations, faiths, and non-faiths routinely converge on college campuses to create diverse and dynamic learning cultures. Many students enter college with similar academic experiences, having met standardized admissions pre-requisite requirements. Truth be told, even in educational settings where students appear, on the surface, to be more alike than different, when you delve below the surface, differences emerge. Homogenous and ethnocentric socialization experiences deny many students of the early exposure to the human diversity commonly encountered in higher education.

Not surprisingly, all students carry with them beliefs that they hold about themselves and *others* whom they may have or no little first-hand knowledge. When the discomfort with the unfamiliar surfaces, students need to be taught how to make sense of their own identity relative to that of others, who they perceive as different. Students must learn about the concept of cultural relativism with the support they need to find their place amongst a multicultural student populace without fear of losing their own identity, or unknowingly or intentionally denigrating others' identities.

Wrong teaching creates wrong thinking and wrong thinking often leads to the wrong actions. Hate crimes, as vile as they may be, are indicative of much more incessant epidemic of intolerance for human diversity. There is a hidden curriculum that passes from generation to generation in spite of legal and social reform.

It seems unfathomable to think that on any given day at dinner tables across the nation, parents are sitting down for a nice home cooked meal served with a lesson on how to be homophobic, racist, sexist, classist, and/or elitist. While this is not likely a common household ritual, oppressive practices and biased thinking directed toward the LGBT community are well entrenched in the American psyche. Young people consciously and unconsciously take mental notes on stereotypes that create one-dimensional characterizations of LGBT *others* who that will invariably define as different from their social construction of the *mythical norm* (Lorde, 1984).

So the question begs, if people can be taught to hate and discriminate based on their preferred brand of prejudice, can they unlearn these biased habits of mind through lessons that support diversity and full inclusion? Unlike other academic content that can be taught by skill and drill or memorization, lessons that seek to dislodge biased thinking, must include student engagement. Student engagement means that faculty members take on a constructivist philosophy when creating learning experiences that will encourage students to unpack their preconceived notions of *others* who they may have decided are different, and perhaps inferior to themselves.

When delving into diversity issues, LGBT issues in particular, it is essential that faculty create a learning culture where all learners feel safe to excavate their baggage and biases without judgment. LGBT issues are especially sensitive because even before birth, once parents know the ascribed genotypic sex of their child, they begin to process of indoctrinating the child into their socially constructed gender identity. Few heterosexual males or females are ever challenged to defend their heterosexuality or whether or not it was their choice or simply innate. The acceptance of heterosexuality sexuality is often taken for granted while members of the LGBT community are regularly expected to justify their right to exist with the same measure of normalcy and acceptance.

Joelle R. Ryan (2009) sought to expand her pedagogical repertoire by utilizing an experiential learning opportunity that allowed students to participate in the Transgender Day of Remembrance. Even though this experience was given mixed reviews by students, Ryan noted upon reflection, "The hesitation that many students felt about moving to a new space and anticipating the unexpected was pivotal if we were to move beyond traditional pedagogy (p. 90)." One can only hope that lessons learned about prejudicial thinking and stereotypes from direct instruction or by inference can be unlearned through teaching that is explicitly geared to challenge intergroup misconceptions and promote unbiased thinking.

When heterosexual students encounter students who do not reflect their own gender orientation, it can be unsettling to comprehend. According to: Koritha Mitchell (2013):

> In this climate, even heterosexuals who do not participate in bullying or gay-bashing benefit from it, because they cannot relinquish the privilege it underwrites for them. The fact that LGBT people's freedom and dignity can be disregarded only reinforces the idea that citizens are heterosexual—that sexual conformity is the sign that someone should be respected and protected. (p. 697)

This is why is why awakening students' consciousness about LGBT issues and perspectives is essential because it is one powerful way to humanize issues that students may not have intelligibly encountered prior to an induction in higher education. As Shelton-Colangelo et al. (2007) note:

> It has become clear that traditional pedagogy and curricula are not suiting the pressing needs of a new generation of learners, our communities, and our world. A class that is based solely on the retention of factual information instead of deep understanding will not produce the life-long learners needed meet the challenges of today's world. (p.179)

Students deserve to be given ample opportunities to interrogate their values and beliefs regarding the LGBT community which will be useful to them when they encounter the unfamiliar in any context.

P.U.L.S.E. Theme 3: Pride in Unmasked Lives to Showcase Equity for LGBTs

Higher education campuses are ideal places for creating inclusive learning environments and other safe spaces for persons who identify as LGBT. Campuses also make ideal crucibles for disrupting patterns of LGBT marginalization. Catherine O. Fox and Tracy E. Ore (2010) note that, "The need for LGBT safe spaces is clear, as high rates of violence, disproportionate rates of suicide and substance abuse, high dropout rates and overall alienation continue to impact the lives of LGBT people on our campuses" (p. 630). The inclusion of places openly as LGBT safe spaces signals university support for LGBT faculty, staff, and students. These designated safe spaces represent institutional policy backed by financial commitment to proactively invest in supporting historically invisibilized populations.

LGBT safe spaces in higher education are comparable to "gayborhoods" which serve as communal enclaves that offer public support for LGBT pride and open acceptance. The definition for *gayborhood* can be found in the online *Urban Dictionary*, which records and defines colloquial cultural slang terms that are not yet officially part of the English language (Retreived from http://www.urbandictionary.

com/define.php?term=Website). *The Urban Dictionary* notes that, "A gayborhood is any neighborhood with a high concentration of same-sex oriented individuals that contains homes, clubs, bars, restaurants, and other places of business and entertainment that are welcoming to the residents and other visiting homosexuals" (Retrieved from http://www.urbandictionary.com/define.php?termGayborhood). According to Cori E. Walter (2011), in *It's a Beautiful Day in the Gayborhood*:

> Gayborhoods started in a dark place in America's history where gays and lesbians were marginalized. The definition of the term and its role has transformed over the years. The gayborhood began as the gay ghetto of containment for the marginalized populations of cities. It then turned into the gay village of sexual entertainment and bohemian culture. The village then transformed into the gay neighborhood of rainbow flags, gay activism, and queer economy. (p. 5)

The transformation of gayborhoods has served as a beacon of hope and a far-reaching catalyst for the evolution of communities that embrace pride in human diversity.

Much like the positive development of communities that has occurred through the formation of gayborhoods, a parallel progression is occurring in higher education. It is becoming increasingly commonplace to see university offices, facilities, and/or employee positions designated to support LGBT students. Their provision represents strategic investment decisions made by higher education administration, commitments that signal the specific provision of resources to LGBT students, staff, faculty, and administrators. The recognition and inclusion of LGBT persons in higher education enhances the collegiate experience for all students. When universities designate safe and welcoming spaces for LGBT students, the doors of inclusion are opened a bit wider for all persons who have ever been made to feel as though they do not belong or are not accepted within dominant culture.

P.U.L.S.E. Theme 4: Practicing Unconditional Love as the Standard for Everyone

Hatred directed at other human beings is foreign to the soul and is a cancerous character flaw. Hate is not innate to the human spirit and is not just a matter of psychological dysfunction. It is a social problem (Whitlock, 2012a). According to sociologist Kathleen Blee, "[t]he role of hate in practices of intergroup conflict and tension is generally regarded, at least implicitly, as a matter of individual psychology (p. 96)." She further stresses that hate must be understood "as a social, in addition, to an individual phenomenon … hate as relational; hate as socially constructed; hate as accomplished; and hate as organized (p. 98)." Blee notes that while a positive individual experience with a demonized group member can challenge overgeneralized hate, disconfirming individual experience does not eradicate hate that is blanketly directed at a universalized group. If hate is indeed a social problem, then all member of societies have an obligation to confront hate in any and all forms not just the brand of hate that resonates on a person level.

LGBT bashing and ridicule egregiously reinforces a culture that fosters *mythical norm privilege*. Audre Lorde (1984) defines what she terms a mythical norm in American as the "thin, white, male, young, heterosexual, Christian and financially secure" individual (p. 589). Lorde (1984) asserts that "the mythical norm" is based on a one size should fit all standard for normality that ignores the multifaceted nature of human identity. This standardization and the extent to which individuals can align their identity with the markers of the mythical norm affords privilege and power.

Consequently, anyone who does not fit into the cookie cutter mold of *dominant culture normalcy* is subject to a form of *deficit discrimination*. Gary R. Weaver (1997) describes dominant culture in the United States saying: "The U.S. is a culturally diverse society. However, there is also a dominant culture.... A more historically accurate metaphor is that the U.S. has had a cultural 'cookie-cutter' with a white, Anglo-Saxon, Protestant, male mold or shape" (p. 3).

Not fitting the mold often leads to the assignment of a perceived "deficit" and subsequent discrimination based on the prescribed deficit. *Deficit discrimination* occurs when any dominant group is seen as the standard for normalcy which sets up others who do not share their attributes to be discriminated against. In hetero-sexual/patriarchal dominated cultures, self-appointed normal folks often assign a deficit value to LGBTs and then proceed to discriminate based on this subjective assignment or watch idly while discrimination occurs.

As well, focusing exclusively on difference leaves us unaware of what Joseph Ofori-Dankwa (2007) terms our *DiverSimilarity*. He explains:

> The DiverSimilarity paradigm advocates the valuing and appreciation of the similarities and differences that individuals and communities have. The DiverSimilarity premise is that to effectively manage diversity, we must also effectively manage our similarities. This is the ultimate diversity paradox. An important aspect of the DiverSimilarity paradigm is the concept of simulation. Given America's history with the assimilation paradigm, it is important to distinguish between assimilation and simulation. Simulation points to the similarities and commonalties that individuals from diverse cultural backgrounds have. Simulation celebrates similarities that individuals have without attempting to modify or change other cultures. (Retrieved from: http://diverseeducation.com/article/7691)

Ofori-Dankwa and Reddy (2007) further purport that DiverSimilarity is, "... based in the competing values model which takes a both/and perspective rather than an either/or perspective.... The DiverSimilarity concept therefore seeks to build on the positive aspects of the similarity and diversity paradigms" (p. 62). In this way, strength emerges from diversity when individuals and groups choose unity over disunity.

PEOPLE UNITED IN LOVE TO STOP ERADICATION OF THE LGBTQ COMMUNITY

I will never forget the day I *came out* as an ally to the LGBTQ community. I was attending evening Bible Study at my church. My pastor was offering yet another lesson that appeared to be *bashing* LGBT people. He often preached sermons and conveyed messages that I thought demonized the lifestyles of LGBT persons. I could not reconcile the contradiction that my Pastor could preach *unconditional love* on one hand while openly disparaging the lifestyles of LGBT Christians on the other. I can remember thinking if, from the Christian perspective, "If we are all sinners in our own right, why do LGBTs have to be singled out as the object of regular discussion and ridicule?"

It is clear to me now that I spent way too long respectfully being quiet while I knew in my heart that I did not agree with the teachings of my Pastor. One Wednesday evening, when I determined that I had had enough, I mustered up the courage to stand at Bible Study during the Question and Answer period and ask my Pastor about his strong views against the LGBT community and why LGBTs were seemingly scrutinized more harshly for what he defined as their "sins" in comparison to heterosexual sinners. His answer was one that he based on his interpretation of the Bible and it never resonated in my soul as being acceptable. I was proud that I challenged what I felt deeply in my heart was wrong teaching and chose to exhibit unconditional love for my LGBT counterparts.

Humanity writ large is both alike and different across an almost infinite number of spectra. In any given context or situation, we can choose to focus on the things that unite us with others or we can fixate on the differences that intensify our sense of separation. In order for progress to occur, the fallacy of separation and otherness must be challenged and replaced with new ways of thinking and behaving that reflect unconditional respect, even love, and acceptance of our fellow human beings. If hate is a learned behavior, people can be taught to relinquish hate and replace it with respect.

CONCLUSION

Hate crimes against LGBTs are an affront to all of humanity and cannot be tolerated. By honoring the deceased Pulse Club-goers, those whose lives were lost as a result of a terrorist, hate-fuelled rampage, we can heighten national and global awareness about the need for LGBT respect, support, and acceptance. Unfortunately, the massive loss of 49 lives, the physical wounding of 53 others, and the grievous injury to innumerable others, while unprecedented, is indicative of an even larger and more incessant aggregate record of LGBT hate crime victims. One can easily make the case that an inexcusable number of daily incidents of intolerance, overt hostility, physical aggressions, micro-aggressions, and macro-aggressions are experienced by LGBTs yet often go unacknowledged, unscrutinised, and unchallenged. Activism that increases awareness about hate crimes directed at LGBTs on college campuses is one step toward unifying the broader society for the purpose of putting an end to hate crimes in any form (Whitlock, 2012a).

We must continuously monitor the *pulse* on our college campuses and hold ourselves accountable for making sure that no person loses their pulse or takes the pulse of another because we have not insisted on the provision of ample opportunities to develop respect for others who may be perceived as different. The time for radical change so that members of the LGBT community are valued is long overdue.

Back in 1993, now more than three decades ago, the late Maya Angelou was honored to be U.S. President William Jefferson Clinton's inaugural poet. She penned a poem, *On the Pulse of Morning* for Clinton's swearing-in ceremony in 2012. Although Angelou's (2015) poem was written long before the atrocities that occurred at the Pulse Club, on June 12, 2016, her words appear to have been prophetic. Excerpts from this poem reveal a prognosis of events that were yet to take place in American history. She writes:

> History, despite its wrenching pain
> Cannot be unlived, and if faced
> With courage, need not be lived again.
> Do not be wedded forever
> To fear, yoked eternally
> To brutishness ...
> The horizon leans forward
> Offering you space to place new steps of change
> Here, on the pulse of this fine day. (pp. 265–266)

Angelou implored her listeners to learn from a past marred by numerous injustices to humanity. She exhibited the wisdom of an oracle with a visionary gift to look back upon the past and from it to extract how to learn and teach lessons that hold the promise of a brighter future.

As a self-proclaimed ally of the LGBT community, I am mindful of Maya Angelou's reminder that each day lived has its own *pulse* and that the actions we take on any given day will shape the collective human pulse. Angelou (2015) beckons the dawning of a new day, and a new human consciousness. She inspires us to embrace each new day as a "fine day," and to collectively create a "space to place new steps of change" (p. 266). Sadly, we may never experience the "Good morning" of a "fine day," for all, unless those of us who are ready to make a change in ourselves, our communities, our societies, and the world, rise on the pulse of each new morning and shine our support on our extended LGBT family to put an end to all forms of hate crimes. We can choose the life-giving "pulse of morning" and look forward to a more civil and humane future, or we can choose the perpetual *pulse of mourning* and more senseless deaths (Angelou, 2015, p. 261).

REFERENCES

Anderson-Minshall, D. (2012, May). *Advocate, 12 crimes that changed the LGBT world*. Retrieved from http://www.advocate.com/arts-entertainment/advocate-45/2012/05/07/12-crimes-changed-lgbt-world?pg=3#article-content

Angelou, M. (2015). *Maya Angelou: The completed poetry*. New York, NY: Random House.

Broverman, N. (2008, March). *Mixed messages*. Advocate. Retrieved from http://www.advocate.com/news/2008/03/14/mixed-messages

City of Orlando. (2016, June 12). *Victims' names*. Retrieved from http://www.cityoforlando.net/blog/victims

Fox, C., & Ore, T. (2010). (Un)covering Normalized Gender and Race Subjectivities in LGBT "safe spaces". *Feminist Studies, 36*(3), 629–649.

King, M. L. (1967, April 4). Beyond Vietnam. Speech presented to Clergy and Laymen concerned about Vietnam in Riverside Church, New York, NY.

Lorde, A. (1984). *Sister outsider: Essays and speeches by Audre Lorde*. Freedom, CA: The Crossing Press.

Mitchell, K. (2013). Love in action-noting similarities between lynching then and anti-LGBT violence now. *Callaloo, 36*(3), 689–717.

Ofori-Dankwa, J. (2007). We need to emphasize similarities as well as differences—DiverSimilarity, the paradigm to effectively manage ethnic similarities and dissimilarities. Retrieved from http://diverseeducation.com/article/7691/

Ofori-Dankwa, J., & Reddy, S. (2007). Diversity management using the DiverSimilarity paradigm: A case study of a major mid-west food retailing and distribution corporation. *Journal of Diversity Management, 2*(2), 61–66.

Roper, L. (2014, August). Name our ignorance in service to our diversity commitment. *Journal of College & Character, 15*(3), 207–209.

Ryan, J. R. (2008, Fall/2009, Winter). Death by transphobia: Increasing gender awareness through teaching the day of remembrance. *Transformations, 19*(2), 80–136.

Shelton-Calonego, S., Mancuso, C., & Duvall, M. (2007). Teaching with joy: Educational practices for the twenty-first century. Lanham, MD: Rowan & Littlefield.

The United States Department of Justice, Office of Justice Programs, Bureau of Justice Assistance. (2001, October). *Hate crimes on campus: The problem and efforts to confront it*. Retrieved from https://www.ncjrs.gov/pdffiles1/bja/187249.pdf

Walter, C. (2011). *It's a beautiful day in the gayborhood* (Masters of Liberal Studies thesis). Retrieved from http://scholarship.rollins.edu/mls/6/

Weaver, G. (1997). *American cultural values*. Retrieved from http://trends.gmfus.org/doc/mmf/American%20Cultural%20Values.pdf

Whitlock, K. (Summer, 2012a). Reconsidering hate. *Public Eye, 27*(2), 1, 17–19, 21–23.

Conclusion ... AND A Call TO Action

LGBTQ+ Inclusion: Getting It Right on Our Own Campuses

VIRGINIA STEAD

This book has addressed crushingly hateful campus exclusion arising from the inherited personal characteristic of LGBTQ+ gender identity. The personal experiences and research findings that these authors have shared create a uniquely informative set of criteria with which to inform constructive activism and ongoing research.

Hopefully, you have acquired new insights and strategies that will strengthen your research and work as activists within your own communities, your states, and the world at large. The time has passed when knowledge of LGBTQ+ exclusion without action is sufficient. What is needed now is immediate and forceful action to integrate members of the LGBTQ+ into "mainstream" campus society and culture.

Readers are invited to contact me with comments on this book and suggestions for additional volumes in the *Equity in Higher Education series*.

Afterword

Ending the Erasure of Trans* and Non-Binary Students Through Higher Education Policy

KARI J. DOCKENDORFF

[*Author's Note:* The term trans* is used to acknowledge a broad array of gender identities. Tompkins (2014) describes trans* as, "meant to include not only identities such as transgender, transsexual, trans man, and trans woman that are prefixed by trans- but also identities such as genderqueer, neutrios, intersex, agender, two-spirit, cross-dress, and genderfluid" (p. 27).]

INTRODUCTION

Campus records and documents are used to track and identify students as they move through their degrees within the institution. But, how institutions place student identities into categories can sometimes lead to the erasure of the student identity, and ultimately the student. For example, when an admissions application asks students to list their gender on the document, oftentimes the student is given two options: male or female. This binary categorization of gender leaves out students who identify as trans* or non-binary since they are not allowed to identify outside of the male/female options.

Some campuses do have policies in place that determine when or if a student is allowed to change their gender or their name, but these policies may actually end up reinforcing the binary gendered system. The aim of this chapter is to explore federal and institutional level policy related to trans* and non-binary students and how they are allowed, or not, to change their name and/or gender on campus records. The chapter will then turn to a discussion of the discourse around trans* and non-binary students and how genderism plays a role in these policies, concluding with a discussion on how we can imagine new policies that do not erase trans* and non-binary students on college campuses.

TERMINOLOGY

In order to understand genderism and how it functions within the institution of higher education, an understanding of key terms is needed. *Sex* and *gender* are two terms that are often conflated and used interchangeably. Nicolazzo (2015) points out that:

> ... the term male signifies one's sex, a designation that is assigned at birth, whereas the terms "man" and "men" refer to one's gender identity, and the term "masculine" refers to one's gender expression, or the embodiment of a particular gender identity. (p. 20)

By conflating these terms, identities that fall outside of the assumption that sex aligns with one's gender identity are erased. Thus, "conflation of sex and gender terminology furthers the cultural unintelligibility of trans* people by rendering their gender identities and expressions invisible, impossible, and unreal" (Nicolazzo, 2015, p. 20).

Heterosexuality is based on the assumption that there are only two genders (e. g. male and female), which are based on the conflation of gender with sex and that these designations are assigned at birth. To further illustrate this point, Schilt and Westbrook (2009) state that:

> Heterosexuality requires a binary sex system, as it is predicated on the seemingly natural attraction between two types of bodies defined as opposites. The taken-for-granted expectation that heterosexuality and gender identity follow from genitalia produces heteronormativity—even though in most social interactions genitals are not actually visible. (p. 443)

Heteronormativity is the dominant ideology that keeps gender locked into a rigid binary of male and female, and assumes that sexuality is also based upon sex. These heteronormative assumptions, about which genders and sexualities are "real", create a gendered hierarchy that determine which identities are seen as, "humans, not-quite-humans, and nonhumans" (Weheliye, 2014, p. 8). From heteronormativity we arrive at genderism which is, "the cultural enforcement of a rigid masculine/feminine gender binary" (Nicolazzo, 2016b, p. 539). Genderism functions on college campuses to maintain the gender binary through the discourse taken up in policies and practices on trans* and non-binary students.

Trans and *non-binary* individuals are those whose gender identity and expression fall outside of the dominant male/female binary. Transgender is sometimes used as an umbrella term to include all gender identities outside of the traditional binary, but the term is also known to represent only those who fall within the trans* identities which maintain the binary gendered system (e.g. male-to-female, or female-to-male) (Tompkins, 2014), which is why the term trans* is taken up throughout this chapter.

The term *cisgender* is used to, "describe individuals who possess, from birth and into adulthood, the male or female reproductive organs (sex) typical of the social category of man or woman (gender) to which that individual was assigned at birth" (Aultman, 2014, p. 61). Cisgender and its use, however, are not without critiques of its own and it is important to note that, "while there is an underlying tension in trans communities about how 'the same side as' reinforces the privilege of non-trans people, the term is useful in eliminating distinctions of 'real' or 'biological' woman/man when making comparative statements" (Marine & Catalano, 2014, p. 137).

The term *non-binary* will also be used throughout this paper. Technically, non-binary individuals are represented within the broader trans* term, however, "those who choose not to biomedically transition occupy a liminal space in which they are neither not trans* enough nor not quite not-trans* enough" (Nicolazzo, 2016a, p. 3), and so, the use of non-binary is a direct push against trans*-normativity within the trans* community.

Trans*-normativity is another way in which gender is policed by the binary structure of gender. Trans*-normativity suggests that, "all trans* people should transition from one socially knowable sex to another (e.g. male-to-female)" (Nicolazzo, 2016a, p. 3). This ideology erases those who identify outside of the male/female binary, and it also assumes that there is only one way for an individual to perform their designated gender. And now, with a better understanding of the concepts of gender, I turn to the context of the discourse of trans* and non-binary students within policy and higher education.

STATE LEGISLATION AND FEDERAL POLICY

Policies around trans* people have been largely debated in the last year at the local, state, and federal level. In November of 2015, voters in Houston, Texas struck down a non-discrimination ordinance (Houston Equal Rights Ordinance § 2014–530 (2014)) that included sexual orientation and gender identity within the classifications of identities protected under the measure; voters feared the ordinance would allow sexual predators into female bathroom spaces to harm women and children (Ura, 2015). Then, in the spring of 2016, a number of states took up legislation that specifically targeted trans* individuals, and their access to public spaces such as bathrooms (South Dakota's governor vetoed HB 1008; Georgia's governor vetoed HB 757). The state of North Carolina became the first state to enact one of these types of laws when their Governor signed House Bill 2 (HB2) into law requiring that people must use the public bathroom that aligns with the sex they were assigned on their birth certificate. In May of 2016, the Department of Justice responded to the state of North Carolina and HB2 by suing the state ("Justice Department Files Complaint Against the State of North Carolina to Stop Discrimination Against Transgender Individuals," 2016, May 9). One of the arguments the Department of Justice points out in the law suit against North Carolina is that this new law puts both the K-12 education system and public colleges and universities in North Carolina in violation of Title IX ("Justice Department Files Complaint Against the State of North Carolina to Stop Discrimination Against Transgender Individuals," 2016, May 9).

Title IX (Title IX of the Education Amendments of 1972. See https://www.justice.gov/crt/title-ix-education-amendments-1972) is currently the only piece of federal legislation that extends protections to trans* students ("Resources for Transgender and Gender-Nonconforming Students," 2016). In 2014, the Office for Civil Rights and the Department of Education issued a clarification on Title IX stating that its protections do extend to trans* students ("Resources for Transgender and Gender-Nonconforming Students," 2016), however there had been no indication regarding how this clarification on Title IX would hold up in court. In the spring of 2016, the first court case to test Title IX protections for trans* students made its way to the 4th Circuit Court of Appeals in Virginia (Grimm v. Gloucester County School Board, United States Court of Appeals for the Fourth Circuit. (2016)). The 4th Circuit Court of Appeals upheld the clarification and sided with a trans* student who petitioned his school to allow him to use the bathroom that aligned with his gender identity. The ruling issued by the 4th Circuit Court of Appeals is currently on hold, however, while the Supreme Court of the United States waits to hear the case in March of 2017 ("Federal judge urges prompt appeal to Court on transgender rights," 2016). These laws and court cases are crucial to follow given that they shape both policy and practices that exist on college campuses.

INSTITUTIONAL LEVEL POLICIES

Because colleges and universities are microcosms of the larger society, where these conversations around policies and laws influence how students, specifically trans* and non-binary students move around the campus, campuses will need to figure out what policies and practices are best for their campus and students. A small percentage of U.S. colleges and universities have implemented policies that determines when or if a student is allowed to change their name or gender on campus records. Currently, there are only 153 colleges and universities that have policies which allow students to use a chosen name on their college records ("Colleges and Universities that Allow Students to Change the Name and Gender on Campus Records", 2016). And, only 54 colleges and universities allow their students to change their gender on college records without medical intervention, and just eight of these institutions allow the change without any supporting documentation ("Colleges and Universities that Allow Students to Change the Name and Gender on Campus Records," 2016). Considering the fact that there are over 7,200 colleges and universities in the United States (The National Center of Education Statistics (2015) reports that there are over 7,200 college and universities in the United States.) the number of schools that do have these types of policies in place is actually quite small.

A closer look at these policies sparks questions like: Are these policies truly supportive of trans* and non-binary students? How do these policies reinforce genderism and how it functions within the institutions? And, what strategies can we take up to create better policies that do not erase the existence of trans* and non-binary students on college campuses? These are questions to hold on to as this chapter moves into a discussion on key concepts within this context of policy and the policy discourse around trans* and non-binary students.

DISCOURSE ON TRANS* AND NON-BINARY STUDENTS

There are three main discourses used when talking about trans* and non-binary students through policy or practice on college campuses: "vulnerability, disability, and resourcefulness" (Dirks, 2016, p. 380). A vulnerable discourse says that trans* and non-binary students need to be protected from these "unsafe" spaces within the institution. Wording policies in this way:

> ... allows the institution to depict itself as concerned for the privacy and safety of trans people without either addressing the larger issue of why gendered spaces such as bathrooms, residence halls, and locker rooms are dangerous places for a transgender person, or confronting cisgender privilege and exploring why gendered spaces were created and how that might change if we challenge unstated cultural norms around gender segregation. (Dirks, 2016, p. 382)

One type of institutional response when thinking about student populations as vulnerable, is to create non-discrimination policies that protect the vulnerable student group (Dirks, 2016; Nicolazzo, 2016b). Non-discrimination policies, however, "have been ineffective at eradicating discrimination on the basis of race, sex, disability, and natural origin" (Spade, 2015, p. 31), and so assuming that non-discrimination policies will protect trans* and non-binary students from homophobia or trans*phobia is not useful and ends up reifying the vulnerable discourse.

Disability is another discourse that is taken up when creating policy around trans* and non-binary students. This discourse situates students as needing to be fixed and, "positions the counseling services of the university as a rescuer of those students, despite the recognition that clinical services are lacking for transgender students" (Dirks, 2016, p. 384). Unfortunately, for trans* and non-binary students, access to adequate health care and counseling services on college campuses is lacking (Beemyn, 2005), and when trans* and non-binary students do seek out counseling services, the mental health professionals often focus on "fixing" the gender problem instead of focusing the stress, anxiety, and other mental health needs caused by coping with the college or university itself (Marine, 2011).

The institutional policies mentioned earlier in this chapter also reproduce the disability discourse by only allowing students to change their name or gender on campus records if they have approval from a doctor or mental health professional. By requiring students to seek support from a professional, the policies are reinforcing the idea that something needs to be fixed and they need to rely on health care professionals that may not be prepared to provide the support the students really need (Marine, 2011). This discourse actually fails to help the student and continues to situate the student as something that needs to be fixed.

One discourse on trans* and non-binary students that does not situate students as needing to be protected or fixed is the *resourceful* discourse. According to Dirks (2016), "the vulnerability discourse positions transgender people's *gender problems* as the ill to be remedied, a discourse of resourcefulness identifies genderism as the problem in need of a solution" (p. 384). By centering *genderism* as the real thing that needs to be fixed on college campuses, this discourse allows policies to be worded in ways that do not situate trans* and non-binary students as needing protection or to be rescued. Nicolazzo (2016b) takes up this discourse by pointing out the resiliency of trans* and non-binary students on college campuses and argues that, "combined with the prevalence of genderism in collegiate environments, higher education becomes an important location in which to stem the gap in the literature regarding trans* student resilience" (p. 539). This discourse needs to be the strategy when thinking of new ways to develop policy that does not erase trans* and non-binary students within campus records and documents.

DISCUSSION

One example of the way genderism functions on college and university campuses is through the policies in place that determine if or when a student is allowed to change their name or gender on college records. Current policies that are in place tend to require that a student has either gone through medical transition from one gender to another, or that the student has the support of a medical or mental health professional ("Colleges and universities that allow students to change the name and gender on campus records," 2016). These types of policies reinforce the disability discourse mentioned earlier, and reinforce the hegemonic assumptions about the gender binary. These types of policies also reify trans*normativity and reproduce the pressures some trans* students may feel to physically transition (Catalano, 2015). One key thought in imagining what types of policies could be created around names and gender changes within college records, is that policies addressing students' needs on a case-by-case basis are not the answer. Policies that treat students on a case-by-case basis put the pressure on the student to find the right person at the right time to get the answers or assistance they need in terms of changing their name or gender; this dynamic also opens the door for some students to be allowed to change their name or gender while not allowing others to do the same. So, what is needed within the institution are policies that center genderism, heteronormativity, homophobia, and trans*phobia as the problems that the university needs to address.

My challenge to higher education leaders and student affairs practitioners is not to pursue "best practices" by creating inclusive name and gender policy for campus records. As is often the case in higher education and student affairs, researchers and practitioners are quick to develop best practices for dealing with a certain type of situation that can be implemented on campuses far and wide. Furthermore, as Nicolazzo (2016a) points out, "the hegemony of focusing solely on implementing best practices may actually further the troubling effects of trans*-normativity, as they are insufficient at recognizing the polyvocality of trans* student experience" (p. 13). As well, I argue that the Campus Pride Index (2016), an illustration of which campuses have what policies, is another representation of best practices. These schools then become the measurement standard for other organizations, even without intentional thought regarding how the individual campuses work or whether they meet the needs of their trans* and non-binary students. As asserted by Nicolazzo (2016a), "... these policies are insufficient at promoting the type of deep unlearning of gender that would proliferate possibilities, especially for how non-binary trans* students can practice their genders and, as a result successfully navigate their college campuses" (p. 12).

CONCLUSION

As this country debates federal and state legislation on trans* and non-binary people and their access to bathrooms and public spaces, now is an important time to explore how we as educators, administrators, and researchers situate trans* and non-binary students on campus. I may not provide specific answers to dictate how policies should be worded in regards to name and gender changes on college campuses, but I suggest that since I do not want to offer best practices, maybe that is okay. I do challenge institutions of higher education to look at their own policies, if they exist, and question how these policies function. Are we framing trans* and non-binary students as the focus of a problem that needs to be fixed or protected? Or do our colleges and universities challenge dominant hegemonic norms of genderism and heterosexuality? Right now, I have the feeling the focus is mainly the student, but I hope we can move to a space where institutions are directly challenging genderism on campus.

REFERENCES

Aultman, B. (2014). Cisgender. *TSQ: Transgender Studies Quarterly, 1*(1–2), 61–62.
Beemyn, B. G. (2005). Making campuses more inclusive of transgender students. *Journal of Gay & Lesbian Issues in Education, 3*(1), 77–87. doi.:10.1300/J367v03n01_08
Catalano, D. C. J. (2015). "Trans enough?" The pressures trans men negotiate in higher education. *TSQ: Transgender Studies Quarterly, 2*(3), 411–430.
Colleges and universities that allow students to change the name and gender on campus records | campus pride. (2016). Retrieved from https://www.campuspride.org/tpc/records/
Dirks, D. A. D. (2016). Transgender people at four Big Ten campuses: A policy discourse analysis. *The Review of Higher Education, 39*(3), 371–393.
Federal judge urges prompt appeal to Court on transgender rights. (2016, June 1). Retrieved August 3, 2016 from http://www.scotusblog.com/2016/06/federal-judge-urges-prompt-appeal-to-court-on-transgender-rights/
Marine, S. B. (2011). Stonewall's legacy: Bisexual, gay, lesbian, and transgender students in higher education. *ASHE Higher Education Report, 37*(4). San Francisco, CA: Jossey Bass.
Marine, S. B., & Catalano, D. C. (2014). Engaging trans* students on college and university campuses. In S. J. Quaye & S. R. Harper (Eds.), *Student engagement in higher education: Theoretical perspectives and practical approaches for diverse populations* (2nd ed.) (pp. 135–148).
Nicolazzo, Z. (2015). "I'm man enough; are you?": The queer (im)possibilities of walk a mile in her shoes. *Journal of Critical Scholarship on Higher Education and Student Affairs, 2*(1), 19–30.
Nicolazzo, Z. (2016a). "It's a hard line to walk": black non-binary trans* collegians' perspectives on passing, realness, and trans*-normativity. *International Journal of Qualitative Studies in Education*, 1–16. doi:10.1080/09518398.2016.1201612
Nicolazzo, Z. (2016b). "Just go in looking good": The resilience, resistance, and kinship-building of trans* college students. *Journal of College Student Development, 57*(5), 538–556. doi:10.1353/csd.2016.0057
Schilt, K., & Westbrook, L. (2009). Doing gender, doing heteronormativity: "Gender normals," transgender people, and the social maintenance of heterosexuality. *Gender & Society, 23*(4), 440–464. doi:10.1177/0891243209340034
Spade, D. (2015). *Normal life: Administrative violence, critical trans politics, & the limits of the law.* Durham, NC: Duke University Press.
Tompkins, A. (2014). Asterisk. *TSQ: Transgender Studies Quarterly, 1*(1/2), 26–27.
Ura, A. (2015, November 3). Bathroom fears flush Houston discrimination ordinance. *The Texas Tribune.* Retrieved from https://www.texastribune.org/2015/11/03/houston-anti-discrimination-ordinance-early-voting/
Weheliye, A. G. (2014). *Habeas viscus: Racializing assemblages, biopolitics, and black feminist theories of the human.* Durham, NC: Duke University Press.

About the Contributors

Dr. Clayton R. Alford, B.A., M.S.E.D., Ed.D. is an educator based in the New York City metropolitan area with an extensive background in Education Leadership, Special Education, and Cultural Foundations of Education. Dr. Alford earned his Doctorate in Education from the University of Phoenix and holds a Master of Science degree in education (MSED) from the City University of New York and a Bachelor of Arts Degree from the Pennsylvania State University. Dr. Alford is active in the American Psychological Association (APA), American Educational Research Association (AERA), and the Black Doctoral Network (BDN). He is also an active contributor to the professional network of LinkedIn. Dr. Alford is committed to social justice and uses the educational platform to address concerns in this realm. Contact: alf1950@optonline.net

Traci P. Baxley, Ed.D. has worked in PreK-20 educational systems for over 20 years, earning a doctorate degree in Curriculum and Instruction with an area of specialization in Literacy. Her areas of scholarship include critical literacy, multicultural literature, and racial and identity development. Much of her scholarship and service is grounded in social justice education that addresses opportunity gaps and the academic and social successes of students of color and students in poverty. She has published in international and national peer reviewed journals and authored book chapters including *Taboo: The Journal of Culture and Education*, *International Journal of Critical Pedagogy*, and *Urban*

Education and co-authored a book entitled "Invisible Presence: Feminist Counter-Narratives of Young Adult Novels Written by Women of Color." Most recently Dr. Baxley was co-editor on a textbook project entitled *Equity Pedagogy: Teaching Diverse Populations*. Contact: baxley@fau.edu

Dr. Brandon L. Beck, Ph.D. is a trans man who teaches Graduate Elementary Education courses at Texas State University. He is chair of the Transgender Education Network of Texas, Vice-President of PFLAG San Marcos, a board member and certified trainer for GLSEN Austin, advisor of Transcend at Texas State, and education director for Alliance of Texas State. Dr. Beck is the 2016 winner of the Texas State Michael Wilkerson Advocacy Award and the 2016 Texas State Excellence in Diversity Award. Dr. Beck presents and writes on transgender inclusion locally, nationally, and internationally, and shares information on trans inclusion at www.transteacher.com. Contact: Brandon@transteacher.com

Nicole Bedera, B.S., M.A. is a doctoral student of sociology at the University of Michigan, Ann Arbor. Her research focuses on gender and sexuality with emphases in sexual violence and masculinity. She is a member of the National Science Foundation Graduate Research Fellowship Program and has published academically about sexual assault prevention on college campuses and the application of feminist pedagogies to study abroad experiences. She has also participated in community service on issues related to sexual violence, including work as a victim advocate, facilitating prevention programming for fraternities and sororities, and creating an educational resource focused on sharing the experiences of sexual assault survivors in their own words. Ms. Bedera's current scholarly work focuses on queer women's experiences with sexual assault in college and college men's interpretations of sexual consent. In the future, Ms. Bedera intends to expand her study of sexual violence beyond college campuses and into an exploration of cases that interact with the criminal justice system. Contact: nbedera@umich.edu

Dr. Jill Bickett, Ed.D. is Director of the Doctoral Program in Educational Leadership for Social Justice at Loyola Marymount University, and a faculty member in the Department of Educational Leadership. She is a lifelong educational leader, serving as teacher and primary administrator in the Catholic secondary school context. Her research interests include Catholic education, single sex education, gender, and social justice in education. Her dissertation research was a case study of a Catholic female single-sex high school exploring student perspectives about, and participation in leadership and service. Dr. Bickett's recent co-authored publications include "Two years of evaluation data from a Jesuit Ed.D. program for educational leadership in social justice" (2013) in *Jesuit Higher Education: A Journal,* and "A decade of impact: The doctorate in educational leadership for social justice." (2015) in V. Stead (Ed.), *The education doctorate (Ed.D.): Issues of access, diversity, social justice, and community leadership.* New York, NY: Peter Lang Publishing. Contact: Jill. Bickett@lmu.edu

Dr. Warren J. Blumenfeld, Ed.D. is a former Associate Professor at Iowa State University's School of Education, and a former teacher at Perkins School for the Blind. Warren is Author of Warren's Words: Smart Commentary on Social Justice, Co-editor of Readings for Diversity and Social Justice, Editor of Homophobia: How We All Pay the Price, Co-author of Looking at Gay and Lesbian Life, Co-Editor of Investigating Christian Privilege and Religious Oppression in the United States, Co-Researcher & Co-Author: 2010 State of Higher Education for Lesbian, Gay, Bisexual, and Transgender People, Co-editor of Butler Matters: Judith Butler's Impact on Feminist and Queer Studies, and Author of AIDS and Your Religious Community. Warren also serves as an editorial blogger for The Huffington Post, The Good Men Project, and LGBTQ Nation Newsletter. Contact: warrenblumenfeld@gmail.com

Carissa Cardenas, B.A. is a Graduate Assistant and Academic Counselor at the University of Redlands. In order to best serve as a social-justice advocate Cardenas has positioned herself in roles were she can learn and attain the knowledge needed to better serve the student population. She is currently assisting with research pertaining to LGBTQ student mentoring and campus climate for students with marginalized identities of gender and sexuality. In addition to a B.A. in Communication Studies from San Francisco State University, Cardenas anticipates receiving her M.A. in School and College Counseling from the University of Redlands, CA in August 2017. Contact: carissa_cardenas@redlands.edu

Dr. Angela Clark-Taylor, Ph.D. is a Visiting Assistant Professor in the Graduate Department of Leadership and Higher Education in the School of Education at University of Redlands. Clark-Taylor's work centers on the relationship between equity in educational access; college student development; and community engagement with a particular focus on populations with minoritized identities of sexuality and gender. Her current research projects focus on feminist university-community engagement, the LGBTQ college student experience, and gender based violence on campus. Clark-Taylor is the managing editor of the New York Journal of Student Affairs and a 2015–2016

Community Innovation Fellow with Re:Gender (formally the National Council for Research on Women). Clark-Taylor received her Ph.D. in educational leadership from the University of Rochester. Contact: angela_clark-taylor@redlands.edu

Susan M. Croteau is a doctoral student in the School Improvement Ph.D. Program at Texas State University. Prior to joining the program, she taught for 15 years at public elementary, middle, and high schools in Texas. Susan belongs to several campus organizations including Allies, Transcend, and the American Association of University Women. She has won several awards including the Texas State University Megan Curran Advocacy Award, the Gloria Mistral Research Fellowship, and the William Boyd Fellowship. Her current research interests include gender diversity, inclusive education, equity and access in public schools, critical theory, Queer Theory, student activism, and social justice leadership. Contact: sc40127@txstate.edu

Christopher A. Cumby, B.A. (any pronoun) is a graduate student in Memorial University of Newfoundland, Canada, studying Counselling Psychology. His research interests involve healthcare, peer support, sexual violence, marginalized voices and social justice. His thesis research focuses on understanding experiences of sexual violence among LGBTQ+ people within the Canadian province of Newfoundland and Labrador. As an activist, Christopher works with local organizations in providing education and training for LGBTQ+ competency, and works with local groups in St. John's and across the province to help elevate the quality of life for queer and trans people. If you have any questions or would like to get in touch with Christopher, please contact: christopher.cumby@mun.ca

Dr. Shiv R. Desai, Ph.D. is an Assistant Professor of Education in the Department of Teacher Education, Education Leadership and Policy College of Education, University of New Mexico. He has been a teacher educator for the last several years at various institutions in Ohio and Kentucky. He was a K-12 teacher and taught in South Los Angeles and New York. Professor Desai was a founding English Teacher for Opportunities Unlimited Charter High School in South Los Angeles, where he utilized Youth Participatory Action Research (YPAR). By making YPAR the focal point of his curriculum, he was able to help his students study the impact of gangs on their community and investigate the school-to-prison pipeline. Prior to coming to UNM, Professor Desai was a founding member of Voices of Freedom at Elementz—a hip-hop based community center in Cincinnati, OH. In this project, he worked with young adults to explore the meaning of spoken word poetry, and how it impacted their lives. He also founded Boyz N Da Hood, an all-boys after-school program at an elementary school in Covington, KY, which tackled issues of masculinity by utilizing hip-hop feminism. Currently, Professor Desai is working with the Juvenile Justice Council (JJC) in Albuquerque, and works with former and current incarcerated youth. Through YPAR, the JJC is documenting and informing policy makers on the changes that need to be implemented in order to improve juvenile detention. Contact: sdesai@unm.edu

Kari J. Dockendorff, M.Ed. is an advanced doctoral student and graduate research assistant in the department of Educational Leadership and Policy at the University of Utah. She is also finishing a Graduate Certificate in Gender Studies. Broadly, Kari is interested in the ways gender and sexuality function on college campuses and how policies work to sort and categorize students on campus. More specifically, Kari is interested in exploring trans* and non-binary student experiences and the nuanced ways they run up against systems of genderism, heterosexism, and transphobia on the college campus. Kari is currently teaching in the Leadership Studies program at the University of Utah and will be teaching in the Gender Studies department in spring of 2017. Upon graduation, Kari plans to pursue a faculty position in a similar department to teach and do research. Contact: KDockendorff@sa.utah.edu

Dr. Emily S. Fisher, Ph.D. is an Associate Professor in the School Psychology Program at Loyola Marymount University. Dr. Fisher's teaching and scholarship focus on counseling, mental health, and promoting positive development for at-risk student populations. She has published extensively on supporting LGBTQ students in schools, including two books: "Responsive School Practices to Support Lesbian, Gay, Bisexual, Transgender, and Questioning Students and Families", and "Creating Safe and Supportive Learning Environments: A Guide for Working with Lesbian, Gay, Bisexual, Transgender, and Questioning Youth and Families." Dr. Fisher's upcoming book, "Counseling Special Populations in Schools", focuses on unique considerations and specific counseling approaches for at-risk student populations, including students who are LGBTQ, students experiencing homelessness, students living in foster care, and students transitioning from the juvenile justice system. Contact: Emily.Fisher@lmu.edu

Dr. Robin K. Fox, Ph.D. is the Associate Dean of the College of Education and Professional Studies at the University of Wisconsin (UW)-Whitewater. Her early degrees are in Early Childhood Education, Child and Family Studies, Special Education, and her Ph.D. is from the University of Wisconsin-Madison in Curriculum and Instruction. While at UW-Whitewater she has been a lead teacher and director of the campus childcare center, a faculty member in Early Childhood Education and a department chair. Before coming to Whitewater she was a teacher and director at Head Start. Robin's areas of research center on children who are gender fluid, how school personnel can welcome parents and children who are LGBTQ, and work with schools to understand the lived experiences of children and families related to adoption. Contact: foxr@uww.edu

Laura D. Gentner, B.A., M.S.E. serves as the University of Dayton's first full-time Coordinator for LGBTQ+ Support Services. In addition to connecting LGBTQ+ identifying and ally students with resources based on current research and praxis, she provides campus programming related to LGBTQ+ support, coordinates the Ally Training Program. She presents to undergraduate students, student employees, faculty, and staff on LGBTQ+ on allyship topics, supports LGBTQ+ inclusive student organizations, and mentors student leaders who work to make campus more welcoming for LGBTQ+ identifying students. Laura has a particular passion for working in LGBTQ+ support services from a faith perspective, rooting the LGBTQ+ Support Services Program in the University of Dayton's Catholic and Marianist values and traditions. Laura earned a Master's of Science in Education in College Student Personnel from the University of Dayton where she served as a Residence Coordinator in Housing and Residence Life, and then as the University of Dayton's inaugural Graduate Assistant for LGBTQ+ Support Services. She earned a Bachelor of Arts in Languages from the University of Dayton. Her research interests include allyship from the perspective of LGBTQ+ identifying students and student leadership development. She has also served for the past seven years as a chapter advisor for Alpha Phi Omega at the University of Dayton, a national coed service fraternity committed to developing leaders through service and friendship. Contact: gentnerl2@udayton.edu

Dominic Grasso, M.Ed. has worked in public education for systems for seven years. He has worked for six years in high minority, low-income Title 1 schools in both Broward and Palm Beach Counties, and has recently transitioned into a district level role supporting LGBTQ & sexual curriculum for Broward County Public Schools. He graduated with a Master's degree in Reading Education, and is a Doctoral Candidate at Florida Atlantic University. He is on track to graduate with a Ph.D. in Curriculum and Instruction with an area of specialization in LGBTQ Issues in Education. He has presented at the National Association for Multicultural Education (NAME) Conference, and contributed to the textbook project titled: *Equity Pedagogy: Teaching Diverse Populations*. Contact: dgrasso3@my.fau.edu

valerie a. guerrero having attended nearly a dozen schools prior to college, has held a lifelong interest in educational inequities and experiences within the United States. She has spent the last 15 years engaged in issues of equity and social justice as related to the college environment. Informed by both academic inquiries and professional experiences working to facilitate more equitable environments and outcomes for students with minoritized identities, valerie has led hundreds of workshops and training sessions on college campuses primarily focused on issues of power, privilege, diversity, social justice, and social identities such as race, gender, and sexual orientation. Inspired by the value of understanding multiple educational and regional contexts, after earning an M.Ed. in student affairs with a graduate certificate in social justice education, valerie moved to Meadville, Pennsylvania to become the Associate Director in the Center for Intercultural Development and Student Success at Allegheny College. Motivated by the potential to positively impact campus climates through faculty and staff development, valerie is currently a doctoral student in the department of Educational Leadership and Policy at the University of Utah. Her research interests within education include critical pedagogies, structural oppression, developing critical praxis, faculty teaching preparation, intersectionality, campus climate, and social justice education. Contact: vaguerrero@gmail.com

Dean Hamer is a National Institutes of Health scientist emeritus, New York Times Book of the Year author, and Emmy Award winning-filmmaker with a long history in communicating complex and controversial ideas to diverse publics. His groundbreaking research on the role of biology in sexual orientation, described in *The Science of Desire*, played a key role in the debate over LGBT rights. More recently his documentary films, such as *Kumu Hina*, have increased public awareness off the rich diversity of human sexuality and gender expression. Hamer has been characterized in a Time magazine profile as "a pioneer." He is a consultant for the BBC and Discovery channels, and a sought-after lecturer and frequent guest on TV documentaries and news shows including Nightline and Oprah. Contact: deanhamer@aol.com

Paul S. Hengesteg, M.Ed. (he/him/his), is a doctoral student in higher education administration at Iowa State University (ISU). He volunteers with the Consortium of Higher Education LGBT Resource Professionals as a member of the LGBT2 Committee and was the inaugural co-chair of the Graduate Student Working Group. While a student affairs Master's student at

ISU, he was the Program Coordinator for Dialogues on Diversity and served as a graduate assistant in Prevention Services. While a Program Coordinator in the Office of Equity and Inclusion at the University of Delaware prior to graduate studies, he provided educational workshops to students, faculty, and staff on LGBTQ ally development, harassment and discrimination, Title IX, sexual violence prevention, and workplace bullying. Additional professional background for Paul includes working at the National Gay & Lesbian Chamber of Commerce and in professional regional theatre management. He proudly serves on the Alumni Association Board of Directors for his undergraduate alma mater, Simpson College. Contact: paulh@iastate.edu

Dr. Karen "Karie" K. Huchting, Ph.D. is an Associate Professor in the Department of Educational Leadership at Loyola Marymount University (LMU). She is also the Associate Director of LMU's Ed.D. Doctoral Program in Leadership for Social Justice and her areas of expertise are quantitative research methodology and assessment. Dr. Huchting's scholarship centers on social justice in the educational context. She has served as the Principal Investigator of several grant-funded research projects and has authored multiple publications examining the efficacy of educational leadership preparation programs to transform candidates to lead their contexts through the lens of social justice. Dr. Huchting also serves as an Editor for the peer-reviewed, academic journal, *Journal of Catholic Education* and she is Chair of the American Education Research Association (AERA) Special Interest Group focused on scholarship in Catholic schools. In 2015, Dr. Huchting was named to the Fulbright Specialist Roster. Contact: Karen.Huchting@lmu.edu

Kristen Altenau Keen, B.A., M.Ed. has been at the University of Dayton since fall of 2012, and currently serves as the Assistant Dean of Students for Education, Support, and Student Empowerment. As a part of her role, she created and manages all sexual violence prevention education for the undergraduate population of approximately 7,000 students, reaching over 10,000 student participants each year. Kristen brought Green Dot, a national bystander intervention program, to the University of Dayton in January 2014, and continues to lead this initiative. She also advises the Peers Advocating for Violence Education (a peer education group charged with sexual violence prevention education) and supervises LGBTQ+ support services. Kristen is passionate about helping college students think about sexuality in more complex ways. Her responsibilities as Assistant Dean include providing trauma-informed individual support to students in distress, particularly those who are survivors of sexual assault, and helping students find paths that will lead them to success. In addition, Kristen serves as an adjunct faculty member teaching human sexuality courses for Miami University and University of Dayton in the sociology, psychology, and family studies departments. She earned her Master's degree in Student Affairs in Higher Education and Bachelors in Psychology from Miami University in Oxford, OH. Contact: kkeen1@udayton.edu

Carol A. Kochhar-Bryant, Ed.D. is Professor and Senior Associate Dean of the Graduate School of Education and Human Development at the George Washington University. For 30 years she has developed and directed advanced graduate programs in education. She has directed initiatives to improve the inclusion and support of non-traditional students on the college campus, and to engage faculty in such initiatives. Carol Kochhar-Bryant is widely published in areas of disability policy and practice; civil rights and inclusive practices; leadership development; and transition to post-secondary and employment for special populations. She consults with public school districts, state departments of education, federal agencies, and non-profit organizations seeking to improve inclusion of individual with disabilities in education, employment and independent living. She has collaborated in research on educational inclusion with the World Bank. For the U.S. Department of Education she has led evaluation teams for the six Federal Resource Centers and has assisted states to develop and evaluate their education improvement initiatives. Contact: kochhar@gwu.edu

Kaitlin Legg is the Director of the LGBTQ Resource Center at the University of North Florida (UNF). She has ten years of experience in developing inclusive and timely campaigns and programs within social justice causes, including previous work to develop feminist leadership, reproductive justice, and LGBTQ initiatives for young professionals and college-aged youth with Planned Parenthood of Central and Western New Yorkand the University of Rochester. Additionally, Ms. Legg has worked within campus-oriented campaigns advocating for diversity and inclusion. She is recognized by the UNF Center for Professional Development and Training as an LGBTQ Subject Matter Expert and trains other professionals on these topics locally and at national conferences. She has lead the way in expanding services and visibility at UNF for trans* individuals, including updated policies and procedures with the University Police Department, the Department of Housing and Residence Life, and Human Resources. Kaitlin is a proud member of the Consortium of Higher Education LGBT Resource Professionals. Contact: kaitlinlegg@gmail.com

Katherine Lewis is a doctoral student in the School Improvement Ph.D. Program at Texas State University. Previously, she was an elementary school teacher in Texas, Colorado, and California. Katherine is a member of several campus organizations including Allies, Transcend, and the American Association of University Women. Her research interests are focused on the social, cultural, historical, and political aspects of education. She presents both locally and nationally on a variety of topics, including: trans inclusion and affirmation, inclusive education, supporting gender diverse students, social justice leadership, and viewing educational issues through a poststructural lens. Katherine has received several awards, including the 2016 Texas State University Megan Curran Advocacy Award. Katherine can be contacted at klewis.teacher@gmail.com.

Dr. Karin Ann Lewis, Ph.D. earned her B.A. in English from Cornell University; she earned her M.S. in Human Development and Education from the University of Rochester and her Ph.D. in Educational and Counseling Psychology from the University of Kentucky. Dr. Lewis is an Assistant Professor of Educational and Counseling Psychology in the College of Education and P-16 Integration at the University of Texas Rio Grande Valley. Her research interests include cultivating resiliency in times of transformative change, personal epistemology development and beliefs about difference and diversity, post-traumatic growth, and how people think and learn during challenging life transitions. She is invested in issues of equity, cross cultural understanding, and social justice. Dr. Lewis offers consulting and professional development locally, regionally, nationally and beyond. Dr. Lewis is also a professional sign language interpreter. Contact: karin.lewis@utrgv.edu

Dr. Kerri Mesner, Ph.D. is an Assistant Professor in the School of Education at Arcadia University in Glenside, Pennsylvania. Kerri is also an ordained minister with Metropolitan Community Churches, a queer theologian, a theatre performer and educator, and an activist. Kerri's current areas of research and writing include gender and sexual diversity in education, trans and gender nonconforming identities, arts-based educational research, contemplative educational practices, and anti-oppressive approaches to education. Kerri brings a background in theology, pastoral ministry, professional musical theatre, and queer activism to these current areas of research. Kerri's doctoral research explored performative autoethnography, queer theology, and anti-oppressive education in addressing religiously rooted anti-queer violence, and included an original one-act play written and performed by Mesner. The play, "Intervention", has been performed to critical acclaim in Canada and the US.

The dissertation was awarded the 2014 AERA Division B: Curriculum Studies Dissertation Award. Contact: mesnerk@arcadia.edu

Camaron Miyamoto is tenured faculty and the Director of LGBTQ+ Center at the University of Hawai'i at Mānoa (2002-present). Mr. Miyamoto continues to learn from his students at UH and is fueled by the belief that we will create a better future through compassion, education, and a steadfast commitment to social justice. Mr. Miyamoto received his B.A. in History from Occidental College (1992); M.A. in American Studies from the University of Hawai'i at Mānoa (1997); and certificate in community organizing from the Center for Third World Organizing (1997). He is published by the Princeton Review, the University of Hawai'i Press and has materials reprinted by Duke University Press relating to queer people of color. His juried presentations include sessions/workshops at national conferences and institutes sponsored by: U.S. Department of Justice/California Coalition Against Sex Assault, National Association for Student Personnel Administrators (NASPA), and the National Gay and Lesbian Task Force. Contact: camaronm@hawaii.edu

Dr. Kristjane Nordmeyer, Ph.D. is an Associate Professor of Sociology at Westminster College in Salt Lake City. Her teaching and scholarship focus on gender, sexuality, research methods, cats, and Scandinavia. She has published academically on intimate partner violence, elder care, and the application of feminist teaching pedagogies to study abroad experiences. Additionally, Dr. Nordmeyer teaches in the Honors Program and leads study abroad experiences in Scandinavia. She also oversees many student organizations on campus, including the college's LGBTQ student group and conducted community-based research on social polices aiming to curb child hunger. Dr. Nordmeyer's current scholarly work focuses on queer women's experiences with sexual assault in college. She also has developing interests in visual sociology and the treatment of animals. Contact: knordmeyer@westminstercollege.edu

Dr. Tara O'Neill, B.A., M.S.E., Ph.D. is an Associate Professor of Science Education, Director of the Institute for Teacher Education (ITE) Secondary Program, Director of the STEMS2 Masters in Curriculum and Instruction, and one of two University of Hawaii Manoa (UHM) representatives on the UH Commission on LGBTQ+ Equality. She specializes in multicultural, place-based science and STEM/STEMS2 education. Prior to accepting a faculty position at UHM, Dr. O'Neill worked for 10 years as a middle and high school science teacher in Boston and New York City. Her scholarly activities focus around three primary areas: (1) science identity development of middle school girls from non-dominate backgrounds (Native Hawaiian, African American, Latino/a, Micronesian, Filipino, and high poverty); (2) the role of place-based education in building culturally integrated STEMS2 (Science, Technology, Engineering, Mathematics, Social Sciences, and Sense of Place) learning experiences; and (3) effective professional development models for building in-serve teachers' willingness and capacity to teach interdisciplinary STEMS2 curricula that integrate Indigenous and Western science knowledge, skills, and practices. Contact: toneill@hawaii.edu

Dr. Sarah Pickett, B.A., M.A., Psych. D., R. Psych. is an assistant professor in the Faculty of Education at Memorial University Newfoundland (MUN) and Registered Psychologist. She is chair of the Faculty of Education Sexuality and Gender Education Committee (SAGE) and faculty advisor to the Gender and Sexuality Alliance (GSA). Her research has focused on LGBQ teacher experience, LGBTQ+ affirming teacher education and sexuality and gender inclusive school culture. Dr. Pickett has studied LGBQ school personnel experiences of sexuality and gender based microaggressions and "outness" in K–12 schools. She developed the pre-service teacher education course, *Sexual Orientation and Gender Identity/Expression in Education Matters*. A multi-year study focusing on the course's overall influence on pre-service teacher's knowledge, awareness and skill and their ability to integrate LGBTQ+ affirmative practice and pedagogy is ongoing. More broadly she is interested in narrative and auto-enothgraphic research, and in how researchers may use these methods to engage in evocative conversations about sexual and gender diversity in education. Dr. Pickett has researched these topics from the position of parent, lesbian/queer, and academic. Contact: spickett@mun.ca

Dr. Laurel Puchner, Ph.D. is a Professor of Educational Psychology and Chair of the Department of Educational Leadership at Southern Illinois University Edwardsville (SIUE). She teaches qualitative research methods and educational psychology in a variety of graduate programs, including K–12 administrator preparation and college student personnel administration. She has published in the areas of women's literacy in developing countries, professional development of teachers, action research, and teacher education for social justice. She is currently doing research on how higher education leaders view their own and their institutions' efforts to promote diversity and to meet the needs of diverse students. She has been active in SIUE's Safe Zone for the past 12 years, serving primarily in the areas of training and curriculum development. Contact: lpuchne@siue.edu

Dr. Barbara Qualls, B. Music, M.Ed., Ph.D. currently serves as the coordinator for the M.Ed./Educational Leadership and Principal Certification program at Stephen F. Austin State University in Nacogdoches, Texas. Higher Education is a relatively new career arc, though. She was part of the Texas public school system for over three decades, serving as band director, curriculum director, junior high principal, high school principal, and superintendent in three different Texas districts. She primarily teaches school law and is involved in legal and advocacy groups at the state and national level. She presented *Looking Down the Barrel: Intentional Weapons in Schools*, both as a research paper and as instructional law at several education and legal conferences as well as a webinar for the Education Law Association. Serving as a contributing reviewer for the *School Law Review Express*, Dr. Qualls publishes briefs of six or more appellate cases in United States district courts related to discriminatory practices in higher education each month. Contact: bquallsbqualls@att.net

Rachael Rehage examines the success of P-20 educator preparation and professional development programs and evaluates their ability to support and affirm students of sexual minorities. Rehage uses queer theory, constructivism, and systems theories combined with narrative inquiry or case study analysis to investigate P-20 education systems and conduct research that seeks to inform organizational and leadership change. Her current research focuses include K-12 campus climate change for students of marginalized gender and sexual identities, and the effects of high school on students of sexual minorities and their decision to disclose in school. Contact: rachael_rehage@redlands.edu

Dr. Pamela Ross McClain, Ph.D. is currently an Assistant Professor at the University of Michigan-Flint in the School of Education and Human Services. She earned her Ph.D. from Michigan State University in curriculum instruction and educational policy with a cognate in teacher and staff development. Dr. Ross McClain's also holds a Bachelor's Degree in English and Afro-American Studies from the University of Michigan and a Master's Degree from Cornell University's Africana Studies and Research Center. Her research interests and academic expertise focus on cultural responsive policies and practices and school improvement in urban public school settings. Dr. Ross McClain is a scholar practitioner, grant writer/strategic planner, community and staff developer who navigates within multiple diverse educational settings. She devises innovative measures that enhance the quality of teaching and learning for under-served/under-performing African American youth in collaboration with various public school stakeholders including administrative and teaching professionals, ancillary staff, parents, students, public service agencies, faith-based and other community-based organizations. Contact: rosspam@umflint.edu

Dr. Pietro A. Sasso, B.A., M.S., Ph.D. is an Assistant Professor and Program Director of College Student Personnel Administration at Southern Illinois University Edwardsville. He has over ten years of professional and teaching experience in postsecondary education. His the author and editor of *Today's College Students, Higher Education & Society, Colleges at the Crossroads: Taking Sides on Contested Issues*, and *The Dynamic Student Development Meta-Theory: A New Model for Student Success.* His research interests include identity construction of traditional undergraduates (college student development), alcohol misuse in higher education (student health outcomes), the impact of the college fraternity experience, and masculinity in higher education. He is a former coordinator in student activities and hall director where he collaborated and facilitated LGBTQIAA programming. Contact: pete.sasso@yahoo.com

Erica Schepp, B.S.E, M.S.E. is the Director of the University of Wisconsin-Whitewater Children's Center. She holds degrees in Early Childhood through Middle Childhood Education and in Curriculum and Instruction. Along with directing the Center she supervises preservice teachers and co-teaches graduate courses in Early Childhood Education. Prior to her current position she was a kindergarten teacher. Erica's research includes developing inclusive settings for children in early childhood who are gender fluid/creative. In developing inclusive settings she studies teacher preparation programs with special attention to how preservice teachers are exposed to gender and specifically moving beyond the teaching of gender as a stagnant, binary notion. She has presented her work locally, and at the state and national levels. Contact: Scheppe@uww.edu

Alan Smith, B.A., M.Div., M.A. is currently an Adjunct Professor in the Philosophy and Religion Department at Arcadia University and in the Black American Studies Department at the University of Delaware. He has taught in K-12 schools and at the collegiate level for 25 years. An activist and artist, Dr. Smith has organized protests, and volunteered for various social justice organizations and political campaigns. He graduated from LaGuardia High School of the Arts in New York City majoring in fine art. At Williams College, he completed a Bachelor of Arts Degree in American Studies and Political Science with minors in African American Studies and African and Middle Eastern Studies. At Yale University he completed a Master of Divinity Degree. At Arcadia University, he completed a Master of Arts in Humanities Degree and is working on a Master of Arts in Education Degree. He has traveled to 46 of the 50 United States and to 23 countries on all seven continents. Contact: smitha@arcadia.edu

Dr. Virginia Stead, H.B.A., B.Ed., M.Ed., Ed.D. (Editor) received her Ed.D. (Educational Administration) at OISE University of Toronto in 2012. She is the founding Series Editor of *Equity in Higher Education Theory, Policy, and Praxis* (Peter Lang). Dr. Stead launched her series with Vol. I, *International Perspectives on Higher Education Admission Policy: A Reader*, which includes research by 58 authors from over 30 countries. This text showcases her qualitative doctoral thesis, *Teacher Candidate Diversification through Equity-Based Admission Policy*, offers new insights into higher education admissions in both undergraduate and graduate programs, and introduces new ways of conceptualizing higher education policy implementation. United States Supreme Court Chief Justice John G. Roberts ordered that this text be among the Justices' materials in the widely influential case, *Fisher v. University of Texas (Austin)* which was decided in favour of affirmative action on December 9, 2015. Dr. Stead's Vol. 6, *RIP Jim Crow: Fighting Racism through Higher Education Policy, Curriculum, and Cultural Interventions* (2016) is a must read for antiracist campus leaders. The full Higher Ed. Series is available at https://www.peterlang.com/view/serial/HET Ideas for future volumes are welcome. Contact: virginia.stead@alum.utoronto.ca_

Dr. Wahinkpe Topa (Four Arrows) aka Don Trent Jacobs, Ph.D. (Health Psychology), Ph.D. (Curriculum and Instruction with a cognate in Indigenous Worldviews) is author of 20 acclaimed books, including *Teaching Truly: A Curriculum to Indigenize Mainstream Education; Point of Departure: Returning to Our More Authentic Worldview for Education and Survival;* and *Critical Neurophilosophy and Indigenous Wisdom* as well as more than a hundred articles and chapters on topics relating to wellness, education, critical inquiry and Indigenous perspectives., he was named one of 27 Visionaries in Education by AERO in their text *Turning Points* and is recipient of a Martin Springer Institute on Holocaust Studies Moral Courage Award for his activism. Formerly Dean of Education at Oglala Lakota College and a tenured Associate Professor at Northern Arizona University, he is currently faculty in the College of Leadership Studies at Fielding Graduate University. He is available for keynotes and can be reached at djacobs@fielding.edu

Travis L. Wagner has a Masters of Library and Information Sciences from the University of South Carolina (USC). He has also earned a Graduate Certificate in Women's and Gender Studies at USC where he currently teaches and pursues a Ph.D. in Library and Information. Travis is a cataloguing intern at the University of South Carolina's Moving Image Research Collections and also works as a consultant to multiple Columbia-based community archives, specifically honing in on preserving and digitizing fragile audio-visual materials. His research interests relate to the role that language-based access plays in content creation and distribution within moving image archives, and he gives specific consideration to how this affects context and interpretation of visual information containing potentially queer and non-gender conforming persons. Furthermore, he is interested in how language-based limitations detract from access for queer identifying persons, and focuses further on the manner in which institutions such as libraries and archives reinforce heteronormative structures beyond information organization practices. Contact: travis.l.wagner@gmail.com

Rae Watanabe has been teaching English at Leeward Community College for 22 years. During that time, she instituted changes to make Leeward Community College safer for LGBTQ+ students. She also served as a commissioner, a chair and a co-chair on the Commission for LGBTQ+ Equality. Through this service, she helped to make the campuses of the University of Hawaii (UH) System safer. Ms. Watanabe is the co-founder (along with the late Joan Souza) of the Safe Zone Program within the UH System. Throughout much of the 1990s, she was a monthly columnist for *Island Lifestyle Magazine*, which was Hawaii's largest LGBTQ+ magazine. In addition, she is the author of a one-act play *The Second Closet*, a play about domestic violence in LGBTQ+ relationships. The play has been performed at UH-Manoa as well as on Maui and was used as an educational tool so that each performance was followed by a panel of domestic violence professionals. Additionally, Ms. Watanabe is a published poet. One of her better known poems is entitled "Rock Garden," told from the point of view of a woman taking care of her best friend in his last days of AIDS. The poem was published by *Makali`i*, the Journal of the University of Hawaii Community Colleges, and republished by *Island Lifestyle Magazine*. Currently, she is a member of Leeward Community College's Writers' Guild and has two short stories in their publication *Kuamo`o Olelo*. In 2015, the guild presented Ms. Watanabe with its Most Valuable Bard Award. Contact: raew@hawaii.edu

Eric J. Weber, Ed.D. Dr. Weber earned his B.S. in Interpreter Training from Eastern Kentucky University; he earned his M.P.A. in Public Administration as well as his Ed.D. in Educational Leadership and Policy Studies from Eastern Kentucky University. Dr. Weber is an Adjunct Professor of Women and Gender Studies at Eastern Kentucky University. His research interests include educational leadership, inclusive services for diverse populations, and social justice and diversity affairs in educational environments. Dr. Weber is also a professional sign language interpreter, nationally certified through both the Registry of Interpreters for the Deaf and the National Association of the Deaf. He has participated in several mentoring programs to share his knowledge and experience with others in the field including interpreting students. Dr. Weber has developed and presented a number of professional conferences and has also written on a variety of issues directly related to interpreting and services for deaf and hard of hearing individuals. Contact: eric.weber@eku.edu

S. Gavin Weiser is a Ph.D. student in the Foundations of Education & Inquiry Program at the University of South Carolina, as well as being enrolled in two separate graduate certificate programs Women & Gender Studies and Qualitative Research Methodology. Gavin's research interests center on intersectional oppressions in the academy and on working toward solidarity and liberation, both of which are related to the professional praxis-based work he has engaged in for over a decade. His previous publications include: Listening to LGBTQ Communities, Practicing LGBTQ justice, An Appreciative Approach to Diversity Training, and A Campus Apart: the Lived Experiences of Student Affairs Professionals of Color. Gavin earned a Bachelor of Arts in Interdisciplinary Humanities with an emphasis on English and African-American Studies from Florida State University and a Master of Education in Higher Education and Student Affairs from the University of South Carolina. Gavin's past work experience includes the Youth Conservation Corps in Waukegan, IL, the Princeton-Blairstown Center, Brown University, the National Student Leadership Conference, and Florida State University Outdoor Recreation Center. Contact: gavin.weiser@gmail.com

Joe Wilson is an Emmy Award-winning documentary filmmaker and human rights advocate whose work explores oppression and empowerment among society's most vulnerable communities. His 2009 PBS film *Out in the Silence* focused on the challenges of LGBT people in rural and small town America and became the centerpiece of a multi-year national campaign to open dialogue and counter school bullying. His 2014 PBS films *Kumu Hina* and *A Place in the Middle* helped bring Hawaiian cultural perspectives to the fore in national and international conversations on issues of gender diversity and inclusion. Previously, Wilson served as Director of the Human Rights and Global Security Program at the Public Welfare Foundation in Washington, D.C., and Producer of Pacifica National Radio's *Democracy Now*. He received a B.A. in Sociology and Economics from the University of Pittsburgh and served as a Peace Corps volunteer in the West African nation of Mali. Contact: qwavesjoe@yahoo.com

Hinaleimoana Wong-Kalu is a Kanaka Maoli (Native Hawaiian) teacher, cultural practitioner, and community leader. Born in the Nu'uanu District of O'ahu, Kumu Hina was educated at Kamehameha Schools and the University of Hawaii. She was a founding member of Kulia Na Mamo, a community organization established to improve the quality of life for māhū wahine (transgender women), and served for 13 years as the Director of Culture at a Honolulu public charter school dedicated to using native Hawaiian culture, history, and education as tools for developing and empowering the next generation of warrior scholars. Kumu Hina is currently a cultural advisor and leader in many community affairs and civic activities, including Chair of the O'ahu Island Burial Council, which oversees the management of Native Hawaiian burial sites and ancestral remains. In 2014, Hina announced her bid for a position on the board of the Office of Hawaiian Affairs, one of the first transgender candidates to run for statewide political office in the United States. Contact: taahine.hina@gmail.com

EQUITY
IN HIGHER EDUCATION
THEORY, POLICY, & PRAXIS

A BOOK SERIES FOR EQUITY SCHOLARS & ACTIVISTS

Virginia Stead, H.B.A., B.Ed., M.Ed., Ed.D., *General Editor*

Globalization increasingly challenges higher education researchers, administrators, faculty members, and graduate students to address urgent and complex issues of equitable policy design and implementation. This book series provides an inclusive platform for discourse about—though not limited to—diversity, social justice, administrative accountability, faculty accreditation, student recruitment, admissions, curriculum, pedagogy, online teaching and learning, completion rates, program evaluation, cross-cultural relationship-building, and community leadership at all levels of society. Ten broad themes lay the foundation for this series but potential editors and authors are invited to develop proposals that will broaden and deepen its power to transform higher education:

(1) Theoretical books that examine higher education policy implementation,
(2) Activist books that explore equity, diversity, and indigenous initiatives,
(3) Community-focused books that explore partnerships in higher education,
(4) Technological books that examine online programs in higher education,
(5) Financial books that focus on the economic challenges of higher education,
(6) Comparative books that contrast national perspectives on a common theme,
(7) Sector-specific books that examine higher education in the professions,
(8) Educator books that explore higher education curriculum and pedagogy,
(9) Implementation books for front line higher education administrators, and
(10) Historical books that trace changes in higher education theory, policy, and praxis.

Expressions of interest for authored or edited books will be considered on a first come basis. A Book Proposal Guideline is available on request. For individual or group inquiries please contact:

Dr. Virginia Stead, General Editor | *virginia.stead@alum.utoronto.ca*

To order other books in this series, please contact our Customer Service Department at:

(800) 770-LANG (within the U.S.)
(212) 647-7706 (outside the U.S.)
(212) 647-7707 FAX

Or browse online by series at www.peterlang.com